The Academic Avant-Garde

The Academic Avant-Garde

Poetry and the American University

Kimberly Quiogue Andrews

JOHNS HOPKINS UNIVERSITY PRESS   BALTIMORE

© 2023 Johns Hopkins University Press
All rights reserved. Published 2023
Printed in the United States of America on acid-free paper
9 8 7 6 5 4 3 2 1

Johns Hopkins University Press
2715 North Charles Street
Baltimore, Maryland 21218
www.press.jhu.edu

Library of Congress Cataloging-in-Publication Data

Names: Andrews, Kimberly Quiogue, 1983– author.
Title: The academic avant-garde : poetry and the American university / Kimberly Quiogue Andrews.
Description: Baltimore : Johns Hopkins University Press, [2023] | Includes index.
Identifiers: LCCN 2022011549 | ISBN 9781421444932 (hardcover) | ISBN 9781421444949 (paperback) | ISBN 9781421444956 (ebook)
Subjects: LCSH: American poetry—History and criticism—Theory, etc. | Experimental poetry, American—History and criticism—Theory, etc. | Avant-garde (Aesthetics)—United States. | Poetics. | Universities and colleges—United States. | BISAC: LITERARY CRITICISM / Semiotics & Theory | LITERARY CRITICISM / Poetry
Classification: LCC PS303 .A55 2023 | DDC 811.00901—dc23/eng/20220707
LC record available at https://lccn.loc.gov/2022011549

A catalog record for this book is available from the British Library.

Special discounts are available for bulk purchases of this book. For more information, please contact Special Sales at specialsales@jh.edu.

The last printed page of the book is a continuation of this copyright page.

Contents

Acknowledgments   vii

Introduction: The 500 Pound Gorilla   1

1 The Dream and the Deed   19
2 Reading Ashbery Reading Ashbery   49
3 Poetry in the Teaching Machine   87
4 Citational Coding   120
5 Archival Authorizations   164

Coda: Toward an Aesthetics of Disciplinarity   205

Notes   215
Index   257

Acknowledgments

The acknowledgments section of a book exists to honor the collaborative and networked nature of what is usually assumed to be a deeply solitary activity. Lately, these sections have also been acknowledging something else: the conditions under which the writing was undertaken, and thus the nature of the collaboration and networking available to the author. This is a good development. I intend to continue it here.

This book was written under conditions that have swung wildly between poles of institutional prestige and privilege. I began outlining its contours at Yale University, where I was afforded years of unfettered time to read, research, and draft the basic concepts that underlie the arguments. I never wanted for a library book, or for access to a database. I was paid basically enough, and had access to healthcare. Barely a week went by without colloquium events, talks by scholars from similar institutions, and other opportunities to build a sense of the profession and to socialize with its most successful members. The book was first drafted under these circumstances.

They are circumstances for which I am extremely grateful, and my thanks in particular go to the folks that had a direct hand in making them conducive for book-writing in the first place. The twentieth- and twenty-first-century literature colloquium read early drafts of some of the material here and provided commentary that shaped my thinking for years afterwards. I owe a great deal of thanks to R. John Williams and Anthony Reed, both of whom read my manuscript with exacting care and attention, and have continued to support me and my work in the intervening years. Any theoretical knowledge that I display with any aplomb in this book is due to the influence of Paul Fry, whose capacious intellect and catholic tastes have proved a model for me not only in my research, but also in my teaching. And of course where would I be without Langdon Hammer, who took this project on when it was barely a project, and who saw it through with care, sensitivity, profound intellectual acuity, and a tremendous editorial pen? I am profoundly lucky to have had one of our greatest scholars of poetry *and* one of our greatest academic prose stylists, in the same person, as a reader and champion.

I left Yale with a tenure-track job in hand at a small, underfunded liberal arts college in rural Maryland. The next four years were thus spent in conditions quite different from those under which the book was conceived. At Washington College, I taught more classes than the average faculty member does at a research-intensive institution, and I advised no graduate students and had no research assistance. There were no colloquia and no scholarly speaking series. There were about one-twentieth the number of library books, and database access was limited. As the institution's enrollment numbers worsened and its structural deficit ballooned, faculty members were regularly threatened with termination, and our pay and benefits were cut. This book was rewritten under these circumstances.

They are circumstances that certainly made the writing of this book more difficult, but they are not comprehensive (and nor are they even *close* to the worst on offer for the majority of scholars attempting to do this kind of work). I was exceedingly fortunate and grateful to receive a number of small internal grants that helped with research and conference expenses, as well as a project development grant from the American Council of Learned Societies geared specifically toward professors at teaching-intensive institutions. And some of my very deepest debts of gratitude go to my wonderful, vibrant, courageous, and dedicated colleagues from departments across Washington College: most of all to Katherine Charles, Meghan Grosse, Jason Patterson, George Keiser, Sara Clarke-De Reza, and Tenley Bick for their enduring friendship and camaraderie. Heartfelt thanks are also due to James Hall, Roy Kesey, Elizabeth O'Connor, Courtney Rydel, Alisha Knight, and Rich DeProspo for their departmental collegiality and their unwavering support of what I was up to both as a poet and as a scholar, and to Jennifer Kaczmarczyk, who I am pretty sure is responsible for anyone in the entirety of Smith Hall being able to do anything at all. Solidarity forever with Clayton Black, Ken Schweitzer, and Robert Lynch, union organizers extraordinaire and actual users of tenure. Particular thanks go to Sean Meehan, who may well be the best departmental chair there has ever been, and who is a model of what a teacher-scholar should be. May we all learn to be both as kind and as fierce as you are, Sean.

Other friends and colleagues along the way have formed the bedrock on which I base any sense that literary scholarship is worth pursuing: Natalia Cecire, for being maybe the sharpest person I will ever know and for reading my work with patience, care, and support even as it was in various stages of disastrousness; Aldon Nielsen, for supporting both my poetry and my scholarship for going on two decades now with not a single fallow period; Abram Foley, for commiseration and mutual materials sharing as we made our way through the publication process; Xiaoye You, even though he probably doesn't know it, for allowing me to write the seminar paper that became the article that became the idea for this book; and for the conference meet-ups and general role modeling ways of Julia Bloch, Sarah Brouillette, Andrew Epstein, Harris Feinsod, Evan Kindley, Evie Shockley, Matt Tierney, Lindsay Turner, and Gillian White. There are others that I am sure I am forgetting in the haze of recirculated hotel air, but know that I have appreciated every conversation and every drink.

Special thanks go to John Keene and Claudia Rankine: Claudia graciously answered early emails asking her about her time writing *Don't Let Me Be Lonely*, and John was *so* generous with his time that we eventually wound up not just being interviewee and interviewer but friends and colleagues. A kinder genius there has never been.

Now I find myself at the University of Ottawa, a circumstance that has brought the resources of a highly unionized, research-intensive university to bear on the ending stages of revising this book. For bringing me here on a wave of truly incredible empathy and transparency (and recipes), I have Jennifer Panek to thank. Thanks also to Sara Landreth and James Brooke-Smith for being the welcome wagon, and to Tom Allen, Jennifer Blair, Andrew Taylor, Lauren Gillingham, and Robert Stacey for the conversations that made this place feel like home before I even got here. Once I did get here, Vicki Burke, Anne Raine, and Geoff Rector all offered kindness, support, and camaraderie. Our department's administrative assistant, Liz White, deserves an acknowledgments page all her own. To Suyi Okungbowa: thank goodness there are two of us.

This book would look very different, and be much worse, if not for the two anonymous readers of this manuscript in peer review. One of these readers was so thorough and careful with my ideas that several of their phrases have made it into the book basically wholesale. Catherine Goldstead, my editor at Johns Hopkins University Press, both found these reviewers and believed in this project from the day we met in a Baltimore café years ago; it is her I have to thank for the fact of this book existing as a book. Hilary Jacqmin was a conscientious and responsive copy and production editor; all typos are absolutely on me. Invaluable assistance with indexing and permissions was provided by Joel Simundich and Kurt Newman; I am *beyond* grateful for their taking care of the details while I pulled my hair out over the big picture.

I am also grateful to the editors of the journals in which parts of this book first appeared, both for publishing my work in the first place and then for giving me permission to collect it here. A highly modified version of the first chapter was published as "'Resisting the Intelligence Almost Successfully': Wallace Stevens's 'Academic' Style" in *Modernist Cultures* 14, no. 1 (2019): 53–69 (reprinted with the permission of Edinburgh University Press); a version of the third chapter was published as "Trade Secrets: Poetry in the Teaching Machine" in *New Literary History* 49, no. 1 (2018): 71–91 (used with the permission of Johns Hopkins University Press); and a small portion of the fifth chapter was published in an earlier form as "Poetry in the Program Era" in *The Cambridge Companion to Twenty-First-Century American Poetry*, edited by Timothy Yu (Cambridge: Cambridge University Press, 2021). An article entitled "What Does Translation Know?," published in *Textual Practice* 31, no. 2 (2017): 339–363, is the earlier and fuller version from which my remarks on Christian Hawkey are drawn in the fifth chapter. It is used with the permission of Taylor & Francis Ltd. (https://www.tandfonline.com/).

Many parts of the revision and production of this book were undertaken during the collective grief and trauma of the COVID-19 pandemic; for me, this period was also marked by circumstances that necessitated my first foray into full-time parental caretaking while I was supposed to be on research leave. To the extent to which I did any kind of adequate job by my mother and father during this time, I was prepared to do so by the very people receiving the care. I'm pretty sure my parents still don't really know what I do for a living, but this has not once stopped them from being unreservedly enthusiastic, supportive, and proud of it. I do not take this circumstance, nor the incredible advantages it has conferred, lightly or for granted.

To the group chat: Bo, Kate, Jenna, Viv, and Jamie. May what started in the squirrel-infested Hall of Graduate Studies never end, and may we know each other for all of our lives.

This book, like basically everything else I've done in my intellectual life, is dedicated to Brian Lennon.

But I dedicate myself, and everything that I will go on to do with both my head and my heart, to Alexander Bowles. Thank you, Alex, for tolerating the mess that this book occasionally made of me, and for weaving around both it and me a life, a love, and a home in which I could think, in joy and otherwise, about the version of existence I venerate in these pages.

The Academic Avant-Garde

Introduction

The 500 Pound Gorilla

"The university is the 500 pound gorilla at the party of poets."[1]
This was Ron Silliman's assessment of the state of the genre in 1990. Three decades later, the gorilla is still very much in attendance—one might, in fact, go so far as to say that it's eaten enough snacks and poured enough drinks to become a proper 800-pound gorilla, the host of the whole affair. There has been no shortage of feelings expressed about this situation. Such expressions are not new phenomena—Matthew Arnold tackled a corollary to the problem in 1888—but the rise and solidification of creative writing as an academic discipline, particularly in the United States, has certainly changed both the tenor and the urgency of the discussion.[2] In *The Program Era*, a book now impossible not to invoke when saying anything about the subject, Mark McGurl describes a "literary journalism" full of a "suspicion . . . that there may be something inherently wrong" with the graduate creative writing program and, thus, its products.[3] Things have not changed appreciably since his writing. In fact, and despite its thoroughgoing optimism, *The Program Era* might have made things worse, occasioning shortly after its publication a collection of essays that appeared in the journal *n+1* and that were eventually grouped under the heading "MFA vs NYC." The handwringing contained therein, combined with the continuing and profound influence of McGurl's work, stands testament to the fact that we still want to know what we ought to think about writers who go through these programs, as if there were any one way to think about them.[4]

The book you have before you is indeed a book about creative writing. Many of the authors in this study attended, founded, or teach in MFA programs. But this is not, I argue, what makes their work fundamentally of "the university."

The purpose of this book is, instead, to make a case for the poetic possibilities of the work of literary studies. It aims to demonstrate the degree to which the practices of a discipline nominally tasked with *examining* innovative literary work have in fact fostered the *development* of such work, and it sees this relationship's strongest effects in poetry. The poetry under consideration in *The Academic Avant-Garde* values the labor of academic criticism on levels both intellectual and aesthetic; one of this book's main arguments is that the recognition of this valuation brings this type of poetry (which ranges widely across forms and commitments) into better view while also giving us, somewhat paradoxically, a particularly clear picture of the building blocks of literary studies itself. The book is structured around these blocks, taking them to be historical, professional, and methodological in turn.

Outlining, and then arguing for, this type of intellection via poetry (as opposed to criticism itself) serves both to highlight the genre as one with even stronger ties to the university than fiction, and to place creative writing as a practice within a disciplinary nexus, rather than treating it as a fully autonomous formation within the humanities. Further, linking critical methodologies to avant-garde poetic production shows that criticism can enrich spheres of writing beyond itself—can, in fact, be used to help that writing find language to ask searching questions about genre, subjectivity, and knowledge work. This picture of interdependence is, I think, a more accurate picture of the aforementioned gorilla. Polarized responses to the success of academic creative writing tend to accept creative writing's own definition of success at face value—success that has, in the "most successful" cases, set up creative writing as a department separate from English. But there are other ways of situating the discipline. In particular, shifting the view of what writers have at their disposal within academic contexts toward what they share with, rather than how they are independent from, literary studies allows us to see the potential not only of poetry written within such contexts, but also of the contexts themselves.

Such an approach makes clear that while the university has certainly affected the forms of twentieth- and twenty-first-century American poetry by dint of credentialing the pursuit of creative writing, it has also affected those forms by putting them into sustained contact with the already-extant academic humanities and the concerns and debates that beset them. That these concerns, "poeticized," tend to take on a character that could be described as avant-garde may seem like a contradiction. Indeed, this is a tension that this book's title is meant to invoke. But although the word "academic" is often a synonym for "boring" or "dry," it also, and tellingly, often means "complicated," or "difficult," or "niche." And while complication for its own sake does not necessarily avant-garde art make, one of the major claims of this book is that the hard scrutiny of language puts real pressure on the language doing the scrutinizing. When that language is further pressed into the service of poetic concentration, the result often takes startling new forms. Each of the authors in this study is widely recognized as being a poetic trailblazer; if I spend time making the case that they are in fact *avant-garde*, it's an artifact not only of the difficulty of the term, but also of the large structural question that underlies this book: is it possible for vanguardist practice to be based on academic institutionality?

This book aims to prove that the answer to this question is yes. It will do so by way of outlining the inextricable links between what that practice looks like and the conditions (present and historical) of its possibility. It does not come to the conclusion that the university is the only possible structure capable of producing this work, but it does assert that in the contemporary United States, it is a primary one, and is worth taking seriously. It thus takes particular interest in the activities that the American academy sustains in the realm of literary studies and writing, and looks for the ways in which those activities have been deployed in the service of avant-garde artwork. One activity sustained on the writing end, of course, is the workshop, and I am lucky indeed that in addition to McGurl, Christopher Kempf has taken on that subject both recently and at length.[5] As the discussion of the creative writing program as such has proliferated over the past few years, however, there's a risk that a picture will develop in which the workshop or the MFA just *is* where creative writing lives in the academy. What other modes of relation serve to produce literary writing within the context of the university? What other modes of *work*? This book wants to answer these questions not simply for the sake of comprehensiveness or whataboutism, but because the answers reveal the extent to which an entire subgenre of poetry has arisen as a result of them.

They reveal, too, that this poetry grapples with persistent questions about the work of intellection as a professional pursuit, and about the formations of knowledge that accompany and result from it. As a phenomenon that generates explanations of its own (and, if you are a literary critic, your own) procedures, then, academic avant-garde poetry bears examining not just as a historical phenomenon but as a theoretical one. This is why this book is organized around broad categories of academic work and labor. One way to think about the conglomeration of writing described in these pages is indeed as a set of effects: a record, that is, of the conditions under which knowledge is gathered and sorted, and then transmitted. To be sure, conditions will be described, and they will also be linked to poetic form. But "form," as Anthony Reed has put it, "is neither a purely creative act nor a predetermined set of significations that bring to consciousness the dynamics of the social system with which it is contemporaneous, but something in between."[6] Ultimately, this study shows how its eponymous writers represent a set of sensibilities with which we can think definitionally: about what both intellectual and poetic work can look like, what its content is and (or versus) what it could be, even to what extent it might play a part in something like an effective alternative to life and work under neoliberalism.

But what is work? In *The Academic Avant-Garde*, the concept will take two broad forms, following in the main the distinction Leigh Claire La Berge makes between *work* and *labor* in *Wages Against Artwork*. "Work," as she has it, "is a local action in which we all engage in order to make our lives both meaningful and possible," while "labor [is] an abstraction through which our work is organized."[7] This is a notoriously tricky distinction to make when it comes to intellectual or artistic or affective work: because these forms of work are often thought of precisely *as* the things that "make our lives meaningful," they have been the foundation of the "do what you love" mantra that allows for the systematic devouring of "creative" labor under capital.[8] La Berge places this tendency under the aegis of real subsumption, that is, "the ability of capitalism to progress, to intensify, to extract more, and to encompass all."[9] The example of teaching is a particularly clear one: in the case of the humanities (which rely in the main significantly less than the sciences do on major external grants for the payment of costs and salaries), it is the activity that is most easily recognized as fitting directly into a labor market that requires a service in need of rendering. At the same time, it is also more often than not framed as a "calling," the assumption of pastoral care for students used as a mechanism by which to extract a maximum amount of surplus value (extra hours, purchasing of materials, content generation, etc.) out of the supposedly "unalienated" quality of the work. In teaching, work—

for the notion of teaching as a calling does in fact come from the sense that there is, as Jorie Graham will tell us later in this book, something truly vital about it—becomes labor disguised as work.

Research takes a similar form. This book assumes that the commodity in question that renders research as labor in literary studies is "the reading" in the form of research articles and books on literature; the work of "reading" thus takes on special importance in terms of what scholars in the field are supposed to provide within the university's relations of production. But like the care work embedded in teaching, indeed perhaps even more so than it, "reading" contains work that exceeds those relations, that "makes life meaningful" in ways that are difficult for capital to capture, try though it may. Methodology—the systematized search for ways of reading adequate to the complexity, importance, or even beauty of the read objects—is one name for this work, and the shared discourses that it makes possible point up both what is most communal and most aesthetic about literary study. Academic avant-garde poetry redoubles this effect. At the very end of her book, La Berge offers a tentative but similar kind of synthesis: she asks "what, then, is the proper place of Marxist cultural critique of art? Might it be understood as partaking in the aesthetic? As considering not a material (re)organization of social life, but of producing a space apart from that material organization that enables reflection on it divorced from a need to act?"[10] The art that she has examined in the chapters leading up to this point lead her to the question about her own work; so too will the poetry in *The Academic Avant-Garde* lead us to a better sense of the possible "space apart" occupied by literary studies. By organizing this study in a way that moves from the labor-conceptions of academic work to the more granular ways in which that work makes meaning, I hope to underlay an ever-present sense, in poetry but also in general, that "wages are needed but wages are not enough."[11]

The book's structure, then, captures one important part of the notion of *avant-garde* that it hopes to sustain over its chapters, one that acknowledges the word's troubled history without relegating it to the status of mere descriptor for a historical series of artistic projects that attempted and largely failed to effect broad political change. There is a kind of hard optimism about the term that I want to emphasize, while suggesting that a narrow view of its success in terms of political efficacy no longer functions very well within poetry's current fields of production (or, indeed, within the juggernaut of global capitalism). Thinking about the avant-garde as existing only "outside" of all possible spheres of commercial, institutional, or hegemonic-cultural influence, as is often done, is similarly unhelpful, reducing the term as it does to a litmus test that no one ever passes.[12] Paul Mann's argument in *The Theory-Death of the Avant-Garde* offers a bit of help: if the narrow view and the litmus-test view would both declare the avant-garde dead, the avant-garde finds its discursive immortality precisely *in that death*, insofar as said death is constantly theorized. Mann reads Peter Bürger's lament for the avant-garde, in this connection, in light of Mann's own cautious optimism: "even if autonomy is false," he argues, "it still functions" as, at minimum, a concept which can be critiqued as such.[13] As a *discursive* phenomenon, the avant-garde's life after death is, in essence, controlled by how it gets talked about as living or dead; "the academy," Mann notes, "approves a space in which the avant-garde can be described as free, then turns around and insists that after all any freedom endorsed by the academy cannot be taken seriously."[14] This is a particularly neat encapsulation of the contradiction at the heart of the literary academy (and thus at the heart of this book), and I will return to it at greater length in the next chapter. In the meantime, suffice it to say that Mann's description certainly captures a form of bad affect that most scholars will recognize: we might be the arbiters of taste at the margins, but simultaneously, somehow, we kill everything we touch.

This form of negative thinking does not stick so firmly to poets, even when they, too, constitute the type of academic "we" that this book attempts to describe—and so it is in poetry that we might be able to see the clearest way around the affective trap just mentioned. It's not that said affect doesn't make sense. The edge of the university, as it were, is always already becoming its center, because edginess is, at least nominally, part of the central mission statement ("advancing human knowledge," etc.). But poetry shows us the vital energy contained in resisting that centripetal pull. If vanguardism can be profitably seen as a set of discursive relations rather than an intrinsic quality, a resistant or inventive way of relating to the academy *itself* can help to move around the boundaries of the latter's imaginary: what it values, and how it values it. This book will thus return again and again to the phenomenology of *reflexivity*—and will argue, throughout its close readings, that it should be thought of as a collective phenomenon. Reflexivity in this account, unlike in McGurl's, is used not to differentiate the individual via a self-conscious choice regarding "life story," but instead to critically examine the conditions that allow (or disallow) such individuation to take place.[15]

This book thus describes what might be called, in Theodore Martin's memorable phrase, "a controlled experiment in historical emergence."[16] It will show how poetry and literary study come to share space, and how the dialectical tensions that result from that shared space give rise to a *sui generis* form of poetic discourse. It will further show how that form of discourse distills a more general discursive culture particular to humanist intellectuals, and what we have to gain from paying attention to that culture as an aesthetic phenomenon. It will not be teleological: one of the rationales for using forms of work and labor as an organizing principle is to avoid an oversimplified narrative of "progress"—always a risk when studying the avant-garde—that would move poetry from point A to point B over the course of the last half century. It is also not an attempt to be comprehensive; insofar as this book is a study of a genre, it contains the necessary omissions and elisions that make any examination of genre possible. For instance: where, one might reasonably ask, are Eliot and Pound and all of their footnotes? What about poets at Black Mountain, which was literally a college? Where are all of the other Language writers? One answer to these questions is that the phenomenon I describe here has less to do with the founding of new institutions, as Pound wanted to do and as the founders of Black Mountain College actually did, than with what can be made of extant institutional structures. I am also interested in what might be a more durable kind of vanguard, because it is in this kind of durability, I think, that lie any hopes we might have of creating a collective picture of a better and richer life. Lest we confuse freedom for happiness, the picture itself is often not entirely rosy: indeed, an essential feature of the academic avant-garde as a formation is a type of pervasive anxiety, a struggle with one's own positionality. But that struggle has a direction, and is, one might say, itself an *ethos*. That the primary site of such a struggle is the modern university guides my choices here; it is my hope rather than my fear that the reader might find other poets and poetries that could fit within this general framework.

That said, there are also thinner ways of conceiving of this framework that this book hopes to circumscribe. To wit: in some ways, the most bluntly avant-garde phenomenon we currently have in poetry is that of the latest form of conceptualism, by which I mean the loose formation of poets and performance artists "led" by such polarizing figures as Kenneth Goldsmith and Vanessa Place. It is a formation, too, that cannot be separated from academia. Goldsmith in particular would seem to be a model of one version of an academic avant-garde: professor at Penn, trained as a sculptor and a darling of New York's Museum of Modern Art, he is the champion of "uncreative writing" as creative pedagogy and the author of such books as *Day*, which is a word for word transcription of a single issue of the *New York Times*.[17] This is deliberate provocation in the Duchampian mode, and there's a way in which its unoriginality is itself (refreshingly?) unoriginal. Such work asks quite directly for critical intervention; indeed, as in Duchamp, its status as art depends upon it.

The work itself, however, is not interested in making these interventions. Insofar as Goldsmith wants a "thinkership" instead of a "readership," it is because the work itself revels in the performance of *not* thinking.[18] To record one's every bodily movement over the course of a day, as Goldsmith has done in *Fidget*, doubtless requires intense concentration, but the result is a form of transcription that (deliberately) contains no imaginative tampering.[19] Hence "conceptual": it is supposedly the concept, not the result, that contains the poetry. A poet like Susan Howe, on the other hand, spends huge amounts of time and space processing her own potential for meaning-making both in and through her work, and to the extent that Language poetry is in some ways complicit in the subject-erasing proclivities exemplified in (to name just one instance) Goldsmith's dramatic reading of Michael Brown's autopsy report, it has also historically been invested in the kinds of autocritical processes that, thus far, neo-conceptualism seems to lack.[20]

"The academic avant-garde" as moniker, then, is not meant to be merely a kind of spatial-temporal metaphor. Conceptual poetry's dependence on structures of academic thought, while both extant and in line with a consistent avant-garde tradition (an interesting turn of phrase), does not show up as a traceable form of *interaction* with those intellectual structures—and as such, the ways in which they might themselves be described as "academic" seem weak for the terminological formulation toward which I write here.[21] As a compound term, the "academic" in "academic avant-garde" is meant to register the aforementioned investment rather than a demand, a grappling with social position rather than simply the social position itself. Such a definition, I think, forms the richest possible picture of what it means and looks like to write contemporary vanguardist poetry from an academic standpoint.

To ground this picture historically, this book's first chapter will offer a sustained look at academicism's modernist inheritance followed by a rapid overview of its submersion (during which period creative writing programs cemented their basic and remarkably persistent structure) and reemergence during the shakeups (good and bad) of the later twentieth century.[22] For now, the theoretical framework I've just outlined will hopefully indicate that despite the stylistic gulfs between, for example, John Ashbery (subject of the book's second chapter) and Claudia Rankine (subject of the fourth), one of the most fundamentally consistent characteristics of advanced poetry in the age of collegiate patronage is in fact a type of reflexivity: the way, in the words of Sarah Brouillette, that "writers appear to experience making culture less [as] an inherently fulfilling self-expression and more [as] an encounter with heightened contradictions."[23] Brouillette is here examining how British writers interrogate the way in which their own work is described by the architects of the "creative economy" under New Labour, but one can see a loosely analogous type of phenomenon playing out in poetry whose experimentalism is bound up with discursive forms usually seen as anathema to creative expression. As Brouillette notes, a "self-critical" stance is at this point an "almost clichéd means for writers to negotiate the terms of their participation in the literary field"—but I would argue (as she implicitly does) that it remains important to look closely at the particularities of those stances.[24] They are, after all, dispatches from the front.

The problem of the avant-garde tends, as I've just shown, to be a categorical one: that is, in our post-Bürgerian moment, its theorization rests primarily on what "counts" (or counted) as it, and thus who's in it, rather than how it works. There is no shortage of explications for how poetry works—but neither is there a shortage of the kinds of generic questions that beset the avant-garde. The polemics surrounding poetry in creative writing programs, for example, have focused in the main on the ways in which those programs have created their own version of an aesthetic "mainstream." Anyone outside the mainstream, regardless of their relationship to the academy, is thus an "outsider" poet. This bifurcation is too easy, and while I don't mean to imply that everyone has so far painted a starkly black-and-white picture of poetry in (or out of) higher educational structures, the fact remains that there has been little room for nuance, on the parts of poets and critics alike, in discussions of the university's effects on the writing of poetry.[25] Calling attention to innovative academic poetry's ways of processing itself—processing that takes place, again, *as* the poetry rather than before or alongside of it—can provide an alternative to the terminologies of "in" (mainstream, bad) and "out" (countercultural, good) when thinking about cultural production in the program era.

Insider-outsider arguments about poetry are both particularly vexed and particularly instructive because of how sharply they remind us of poetry's deeply oblique relationship to the market (of both labor and goods). It's not controversial or surprising to point out that there are vanishingly few ways for poets to carve out real cultural space for themselves. The fact of social media has ameliorated this situation somewhat, with slam and spoken-word poetry finding wide audiences via YouTube and other video apps, and a type of highly condensed lyric poetry being wildly popular on Instagram.[26] But because of the extremely restricted playing field on which most poetry operates, the fact remains that for the overwhelming majority of poets attempting to ply their trade in the United States, the insider/outsider distinction is in fact essentially meaningless, which results *affectively* in a type of collective grasping at straws. Any argument about reflexivity, in this connection, is also an argument about genre.

When McGurl uses the phrase "reflexive modernity" as a touchstone throughout *The Program Era*, he is referencing a phenomenon that is significantly less novel in a genre that has had since at least the Romantic period a type of "self-creation" as a major mode. In the postwar novel and short story, McGurl argues, "autopoiesis" is a way of writing the self into fictional texts: the reflexive point of view allows for an "autobiographical drama of self-authorization" that validates and individuates the author in a professional context.[27] To be sure, the semi-autobiographical speaking voice in poetry—what is often simply referred to as "the lyric I"—almost always evinces a type of reflexivity. But it is one whose development has not been caused by the systematization of poetry writing within academia, no matter the ways in which that systematization may have later affected its forms.

As might be clear by now, the type of reflexivity with which I'm concerned does in fact have its origins in the proximity of poetry writing to work in the academic humanities—as Gillian White has put it, a "dizzying hyperawareness of a critical process" from which it has become "less and less distinct."[28] But this awareness produces some startling results. As this book demonstrates in the cases of Wallace Stevens being troubled about the purpose of study, John Ashbery reading himself, Jorie Graham thinking about pedagogical epistemology, John Keene and Claudia Rankine poeticizing Black studies, and Susan Howe creating a familial archive, the thinking about thinking that academic avant-garde poetry tends to do effectively inverts the effect of self-creation in fiction: that is, it radically brings into question the notion that the individuating process of authorial invention represents a kind of freedom. Precisely because the workshop has created such a solid mythology of this trajectory ("find your voice!"), we might well expect for there to be some interrogation of the model, now that the dust has settled somewhat and the ways in which systematized creative individualism can be co-opted by capital have become clearer. The tricky task of resisting this mythology while trying to put other models of subjectivity in place creates an intensely ruminative, sometimes fragmented, highly discursive form of poetry. One might call it a form of lyricized critical thinking.

This is a truly difficult phrase. But I want to stick with the idea, as examining it in conjunction with poetry's generic idiosyncrasies may prove mutually clarifying. To *think critically*: surely, given the anodyne nature of most administratively approved ways to characterize an education, this cannot mean much. As it stands, the term is one that is nigh impossible to avoid when considering the "mission" of tertiary education. (That said, as of this writing, I have failed to find it in my own institution's set of "core aspirations," the language of thinking having been replaced by the language of "preparation.") Because of the phrase's general saturation, the definition of "critical thinking" usually winds up boiling down to a bland both-sidesism: the ability, that is, to ferret out and eliminate *bias*, that most insidious enemy of proper intellection (and, not coincidentally, of "civil debate," another mission-statement darling). What might it mean for "critical thinking" to regrow some of its teeth? To move toward, in that most wonderfully bombastic of Marx's titles, "a ruthless criticism of everything existing"? To be sure, there's nothing so strident as that in a John Ashbery poem. But even he finds himself asking: "if each act / is reflexive, concerned with itself on another level / As well as with us, the strangers who live here, / Can one advance one step further without sinking equally / Far back into the past?"[29] This form of thinking has very little to do with the cultivation of "objectivity." It is instead a type of hyper-awareness of one's own effect on, and ability to process, the world.

The cultivation of such awareness can happen in many ways, but it remains the case that even given the hijacking of the phrase "critical thinking" for use on the splash pages of university websites, the academy is (and the humanities in particular are) a primary structure capable of systematizing the ability to think in a "reflectively skeptical" manner.[30] Gayatri Chakravorty Spivak has put it succinctly in "Thinking About the Humanities," a lecture given at Columbia in 2007: the humanities "train, enrich, and strengthen thinking—improve its range and scope—in its own terms."[31] The humanities, in other words, are (ideally) fundamentally reflexive: they teach you to think about how you think. By doing so, Spivak goes on, they allow one to cultivate one's "imagination," a term which she takes pains to distinguish from the "creative" imagination. The latter, though important, is a type of isolation; it "exercis[es] itself by itself." The humanistic imagination, on the other hand, is projective; it "teaches the student to suspend herself into" the object of study.[32] This relational form of thinking recognizes the self as radically contingent. You don't "find your voice," you throw it.

Ultimately, Spivak brings her talk around to the "double bind" that the humanities find themselves in in an age of globalization; in this context, thinking "beyond self-interest" takes on a specific political importance.[33] But even in the more hermetic context of critical thinking within literary thinking, the implications are significant, and they bring us back around to the question of genre. Poetry's intimacy, its closeness to the innermost self, is often taken as a given, even though the development of that assumed proximity is in historical terms a relatively recent one.[34] In struggling to move beyond that now-solidified set of assumptions, academic avant-garde poetry often confronts itself on the level of genre: that is, if the goal isn't to (say) revert back to the epic, and if the immediacy of the natural sign no longer seems a possibility, then how might poetry be definable as such when tasked with forming new modes of speaking subjectivity? When formed, would—or could—those subjectivities remain poetic ones?

These are non-rhetorical questions. The quest to answer them is thematic in the writing of each of the poets under consideration here. In the very near background is thus also the question of recognizability: of knowing, to slightly modify Stanley Fish, a poem when you see one. Fish's essay, whatever you think of the credibility of an experiment involving hoodwinking your students into believing that a list of names is in fact a devotional poem, is also deeply concerned with the cultivation of knowledge forms, and while he's using the example he knows professionally, it's significant that the knowledge form in question involves reading—recognizing—poetry in a collegiate lecture hall. The collective setting of education, in other words, produces a series of "communal or conventional categories of thought"; poetry, as a genre that (we have communally decided) requires more interpretive work than most, brings the contours of these communal categories into particularly sharp relief.[35] When the poets *themselves* become part of this scene, it is perhaps only natural that they display a heightened concern about the ways in which the definition of what they're doing is affected by their involvement in the very "interpretive communities" tasked with scrutinizing their work.

This book suggests that this concern manifests itself in two very broad ways: in Ashbery and Graham, as a reflexive anxiety about what kinds of knowledge poetry can both produce and transmit, and in Rankine, Keene, Howe, and others as poetry so dedicated to finding new ways of conveying that search for knowledge that it overspills its own generic boundaries. The question of what a poem *is*, in this context, is yet another chance to engage with the work of literary analysis, but in a way that explores the aesthetic possibilities of hermeneutics and (yes) critical thinking. How does critical discursivity respond to the line, and vice versa? What leaps in logic can a poem committed, in a sense, to explaining itself still sustain? What remains of the image in the wake of linguistic positivism? These questions are everywhere in the background of academic avant-garde poetry, and to the extent that they are "merely" aesthetic questions, they are also and crucially questions that require more than a journey of self-discovery to answer, even if self-discovery is part of the picture. They require, in the most strenuous cases, an entire culture of discourse, one learned and practiced and transmitted in a deliberate manner by intellectual workers.

If one "double bind" of the humanities is, as in Spivak's view, the dialectic between being opposed to and being supported by globalization, another emerges from the situation just described: the bind, that is, between democratization and elitism. Artistic avant-gardes are almost by definition elitist; their claim to novelty is by necessity based in scarcity (*we're the only ones doing this*). And as the humanities become ever more marginal to the mission of higher education, arguments for their continued survival bifurcate according to one's attitude toward vanguardism as a social position: more "public" humanities, if one is not inclined to be sympathetic, and an increased insistence on the value of specialized analytical discourses, if one is. I will not mince words here: I do not think that the salvation of literary studies rests in more of its professors writing for *The Atlantic*, and no amount of clear, succinct, and plainspoken lyric (the caricature of the "workshop poem") has managed appreciably to budge the public market for poetry readers, aforementioned social media notwithstanding. I think it is useful and worthwhile to ask what function advanced artistic and scholarly work might serve in the imagining of a good and fulfilling life. To radically democratize *that*, then, would be the goal.

This is essentially John Guillory's argument at the very end of *Cultural Capital*, and I will return to it in the next chapter.[36] That chapter seeks to ground the book's historical argument by looking back, first, to modernism and the university at the turn of the century—a time in which educational reformism began to take the career-oriented, individualist shape we recognize today. Taking Wallace Stevens as my primary case study, I show that Stevens's enduring commitment to the kind of intellectual work he learned to do at Harvard is clearly legible in his (in)famously abstract, philosophical poetry. I want to suggest that that poetry, the overwhelming majority of which he wrote while working in insurance, served as an antidote to workaday life—a way to keep the most pressing conversations from his undergraduate years alive. This sense of intellectual labor as a type of freedom, even if a difficult and often melancholy one, is a sense that continues to shape both how study in the humanities is justified and the self-perception of workers therein as a class, even if that class is increasingly fractured along the lines of who has a stable job and who doesn't.

The second half of the chapter makes a rather dramatic leap from the early part of the century to the later part, specifically to the eighties and nineties, during which time Language poetry made lasting inroads into the academy—inroads made because of a complex combination of the canonicity of modernist experimentalism, the rise of literary theory, and perhaps counterintuitively, the advent of the modern form of discourse surrounding the ongoing "crisis in the humanities." If Stevens used poetic reflexivity as a way to keep the "dream," as he put it, of a creative life in sight, innovative poets in the academy in the later twentieth century use it to resist some of the more calcifying rhetorics of creative writing programs. I briefly fill in the gap between these two periods by outlining the formation of the academic "mainstream" poetry (what Charles Bernstein calls "Official Verse Culture") that these programs supposedly produce, giving shape to the intra-academic dynamics of vanguardism that characterize the contemporary period.

Taken together with this introduction, the book's first section lays out the major theoretical concepts that structure each chapter as well as a historical trajectory that forms the general backdrop for this book's intervention. While I am primarily concerned with the contemporary period (if indeed there is such a thing), the very slipperiness of the present as a period requires both a bit of an anchor in a slightly less mobile bit of history—modernism— as well as an organizational strategy that does not pronounce periodicity where there perhaps isn't one yet. Thus, the book's first section serves as that anchor, while each chapter in the second and third sections takes on a very broad category of the activity of literary studies, providing provisional definitions of each type of activity but spending the bulk of its time demonstrating the pressures that poetic discourse puts on those very definitions. In turn, a subsidiary aim of each chapter is to help us rethink not only the work of literary scholarship, but also the work of creative writing. The overarching goal is to show conclusively that there is a spectrum of interdependence between them, and that understanding that spectrum is one of the most important tools we have for comprehending the field of poetic production in our time.

In the next section of the book, then, I take up broad categorizations of *labor*: in the second chapter, *professional reading*, and in the third, *teaching*. The first claims under its auspices both the legacy of the New Criticism as well as the challenges to the very idea of "reading" a text posed by deconstruction. For poets who find an academic reading public in this period, the question of what it means to read a text professionally gains a particular urgency. Chapter 2 discusses the poetry of John Ashbery, possessor of one of the widest and most solid academic audiences of the last hundred years. Ashbery is an academic poet less for his own participation in the world of colleges and universities than for his outsized impact on it; as one of the most written-about poets of his time, his brand of difficulty and poetic intellection has left an indelible mark on both the study and practice of the genre. Ashbery's writing, which (like Stevens's) has a tendency to read itself, does so anxiously, rather than authoritatively; in so doing, it registers a nervousness about obscurantism, abstraction, and its own relevance. These are some of the things that academic literary critics also have a tendency to get worked up about, not only for the justification-related reasons discussed above, but also because such justification, even though "outwardly" directed, also forces academic intellectuals to (re)evaluate the terms on which they base their own class imaginary. The chapter ends with a brief look at the poetry of Mei-mei Berssenbrugge and the evolution of this auto-analytic style.

If the notion of "professional reading" requires some untangling of disciplinary history, the notion (if not the practice) of teaching seems self-explanatory—teaching is teaching; you know it when you see it. I will argue to the contrary that the labor of teaching encodes complex epistemological concerns that are of particular interest to poets, working as they do in a medium that is often seen as something that cannot (or even should not) be taught. Chapter 3 thus turns to the epistemological pedagogies of Jorie Graham's poetry in order to look at the ways in which theories of teaching, inscribed within theories of knowledge and transmission, become vehicles for thinking about hierarchy, generosity, and avant-garde acceptance in a higher educational context. In particular, contained within Graham's tendencies toward the romantically obscure is a deep ambivalence about divulgence: how much, in other words, to "give away" in the writing. This ambivalence is particularly prominent in *The End of Beauty*, a volume much talked about for its formal innovation and related difficulty. I suggest that Graham's poetic epistemology in this book, which is filled with gaps and withholdings and references to secrets, is simultaneously pedagogical within those very gaps.

The third section of the book takes the concept of "reading" and makes it a bit more granular, looking at the way in which critical methodologies, i.e. the *work* of literary study, show up in a wide range of contemporary poetry. The fourth chapter describes the uses and re-uses of *disciplinary theorizing* in poetry seeking to renegotiate the terms of identity writing; the fifth chapter looks toward poetic uses of *archival historicism* as a way of situating even the most intimate acts of self-expression within their (sometimes jarring) historical contexts. In the former, John Keene and Claudia Rankine are discussed in tandem as a way of charting how the use of theoretical-philosophical paradigms in contemporary Black experimental poetry can reframe both the cited paradigms and the specific kinds of autobiographical expectations often imposed upon writers of color. The first reframing allows us to see the deep symmetries between the intellectual projects of these poets and the development of African American studies as an academic discipline, while the second sheds light on the way in which those symmetries shift questions of self-expression away from authorial invention and onto large, networked narratives of identity and belonging.

From there, the fifth chapter examines a broad network of poets whose writing is dependent on, even as it is suspicious of, a type of empirical historicism. As the writing of poetry has professionalized within the orbit of the university, when it does take on the subject of history, it both assumes some of the characteristics of academic literary historicism—because it has access to the same materials—and uses these characteristics to push back against a traditional notion of lyric autobiography propagated by workshop practices. Nowhere are these tendencies more pronounced than in the work of Susan Howe, and the bulk of the chapter focuses on her hybrid-genre work. Howe, like Ashbery, is not a product of a creative writing program. But her life and writing are marked all over by her proximity to universities, both positively (in terms of her love of libraries and special collections) and negatively (in terms of being and feeling barred from those collections). Fiercely attached to the materiality of texts, she has intervened in numerous scholarly debates about collation and editing and biographical interpretation, particularly regarding the works of Emily Dickinson but also, I argue, regarding her own life as archivist and archival subject. Using a capacious definition of archive that attempts to encompass both the Foucauldian sense of it as a category marker and Derrida's notion of archive as desire, I situate Howe's archival autobiography at the forefront of a wave of concern, visible in the writing of authors such as Myung Mi Kim, Catherine Taylor, Jena Osman, and Christian Hawkey, about the sourcing of the self.

These broad categorizations of what it means to do academic work in the humanities are in no way mutually exclusive. To return to Ron Silliman's metaphor, and at the risk of really overextending it this time, they are instead some of the buffet stations that the university-gorilla has set up at the party of poets. And if you think (as I do) that it would be worthwhile to answer Silliman's call for "a far more critical and specific taxonomy of the divergent writings" produced from within academic institutions, then it is time to look at the plates that have been assembled.[37] They can, as I'll point out in a brief coda, nourish us, too. For those of us that see some version of our own bricolage of commitments in them, they can help restore our belief in the value of what we do (even as they show us, in the process, the ways in which we distort ourselves with worry); for those that encounter them earlier in their educations, they can create an enriched sense of what it is possible to do with the kinds of analytic techniques usually seen as fusty, dry, or irrelevant. Above all, they can help us see the ways in which "critical thinking," normally a milquetoast bucket into which we put vague hopes of a better citizenry, can be honed into as sharp and fine a point as you'd like, capable both of cutting into and around the bruised and broken bits of our academic culture, and of suturing the whole thing up into new shapes.

In a talk entitled "Cultural Studies and Its Theoretical Legacies," Stuart Hall presents a central dialectical tension besetting those trying to do cultural-analytical work: the idea "that culture will always work through its textualities — and at the same time that textuality is never enough."[38] It's a particularly vexing problem for literary studies (where the primary objects of study are texts). But as Hall suggests, perhaps there is a solution in the struggle toward a "genuine cultural and critical practice," one in which frameworks of analytical thinking form the basis for collective life.[39] The writers considered in this study, in their various and oblique ways, invite us to look with fresh eyes at this struggle, at its dangers and opportunities. It is truly difficult to say what the future of the academy will look like, and it is easy to imagine it as bleak. But fatalism gets us nowhere, and it may well be true, as Robert Cashin Ryan has put it, that "the apparatus that has kept us endlessly in wait might have granted us resources completely antithetical to market-expectation."[40] So let's take stock of what weapons we have, and then figure out how to deploy them.

1

The Dream and the Deed

Wallace Stevens was not exactly an enthusiastic student. He was a good one, earning mostly As and Bs during the course of his three-year special program at Harvard, but on the whole he took a dim view of the process of book learning. A journal entry toward the end of his studies will sound familiar to anyone who has ever suffered from the American educational illness often dubbed *senioritis*: "I shall be rather glad to forget many things that have happened. Nine months have been wasted. In the Autumn I got drunk about every other night, and later, from March until May, and a good bit of May, I did nothing but loaf."[1] These are not the words of a diligent studier of texts—but they contain, too, a twinge of regret, a frustration about time wasted not *with* schoolwork but with *not*-schoolwork. In the back of his head were likely his father's regular reminders to "keep hammering at your work, my boy," as "time mis-spent now counts heavily."[2]

It's hard to say what, exactly, counted as time misspent for the younger Stevens. Shifting constantly between a paternally inherited conviction that education was a tool (specifically a bootstrap), the opposing conviction that it was an end in itself, and the romantic notion that nothing one learns in a classroom compares to first-hand observation of the natural world, Stevens spent a lot of time thinking about how best to "realize to the last degree any of the ambitions [he had] formed" during his student years.[3] Those ambitions were themselves tangled: in the same journal entry, Stevens proclaims his split allegiance between the "dream" of creative activity and the "deed" of practical work, between wanting his literary "powers to be put to their fullest use" and not wanting "to have to make a petty struggle for existence—physical or literary."[4] And during his attempt to make it as a journalist in New

York—a career that would not in the end pan out for him, leading to his enrollment in law school—he asked himself very bluntly a still relevant question: "Is literature really a profession? Can you single it out, or must you let it decide in you for itself?"[5]

The creative writing program, of course, had not yet sprung up to tackle those questions, leaving us to speculate what a writer like Stevens might have done had he the opportunity to pursue his "literary existence" at the university level. Aside from turning in a set of sonnets as his long theme for English 22 in the spring of 1899, Wallace Stevens's studies at Harvard were relatively staid, consisting mostly of courses in English, French, and German language and literature, with a smattering of politics, economics, and history thrown in for good measure.[6] As a special (non-degree) student, Stevens was freed from the course constraints of any one department, making him one of the earlier examples of the modern liberal-arts major. This freedom collided with familial expectations in odd ways: on the one hand, Stevens could in theory pursue study that pleased him (see: the sonnets), but on the other, he was constantly reminded that what *ought* to please him should be a profitable job. "It will not do," intoned his father, "to put off the thought of subsistence as a drone matter."[7]

In *Modernist Quartet*, Frank Lentricchia details the ways in which modernist philosophy grappled with the "genteel tradition" of "Pateresque aestheticism" by linking poetic perception to structures of work and labor. Describing George Santayana's Marcusean utopian aesthetics, in which the "joyless grind known as *work*" would be annihilated by the triumph of "aesthetic play," Lentricchia invokes precisely this tension that characterized Stevens's time at Harvard: an environment where upper-crust intellectuals grappled with the desire to have an "intensity and purity of perceptual pleasure" while acknowledging the driving need to have a functioning career. Ironically, he notes, such pleasure did not at all come in the form of the clear image in a pure poetry: instead, the "reality" of Stevens's work is that of "self-conscious... dense and difficult substance," aimed at "those with the most patient critical attention."[8] Santayana's critique of modernism, which Stevens doubtless absorbed, centered on its dangerous nostalgia for "primitive innocence," symbolized by the unity of word and thing. His "antidote," Lentricchia writes, "is what he called the philosophical poem," one that in its modernist instantiation would "subordinate image and character to their 'effects and causes,' their context and condition."[9] Stevens, from his first days in Cambridge a reluctant joiner of the workforce, found in this sort of philosophical poetry a temporary respite from the drudgery.

Poetry, for Stevens, was thus always a form of resistance. This fact has not gone unremarked by critics, who have read in his work a host of things against which he was wont to push.[10] In the well-known opening of "Man Carrying Thing," Stevens remarks upon it himself: "The poem must resist the intelligence / almost successfully."[11] As Bart Eeckhout has pointed out, much depends on that little qualifier "almost": "if Stevens wants the intelligence to be resisted," he writes, "he does not want it to be ultimately defeated. In one of several possible readings, he continues to long for the serendipity of *some* sort of intelligence, even if (and perhaps because) it will be hard to come by."[12] That "*some* sort of intelligence," presumably, has little to do with the pragmatic and rational rituals of career preparation—the kind of intelligence, in other words, embodied by his father Garret, a successful schoolteacher-turned-lawyer whose belief in the power of the Protestant work ethic bordered on the dogged. The poem must resist that type of intelligence, we can safely say, more or less entirely.[13] To what, then, must it give in, after a struggle? What spark in the mind results in the appearance of "the bright obvious," as the last line of the poem reads, "motionless in cold"?

In what follows, I want to suggest that such an intelligence, resisted and resistant, is the feature of Stevens's style that most fundamentally undergirds the poetics of the academic avant-garde. Marking Stevens as a precursor to anything one might call "avant-garde" may sound like a stretch; certainly Hugh Kenner and Marjorie Perloff, two of the great champions of Ezra Pound, have made it a difficult claim to make. But I am nevertheless making it, and I am not the first one: Srikanth Reddy, in a reading of Stevens not so far from my own, has argued for Stevens's "discursive activism," in which "description may be revelation, but digression is revolution."[14] Reddy's analysis sees the artful changing of the poetic subject, as opposed to the more "postmodern" tradition of poetic fragmentation, as a central effect of modern poetry's grappling with Enlightenment subjectivity. I'd argue that modern poetry's grappling with Enlightenment subjectivity takes place increasingly on the terrain of the university, and so it makes sense to also look at the effects of that shift in locale. But I also do not want to overlook the even larger, more generally structural forces that have shaped that site of production, and it is at this more abstract level that it makes sense to begin this story with Stevens, rather than with, say, a mid-century poet who took a degree in creative writing. For Stevens's discursive style presages, in many ways, the discursive stylings of an entire emergent class—one that has been framed as itself a type of vanguard.

In "Sailing After Lunch," Stevens's wandering proposals include the following: "The romantic should be here. / The romantic should be there. / It ought to be everywhere. / But the romantic must never remain, / Mon Dieu, and must never again return."[15] This startlingly direct thesis on modernist poetry in the middle of a modernist poem is a crystallization, I'd argue, of something that in later decades becomes a *culture of class feeling*: one based upon what the sociologist Alvin Ward Gouldner has identified as the "culture of critical discourse," or CCD. This type of discourse, Gouldner argues, is the defining rhetoric of what he calls the "New Class" of professional-intellectuals, "neither identical to the old working class nor to the old moneyed class."[16] The CCD, in his description, is *fundamentally* reflexive: that is, it is "self-monitoring, capable of more meta-communication, that is, of talk about talk"—further, it is "able to make its own speech problematic . . . the CCD thus requires considerable 'expressive discipline.'"[17] As a form of discourse concerned above all with *justification*, as Gouldner has it, the CCD is perfectly suited not only to a profession that creates texts about texts, but also to one that sees itself as having to argue in a near-constant way over and for the terms of its survival.[18]

In Stevens's poem, we encounter a dark form of this "self-monitoring" on planes both stylistic and temporal: jokey musings about romanticism try, and largely fail, to lend an air of nonchalance to what are essentially grave concerns about the state of poetry in the early part of the twentieth century. The "heavy historical sail" under which Stevens's boat is circling impotently is "wholly the vapidest fake"—a vicious rebuttal of exactly that sense of historical nostalgia about romantic immediacy that the poem had just expressed. Such auto-critique is a way of working through the vanguardist desire for a complete breakage from the past with an awareness (however grudging) that the sail of history cannot simply be torn down but must instead be somehow adjusted (given, in the words of the poem, a "slight transcendence") in order to put the boat on course. On course toward what? The poem's paper-thin allegory doesn't say; it says only that one ought to leave fossilized tropes behind and be, instead, "a pupil / Of the gorgeous wheel," by which he means the steering apparatus of one's own ship. To be a pupil, thus, remains central: the question then becomes who, or what, makes up the wheel of this pedagogical vessel. There is a real sense in which Stevens thinks that it could be (modern) poetry that teaches us how to think about the world—but before it can do that, its authors must figure out what poetry is. It is this reflexive theorizing that takes place with unprecedented explicitness in our contemporary era—not coincidentally, an era in which it is relatively hard to get an education in literature without encountering Wallace Stevens.

Gouldner's theory of the intellectual class remains deeply compelling, I'd argue, precisely because it is also a discursive theory: one that asserts that class sensibility can be *formed* through language, rather than language being merely an effect of socioeconomic positionality. Stevens was, in the end, a member of what is often called the professional-managerial class.[19] But he was also a "humanistic intellectual" as Gouldner defines it: his interests, in plentiful evidence throughout his poetry, were "critical, emancipatory, [and] hermeneutic."[20] Gouldner goes on to say that such a combination often winds up also being "political"; this is the extrapolation that Reddy would have us make about Stevens's fixation on change. I don't want to make too much of the immediate political implications of Stevens's ways of handling language. I do, however, want to make a case for that handling being both more radical and more prescient than we might normally think, which is why I'm linking it to a sociological theory developed in the late seventies, precisely when the remainder of this story as told in the chapters that follow begins to unfold. The dialectics that Stevens creates—between Romanticism and modernism, between "literature" and "profession"—are ones that persist, and they persist in the culture of critical discourse that now produces both literary studies and a growing share of the literary itself.

Gouldner recognized this facet of the New Class's political economy as well, and his description of the contradictions at the heart of the modern university in sections 7.3 and 7.4 of *The Future of Intellectuals and the Rise of the New Class* is perhaps still the best that we have:

> Academicization often withdraws concern for the major crises of society, sublimating it into obsessive puzzle-solving, into "technical" interests. Obsequious professors may teach the advanced course in social cowardice, and specialists transmit narrow skills required by bureaucracies. But Ronald Reagan did not set

out to curb the University of California because it was a servant of capitalism. [. . .] Like the patriarchal family, the school is surely conceived by its managers as an instrument for the self-perpetuation of the *status quo*. And yet, in both cases, while it rarely *teaches* rebellion, many young people learn it during their education.²¹

How does this happen? In this study's introduction, I pointed out that however bowdlerized the phrase, "critical thinking" can still point to a set of intellectual and discursive practices designed to produce some level of dissatisfaction with said *status quo*. Gouldner would call this the culture of critical discourse. In the modern university, this culture is perhaps one of the only things holding together a discipline like literary studies, particularly given the increasingly strong economic stratification from which it suffers. We know by now the widening gulf that yawns between the working conditions of, for example, a tenured faculty member at an R1 university and those of the legions of contingently employed instructors, many of whom have doctorates from these very universities, that are now responsible for the bulk of tertiary education in fields like English and modern languages. What they share is a dedication to (and expertise in) the culture of critical discourse that Gouldner identifies. What they cannot share is his feeling that this discursive class formation will come someday to a universal, even revolutionary, success—but even here there is some small form of optimism about the CCD *itself*.

That is to say, a belief in the power of reflexive critical thought—thinking about thinking, being able to express the very conditions that allow oneself to have expression—persists in driving the praxes of humanistic scholars both permanent and precarious, and yokes them together (however unsteadily) in a cultural-political formation based upon this broad category of intellection and discourse. When Jerome McGann praises, somewhat eye-openingly, both Susan Howe *and* Harold Bloom in the same sentence as writers for whom "the scholarly event is pursued as an archaeology of knowing," it is their dedication to the infinitely multiplying complications of the culture of critical discourse to which he points.²² When Charles Bernstein, a writer to whom I'll return later in this chapter, envisions an ideal university in which scholars and poets "reorient themselves toward a kind of inquiry in which there are no final solutions, no universally mandated protocols," it is the culture of critical discourse ("the refusal," as Gouldner puts it, "to let things simmer down") that he venerates.[23] And while there is real risk here of glorifying argumentation as itself a politics, the cultivation of inquiry as a *capability*, one which might prime those in whom it is cultivated to "examine the life [they] lead rather than just enjoy or suffer it," certainly has real political potential. Critique, after all, is a harder activity for capital to co-opt than that of expressing oneself. As an *aesthetics*, then, the culture of critical discourse is that interrogative capability made manifest in art. The functions that such manifestations perform vary widely, but they are all invested in the "restlessness" of the critical viewpoint, that is, the viewpoint that refuses to naturalize "the present and the assumptions it uses."[24]

It is this difficult restlessness—one that looses the poem from external referent while introducing thematic questions about the nature of that loosing—that has been glossed in Stevens criticism for decades but has not yet been recognized for what it now is: a form of cerebral modernism particularly well-suited to a later era in which a huge number of published poets have advanced degrees. Marjorie Perloff herself, interestingly, dismisses Stevens's innovations precisely on the grounds that they are, in fact, too much an "advanced form of 'interpretation'"; for her, Stevens is too interested in his own "strenuous effort to reimagine what he calls the First Idea."[25] Helen Vendler has called it his "pensive style," but she is generally uninterested in the implications of this style for Stevens's place in the modernist canon—or for his place on the syllabus.[26] Instead of viewing Stevens's poetic thinking as a circular hermeticism, no matter how interesting, or as the lens through which he processes the entirety of his "contact with life at large," I propose a terminology of vanguardism reframed around the possibilities opened up by the legacy of his poetic auto-reflexivity.[27]

For while not as referential as Pound, nor as linguistically and formally experimental as Stein, Stevens is perhaps American modernism's most radically philosophical poet, less interested in the imagistic collage and disjunction that more obviously marks the modernist avant-garde than in highly consistent, abstract meditations on perception and ontology—the stuff, that is, of which poems are made. And in this abiding, reflexive concern with how poetry works, one finds tonal modes and sets of concerns that resonate deeply with those of literary criticism, highlighting the reciprocally sustaining relationship between the two modes of writing that would more explicitly come to characterize an era in which both, for good and for ill, are "really a profession" within the structure of the academy. In the early poem "The

Weeping Burgher," Stevens opens with the lines "it is with strange malice/ that I distort the world," capturing a poststructuralist sensibility *avant la lettre* both in its focus on how the word mutates the world (a prelude to the deeply canonical "Anecdote of the Jar") and in the resultant reflexivity about the nature of the poem's own discourse.[28] Stevens's views on the work of poetry—those distortions as well as its unavoidable interpretations, and the relationship between the abstract and concrete—turn out, that is, to mesh very well with the evolving work of literary study in the later part of the twentieth century, giving him an outsized presence in the academic criticism of the last seventy-five years.

In *Wallace Stevens and the Limits of Reading and Writing*, Bart Eeckhout lays out the situation succinctly: "reading Stevens, as a literary critic, can no longer be done without confronting the full-blown critical industry that has sprung up in the poet's wake."[29] He goes on to describe the disciplinary situation that gave rise to such an industry, tying it to "the boom years of educational democratization" (the sixties) and the developing backlash against the interpretive methods of the New Criticism. Where Eeckhout differs from historicist critics such as John Timberman Newcomb is in his focus on "the qualities of the poetry *itself* as those qualities *interacted with* those institutional practices."[30] Identifying broad and well-known characteristics such as "ambivalence" and "liminality," he explores how the indeterminateness of such between-states allows professional studiers of literature to do their jobs: if a poet is endlessly interpretable, then the task of the literary critic is never finished. And Stevens, it is implied, is one of modernity's very best suppliers of infinity.

This keeps the ink flowing, to be sure—but there is more to Stevens's persistence of legacy than his poetry's enticing ambiguity. His "malicious distortions" reflect not just a commitment to a modernist sensibility concerned with "making it new," but also a real concern with the analytic possibilities of poetic language—concern that would find its way, in significant part via modernism's (and thus Stevens's) canonization, into the poetry of experimental writers who hone their crafts within the university system. The link between Stevens's work and the poets who are the focus of the bulk of this study, then, has less to do with Stevens's career (unlike Pound, he was never a professor) or even his more obvious proclivities (unlike Eliot, he wasn't the most dedicated student), but rather in the fact that *despite* his ambivalence toward academic institutions, he produced some of the most influentially ruminative poetry of the early twentieth century. This poetry, as Simon Critchley has put it, uses as its driving mode of discourse the language of philosophical "theses, hypotheses, [and] conjectures."[31] These thought forms pre-empt the philosophical reader, as it were, in a way that signals a shared commitment to that very language: to its seriousness and importance, and to its potential role in creating an autonomous space for cogitation free from practical necessity and not secondary to some transcendental "real." (It is not a coincidence that university study is so often placed in opposition, as a rhetorical jab, to the "real world.")

The truth in poetry, or its access to the "real," exists for Stevens in multifaceted attempts to get as close as possible to the mechanisms of thought: to be able to say with more or less certainty that "I know, too, / That the blackbird is involved / In what I know."[32] Such epistemological reflexivity is a crucial part of the cultural-class formation of the academy and its surrounds, and it is less concerned with certainty than it is with examining the quality and conditions of "certain-ness." Stevens's professed aversion to academic study, it's important to remember, is an aversion to a very different kind of study from the web of methodologies that make up contemporary literary analysis. To yearn for immanence is not the same thing as a desire for scientific rationality, and the dominance of philology in turn of the century English departments evinced a much more vested interest in the latter than the former.[33]

Such insistence on the justification of literary study via quasi-scientism was, predictably, unappealing to modernist poets, who wanted space for the aforementioned "poetic reality" distinct from the airlessness of philological quantification. "Is the function of the poet mere sound . . . to stuff the ear?" asks Stevens rhetorically in that tantalizingly titled poem "Academic Discourse at Havana."[34] He worries that it might be—his poems are exceedingly attentive to the sounds of words—but in the end, "let the poet on his balcony / Speak, and the sleepers in their sleep shall move, / Waken, and watch the moonlight on their floors." Both ears and eyes are unstuffed, as it were, in these lines. The type of observation to which the poet exhorts his listeners is not the rationality-seeking observation of scientific inquiry but rather "an infinite incantation of our selves": a constant reiteration of the poetic act. Indeed, "Poetry is the subject of the poem," he writes in "The Man with the Blue Guitar," "From this the poem issues and / To this returns. Between the two, / . . . there is / An absence in reality, / Things as they are."[35] Endlessly preoccupied with the distortions of which poetry is made, Stevens's brand of difficulty stems from how hard the poetry thinks about itself—and thus, how hard it makes the reader think about what it is.

Stevens's poetry may be difficult, in other words, but it's difficult in a strangely explanatory way. Not content with merely presenting or even carefully arranging empirical details, Stevens more than any other modernist wrote poems that are arranged like argumentative propositions. To return to the opening of "Man Carrying Thing" at this point requires the addition of a few extra lines: "[t]he poem must resist the intelligence / Almost successfully. Illustration: / A brune figure in winter evening resists / Identity."[36] Written in 1945, a full four decades after Stevens left Harvard, the poem uses a lyrical image (as it were)—the figure in the winter evening—as an example to support an assertion, which is that its reality is secondary to our thoughts about its reality, and that this state of affairs is distressing but unavoidable. Stevens's reaction to this unavoidability is to confront it head-on: to attempt, as I am doing now, to examine the tensions that exist between talking about the world as empirically verifiable and thinking about it as a series of linguistic slippages. And as literary study moved away from philology over the course of the twentieth century—a move that Stevens hoped for and, indeed, encouraged—it moved toward texts whose esotericism more closely matched its own interests in the generative logics of autopoesis.[37]

This multivalent shift in the aims and methods of professional literary reading is in large part how modernism gets canonized, and it is also at the root of the strange forward-backward definition of *academic* that plagues all attempts at a taxonomy of the word's relationship to the arts. To wit: the academy is at once conservative and radical, didactic and obscurantist—and modernist poetry, which explains itself while simultaneously demanding that its reader possess a certain training in order to read it, also occupies these contradictions. Aestheticized in the play between clarity (Williams's famous and meme-able plums in iceboxes) and opacity (the same author's *Paterson*, a book of referential pastiche that attempts a mystical total history of the eponymous New Jersey town), modernism's poetics are, to echo Gail McDonald, a record of the uses to which these poetics have been put by both writers and critics in the American university.[38]

The dominance of the Poundian paradigm for thinking about the avant-garde has obscured some of these uses, and we ignore them to our detriment. Stevens, as we know, was not interested in *Cantos*-esque pastiche; from the point of view of *techne*, it would indeed seem that the formal methods of a poet like Susan Howe, the main subject of this study's fifth chapter, look much more like MAKING IT NEW than like any idea of order, at Key West or no. But as I laid out in the introduction, there is in reality little in common between the world that Howe patches together and the "uncreative" writing that Perloff sees as the most lasting legacy of Pound's work.[39] Recently, Howe has in fact written on (and, as she is wont to do with her literary forebears, with and around) Stevens, in particular Stevens's formative encounters with pragmatic and epistemological philosophy during his undergraduate days:

> How can the chosen words "philosophy and "poetry" ever attain true harmony? Intent on one disciplined desire, you stare longingly at qualities acting and being acted on in the other ("I quiz all sounds, all thoughts, all everything / For the music and manner of the paladins / To make oblation fit. Where shall I find / Bravura adequate to this great hymn?" ["Le Monocle de Mon Oncle," 1923]). Perhaps, at 73, remembering the hero [George Santayana] of his early college days, Stevens could look back and recognize that his necessary calling, its faith and risk, was to address poetically the search for truth Santayana, inspired by his master and model Spinoza, had addressed discursively.[40]

In this formulation, Stevens's "necessary calling" was to be a poetic philosopher—to turn a discursive search into a poetic one. What Stevens did, in the end, was to make a discursive poetry, one which has clear resonances with Howe's intertwining of lyric compression and essayistic exegesis. Howe may take her formal cues from the radical fragmentation of Pound and Stein, in other words, but the way in which she presses that fragmentation into the service of coherent argumentation tells a more complicated story.

That story involves Stevens's persistent concern regarding the artistic capabilities of abstract cogitation, something he puts into uneasy contact with a more intuitive notion of "natural" positivism. This contact, I've suggested, manages to resist both the pull of romantic transcendence and fin-de-siècle discussions about educational rationalization via a similar form of reflexive critical thinking. By foregrounding the tension between the "real" and thinking about reality (or as Howe might put it, the truth and one's searching for it), Stevens's poetry enacts on the page the struggle to carve out a place for the difficult, impractical effort of interrogating what we can know about the world. And while nobody was yet thinking about "tenured radicals" in 1899, the tensions that would come to characterize the university as simultaneously a haven for cutting-edge thought and a bastion of traditionalism were already beginning to be pulled taut. Then and for a whole career thereafter, Stevens grappled with his own nostalgic tendencies via a melancholy, knowing skepticism that he developed while navigating what it meant to get an education. His "poem[s] of the act of the mind," as he puts it in "Of Modern Poetry," are poems that evince the lasting impact of the "reactionary" strain of academic humanism that now, in our moment of hyperpragmatism, seems radical indeed.

So: in his grousing about schoolwork or lack thereof, Stevens slogs semi-reluctantly through one version of the academy—but in his poetry, we find another, much less reluctant version, one that explains not only his remarkable popularity among literary critics in the later part of the century but also the persistence of his discursive style in the work of the writers that form the bulk of this story. The first version was his father's, consummate believer in the career-preparation model of education that he was: he never missed an opportunity to remind his son that he was "not out on a pic-nic—but really preparing for the campaign of life—where self sustenance is essential and everything depends upon [one]self."[41] Stevens, as we know, found this individualistic pragmatism persuasive. But the second—that "intelligence" acquiesced to in "Man Carrying Thing," which allows one to see the world for what it is—is, while deeply introspective, not exactly individualistic (the "figure" that the intelligence is almost seeing "resists / Identity") and certainly not pragmatic. It is instead, as we have seen, a version of learning that makes a home in its own processes, that tarries and seeks, in a sense, only itself. That such contradictory models of education could coexist testifies to the upheavals that marked the turn-of-the-century academy—upheavals that continue to complicate what we mean when we describe something literary as also something *academic*.

Indeed, Harvard in 1901 was an active laboratory of educational policy. Although the idea of the creative writing workshop wouldn't be floated for some decades, the conditions for the convergence of the literary arts and the university were being set as many of America's most influential modern poets were setting their things down in dormitory rooms. As is well known but rarely discussed as such, American high modernism is a product of the

Ivy League and the Seven Sisters, be the poets under consideration Eliot and Stevens at Harvard, Stein at Radcliffe, Pound at Penn, or Moore and HD at Bryn Mawr.[42] And it was in these elite institutions that the "progressive reform" movement in tertiary education took hold, coaxed along by Charles W. Eliot, relative of T. S. and president of Harvard from 1869 to 1909. This movement oversaw the relaxation of core curriculum requirements and the introduction of electives, changes designed to encourage individualized development and workforce readiness.[43]

Unsurprisingly, these reforms were met with a backlash from certain faculty members who viewed such professionalization as antithetical to the mission of higher education. One of these faculty members was the philosopher George Santayana. Santayana's relationship with the young Wallace Stevens has been documented most thoroughly by Al Filreis, whose extensive chronicling of Stevens's life through the 1930s gives an indispensable sense of what academics were reacting to at Harvard in the early 1900s and how that reaction lines up with much later pushback, primarily in the humanistic fields, against the transformation of higher education into vocational training. In particular, Filreis traces the ways in which Stevens absorbed both Santayana's philosophical writings and his views on the value of college "as a retreat" from "the pressures of daily life" rather than as preparation for them. "I wish reformers," Santayana wrote, "instead of trying to make the colleges more useful and professional, would try to make the world more like the colleges."[44]

This skepticism toward curricular liberalization resists easy political categorization. Filreis describes the "Harvard resistance," by which he means that "vocal minority" of professors just described who were unhappy about President Eliot's modifications, as "reactionary" and "antimodern," both of which judgments are in a sense literally true.[45] Their specific objections, however, which included a distrust of positivism and "utilitarian optimism," a belief in education as an end in itself, and a will to shield universities from the whims of the free market, sound very much like later critiques of higher education's more corporatist tendencies that tend to come from the left.[46] These later critiques, of course, do not share the earlier's desire for a return to the days in which the university's purpose was to afford genteel young men some time to learn Latin and Greek. Instead (in the best cases), they envision an academy in which access to the time and space needed to develop one's brain is more, rather than less, democratized. But in both cases, departments of classics tend to get defended—an interesting proxy for the perceived threat that the world of business poses to the world of the academy.

Students need jobs after they graduate: it is true now, and it was true for Stevens. But in the time that Stevens had to enjoy a broad-based humanistic education, he discovered both the pleasures and the pains of cogitation unmoored from practical necessity. While the elimination of Harvard's common curriculum was designed to allow students to choose electives better suited to the eventual development of their prospective careers, Stevens's studies as enumerated above reflected a real inclination toward something like the old "*Ratio Studiorum.*"[47] Stevens demonstrated, in other words, an aestheticist's interest, not a businessman's (that class in economics? He got a C). And he was thus exactly the kind of student with whom Santayana could exchange sonnets concerning natural and religious design, and who would count such an exchange as time well spent.[48] His enduring commitment to such exchanges in the eventual absence of intellectual partners like Santayana manifests itself in poetry full, as Filreis puts it, of "introspection and self-analysis for its own sake."[49] But "analysis for its own sake" brings with it melancholy realizations about the nature of reality for a poet with Romantic leanings. Stevens puts it clearly in a famous but often misread line from "The Emperor of Ice-Cream": "Let be be finale of seem."[50] Followed by an elaborate image of a corpse in a shroud, this line asserts that death is the only thing we can know for sure: everything else merely "seems." The penultimate line of the poem, "Let the lamp affix its beam," sheds light not on some positive reality but on the intractable presence of metaphor. As much as Stevens might have wanted to break through to "that for which the symbol stands," he found himself working with the models of auto-reflexive thinking that he had acquired at Harvard.[51] Out of Santayana's academic anti-liberalism, then, comes Stevens's version of academic radicalism: having absorbed the conviction that there ought to be something beyond "merely useful knowledge," his poetry enacts both his mournful, "wintry" separation from Romantic notions of poetic transcendence and his resolve to carry on writing in the face of more immediate, materially focused concerns.[52]

All of this is to say that, as the complications of even this narrow slice of history show, the modern academy is not a monolith, and it therefore stands to reason that art produced from within its cultures and competing values will not be either. The possibility that an institution such as the American university could foster vanguardist thought and aesthetics should not be foreclosed simply because the institution itself occupies a dominant position within its sociocultural field.[53] To extend the Bourdieuian metaphor, the case of the academic humanities in this century is an instructive one: they occupy a dominated position within the space of the university (witness the overarching political emphasis on the development of STEM fields), but the university itself has a tendency to reproduce hegemony within the larger field of class relations. This doubleness is the mechanism by which an institutional insider—Santayana surely, but Stevens too—can come to feel very much like an outsider. In the case of writing poetry, bereft as it is from any real access to commercial support, the tension between Stevens's "dream" (of autonomies both intellectual and financial) and "deed" (food on the table) is particularly acute. Stevens's life can thus function as an institutional bellwether: well before both the advent of creative writing and the collapse of the academic job market would make such choices the topic of near-constant debate in the literary realm, he picks the deed, but uses the dream to resist it. Produced as alternative to and respite from his sensible career, and as an alternative to the notion of Romantic immanence (no matter how much he might have desired it), much of Stevens's work relies upon a form of thinking made available to him at university—thinking, that is, for thinking's sake.

Indeed, Stevens's earliest efforts to triangulate the roles of creativity and freedom with tradition and necessity show his work to be remarkably reflective of persistent tensions in the debate over what the American university is *for*, and where the concept of "creativity" (with its associated autonomies, freedoms, impracticalities, and co-optations) fits into that purpose.[54] Writing during summer vacation, a time he relished as it gave him the chance to have "green fields and woods" instead of the "bad photographs and reproductions" of art and literature, Stevens ruminates on the idea of the learned artist:

> Livingood says that I would be surprised at the amount of learning possessed by the English poets. Not at all. But I doubt if he can explain the reason for their acquiring that learning. He thinks they did it as a part of their trade. On the contrary I think they used study as a contrast to poetry. The mind cannot always live in a "divine ether." The lark cannot always sing at heaven's gate. There must exist a place to spring from—a refuge from the heights, an anchorage of thought. Study gives this anchorage: study ties you down; and it is the occasional willful release from this voluntary bond that gives the soul its occasional over-

powering sense of lyric freedom and effort. Study is the resting place—poetry, the adventure.[55]

The contradiction that Stevens sets up between something being "a part of a trade" and it being in contrast to that trade is an odd one: if study is the place from which poetry springs, could poetry exist without it? In his desire to preserve the realm of poetry as one of pure emancipation (presumably from the creativity-stifling burden of literary tradition, or the aforementioned memorization), Stevens articulates a position that would in some sense become the rallying cry for creative writing programs. But by framing his opposition as a dialectic, he also manages to espouse a view that would keep "learning" and the writing of poetry very tightly bound indeed.

"Thought," as the necessary springboard, prevents the poet from imagining themselves too close to the divine. And in so doing, it also bars the poet from an unmediated sense of the positive: thinking about something, that is, always overshadows the thing itself. Stevens's last poem, "Not Ideas about the Thing but the Thing Itself," never achieves, knowingly, that which its title promises. This, too, is a dialectic: one between the world and one's thinking about it. As with poetry and study, the question of whether the two are mutually constitutive or mutually exclusive is one of Stevens's constant preoccupations. In his surreal *Bildungsroman* (*Bildungsgedicht*?) of intellectual development, "Comedian as the Letter C," the title character Crispin is described as the "Socrates of snails," and the poem repeatedly professes a desire for or insistence upon something like natural immediacy, despite the poem's obvious sonic constructedness. Take, for instance, the assonance- and consonance-rich line "the plum survives its poems."[56] To say that a plum survives its poems is not exactly to describe the plum, but rather to theorize about it. To say that "the melon should have apposite ritual" and that "the peach . . . should have an incantation"[57] is not to be either a ritual or incantation but to propose one. The claim, just prior to the line about plums, that "the words of things entangle and confuse" is similarly propositional, but with an added note of wry knowingness (that, it should be noted, again prefigures the deconstructive impulse): Stevens's language is only ever approximate, but it's the only language he has. The yearning for the "real world" and its literal fruit might be there, but the purpose of poetry, in this instance, is to meditate upon rather than inhabit it.

Stevens's preoccupation with the concept of semiotic form ("this invented world," as he puts it in "Notes toward a Supreme Fiction") is a deeply hermeneutic concern, one that he shares with the modern literary critic. Indeed, in "The Idea of Order at Key West," Stevens addresses a real scholar, Ramon Fernandez, in a way which links the critic and poet in a shared philosophical project: "Oh! Blessed rage for order, pale Ramon, / The maker's rage to order words of the sea . . . / And of ourselves and of our origins."[58] Fernandez's "rage for order" would turn out to be fascistic, though Stevens could not have known this; he is here grappling with his own worry that to be human is simply to live in form, "that there never was a world" for the poet "except the one she sang and, singing, made."[59] The critic's predilection for interpretation is a bit of a curse for the poet, denying as it does any hope for artistic transcendence, but in asking a critic to "tell me, if you know . . . / why the glassy lights . . . / Mastered the night and portioned out the sea," Stevens recognizes that it will not suffice to pretend they are not, here, searching for answers to strikingly similar questions.

Thus far, I've been tracing two basic strands of parallelism that link Wallace Stevens to what I am calling the academic avant-garde: his reflexive poetics and his institutional situation. These things are, as I've tried to show, deeply interrelated; so too will they be for the poets that follow this chapter. But the reflection in the mirror that Stevens holds up to the present isn't a perfect one. The university at the end of the twentieth century doesn't look much like it did at the beginning of it, even as there is a lot in the foregoing that I've pointed out as prescient. And so while histories of the American university have been done at much greater length and with much richer detail than I'm capable of in these pages, I want to dwell for a bit on the developments that have brought poetry writing and literary studies even closer together within the space of the university, a space that has become more amenable to the production and dissemination of avant-garde work even as it retains both its literal conservatism and its increasing dependence on market logics.

Indeed, the fact of neoliberalized higher education, which specializes in manufacturing the very "student demand" toward the requirements of global capital to which it says it is merely responding, puts a fine point on the question of whether or not it is possible for a vanguardist poetic vision to be based on conditions of institutionality. And it would be remiss to ignore those institutions' long ties to "state containment," as the bracing work of Juliana

Spahr reminds us.⁶⁰ But to the extent to which those conditions and institutions can, in spite of everything, be conducive to the work of producing and thinking about language, it is useful to examine the ways in which that question has been answered in the affirmative, even with the necessary caveats.⁶¹ The rise of creative writing over the course of the twentieth century has created one of these caveats in the form of some structural complications that avant-garde poets must confront, perhaps particularly the coziness that has developed between its appeal to individualistic freedom (in the form of "expressing oneself") and the goals of the market-liberalized academy described above. Where to turn when you find yourself suspicious of that co-optation? When the workshop, under the guise of nurturing individual talent, seems instead to produce only tradition?

This latter question caricatures the writing program in a way that is easy to disprove at the level of the individual writer while also remaining remarkably durable at a structural level, a signal of the deep contradictions that accompany any attempt to systematize the creative arts. The concept of "individuality" in poetry is, after all, so vague as to be essentially meaningless: from the "find your voice" mantra of the creative writing program brochure to its countercultural resistance to commercial co-optation of the uninstitutionalized avant-garde, nearly any form of poetry can be yoked to some form of what it means to be an individual (including the idea that individuality doesn't exist). One response to there being "no way out of the game of culture," as John Guillory has put it, is to look at the game itself; while this is far from a cure-all, it has broad implications for the poets who are wary of the claims of their own craft, and for who winds up being available as their interlocutors.⁶²

Take the example of Charles Bernstein. A particularly outspoken example of a poet who has embraced his semi-contradictory position as an outsider poet on the inside, Bernstein never attended a graduate program in creative writing but nevertheless helped to found the Poetics Program at SUNY Buffalo, and ended his career as a distinguished professor of English at the University of Pennsylvania. As an undergraduate, he studied philosophy at Harvard with Stanley Cavell. This training in philosophy (and its echoes of Stevens's relationship with Santayana) is telling. His poems, not too dissimilarly from some of Stevens's, are sometimes structured like propositional exercises, although never without an impertinence that can seem, at times, like a flag that points up his avant-garde credentials. In "A Defence of Poetry," a poem whose title he takes from Shelley and that is dedicated to the literary scholar Brian McHale, Bernstein gives us misshapen theses on poetics: "My problem with deploying a term liek/nonelen/in these cases it acutually similar to/your/cirtique of the term ideopigical/unamlsing as a too-broad unanuajce/interprestive proacdeure."[63] Bernstein is responding to an essay by McHale entitled "Making (Non)sense of Postmodernist Poetry," and the blunt object of his misspelling (look! Nonsense! *Or is it*) exists in a strained relationship to the words' conformation to a type of agreed-upon method of academic discourse.[64] In this case, Bernstein is acknowledging the intellectual contribution of his interlocutor while voicing a reservation about that contribution in a specific instance. This way of "speaking," as it were, is the kind of thing that one learns in graduate school or, in the case of Bernstein, through a long relationship with the academic humanities that has been well-documented in studies of Language poetry more broadly.[65]

This relationship, for Bernstein, has produced not only the knowing, nose-thumbing poetry just quoted but also much more serious, decidedly not-misspelled defenses of the possibility inherent within the academic humanities. In *Attack of the Difficult Poems*, a collection of essays, poem-essays, and poems geared toward assessing the state of challenging poetry in the contemporary sphere, Bernstein updates an essay first published in 1997 in a special issue of *Daedalus* dedicated to the examination of the academic profession. In it, he praises the ability of the university to be profoundly multivalent: "the academic profession is not a unified body but composite of many dissimilar individuals and groups pursuing projects ranging from the valiantly idiosyncratic to the proscriptively conventional."[66] While here, too, we find the kinds of knee-jerk critiques often leveled at and within the academic humanities—that it promotes "lifeless prose, bloated . . . with compulsory repetitive explanation," that its "austere probity" is insufficient to effect change, that he submitted an essay to *PMLA* and was rejected—we also find a sincere and stirring belief that, at its best, the literary academy can realize a "grand democratic vista" that looks forward toward "what it is possible to do" in art and letters.[67] Bernstein's, in other words, are not bad faith critiques: he is genuinely interested in making the project of tertiary education the best thing that it can be in the face of what he sees as an unprecedented attack from the forces of the corporate marketplace. For an avowed avant-gardist to be so committed speaks volumes about the ways in which the literary academy has come to imagine itself—politically, culturally, stylistically—in recent years.

But there is, of course, a flip side, and it's one that bridges the gap between Stevens's time at Harvard and Bernstein's time at Buffalo over 80 years later: Bernstein is also the coiner of the term "official verse culture," which he uses as a thinly veiled stand-in for the economies of poetic circulation propped up by the proliferation of academic creative writing programs.[68] While this proliferation began in earnest in the 1960s, a term like "official verse culture" points (intentionally or not) to a longer history that encompasses the very advent of these programs. It has embedded within it as well, this time very unintentionally, a picture of the constrained quarters of the struggle itself. Because Bernstein remains sanguine regarding the possibilities for creativity within the academy, his definition of "official verse culture" must encompass that against which he, in his position as a professor, is working: the pedagogical and curatorial idea, that is, "that innovation and originality are not criteria of aesthetic value."[69] The mass production of writers within the professionalized creative writing system would seem to feed right into such a culture—after all, what can mass production produce besides products for the masses?

The problem here is that there is virtually no mass market for poetry.[70] Certain forms of social media poetry aside, even a poet like Billy Collins could never hope to reach the sales figures of a writer like Jonathan Franzen or David Foster Wallace, the latter of whom is usually regarded as on the more cerebral end of what the general reading public will tolerate. Thus, the "professionalization" of poetry writing within graduate programs in the United States is met with an oddly hermetic kind of suspicion: there's the general feeling, expressed with clipped precision by Marjorie Perloff, that due to the expansion of programs in creative writing, "the sheer number of poets now plying their craft inevitably ensures moderation and safety. The national (or even transnational) demand for a certain kind of prize-winning, 'well-crafted' poem—a poem that the *New Yorker* would see fit to print and that would help its author get one of the 'good jobs' advertised by the Association of Writers & Writing Programs—has produced an extraordinary uniformity."[71] Perloff, here, combines an aesthetic concern with an economic one: poetry is boring, she claims, because you have to be boring in order to get a job teaching others to produce boring poetry. There may be no "mass culture" for poetry, but it manages to have enough devoted adherents to have a definable center against which advocates of more "innovative" work can push. This center is the place from which the creative writing ideological apparatus reproduces itself, and from Perloff's point of view, it's a disaster.

This assessment of the state of American poetry is telling for a few reasons: it displays the extent to which poetry writing at both the apprentice and mentor levels is supported and reproduced by the academic system, and it views that system as having walled creative writing off into a series of self-replicating gardens. In *The Elephants Teach*, the standard history of the development of creative writing as academic program, D. G. Myers laments that by the mid-1970s, "what had begun as an alternative to the schismatizing of literary study had ended as merely another schism": in other words, by 1976 (the last year mentioned in Myers' work), creative writing as such had become so successful that it no longer needed to acknowledge the fact that what put it in place as an academic discipline was, in fact, a group of poet-*critics*.[72] Myers refers here to the *Fugitive* poets and New Critics (not identical but with significant overlap) who gathered at Vanderbilt in the 1920s and '30s to try and reimagine both literary analysis *and* the practice of writing within the academic institution. Evan Kindley traces a similar kind of history in *Poet-Critics and the Administration of Culture*, and while he casts a broader occupational net, surveying a range of ways in which poet-critics justified the pursuit of their art to the American state, he too notes that the introduction of poets into the academy in the early part of the twentieth century was invariably tied to the burgeoning discipline of criticism.[73]

As the years wore on, however, we know what happened. While taking pains to emphasize the degree to which the figure of the poet-critic was one that overspilled the confines of the university, Kindley provides a helpful summary of where things in the university did in fact wind up, bringing together Myers, Gerald Graff, and McGurl in a type of general consensus that "once [creative writing and academic criticism] had gained sufficient prestige from the other," they went their separate ways.[74] It is Myers who is most pointed about the causality of this split, ascribing it, in so many words, to what Kelly Ritter and Stephanie Vanderslice would later go on to call "teaching lore," by which they mean a system that reproduces teachers while inculcating a generalized avoidance of any sustained discussion about pedagogical theory. Instead, protected from scrutiny by the pervasive (and contextually confounding) myth that writing cannot be taught, poets and novelists in the academy have enjoyed a form of autonomy that allows them to perpetuate the creation of literature as "a Romantic process that exists outside the boundaries of the classroom."[75] Creative writing, the story goes, has managed to pull the ultimate fast one on the literary academy: it takes the money and runs.

It's both a good and persuasive story. After all, the creative writing workshop has changed very little since its separation from literary studies—writers still take in criticism from their peers and venerate (and gossip about) their mentors, despite handfuls of panels at every annual meeting of the Association of Writers & Writing Programs that offer this or that new pedagogical suggestion. Iowa's mission statement still includes the strangely equivocating "writing cannot be taught . . . [but] talent can be developed" sentence. The poetry that accompanied this solidification of the discipline is both cause and consequence thereof; as the entrée of writers into the academy exposed them to the university's function as a professional "training ground" (as R. P. Blackmur feared it might), the program both needed and produced writers whose work might reflect an ability to establish human capital. Enter the poetry of intimate personal experience.[76]

I am about to do that poetry a grave injustice here. It is a rich and, contra Perloff, in fact varied tradition that both deserves and has received its own study. But for the purposes of our story, it will have to suffice to cast it only the briefest of glances, to sketch in that sense of "official"ness against which the academic avant-garde sets itself. To do this, I will turn to the tradition's most obvious exemplar. Between setting up a tent on Allen Tate's lawn and being a profound influence on poets such as Sylvia Plath and Anne Sexton (both of whom were his students), Robert Lowell occupies a transitional, mid-century space that connects and merges in complicated ways the reserve and formalism of his poet-critic mentors with the visionary self-expression that would become his, and then so many other poets', hallmark.[77] The publication of *Life Studies* in 1959 is the (in)famous flash point here; in it, Lowell veers sharply away from the measured quatrains and intricate fictionality of earlier volumes such as *Lord Weary's Castle* and toward a graphically autobiographical exploration of mental illness and skeletons in various familial closets. Instead of writing the kinds of poems expected out of an educated New England blue-blood, he wrote *about* the vicissitudes of being an educated New England blue blood. Describing his family's summer retreat in fashionable Mattapoisett, Massachusetts, Lowell cuts a vicious double picture of horror and refinement:

And I, bristling and manic,
skulked in the attic,
and got two hundred French generals by name,
from *A* to *V*—from Augereau to Vandamme.
I used to dope myself asleep,
naming those unpronounceables like sheep.[78]

Whether or not the "I" in *Life Studies* is the "*real* Robert Lowell" (as he put it in an interview with the *Paris Review*, in which he seemed to indicate the answer as being both yes and no), the intimacy of it would come to define a generation of poets—and these poets were, increasingly, trained in writing workshops.[79] So even if *Life Studies* marks a definitive *stylistic* watershed for Lowell, it would be too simplistic, as Langdon Hammer has shown, to say that it represents a full-scale break from the formal precisions of the work of Tate and Ransom.[80] More accurately, it serves as a prescient indicator of what scholasticism would become for creative writing.

Thus it is that the "cannot be taught" school of thinking runs up against the very fact of it being taught: proper and true self-expression, as intimacy, can only be brought forth through an Iowa-esque "nurturing of talent," but self-expression is simultaneously necessary for an educational enterprise in which "creativity" becomes "a value beloved by American artists and scientists and corporate types alike—by everyone, really."[81] For what is creativity in late capitalism, in essence, if not a series of personal quirks that can somehow be monetized? For poets, the money is more or less out of the question—but as holders of a kind of symbolic capital, it is their self-expression, perhaps, from which all other kinds of creative self-expression follow. Lowell, who moved between prestigious teaching posts at places like Iowa and Boston University after the publication of *Life Studies*, did manage to monetize his own sense of intimate mysticism, proclaiming that poetry writing "isn't a craft, that is, something for which you learn the skills and go on turning out. It must come from some deep impulse, deep inspiration."[82] This is teaching lore at its finest, but whether or not you believe it, it remains true that it is in some ways much more expedient—not to mention more philosophically consistent, in this instance—to teach students how to write clear narratives about personal turmoil ("Mother! Mother!/as a gemlike undergraduate,/part criminal and yet a Phi Bete,/I used to barge home late")[83] than it is to strenuously inquire after the cultural frameworks, assumptions, and allowances of such narratives.

Lowell's remarkable ability to capture the swinging polarities of his public and private selves is, of course, anything but easy. His work reflects not only a tremendous amount of skill but also an articulate honesty about his own historical positionality; if those detractors of the "McPoem" (as Donald Hall has called it) have Lowell to blame for anything, it might be for being too good at his job.[84] His exacting type of clarity, in which a defiant skunk can carry the weight of crushing self-hatred, requires not unfettered display of emotional life but rather a form of control over that life that invests its energy in imagistic specificity. Insofar as the writing of poetry *can* be taught, the goal of metaphoric precision is one that responds well to the kinds of scrutiny that a poem will receive in a workshop: group-oriented scrutiny, that is, that often revolves around questions of exactitude. Is the imagery "sharp" enough? Is the situation "clear"? Are the emotional stakes appropriate to the subject matter? These are the kinds of microscope lenses under which Lowell's poetry shines. And such lines of questioning, then, become the primary form of interpretive labor practiced by poets within the semi-autonomous institutional space of creative writing programs.[85]

This form of semi-autonomy performs a role both as itself and as its opposite: on the one hand, the insularity of the program and the ensuing (perceived) homogeneity of its products is the feature against which poets like Bernstein and Hall and critics like Perloff, Myers, Ritter and Vanderslice bristle. On the other, it functions as a signal of the program's total absorption within the academic institution, when said institution is seen as the reproducer of a dominant cultural mode. This is a lose-lose situation: creative writing is chastised for losing its autonomy in favor of academicity, and then for being too autonomous within that academic space. If the forms of labor performed in the semi-detached creative writing program stand in for institutionalization gone "wrong," however, there remains a powerful sense—evinced, perhaps despite himself, by a figure like Bernstein—that there is such a thing as institutionalization gone *right*: that there must be some way for poetry writing to exist as a discipline that does not succumb to, or at the very least complicates, the program's "fiction of autonomy."[86]

Outside the workshop, the English department.

If the study of literature and the writing of poetry were bound closely together throughout the early part of the twentieth century, only to be separated somewhat by the development of creative writing programs, the analytic proclivities of the academic avant-garde might be said to represent a type of return. But although the heightened critical discursivity that is the hallmark of this poetry hearkens back to Stevens's modernist sensibilities, the forms that that discursivity now takes also reflect the major shifts that have taken place in literary studies in the relatively recent past. In this last part of the chapter, I want to briefly chart some of the causal and consequential terrain of those shifts, arguing in the main that the contemporary academy is particularly primed to be the site of avant-garde struggle in the literary realm. This isn't necessarily a good thing, given what it implies about the remaining terrain for such struggle. But it is still terrain, and in the degree to which the academic avant-garde finds in contemporary critical practices the foundation for a vision of poetic life, a picture emerges, if not of unfettered optimism, then of genuine belief in the power of the joys and frustrations of scholarly work. It would be a mistake to dismiss that belief as mere hermeticism or, more generously, vulgar idealism.

To begin by stating the obvious: the last half-century, not unlike Stevens's turn-of-the-century Harvard, has seen remarkable shake-ups in the *what* and *how* of literary study, as well as the marketplace for that study. This is true even if you exclude the rise of creative writing from your scope: the last fifty years have seen the rapid growth of gender, cultural, media, and ethnic studies, not to mention the various theoretical "turns" (semiotic, historical, material, affective, institutional) in literary criticism, all of which have vastly widened the scope of what can conceivably fall under the disciplinary rubric of the study of literature. Simultaneously, and seemingly counterintuitively, the field of literary studies in English (as a proportion of what one can now study at the tertiary level) has shrunk drastically, with falling enrollments, a moribund job market, and crushing adjunctification all contributing to the sense that the very endeavor might be at risk of being snuffed out.[87] Humanities departments that aren't English—modern languages, philosophy, comparative literature, and so on—tend to be in even worse shape, and so a general existential malaise more often than not accompanies any discussion or even defense of "the humanities" as a group.

As Chad Wellmon and Paul Reitter have recently argued, this malaise is not only not new, but has in fact been fundamental to the self-conception of the humanistic disciplines since the eighteenth century.[88] But while the phenomenon of literary studies seeming to collapse as it expands is one that fits into their general narrative that "the humanities" have always bitten off more than they can chew, it has not been well-documented as a relation in and of itself.[89] For the situation of both humanist academics' current sociocultural imaginary, as well as for the contemporary writers whose work has found a durable place in the criticism of those academics, this relation is a crucial one, for the study of contemporary avant-garde literature as an academic pursuit is in essence allowed by it.

The expansion of the disciplinary field demonstrates the degree to which the university has become a way to sustain various kinds of ideological struggles, even as it also props up "industrial- and informational-corporate economies." Pessimistically, these things go hand in hand; if you can keep the dissidents on your watch, you can make sure that they don't pose a threat to your social order.[90] But even as it's overblown to claim that the humanities are the sole conservator of our species' "transcendent needs," it's too glib to dismiss something like literary study as just a way of greasing various squeaky wheels.[91] There's a reason, in other words, why John Guillory closes *Cultural Capital* with a call for nothing less than the radical redistribution of the university's means of producing the book's titular phrase, and why Nick Mitchell argues that "in the critical pivot in ethnic studies, there's a real opportunity to build a framework that can reinvigorate social movements."[92] In the wake of widespread deindustrialization and the resulting expansion of educational credentialism, as well as the concomitant solidification of the university's role as the dominant vehicle of corporate-workforce reproduction, the university may seem like a shrunken battlefield, but it's a very important one.[93]

Literary studies' role in both the conservatism and radicality of American higher education is in many ways reflective of the larger structural complexities that accompanied the demographic expansion of the university over the middle part of the last century. Mitchell, this time writing with Abigail Boggs, reminds us that the aforementioned widening of literary studies' objects of analysis was not the result of some natural leftward shift on the part of English professors. Rather, "English departments were among the disciplines most regularly tapped (and funded) to manage the crisis wrought by the incorporation of historically excluded populations"—a container within a container.[94] But if literary studies was supposed to render interventions like Black studies, Asian studies, and women's and gender studies blandly palatable to university management, it did not succeed. In fact, it wound up *itself* as a discipline on the receiving end of reactionary backlash, both from within its ranks (in the form of the canon wars) and from outside the academy altogether (in the form, among other things, of the coverage of the canon wars).[95] Combined with earlier anticommunist repression that continued well into the seventies, the study of literature has been in the crosshairs of both university and state management for decades. It is no wonder that its practitioners, particularly its newer ones, feel like they're teetering on the edge.

In this connection, the more recent past, which is to say the situation following the 2008 financial crisis and perhaps culminating in the mid-pandemic protests following the murder of George Floyd in the summer of 2020, has made the contradictions besetting literary studies (and, in fact, creative writing) even starker. The renewed administrative commitments to "equity, diversity, and inclusion" occasioned by the latter event are rendered toothless by the austerity imposed by the former, and so even as what hiring there is in the field is now more geared toward the study of minoritized work, the absolute numbers are still abysmal. Creative writing, despite it, too, enjoying relatively robust student interest, also produces vastly more qualified holders of graduate degrees than there are stable jobs available for them. But because academic creative writing has both a much shorter history and a semi-functional economy outside the institution, that lack of employment does not register as an assault on the activity in quite the same way as it does for the analytic humanities. You cannot say, as Reitter does, that Alexander von Humboldt voiced still relevant concerns about your discipline if your discipline was invented less than a century ago.[96] And if the academic field of creative writing disappeared, people would continue to write and publish novels and essay collections and poems. Could the same be said of literary studies and monographs like this one?

It might seem that avant-garde writers, defined as they traditionally have been by their *opposition* to institutionality, would be perfectly fine with the demise of the English department. But the truth of the matter is that—both like and because of the scholars who read their work—the forms of cultural production in which these writers are invested have found a more robust economy of circulation inside the university than they could reasonably expect to find outside of it. The partial radicalization of literary studies occasioned by the expansion/collapse dialectic just outlined, while not the first catalyst for the introduction of avant-garde works into regular scholarly circulation (modernist poets, for instance, were by and large canonized by the New Critics and their contemporaries), did create a situation in which the sociocultural imaginaries of critics began to line up with their avant-garde counterparts in creative writing. As academic humanists have come to see themselves—ourselves—as having to fight for various kinds of visibility and legitimacy, there is a sense (however conflicted) that we, too, exist at the margins. And because our jobs are so often framed in terms of advancing human knowledge, even of creating a better society, there is a sense (however conflicted) that we, too, are a strange kind of vanguard.

We may not, as Joseph North has bracingly argued, be generally correct in that sense.[97] But even if the broadening of the discipline has not resulted in the triumph of the political sensibilities of those responsible for it, it remains the case that it has carved out space within the literary academy in which work that continues to try and envision a real and democratic future for rigorous intellection can be both produced and examined. This is work in which "Life consists / Of propositions about life,"[98] to return to the writer whose poetry made for him such a life, one that ran melancholically parallel to the life that he so dutifully built according to his father's wishes.

The romanticism with which Stevens expresses his sense of literary vitality captures the hope and the promise, however often thwarted, of both academic humanism and creative writing; in a long letter to his fiancée in 1909, he writes "we all cry for life. It is not to be found in railroading to an office and then railroading back. [. . .] But books make up. They shatter the groove, as far as the mind is concerned. They are like so many fantastic lights filling plain darkness with strange colors."[99] One of the great tragedies of the modern university is the degree to which it actively forecloses alternatives to "railroading to an office," even as it exposes students each day to the "strange colors" of such an alternative. Stevens's poetry, as we have seen, is decidedly less romantic than his love letters, even as it contains a similar sort of yearning. "It would be enough," he writes, "if we were ever, just once, at the middle, fixed / In This Beautiful World Of Ours and not as now, / Helplessly at the edge"—here, the poetry does not "shatter the groove" so much as it makes one painfully aware of the groove itself.[100] The use of the first person plural feels in this passage universal, but the poem's opening narrows it down: "the lecturer / On This Beautiful World Of Ours composes himself." "We" at the edge are in a classroom, and "if the day writhes, it is not with revelations. / One goes on asking questions." Stevens's romanticism turns always against itself, by turns fiercely and sardonically and sadly, and if this dialectic is what makes his work feel critical in that word's senses as both *urgent* and *analytical*, it is also a criticality that has become a culture of critical discourse, carried forward by writers and intellectuals who both prop up and are propped up by what remaining claim the university still has to affording people the chance to imagine, in language, a better world.

For this is the crucial conceptual elision that Stevens's poetry emphasizes: that while there might be an outside to language ("This Beautiful World"), what we *know* is only language. Our world, beautiful or not, is conceptual and linguistic. To work with language is thus to work with what we fundamentally are, and if this creates the dangerous romance of both creativity as solipsism (as Stevens recognized) and its more marketable cousin, creativity as personal branding, it creates, too, the possibility of recognizing that this labor can be otherwise. The university, which has long placed the production of a thing and the study of that same thing in very close quarters, holds both the danger and the possibility at once. The relatively short amount of time in which this has been the case for creative writers and their critics allows us to take a relatively wide-angle view of its history, as I've attempted to do in this chapter; if we can see in Stevens the first inklings that sonnets and study must perform a delicate dance with one another, by the 1970s, the academy was shaping the production of poetry in multiple and sometimes contradictory ways.

The place of Stevens's modernism on this compressed and rapidly evolving timeline is not merely at its beginning, nor does it thread its way to the present merely by dint of canonization. As a version of Stevens's worries about the dream and the deed became paradigmatic for generations of scholars and writers in the corporatized university, his poetic focus on the dream— of unfettered time to write and think, of a poetry that could enact thinking even if it could not make it through to the "real"—continues to bear a striking resemblance to the heightened reflexivity of both scholarly thought and the poetry that has found mutuality in such thought. In the next chapter, I want to argue that we must understand the poetry of John Ashbery, the writer most often said to be Stevens's most prominent literary heir, not only as a continuation of Stevens's post-Romantic tonalities but also as a version of Stevens's relationship to the idea of the life of the mind. It is, naturally, a version inflected by the academic era I have just described, in which the labor of the scholar and the writer feels particularly limned in brightness because under particular threat. "From this," writes Stevens, "the poem springs; that we live in a place / That is not our own and, much more not ourselves / And hard it is in spite of blazoned days."[101]

2

Reading Ashbery Reading Ashbery

Toward the beginning of *Houseboat Days*, John Ashbery's eighth full-length book of poetry and the book that immediately followed the remarkable critical success of *Self-Portrait in a Convex Mirror*, there is a poem entitled "The Explanation."[1] In some senses it is a "typical" Ashbery poem, insofar as such a thing exists: lightly funny in a melancholy way, atopic, ruminative. "What am I doing up here?" the poem asks, after figuring its voice as a conductor in front of an orchestra at a gala and as a "ruler" sitting atop a "teddy-bear throne." The answer: "Pretending to resist but secretly giving in so as to reappear / In a completely new outfit and group of colors once today's / Bandage has been removed, is all." Using the day's wound as an opportunity for transformation, the end of the poem nevertheless looks a bit nervously toward the future, in which the figure "up here" yields to a force that, earlier in the piece, had "thrown" it "to one side / Into a kind of broom closet as the argument continues carolling."[2] As an explanation, "The Explanation" reads at first as anything but: we do not know *what* the poem tries to resist, or *where* "up here" is, or even *who* is in the poem. But these observations don't necessarily mean that "The Explanation" is simply a tongue-in-cheek instance of titular irony, or lead to the further conclusion that John Ashbery is therefore uninterested in explanation as a category of discourse. He might "pretend to resist," but he not-so-"secretly give[s] in," enjoying in spite of himself all the new outfits and colors given to him by his work's ever-growing number of explainers.

And Ashbery has, as we know, a lot of explainers—more of them, perhaps, than any other American poet in recent history.[3] This chapter is interested in why that is. There are some obvious reasons, one of which is that his poetry does in fact seem to need quite a bit of explaining, given its syntactical and paratactical difficulties. But there are a lot of difficult poets whose work has not occasioned such a volume of analysis. What there are fewer of are poets whose difficulty looks quite a lot like literary critical difficulty, who came to prominence at a time when that difficulty was arguably at a zenith, *and* who also seemed to be aware of this state of affairs. At the very beginning of his first lecture as the Charles Eliot Norton Chair at Harvard, Ashbery speculates with characteristic self-deprecation as to "why [he] had been chosen for this honor," and then gets right to the point: "I am known as a writer of hermetic poetry," and so "in the course of lecturing I might 'spill the beans,' so to speak: that is, I might inadvertently or not let slip the key to my poetry." He goes on: "there seems to be a feeling in the academic world that there's something interesting about my poetry, though . . . considerable confusion about what, if anything, it means."[4]

The mode of modesty doesn't do a particularly good job of masking the satisfaction that comes with being the one holding the beans. But he also insinuates that the beans have been there for the taking all along: he can't "explain" his poetry, he says, because "my poetry is the explanation. The explanation of what? Of my thought."[5] If this sort of explanation nevertheless remains "hermetic," we must assume, as Ashbery does, that the critics will arrive to try and explain the explanations. With an erudite sensibility inherited from modernisms early (Stevens) and late (Auden), combined with a penchant for surreally philosophical abstraction, Ashbery's difficulty is a difficulty that imagines its reading public in scholastic terms, and it allows us to see the beginning of the current period of relations between poetic and critical discursive modes as each struggles with its own relationship to centrality and vanguardism. Contained in the dialectical play of Ashbery's poetry, between the "broom closet" and the "throne," is a reflection of the shifting polarities of the cultural worker's positionality: as if heeding Adorno's call, here we find something that is "uncertain of itself right into its innermost fiber."[6]

That uncertainty has seeped into any number of debates about the status of English, creative writing, "the humanities," even the university as a whole. This chapter focuses on the status of the act of academic reading: the labor that is the site of contact between writers and critics, and which produces the writings that are often in fact simply called "readings." What these readings are, who they are for, and how they should be conducted have all become, for better or for worse, stand-in questions for the larger question of the "value," material and otherwise, of the study and production of difficult literature. As Andrew Epstein has argued, Ashbery had some corollary concerns, his poems "self-consciously chronicling his own navigation of the literary field"—and while Epstein takes a usefully wide-angle view, examining Ashbery's relationship to the concepts of individuality and communality writ large, I think it will be illuminating to focus on the more specific interplay between Ashbery's poetry and the institution of literary criticism that has found so much to say about his work.[7] For indeed, if Ashbery can "remain neither *in* nor *out* of the center or the collective," that's a self-conscious wavering common to most literary writers and literary critics.[8] The unreliability of the narratives of positionality that come from such wavering is why this study is not particularly interested in biographical surveying either of poets or of critics; as Nick Lolordo has provocatively put it, "claims of marginalization and disavowals of dominance have become so prevalent in poetry circles as to evoke a reversal of the famous image: the poetry world is a circle whose circumference is everyone, its center no one."[9] Although their reasons are often different, creative writers tend not to want to be associated with literary studies, and the reverse is true too. Forging links between them will involve not taking anyone, really, at their word.

And so we come again to the matter of the odd choice: Ashbery isn't an "academic" in any robust sense of the word. He nominally taught at both Bard and Brooklyn Colleges, which is significant insofar as it means that at some point, bills were getting paid via the teaching of creative writing, but it would be hard to say that his identity as a poet was meaningfully tied to his work as a professor. I want to suggest, as I have with Stevens, that this direct, one-to-one type of relationship is not the only one capable of demonstrating an intimacy between poetic and literary critical modes of expression. Ashbery, after all, was a deeply literary-minded student encouraged by his teachers, and he spent decades writing regularly and professionally as an art critic. Karin Roffman and Jesse Zuba give us picture after picture of the former situation: he was an enthusiastic "quiz kid" who was mentored early on by the University of Rochester's Katherine Koller, and by the time he first set foot on Harvard's campus for his undergraduate degree, he had already begun to form a theory of the contemporary poet as one who "turns from the outside world . . . and feeds on the process and intricacies of his own mind."[10] As for his work as an art critic, David Bergman's introduction to

Reported Sightings is clear enough, placing a passage from a review of Esteban Vincente alongside one from *Three Poems* and declaring that "stylistically, the two passages are quite similar."[11]

It's worthwhile to take a brief look at that passage from the Vincente review. It reads as follows:

> The window . . . is a source of light, and while hinting at those menacing outside forces, it remains a feature of interior architecture; what we see is somehow always related to what we see inside, whether it be the figure, whose nature coalesces only within the four walls that Pascal advised us to stay within, or in unidentified phenomena which appear as functions of the carefully guarded and tended "intimacy and clarity of the interior life."[12]

The extrapolation from the figure of the window to its significance to the tenor of the painting, its careful play of "outside" and "inside," is a nuanced and sophisticated act of reading, one as attentive as any act of literary or art historical criticism to how a piece of art works on its audience. Bergman goes on to say that the passage "reinforces an idea about which Ashbery is especially intent—the relationship between one's environment and one's capacity for self-analysis and self-definition."[13] For Ashbery, that environment might not have been the school *precisely*, but it was nevertheless one defined in large part by professionalized acts of reading. Much later in his career, in the same Eliot lecture quoted above, he would provide a concise picture of this type of work: remarking that John Clare's *The Shepherd's Calendar* is oftentimes "monotonous," he argues that "it takes a special kind of reader to appreciate it for what it is: a distillation of the natural world with all its beauty and pointlessness."[14] It is "this special kind of reader" that is the focus of what follows.

Criticism on Ashbery has approached this subject from various angles, but none directly. Bonnie Costello remarked in 1982 that "reading is as much Ashbery's subject as writing is," an important observation to which my follow-up would be to ask which readers he tends to reach, and thus of what the activity of reading as Ashbery imagines it might consist.[15] Daniel Cottom's 1994 analysis of Ashbery's ubiquitous "it"—most often a pronoun without an antecedent, leading to a series of linguistic marks without referent—does specify the "academic readers . . . who compose so much of the audience for poetry these days," but denies that Ashbery might have any relation to said audience other that a kind of vague hostility, an intelligence that refuses ideas via constant deflection.[16] Such a reading tries, as so much work on poetry does, to keep Ashbery out of the center of the aforementioned poetry-world circle, placing "academic readers" there instead. Curiously, those "academic readers" never seem to be the readers doing the reading; they are always elsewhere, shutting out the avant-garde and, by extension, its studiers. When basically everyone feels like this, we see that Lolordo's formulation is apposite not only for poets, but also for poetry's professional analysts. Zuba, in an analysis of *Some Trees*, Ashbery's first full-length book and winner of the Yale Younger Poets award, comes closest to putting his finger on the situation when he aligns Ashbery's earlier work with the New Criticism, noting that the book "put[s] New Critical prescription into practice with an almost programmatic comprehensiveness."[17] By this he means not that Ashbery was somehow a covert conservative (though he is trying to point out that *Some Trees* isn't the kind of radical break that many scholars have claimed it was) but rather that the New Criticism in fact responded most enthusiastically to a type of "experimentalist aesthetic."[18] If this marks the very beginning of the academic acceptance of avant-garde work, that affinity would only grow stronger as the position of the literary critic became less and less central to culture both inside and outside of universities.

The claim of this chapter is that this shared sensibility about the (de)valuation of literary-interpretive labor has a discursive form, and that Ashbery is a foundational figure in introducing this form into contemporary poetry. When we understand things in this way, we understand too the centrality of Ashbery to the academy without either overblowing the biographical case or "normalizing" his style.[19] I look in the main at "Fantasia on 'The Nut-Brown Maid'" and "Litany," two of his longer and more discursive poems that appeared in books directly following *Self-Portrait in a Convex Mirror*. These dialogic poems literalize Ashbery's dialectic reflexivity; in them, explanatory self-awareness is as fretful as it is proud, tragic as it is triumphant, collective in its own, strange privacy. I ground these dialectics as ones particularly pertinent to the academic humanities in a return to the culture of class feeling described in the previous chapter; I will then briefly juxtapose Ashbery's poetic with that of the poet Mei-mei Berssenbrugge, whose reflexivity mirrors his but whose relationship to institutions of higher education is substantially tighter.

Berssenbrugge—Columbia MFA and a longtime professor of creative writing—writes poetry with an abstract, ruminative quality much like Ashbery's but with a significantly more obvious commitment to argumentative statement. In other words, while Ashbery tends to avoid coming to a point (even if he sometimes can't help it), Berssenbrugge's poetry contains thesis-like objects that move the work forward. For her, poetry-as-process-analysis sidles even closer to literary critical argument:

> Taking advantage of the relationships and interaction, which actually exist between what happens
> to her and her desire, she creates some metaphors both obvious and opaque, as screens of rays crisscrossing
> the landscape in which herself and what she expected from you in the way of support coincide,
> so that you and I resemble each other, now.[20]

Organized into clauses that explain an intellectual action, clarify that action, describe the written outcome, and then move outward toward a broader consequence, the opening of "Forms of Politeness" marches through the motions of argumentative writing while infusing that structure with the antecedent-less abstraction that is one of Ashbery's most well-known hallmarks. The shape of explanation connects writer and literary critical reader on a technical level ("you and I resemble each other, now"), while the deliberately opaque language contained in said shape proffers an invitation to professional interpretation. With its multifaceted appeals to the analytical imagination, Berssenbrugge's metanarrative poetry can show us how a scholastic sensibility such as Ashbery's, which is in the main aloof, becomes even more connected to the discipline of analytical reading as both genres come to ruminate upon their place in the world.

In the last chapter, I touched upon Alvin Ward Gouldner's analysis of the intellectual class position as one formed in the main discursively—a difficult claim, but one that does in fact help us recognize the fuzziness of the cultural status of those who, for instance, come up with theories of class positions. In both *The Future of Intellectuals and the Rise of the New Class* and earlier in *The Coming Crisis in Sociology*, Gouldner is blunt about the oddly democratic elitism of intellectual discourse's metacritical nature. For Gouldner, the culture of critical discourse—as previously outlined, the "grammar" that is the "deep structure of the common ideology shared by the New

Class"—is both convinced of its own superiority ("the grammar of critical discourse claims the right to sit in judgement over the actions of and claims of any social class") *and* "willing to talk about the value of talk itself and its possible inferiority to silence or to practice."[21] Critical discourse, in other words, is always reading itself, and it has a tendency to think that such a practice is both a good thing and, crucially, a teachable thing: for if you can learn the discourse, presumably you can learn to be a member of the "new class." And if you learn the discourse particularly well, and have some particularly good luck, you can earn a living perpetuating it. This is the universalist promise and scarcity-bound reality of the culture of critical discourse, and in the corner of that culture inhabited by literature and literary studies, it produces the deep-seated uneasiness around both the value of professional reading and the willingness to even name it as such.

For to call thinking and writing about literature, or writing literature itself, "professional" is to recognize in some way its status as labor, its entrance into a market of exchange from which it is often imagined (however idealistically or erroneously) to be exempt. It doesn't help that the profession of reading is a slippery one: academic humanists are not, certainly, the only people in the world who can say that they read for a living. They (we) have, however, some strong claims upon the philosophical and/or meta-discourse about what reading *is*, and so it seems all the more important to consider in this connection schematics like Gouldner's and Magali Sarfatti Larson's, which posit a fundamental friction between the desire to democratize the culture of critical discourse and its concomitant ways of reading the world, and the sense that such a democratization must be *led* by a class of people who already possess those discursive and reading skills and are capable of disseminating them.[22] Atop this tension sits another: the fact that these would-be disseminators—philosophers, literary critics, writers, cultural interpreters—are somehow both wary of and feel undervalued by the labor market.

These feelings have something to do, no doubt, with the fact that what the market *does* value—technological "innovation," salable products, patents, and other forms of intellectual property—is not particularly amenable to the thing being peddled by humanist intellectuals: critical discourse, or being a "special kind of reader." Relativist, iterative, slow-moving, and skeptical, the CCD inculcates in its users what Gouldner names a "status disparity": a gap between the work required to achieve advanced literacy and the "power and wealth" that should, but doesn't, remunerate it.[23] Ashbery himself puts it another way: one "so often feels oneself" an "underdog... when one embarks on the risky business of writing."[24] But this lack of status, in a way that will sound familiarly Bourdieuian, is also what makes the avant-garde legible: you have to be on an edge to be cutting-edge. As the labor of reading and producing difficult texts is pushed ever-farther toward the edges of cultural production, and yet remains central to the job requirements of academic writers and readers, a belief in the power of fine-grained reading, reading which reveals the instability of language's relation to the world ostensibly outside of it, comes to seem like a particularly sharp double-edged sword.

I suggest that Ashbery's long dialogic meditations explore precisely this pointy discomfort, illuminating the dialectic between institutionalized power and the precariousness of vanguardism—as Jasper Bernes has put it, between being a "boss" and a "subordinate"—that characterizes the imaginary of literary studies in the academy.[25] After all, Ashbery, like most artists, wanted to be successful. Recounting his long rise to fame, he admits to a crisis in conscience (and confidence) upon not reaching the audience he had hoped for:

> When I first started writing poetry I thought, *this is great, people will love this, I'll become a celebrated poet*, and that turned out not to be the case at all. My first book *Some Trees* (1956) published in an edition of 800 copies, took eight years to sell out. And the next book, *The Tennis Court Oath* (1962) was even less successful. So then I thought, *well people aren't going to think I'm a great poet*. So what do I do?[26]

Thankfully for us, Ashbery persisted, claiming an ever-larger piece of the poetic-cultural pie while insisting, regarding his audience, "*to hell with them.*"[27] This simultaneous desire for and disavowal of popular appeal both describes the tricky positionality of the artistic vanguard and, in Ashbery, manifests itself in a style that refuses clarity but recognizes, in this refusal, that "the people [who] will love this" might be gatekeepers of a different sort. There is no neat solution proposed here: what the poems do, in recompense, is to try and "talk through" the problem, perhaps in the hope that exposing it is a virtue in itself. While this talking through arguably reaches its apex in *Flow Chart* (1991), it established itself much earlier in his career, and these nascent thoughts, I believe, can best reveal how reading Ashbery in the world of literary studies has come to be a type of reading *with*.

At this point we can begin to see two narratives beginning to form: a disciplinary-historical one about the role of reading as professional practice, and an aesthetic one that has to do with Ashbery's style and its reception among those readers. I propose that these two narratives are linked on two planes: one that sees both as the starting point for a contextual definition of *thinking*, and a related affective one that registers hopes and concerns about that thinking in the world. The occasional fierceness with which scholars argue about how reading should or should not be conducted—whether, for instance, "critique" has or has not "run out of steam"—is a telling phenomenon in the disciplinary history of the present.[28] How we read is seen as so close to how we think, in other words, that entire political agendas get tacked on to reading methods: Mitchum Huehls claims, hyperbolically, that "it's actually the politics of oppositional critique that remains perpetually complicit with neoliberalism, while it's those post-normative ontological forms and modes, which might at first glance look like mere capitulations to neoliberalism, that offer the most possibility for undoing neoliberalism as we know it."[29] Whether or not one thinks this claim is true (I do not think it is), it points up just how high the stakes can be set for a form of increasingly precarious labor that requires long years of "training and experience" within a disciplinary apparatus.[30]

The quoted phrase comes from Elaine Auyong's recent attempt to answer the question of what professionalized reading actually is. It is, she argues, an activity fundamentally different from, although always inclusive of, nonspecialized reading practices, and it organizes the "systems of values" that shape (however loosely and unconsciously) the discipline of literary study. Those values include, importantly, privileging the types of "background knowledge" afforded by that aforementioned training, as well as a desire for argumentative "coherence" *beyond* comprehension that forms, as Jonathan Kramnick has detailed, a type of unacknowledged aesthetics.[31] And although she acknowledges that specialized reading "may not—and need not—serve a broader instrumental function," the terms of Auyong's argument—the embeddedness, in any definition of reading, of whole matrices of values, experiences, and goals—make clear the degree to which the work of reading comes to stand in for the thinking subject doing that work. After all, reading forms the cornerstone of everything else that literary critics do: we read (hopefully) before we write, we teach our students how to read (perhaps especially when we teach them how to write), we read each other's work. It's as close to a universal workplace condition, as it were, as it gets, and as such, normative claims about how to go about doing it are going to seem like normative claims about how to *be*.[32]

Underpinning this current wave of disciplinary reflexivity is an older one that refuses (much like the avant-garde) to go away despite repeated obituaries: the institutionalization of literary theory. As a fairly late bloomer in terms of publicity, Ashbery had finished his education (a bachelor's at Harvard in 1949, and an unhappy stint as a graduate student in Columbia's English department that ended in 1951) well before his work took off—but when it did, it did so alongside that of the likes of Paul de Man and in the middle of the career of Harold Bloom.[33] Bloom's championing of Ashbery's work, and Ashbery's ambivalence about it, is relatively well-documented.[34] One might even call *Other Traditions*, the lectures described at this chapter's opening, a type of response to Bloom's way of canonizing him.[35] But Bloom wasn't the only giant of criticism to whom Ashbery felt he had to answer. In a 1989 interview with Vasilis Papageorgiou, Ashbery provides a typical-for-him response to the question "[what] is your attitude towards the new literary theories?" by saying "I don't really have any because I don't follow them. I hoped you weren't going to ask me about this because people are always asking me what I think of Derrida and Deleuze and I have to embarrass myself by saying I haven't really read them."[36] So much, then, for any notion of direct influence. Nevertheless, what this moment signals is a thoroughgoing awareness of the constant *expectation* that he would have thoughts about "the new literary theories," and thus that may of his readers were the type to already have such thoughts.

Though by now a type of disciplinary bedrock or even background noise, it's relatively uncontroversial to point out that in their academic heyday, these highly abstract, philosophical modes of reading were seen, not only by other scholars but even to the mainstream media, as a truly radical shift in the way such studies were conducted. If there could be said to be an avant-garde way of studying literature, the popular perception in the last decades of the 20th century was that deconstruction was it. Though this obscures, of course, any number of ways in which radical theories of reading and aesthetics have been developed outside of the university, the charismatic infamy of the academic version of "theory" lent a new and surprising edginess to departments of literature. Ashbery's reticence about being linked to such institutional vanguards probably stems from the fact that in his view, like that of many others, the phrase "institutional vanguard" (or indeed the title of this book) would indicate precisely the kind of "vast and well-equipped regiment" against which experimental artists must "fight [in order] to preserve their identity."[37] His post–*Self Portrait* writing, as I'll show, thus bears the marks of his preoccupation with his own trajectory as a poet during a time when the possibility of an extra-institutional counterculture began to seem more distant. But the institutional counterculture, as it were, was having identity struggles of its own, and so instead of Ashbery's poetry finding receptive readers (as it had with *Some Trees*) who saw in it a chance to exercise a method, it found readers, receptive and not, who saw (and continue to see) in it the method itself, reflexive obsessions and all.

The aesthetic features of his work, in other words, carry the kinds of ambivalences about the purpose of art that also burden critics regarding the purpose of criticism. To look at Ashbery's reception in the late seventies and eighties, even briefly, is to sketch for oneself a picture that looks very much like the reception of poststructuralism around the same time. Paul Breslin, writing in *Poetry* magazine in 1980, grudgingly admits that Ashbery is a central figure in American poetry even as "his relentless self-cancellation takes away almost all that his lyrical genius gives" and takes David Shapiro, the author of *John Ashbery: An Introduction to the Poetry*, to task for being "unrelievedly pretentious," mostly due to his "ostentatious display[s] of learning" which include references to the likes of Derrida, de Man, Lacan, and Hegel.[38] Claude Rawson, six years later, is hardly more sanguine than Breslin: while he too admits Ashbery's centrality, ultimately "Whitman's metrical capriciousness turns in Ashbery into a fussy exercise in extended pointmaking."[39] It is difficult to see how a "self-cancelling" poet could also be involved in the business of "extended pointmaking"—but it is precisely this dialectic between exposition and negation that makes Ashbery so amenable to critics like Shapiro, who see in Ashbery's work both "a model of our most difficult aesthetic desires" and something that can "break down the usual opposition of criticism and creative work."[40] For these critics, Ashbery's style of poetic thinking registered either as an assault upon or a paean to not only what *poetry* ought to be doing, but also what *criticism* saw its most pressing task to be.

That is to say, there's a resistance to Ashbery's form of fussiness—its contradictory meanderings, its unabashed abstractness, its obvious difficulty—that mirrors resistance to certain kinds of academic prose.[41] Such resistance, I'd argue, stems from a persistent, justifiable anxiety in the humanities about the tension between inward-facing specialization and outward-facing modes of justification and access. Praise for Ashbery's work, on the other hand, translates "fussiness" into or as a type of rigor, one concerned with the active performance of intricate meaning-making (and meaning-questioning) processes. In Shapiro's case, while the claim that Ashbery "break[s] down the opposition of criticism and creative work" overstates things somewhat, there's no doubt that Ashbery's poetry is indeed concerned with analytical work: work that his poetry both performs and distrusts.[42] The performance evinces a conviction about the poetic power of documenting a mind reading its own machinations, a process simultaneously absolutely personal and radically communal. The distrust demonstrates the extent to which such convictions are accompanied by the fear that a dedication to the cerebral amounts to a kind of snobbery, a deliberate turning-away from "how things are." In "Business Personals," Ashbery writes: "Such simple things, / And we make of them something so complex it defeats us, / Almost. Why can't everything be simple again"[43]—it's a romantic notion, to be sure, but there is much to be said about the romanticism of Ashbery and academics alike.

Insofar as "romanticism" often gets conflated with a naive sentimentality, and is thus used as an epithet, I do not mean for it to be so used in this case. Instead, I read Ashbery's resistance to the complexities of his own work as a strange byproduct of the attempt to retain "outsider" credentials as he finds himself inside the literary-cultural spotlight.[44] If a poet like Nathaniel Mackey, as I discuss in this study's conclusion, refigures learnedness and jargon as a form of vanguardist reclamation of an exclusionary discourse, it is a move that Ashbery cannot make: for him, the concern lies in how to deal with his own position as a lover of complexity who is nonetheless nostalgic for the "simple," knowing full well that such a nostalgia cannot form the basis for the kinds of truths he wants his poems to impart.

It would be easy to say, at this point, that Ashbery's poetry thus speaks out of both sides of its mouth regarding the issue of how poetry ought to look and whom it ought to reach. The same, uncharitably, could be said about intradisciplinary debates about literary criticism. Neither claim would be true, for either would reduce real struggles toward relevance and sophistication to mere cynicism. Instead, I'd suggest that while there is of course no total escape from the jockeying for position that happens in any area of life, the positions of the literary arts and humanities in the 1970s were being jostled more severely than they had been in decades, and as a result, debates about difficulty and obscurantism took on a new kind of urgency. In Ashbery's case, his vision of poetic labor sidles close enough to that of critical labor that it becomes vaguely uncomfortable—to put it another way, if theory makes (or made) it *de rigeur* for critics to point out the radical indeterminacy of literary speech, Ashbery's "poetics of indeterminacy," to borrow a phrase from Perloff, might make him "just" another critic. To mitigate this discomfort, Ashbery appeals to a tongue-in-cheek type of positivism: in "Pyrography," also in *Houseboat Days*, he argues that

> To be able to write the history of our time, . . .
> It would be necessary to model all these unimportant details . . .
> So as to be able to include them; otherwise the narrative
> Would have that flat, sandpapered look the sky gets
> Out in the middle west toward the end of summer,
> The look of wanting to back out before the argument
> Has been resolved, . . .
>
> . . . .
>
> Therefore, since we have to do our business
> In spite of things, why not make it in spite of everything?
> That way, maybe the feeble lakes and swamps
> Of the back country will get plugged into the circuit
> And not just the major events but the whole incredible
> Mass of everything happening simultaneously and pairing off,
> Channeling itself into history, will unroll
> As carefully and as casually as a conversation"[45]

Ashbery, as a poetic historian, makes gestures here toward Whitman—but instead of a complete history being written *because* of, say, America's multifaceted greatness, it's being theorized (and not written) *in spite* of it. Ashbery is not writing "the history of our time" that he describes; his poetry isn't really interested in "feeble lakes and swamps" in any descriptive sense.

All the same, passages like these appeal to the sense that poetic work *is* descriptive in some positivistic way that is fundamentally different from that of analytic humanism, even as that description never gets carried out.

In the end, Ashbery never really gets away from the poetics of process, argumentation, and proposition—the poetics, that is, that make it seem as if Ashbery is constantly performing readings of his own work as the work itself unfolds. Calling up an image of a "garden of violet cabbages," as he does in "On the Towpath," turns into an examination of whether or not "these and other things could stay on / Longer, though not forever of course; / [. . .] No, / We aren't meaning that anymore."⁴⁶ There is no suggestion as to what ought to replace the cabbages other than the discourse proclaiming their unsuitability; meaning, such lines imply, adheres no longer to natural particulars but instead in how the mind works them over. The privileging of intellection—even if begrudging—that lends Ashbery's poetry much of its distinctive character (and which explains the critical near-consensus about the connection between Ashbery and Stevens, a consensus that I think in the main is warranted) is also what makes his work so important to the relational history between poetry and academia in the late twentieth century. As a closer look at some of his more expressly "conversational" poems will show, his poetry takes up residence in the gap that confronts the literary professional: the one that yawns between the sense that art ought to reflect "our most difficult aesthetic desires" (to re-quote Shapiro) and that which yearns toward something like a universal appreciation for critical thinking and attentive reading—tasks which are, in short, the work of the humanities.

"Fantasia on 'The Nut-Brown Maid'" is the final poem in *Houseboat Days*, and it takes its dialogic form—a series of vignettes told alternately by a "He" and a "She"—from its source text. Like "Self-Portrait in a Convex Mirror," "Fantasia" has a concrete historical allusion as its starting point: in this case, an anonymous fifteenth- or sixteenth-century ballad that has been reprinted in a couple of eighteenth-century magazines and anthologies.⁴⁷ The ballad is told as a secondhand story in which a woman tries to persuade her lover to allow her to accompany him into exile, only to find out that he is not banished to the forest but simply testing her fidelity. In Ashbery's hands, the poem becomes an occasion to create a dialogue with the self, the "He" and "She" figures merging and separating "together yet apart, in a give-and-take, push-pull / Kind of environment. And then, packed like sardines / Our wit arises, survives automatically."[48] There is, as is typical of Ashbery, no good way to summarize the piece; the closest one might come is to say that it outlines an internal argument about the role of the empirical world, with "he" wanting very much to believe in "distant factories, / Tall smokestacks, anything," and "she" insisting that there is "nothing solid, nothing one can build on."[49]

In one of the few analytical treatments of the poem, David Herd describes the ballad as "predicated on the communicability of life in the forest, its interlocutors occupying a space between the forest and society," and reads Ashbery's interest in it as a chance to ask, expansively: "how can poetry which is permanently engaging with the present situation offer the kind of cultural support that in a period of civilities would have constituted its role?"[50] The "present situation" he refers to is the period of intense public scrutiny that Ashbery underwent after the publication of *Self-Portrait*; Herd argues that "Fantasia" is essentially a long meditation on whether or not poetry can serve a communal function in the modern era. The examination of communication, I'd suggest, is one way of describing the act of reading, and in "Fantasia," Ashbery grapples with who can, and does, read poetry that works through the separation between language (as aestheticized concept) and communication (as empirical or pragmatically oriented).

Ashbery himself as late as 2013 put it thusly: "[t]he bond between language and communication . . . is something that preoccupies me. Language has its own meaning, which is separate from meaning as communication, or so it seems to me."[51] In its theorization of language as an entity separate from its application, Ashbery's thinking about "the meaning of language" as opposed to the meaning of communication has an important correlative in the interplay of the abstract/general and the concrete/particular.[52] "Language," in Ashbery's formulation, exists in an ethereal state "beyond expression," and lies on the most general of conceptual planes; as such, it manages to be simultaneously universal (as in Benjamin's formulation of language as the power to name) and highly elusive.[53] Communication, on the other hand, is more concrete and specific, sharing a root with *community* and *communal* and in this connection belonging to a group of words specifically geared toward outlining the boundaries (hard or porous) of group formations.[54] As Ashbery plays with the idea of communication in the dialogic form of "Fantasia," he literalizes the self-reflexive struggle to communicate difficult ideas about language beyond communication, and demonstrates a familiar anxiety over what kinds of communities he does or does not reach in documenting such a struggle.

The relationship between self-reflexivity and abstraction is Ashbery's modernist inheritance: as Charles Altieri has analyzed at length, abstraction functions for high modernist poets as the scrutiny of self or form that allows them, without the burden of definitive external reference, to avoid solipsism and break outwards into another possible world.[55] But here, as in much modernist poetry, there is pessimism of the intellect even as there is (perhaps) optimism of the will. Toward the end of the poem, the interplay of "he" and "she" in "Fantasia" solidifies somewhat into a dialogue about the follies of external referentiality and, relatedly, the relationship between the artist and the critic, formed as a "we" meditating on the "diffuse quality of our literature."[56] As the "she" figure refers back to the poem's reflexive form in the lines "Patience / Of articulation between us is still what it is, / No more and no less," "he" laments, Ashbery's long lines suddenly giving way to prose: "You're making a big mistake. Just because Goofus has been lucky for you, you imagine others will make a fuss over you, all the others, who will matriculate. You'll be left with a trowel and a lot of empty flowerpots."[57] The "he" figure is worrying about and reacting here, as he does in more indirect fashion for most of the poem, to the "she" figure's insistence on the acceptability of a world riven from the notion of positive reality, a world reflected in the poem's own obsession with internal contradiction: "there are lots of differences inside. / There were differences when only you knew them. / Now they are an element, not themselves."[58] The success of "Goofus" (a probable reference to *Self-Portrait in a Convex Mirror*) is rendered anxiously as a fluke, as if it were not possible for poetry so concerned with examining its own utterances (the "articulation between us," which are the "differences inside") to hold the attention of those who will, in a telling word choice, "matriculate."

Ashbery's conflation of concerns surrounding poetry's ability to index the real world and its critical reception is overdetermined, the result of a set of formal and thematic registers which coalesce into a complex picture of poetry's social and asocial networks. The breakdown of the line into prose in the passage above, for instance, signals an affective state as close to panic as Ashbery ever comes—the poem's need to be-for-another (to *communicate*) colliding with its desire to dig beneath the surface of its own machinations (to read its own *language*) causes the poem to lose hold, as it were, of its formal control. As it attempts to wrestle with what constitutes the poem's communicative base (is it merely those "who will matriculate"?), the referential grammar breaks down further even as it becomes more professionally particular: "that the glint of light from a silver ball on that far-off flagpole is the equivalent of a career devoted to life, to improving the minds and the welfare of others, when in reality it is a common thing like these, and less profitable than any hobby or sideline that is a source of retirement income."[59] The relative particularity of "that flagpole" gives way immediately to the abstractions of "career," "life," "minds," "welfare," and "a common thing," and the word "these" has no antecedent except perhaps for the totality of all metaphoric equivalencies, turning the poetic gaze inward at the sum of all its potential (non-)accomplishments. The extreme reflexivity of this gesture is tempered and indeed antagonized by thematic content: that poetry in its inaccessibility and abstractness could be the same as a life devoted to "improving the minds and welfare of others" is posited as ridiculous, but (or and) it is precisely what "he" is accusing "she" of imagining. What Ashbery is worrying about in this moment is a form of *justification* for the literary act, particularly as that act detaches from empirical referentiality.

Justification is, of course, something that has preoccupied professional humanists for decades, but I would suggest that its thematic appearance in Ashbery's poetry signals an important confluence between literary practitioners and critics. One of the crucial components of justification as an impulse within the literary humanities in particular is the way in which it forces into contact the ideal and resistant "worlding" of the literary act (to borrow a Heideggerian formulation) with the economies of the "real" world. Ashbery expresses this collision both directly and semi-metaphorically, in the voice of the calming "she" that follows the non-lineated text above: "But the real 'world'/Stretches its pretending into the side yard/Where I was waiting, at peace with my feelings . . . /We were walking/All along toward a door that seemed to recede/In the distance and now is somehow behind us, shut,/Though apparently it didn't lock automatically."[60] The threshold that is now suddenly behind them but not retroactively uncrossable becomes an acknowledgement of the movement between poetic abstraction and "a career" that partakes in an existing economy of production and consumption that requires things like "retirement income." Ashbery's deep inhabitation of the conflicts between the desire for poetry to reflect particular experiential states that are socially legible, and its desire to break away from empiricism and into the realm of the more nebulously cerebral, has important parallels to the crisis of purpose that continues to shape how literary criticism performs its own versions of self-reflexive critique and conceptual idealism. In this connection, I argue that his vacillations between a commitment to the quotidian particularities of sensoria and the rarefied philosophical diction that links him to a critical community form what one could call an aesthetics of intellectual class feeling.

In an exploration of the poet-critic R. P. Blackmur's involvement in midcentury anxieties over the commodification of literary culture, Evan Kindley begins to delineate the importance of critical justification in the production of circulatory economies for literature during and after modernism by noting that the philanthropically funded literary critical industry (if it could be so called) "was born out of a collective realization that American literary culture would need to grow but also a collective fear that that growth would be wild, unrestricted, and personally damaging to the literary intelligenstia."[61] To keep literature viable as an object worthy of charitable funding, in other words, it must have an oblique relationship to the market and, because of this, be justifiable as an autonomously valuable thing. The apparatus of criticism thus exists in its current form as one that both fields demands for justification from outside sources and provides in the form of theory its own demands for continued justification and examination of literary objects.[62]

Justification, in this incarnation, becomes both a symbol of the literary critical institution's relative autonomy *and* the extent of its need to communicate in a particular way with the rest of the world. I would like to draw a parallel here between this dialectic and the planes of referential relation that inhere in poetry such as Ashbery's. In the same way that meta-disciplinary debates in the literary humanities grapple with resistance to and dependence upon the mechanisms of late capitalism, Ashbery scrutinizes the relationship between cultures of poetic discourse: between the rendering of empirical particularities and the desire for a more autonomous, abstracted form of thought that resists its own status as institutionally produced for the sake of the preservation of vanguardist poetical thinking. As the university retains its status as a hegemonic administrator of culture, but turns its administrative interests away from humanistic pursuits even as it remains a major patron of poetry, the perception of threat and the subsequent affective responses to it—from anger to anxiety to resignation—come to be shared among artists and critics alike. This form of solidarity, however tenuous, is expressed most interestingly in the aesthetic of the academic avant-garde as it attempts to stay afloat within the disciplinary institutions of its patronage while using the discipline's own discourse modalities as a form of critique.[63]

The result is a kind of funhouse mirror: the viewer might laugh at what she sees, but it's also hard to avoid thinking about the concept of reflection and the truths that distortion proffers. Ashbery's form of distortion projects back upon his reader an image of the thinking self as a series of dialectically interwoven affective stances: earnest and ironic, bumbling and sharp, confident and insecure, specialized and universal. Ashbery is difficult because his dialectics, *pace* Hegel's and like Adorno's, don't ever really resolve, nor do they ground themselves in imagistic particulars. The resistance to clarity is both the invitation to critical reading and a type of performance thereof; if academic prose is "at its best" lucid and punchy, it nevertheless stands that much of the task of literary analysis is in fact to complicate things. Not for nothing is the phrase "reductive reading" usually used as an epithet. In this connection, the questions that animate the monologic dialogue in "Fantasia" are not only about the relevance to poetry of the empirical world, but also about the relationship between that relevance and navigating elite cultural status: of what kind of culture, these poems ask, are they now the guardian? Who now are their readers, and what ought they now tell them (and in what register)? What is the purpose of the production of cultural artifacts?

These are all questions, in a sense, *about* access; thus the (in)accessibility of poets like Ashbery is not only a matter of style but also of substance. As he writes toward the beginning of "Fantasia": "It's as I thought: there is / Nothing solid, nothing one can build on. . . . We may as well begin the litany here: / How all that forgotten past seasons us, prepares / Us for each other, now that the mathematics / Of winter is starting to point it out."[64] The levels of inaccessibility here are multiple: there is no antecedent to "there," and so the lines remain suspended in space, abstracted from any given locale. "That forgotten past" is both abstract and literally inaccessible, as it has been forgotten. The idea that there is "nothing solid" to "build on" registers a lack of access to an abstract concept: the materially or empirically verifiable real. This lack, however, does not stop the poem from continuing. Indeed, it is precisely upon the idea of the inaccessible that "we may as well begin the litany."[65] Thus the project of building something (a poem, a relationship between two people) begins from the admission that there is nothing to build with, that building is impossible.

The lines above are spoken by the poem's "she"; in the following stanza, "he" agrees and adds a further complication of his own: "It is true, a truer story: / Self-knowledge frosts each action, each step taken / Freely: Life is a living picture."[66] The abstract totality of human action is arrested (or, dialectically, sweetened) by "self-knowledge"; we are constantly being stopped by "much that might be / Examined for the purpose of examining it." This type of reflexive analysis, or what Gerald Graff might call "theoretical awareness," is both what the poem performs—each piece of dialogue, however obliquely, being a sort of reading—and a major contributor to Ashbery's inescapable presence in discussions of contemporary poetry.[67] As these discussions take place more and more among analysts connected with departments of English, Ashbery's anxieties about communication and clarity, abstraction and ephemerality, and the regulatory cultures of discourse that surround these concepts come to seem more and more like poetic paradigms for thinking through the institutional situation of the literary humanities writ large.

If the most obvious overlap between the situations of poetry and of literary criticism has to do with the aforementioned conundrum of justification—answering the question, in other words, "but what is it *for*?"—a corollary question surrounds it as both cause and effect: "but what does it *mean*?" The affective valence of this question is disciplinary-dependent: complication being (mostly) a cause for respect and admiration in the sciences, and of accusations of snobbery or meaninglessness in the humanities. Dismissal of the abstract or labyrinthine artwork has long evinced the interplay of disdain and fear that, paradoxically, serves both to marginalize the humanities and to give it its cache, however tenuous, of cultural capital.[68]

As I mentioned just above, the poles between which Ashbery's work tends to shuttle do not settle into a Hegelian synthesis; Ashbery's "negative capability" is instead Adornian. Of the theorists regularly deployed in literary analysis, Adorno has most extensively elucidated the dialectical parallelisms between discourse about art and art itself; in *Aesthetic Theory*, he consistently emphasizes the reflexive confrontation of opposed concepts as the key to understanding the relationship of art to the many forms of the social. From the very beginning, "absolute freedom in art ... comes into contradiction with the perennial unfreedom of the whole," in which "unfreedom" refers to the ways in which art invariably touches upon the commodity form.[69] The genuine artwork, Adorno insists, knows and confronts this contradiction, fusing its "truth content" with its "critical content."[70] But the methods of possible confrontation that Adorno then outlines are far from direct, consisting instead in the main of incomprehensibility and abstraction as ways of forcing conversation about both the nature of hermeneutics and the role of the empirical in art. Meaning, then, comes into view most clearly (as it were) as it is being systematically denied the reader or viewer. The meaning of poetry is to be found in a chorus of readers asking "what does it mean?"

Crucially, it is the assumption that to deny meaning is to assert its impossibility that leads to the general exasperation with (but also, in a way, the magnetism of) analytical methodologies like negative dialectics and deconstruction, and with poetic styles like Ashbery's. In this reading, the idea that a work's meaning exists in its lack is a kind of nihilism. It doesn't help that Adorno, usually relentlessly judgmental, is even-handed when it comes to the spectrum of the comprehensible and the incomprehensible. The most enigmatic artworks, in the world of *Aesthetic Theory*, are the ones that become the most well-understood because of the way in which they demand explication, while the mysteries present in less difficult work fly under the radar.[71] One of the most challenging things about Adorno's critical method is that its emphasis on the interplay of opposites can overshadow the importance of the trace of the other that remains as a constant presence-in-tension at any given pole, without which the dialectical conversation stops and the work solidifies into ideology. To overcome this stagnation, the work must display its own struggle in the "intensive aiming of words toward the nucleus of the innermost muteness."[72] The conscious courting of impossibility described here is a characteristic feature of Ashbery's auto-analytics, as he grapples with the question of what his poetry, suddenly important, should be for.

In Ashbery's dual-vocal poems, what appears as the play of opposites (in "Fantasia," the "he" and "she" characters, and in "Litany," as we will soon see, the dual columns of text) is a device by which one poetic voice can inhabit its contradictions, foregrounding the process of self-critical struggle as a general and generative form. For Ashbery, the subject matter upon which this criticism is turned is framed as unimportant, as "he" says in "Fantasia:" "you chose a view of distant factories, / Tall smokestacks, anything. It didn't matter / So long as it was emptied of all but a drop / At the bottom like the medicine bottle that is thrown away."[73] But the smokestacks of the view are never fully erased by the inconsequentiality of the choice of landscape; in a move that very much backs up Shapiro's assertion that Ashbery performs a type of deconstructive theorizing, the "drop" in the metaphorical medicine bottle exists not only as a fact but indeed as an imperative: "it doesn't matter / *so long as*" the trace remains.[74] The trace of referentiality is both what's left after a long emptying process involving the extraction of the general from the particular—any landscape from a smokestack landscape—and the particle of specificity used to build outward *into* the abstracted, idealized form.

This movement toward the Platonic is an always-already failed attempt to be both everywhere and nowhere; rather than having a descriptive or communicative goal, it describes instead a general procedure for thinking through what constitutes "a view." This emphasis on proceduralism—legible in the difficulty one often has in describing what, concretely, a given Ashbery poem might be "about"—draws the readers' attention to the broad applicability of Ashbery's poetic concerns while refusing to attach those concerns to anything in particular. But it is in that refusal that we find the anxiety that most pervades these long poems: that detachment from the concerns of the material world risk relegating poetry to irrelevance. Or that dialogic poems that are actually monologic are *actually* solipsistic. As in Adorno: "art's double character—its autonomy and *fait social*—is expressed ever and again in the palpable dependencies and conflicts between the two spheres."[75] Between the half-ineffability of the poem's particularities and the larger formal device that registers a shuttling of voices without ever quite fully performing the play of otherness, both the micro- and the macrostructural elements of Ashbery's multivocal poems register this conflict.

Being-for-itself versus being-for-another is one of the most common poetic conundrums of the modern age; what Ashbery's significance to professional literary studies in that age suggests is the degree to which the social value of analytical reading and the idealized autonomy of the work of that reading find themselves in tension. Ashbery's poetry resists its own penchant for the ineffable (claiming, as he does in "Litany," the existence of "solemn abstractions that were crimson / And solid as beefsteak")[76]; literary criticism, as it fields ever more pressing calls for social justification, works through a similar cognitive dissonance regarding the value of its work as difficult, specialized labor versus its desire (and/or need) to be a public good. This play of desires, of admission and resistance, forms the nexus of communality between Ashbery's multivocal, auto-analytical aesthetic and the troubled imaginary of the academic literary community in which his work has found such a secure home.

And indeed, one of the effects of Ashbery's notoriously inscrutable use of pronouns—indeterminate "you"s, "he"s, and "she"s, and the rare use of the first person—is to foster a sense, however strange or vague, of sociality in a genre whose production is often seen as a lone pursuit.[77] Reading, too, is work most often done alone—but the *profession* of reading, and writing readings, relies upon a sense of group identity and at least some semblance of a shared goal. The intense citationality which is now standard practice for most acts of academic literary criticism points toward a fundamental concern for the upholding of conversational appearances; indeed, one of the pillars of the discipline is ostensibly *not* to make points in a void but rather to engage with a community, albeit a specifically trained one. In this connection, Ashbery's poetic conversation in "Fantasia" takes on a loaded "we":

> Further on it says
> That all the missing parts must be tracked down
> By coal-light or igloo-light because
> In so doing we navigate these our passages,
> And take sides on certain issues, are
> Emphatically pro or con about what concerns us,
> Such as the strangeness of our architecture,
> The diffuse quality of our literature.[78]

The conversing "we" in this passage may be "emphatically pro or con" a given issue, but they are nevertheless in the same, perhaps here literal, boat. The dialogic structure of the poem coalesces into the solidarity of a shared journey, one in which the participants jostle through their disagreements in order to perform the labor of illuminating a way forward.[79]

The end of the stanza turns back on itself, as both a commentary on Ashbery's own "diffuse"ness and as a placing of the poem into something that could be called "our literature." Is "our literature" the whole of global literary production? Multigeneric but Anglophone texts? Poetry produced in the United States after 1945? There is a sense here that historical, geographical, and linguistic categorizations are less important than the simple act of forming a constituency that moves beyond the dialectical vocality of he/she and into a larger but still guild-ed (as it were) group of "light"-holders with which to illuminate the "passages" of mental and dialogical activity. In a way, Ashbery here inducts himself into the society of people who critically debate whether or not the "diffuse quality" of his writing and the "strangeness" of his form are indeed something that deserves celebration. By situating the poles of both dialogic and critical-guild communality as co-constitutive, and by performing that situating on an abstract plane with no particular reference other than what might best be called the constitutive parts of the self, Ashbery's reflexivity becomes not only a way to foreground the internal intellectual processes that go into poetic communication but also to force that internalization outward, onto a larger discourse community whose primary interests involve scrutiny and argumentation.

If "Fantasia on 'The Nut-Brown Maid'" formalizes its dialectic and its relational scrutiny through characters that speak in turn, "Litany" radicalizes the interpenetration of voices by positing them as literally simultaneous. The poem stretches to about a hundred pages in the Library of America's edition of his collected early poems, and it consists of two columns of text on each page, meant to be read at the same time—one in italics, one in standard typeface. As in "Fantasia," the two modes of speaking do not situate themselves on ends of an argumentative pole but instead seem to be gently competing facets of the same voice. For all of its formal innovation, "Litany" was initially received as one of Ashbery's more straightforward poems, often in a way that is tellingly relieved: "Of Ashbery's rudderless long poems . . . 'Litany' strikes me as the most interesting. In addition to the perennial theme of indeterminacy, it contains excursions into the problem of ageing and death, and an atypically straightforward verse-essay on poetry and literary criticism." Or "Ashbery has allowed himself startling fits of clarity . . . we get long discursive passages—on the state of poetry, the need for humanistic criticism, or the need to be taken care of, all written in the baldest prose."[80] Longer forays into academic criticism of the poem (of which there are vanishingly few) move through its pages, attempting to summarize.[81]

Only Ann Lauterbach, recounting her experience of reading the poem out loud with Ashbery in Saratoga Springs around the time *As We Know* was published, seems to afford to "Litany" the kind of difficulty and evasiveness that critics find to be the defining feature of Ashbery's poetry: speaking of the efforts to distinguish the voices from one another, she remarks that "they are the curse of a desire to make meaning align with sense through operations of the analytic . . . whereas the poem, like so much of Ashbery's work, insists that meaning and sense making, how we come to know what we know, are more complicated, intractable, and irretrievable, than we care to admit."[82] In my reading of the most "straightforward" section of "Litany," I want to put this by-now typical reading of Ashbery's avoidance of meaning into contact with his more essayistic grammar, not merely in order to show that things are more complicated than they seem—a move that, along with demonstrating how things are *less* complicated than they seem, makes up a large amount of the extant criticism on Ashbery more generally—but in order to demonstrate the inextricability of his meaning-making from his relationship to the intellectual class.

This inextricability has implications that reach beyond Ashbery's reception and into the broader imaginary of poetry writing as "creative writing." Though it is doubtless true that literary analysis as a discipline has moved away, even pedagogically, from asking directly and New Critically "what does it *mean*?", the problem of meaning remains in the air, not as a question of epistemology, but as a question of labor. Critical analysts of literature, explicators as we are, remain dependent on a certain degree of literary opacity, whereas the structure of the writing program, in which students must be taught how to "do" art, depends upon an epistemological stability. The workshopped writer is, after all, constantly faced with criticisms that begin along the lines of "I don't understand what you mean by" this or that stylistic choice. But both, crucially, depend on a measure of hermeticism surrounding the way that *thinking* gets done: the relative difficulty of articulating an empirical and transferable skill set related to "thinking" in both an artistic and critical sense is what allows the myth that writers are "born and not made" to persist and, relatedly, what secures the cultural class position of the intellectual. Paradoxically, however, as Gouldner and others have shown, it is the broad accessibility of thinking that also allows the professional intellectual class to claim permeability for its borders.

The academic avant-garde—caught in the odd triangulation of resistance toward the kind of clarity sanctioned by professionalized creative writing, desire for social relevance and life, and dependence upon an increasingly academicized reading audience (which also governs conditions of employability)—must carefully negotiate its stance toward the conditions of its possibility. In this way, the question that Ashbery asks, and the quasi-answer he gives, at the very end of "Fantasia" take on a deeper significance for things to come: "Responsible to whom? I have chosen this environment and it is handsome."[83] The line contains the disingenuousness of the poem's literary source: faking exile, the knight in "The Nut-Brown Maid" has indeed "chosen this environment." The task, then, is to make of that environment something livable and workable. Ashbery writing, as we have seen and will continue to see, is Ashbery reading both his contextuality and his own writing's response to it; within these readings, the dialectics of universality and particularity, meaning and meaninglessness, elitism and egalitarianism attach themselves both to art as such and to the changing world in which it is produced and consumed.

Most probably, "Litany" is seldom written about not simply because of its daunting size—the enormous *Flow Chart* has been quite popular among literary critics—but because of how firmly its structure resists anything like a coherent statement of thematics. Most Ashbery poems are, as I've mentioned, difficult to summarize, but "Litany" is *designed* to descend into incoherent babble as the columns of text are read together. On the page, of course, the situation is somewhat different, but the sense of mild chaos is similar: the eye moves back and forth between the columns, reading a bit here, a bit there. The result is that Ashbery's already heavily abstracted aesthetic becomes even more so, as chunks of the poem seem to float away from the rest of the text and then back to it again in a dance whose steps are determined by each individual reader. This doubled non-linearity gives Ashbery the chance to test and re-test his stylistic and thematic predilections in multiplying combinations; as in "Fantasia," there's a preoccupation with the positivistic world and an anxiousness about leaving it behind, but with so much more room, the poem's explanatory tendencies are given even freer rein.

"*So long as the buoyant opening/Of a vacant career stand around healthily,*" Ashbery somewhat ungrammatically muses, "*There is no need to ascertain/The pink and red paper stratosphere/Balloons*"[84]—again we see the ambivalence regarding the profession, as it were, of abstraction. No longer needing to "ascertain" the real (where, he goes on to say, "*color cannot have ever been,*" where "*expressions . . . were never there to begin with*"), the poet has been set perilously free by this "vacant career" in which his job now appears to be to theorize about its lack. Meanwhile, in the opposite column, "colors" attach themselves to "tiger lilies" and "forgetting-grass," a gesture of specificity that never really settles into a counter-argument but rather hovers in the space between nostalgia and the self-awareness of the italicized column, which notes that "*I too/Was once captured this way.*"[85] Flip to almost any page in "Litany" and you'll find some example of this form of auto-analysis: listing an improbable array of things that might appear in a shop ("*a pile of ventilators next/To a lot of cuckoo-clock parts,/Plus used government documents and stacks/Of cans of brine shrimp*"), Ashbery pauses to reflect that "*you/Pick up certain things here, where/You need them, and/Do without the others for the moment,/Essential though they may be./Every collection is as notable for its gaps/As for what's there.*"[86] As with the smokestacks in "Fantasia," the material world in this poem is important not as fodder for description, but as the trigger for ruminations upon the workings of the mind in, or apart from, that world.

For indeed, Ashbery's success in the late 1970s and beyond are inextricably tied to his ability to capture a literary and literary-critical moment in which hermeneutic "ideas/Of what else may be there" are left "standing around looking at/The hole left by the great implosion."[87] As I've argued in the last chapter and at the beginning of this one, the literary arts and the academy have been wracked over the past half century by various kinds of implosions and explosions, most of them overdetermined—and thus the image of some loose collective of thinkers standing around a giant crater is evocative on multiple levels. This is the affective matrix into which Ashbery's poetry taps so effectively: nostalgia for a pre-implosion past tempered by a forward-looking conviction, confidence that the crater can be worked with tempered by fear that maybe it cannot.

Ultimately, Ashbery's various categorizations of his work—as referential, as philosophical, as comic, as earnest, as socially dialogic, as inwardly dialogic—are not containers into which various things are dropped. Instead, they are mutually constitutive regions whose consistently recognizable feature is an analytical or explanatory diction that parallels that of critical reading. Persistently self-signaling and universalizing as regards its potential subject matter but simultaneously desirous of a delineated interpretive community, this reading-diction implicates everything from brine shrimp to "the event itself" (which is how Ashbery eventually, and tellingly, categorizes those "ideas / Of what else may be there") in the affective dialectic of the professional intellectual class-unit. My reading of the aesthetics of institutionalized literary production, then, rests in Ashbery's case not on the empirical delineation of the institutional forces that press in on the work from without, but rather in analysis of this anxiously deracinated grammatical presentation. This differentiation becomes harder to see when we are suddenly presented with the specter of clear and professionally relevant subject matter, but I believe it is still visible, and so the portion of "Litany" in which I am most interested is in fact the same portion that the poem's critics gravitate toward for being refreshingly straightforward.

In the lead-up to the moment where Ashbery plunges fully into the waters of what he thinks "criticism" ought to be doing, he uses the word "institution" only once: during a moment when the non-italicized column is absent, we read:

> *You were promised safe-conduct*
> *From a brief, mild agony*
> *To these not-uninteresting pangs of birth*
> *And so, and so, a landscape always seen through black lace*
> *Became this institution*
> *For you, inflected, as we shall see,*
> *From time to time by discreet nautical allusions*[88]

Leaving aside the fact that I have, in fact, already used a boat metaphor to stand in for the academic community, the heavily metaphorical language that surrounds the clearest point of reference for academics falls into place around that metaphor, hinging on the verb "become": the "birth pangs" place one into the "landscape" which is now an "institution." Even though the grammar in this passage is, as in most of Ashbery's poetry, relatively indefinite ("these," "a," "this"), we read it as a relatively smooth narrative of career development—the entering into a landscape in which we are all, again, in the same boat. But what to do with the "black lace," which partially obscures our vision? The semi-transparent film that Ashbery places between us and our institutional landscape registers on two levels: first, as a failure to appreciate one's social situation, the romanticized view through "black lace" solidifying eventually into "this institution." It is also a commentary on the incomplete power of metaphorical speech, turning the passage in toward itself and its activities. This passage is perhaps especially vulnerable to interpretation in this way, but it nevertheless registers the ease with which one can find one's own academic-critical-consciousness portrayed in Ashbery's verse.[89]

As the poem moves toward its most direct treatment of the relationship between poetry and criticism, the non-italicized column reappears, asking "yet whereto?"[90] A possible named destination is "Cloud-Cuckoo-Land," at once a reference to Aristophanes and a comic deflection that reveals a lot about what the poem is about to do. Consider the cloudiness of this statement, for instance: "*Just one minute of contemporary existence / Has so much to offer.*" Invoking both the whole of experience and of the potentially infinite subject-object relations within it, the poem then goes on to assert that sorting all of this out is in fact what critics "*are supposed to be doing.*"[91] The blatant impossibility of this task goes unacknowledged, the lack of a universal poetry-criticism being blamed instead on the fact that "*today / Nobody cares or stands for anything / Not even the handful of poets one admires.*"[92] This is exaggeration to the point of satire, as the absolutes "nobody" and "anything" universalize the discourse to the point where it fails to make any sense. The poetry is literally *senseless*: it is both an impossibility (everyone cares about *something*) and invokes no sensory stimuli. What seems like an attack on the unprincipled passivity of the creative-critical class, however, if we allow ourselves a satirical reading through the lens of this universalized and indefinite syntax, becomes a place from which Ashbery can mount a critique of a false universality, one that repudiates the very capaciousness that it invokes.

What Ashbery is satirizing with these blanket statements about critical labor and artistic principle is, essentially, himself: his own propensity to hover in an abstract space away from "anything" while still caring deeply about the realities of quotidian existence.[93] The affective state that this kind of tonality produces is that of the culturally embattled artist in the age, as it were, of mechanical reproduction—distant and judgmental (in the Gouldnerian sense) while feeling pangs of guilt about that distance and judgement. This emotional matrix, upheld by Ashbery's signature grammar, rebuts those assertions of self-cancellation made by his early (and some of his late) critics. Instead, it renders his play of opposites not as mutually exclusive but as mutually *constitutive* of an auto-analytical project of critique.

In this connection, "Litany" does not mount (or amount to) a wholesale attack upon the institutional production of literature and criticism, but nor is it allowing that the present state of affairs will suffice. It is, as Adorno notes of Beckett, passing "historical judgment over these categories as such, faithful to the historical innervation that there is no more laughing over the classics of comic theatre except in a state of renewed barbarism."[94] Ashbery's "classics of comic theatre" are in "Litany" the *"great poets of the past,"* whom he reads as having created *"the exact feel / And slant of a field"* such that the reader, *"for better or for worse,"* can find *"no / Conceivable way of getting out."*[95] One thinks again, though this is not the original point of reference, of the systematicity of Bourdieu, in which cultural producers position themselves within fields produced and realized by the accumulation of history—specifically the relations of the means of production.[96] To imagine "not standing for anything" is thus to imagine oneself outside of an all-encompassing field—and if we think of the phrase's more linguistic definition, it also means not to *represent* anything. The language of emancipation becomes paradoxically both that of a universal grammar of generality (invoking "nobody" and "anything") and the incredible particularity of individual experience—for if the culture of critical discourse has its roots in anything, it is in the belief that a universalized self-reflexive discourse of evaluation is the best way to realize what can possibly be realized of individual autonomy and self-actualization.

So when Ashbery says that it *"behooves / Our critics to make the poets more aware of / What they're doing, so that poets in turn / Can stand back from their work and be enchanted by it,"* the phrase "what they're doing" references not only the poets themselves, who need criticism to become fully aware of their own work, but also back to another abstraction: the idea that critics should make poets aware of the fact that they do not "care or stand for anything."[97] Far from this awareness being a critique, it becomes a celebration: both the poets and the *"general public"* are meant to be enchanted by the results of professional reading. In this way, the poem relentlessly implicates itself in the very systems of which it is suspicious; its satirical portrayal of the comportment of cultural arbiters is a reflexive critique (but not a disavowal) of the speaker's own real hope: *"If only / They could see a little better what was going on / Then this desirable effect might occur."*[98] The effect in question is the rescuing of the general public from *"the desperate, tangled muddle of their / Frustrated, unsatisfactory living."*[99] The absurd adjectival piling takes a key facet of academic and artistic class consciousness, particularly the *vanguard* of that consciousness, to task: namely, the very representational idea that poets and critics could form a "moral Guardian[ship]" of the unthinking and therefore immiserated mass public.[100]

The concept of a universal poetic-critical discourse, however, is not simply written off as stupid or impossible. The critique here is of a universality that thinks of itself as pure salvo, that does not simultaneously recognize within itself its immanent threat to potential autonomy. It is, in fact, a disassembling of any pretenses to a non-reflexive criticism, one that echoes Gouldner's monumental efforts to urge his sociologist colleagues toward a richer "sociology of sociology."[101] The presumptions of an aesthetic and its attendant theory that could swoop down upon the late-capitalistic multitude and offer them the *"outside or part-time help"* for which they are not asking but which they nevertheless desperately need removes the possibility of an individual will and subsumes it under the aegis of guardianship. The self-judgement that leads to self-appointment is, in this case, anything but immanent criticism.[102]

The satirical portrayal of the discourse of guardianship in this section of "Litany" operates partly in the play of pronouns: the first-person plural is invoked just as the poem moves into a description of the "new criticism." And it is precisely the first-person plural that the new criticism cannot at first approach: it should

> *Not be too eager to criticize us: we*
> *Could do that for ourselves, and have done so.*
> *Nor*
> *Should it take itself as a fitting subject*
> *For critical analysis, since it knows*
> *Itself only through us, and us*
> *Only through being part of ourselves, the bark*
> *Of the tree of our intellect.*[103]

The extreme solipsism of this passage, in which the activity of self-reflexiveness is posited as an historical fact not in need of extension or repetition, satirically nominates itself for the position of ultimate cultural arbiter, as the all-encompassing "intellect" whose autonomy is protected precisely by its claim to the guardianship of those who need assistance in *"assimilating and enjoying whatever it is."*[104] "Whatever it is" stands in as a comical abstraction of culture writ large; the potential truth of the universal concept of art escapes meanwhile through the trapdoor of a false concept of universality. Ashbery's seemingly straightforward delineation of a new kind of criticism—one that can save one's life, if one can only see beyond the morass of contemporary existence—asks in reality for an incredibly nuanced way of thinking about the representational function not only of language itself but also of those who claim to reveal to us the ways in which we are always in chains.

In other words, the freedom promised by the autonomous labor of poetry is paradoxically achievable only with the assistance of the analogous project of criticism; the very non-representationality of language not only unmoors poetry from the confinement of reified methods of linguistic access, but is also the site at which poetry invites criticism into itself as the "philosophical reflection" without which art says nothing at all.[105] In Ashbery's work, the invitation is accepted with typical unease. Muddling the poetic-critical communality of the "we" of the previous stanza, the voice in the second column of "Litany" indicts itself for allowing its criticality to eclipse its poeticality:

> So that it takes over, seizes the glitter
> And luminosity of what ought to have been our
> Creative writing, even though it is dead
> Or was never called to life, and could not be
> Anything living, like what we managed
> Somehow to get down on the page.
> And the afternoon backs off,
> Won't have anything to do with all of this.[106]

The rejection of the critical text is not a manifesto. It is, instead, the painful admission that the deracinated grammar of this poetry, shorn as it is of the "glitter" of representational thought (a kind of thought which, presumably, would allow the relative particularity of "the afternoon" to stick around), still speaks the truth of aesthetic experience better than the alternative: "*Yet the writing that doesn't offend us / (Keats' 'grasshopper' sonnet for example) / Soothes and flatters the easier, less excitable / Parts of our brain.*"[107] Keats's meditation on "the poetry of earth," which as the voice of the grasshopper in spring and the indoor cricket in the winter is always and fundamentally reminding the listener of its aliveness, is presented as an Arnoldian consolation, something that allows us to avoid thinking about critical discourse and instead gives us an easy "*grasp of a certain level of reality that / Is going to be enough—will have to be."*[108] This is a highly and deliberately simplistic reading of Keats's sonnet, the end of which invokes through a slumber scene the rising heat and delirium of fever. Thus when this section of "Litany" itself dozes off to sleep, the peace of it is hardly such that *"no one is to blame, and no reproach / Can finally be uttered as the lamp / Is trimmed."*[109] A sonnet about a grasshopper that is not actually about death might be something that can be imagined, but it is not what Keats wrote, and it is emphatically not what "Litany" is, or strives to be.

Through its emphatic disingenuousness, the poem argues simultaneously for both refusal and admission of the reciprocal relationship between poetry and the social formations in and around which it arises—in this case, the formation of literary criticism. But again, rather than resulting in a sort of paralysis-of-principle, such a dual mindset generates a self-critical sensibility informed by a desire to move beyond representational poetics and the recognition of the company one then keeps upon doing so. The professional academic reader needs the inaccessible nature of poetic non-representationalism in order to perform her constituent labor, while poetry's claim upon the truth of language beyond positivism hinges on the accumulation of particular instances of radical abstraction that ask for philosophical-critical language to complete and sustain it. This mutual dependency paradoxically reinforces the notion that the institutional positionality of both poetry and criticism in fact allows for the possibility of artistic and intellectual autonomy—not to be construed as a complete and solipsistic independence, but rather a solidarity that provides at least one form of defense against the encroachments of instrumentalism that have long threatened the project of critical inquiry.

Confronting the uncertain, of course, can take many forms. As we will see in the next chapter, it can be turned into an entire pedagogy—or it can be generative as a nearly bottomless well of analytic possibility. Taking this latter position is the poet Mei-mei Berssenbrugge, whose work bears some of Ashbery's hallmarks (a loose play of pronouns, heavily abstract diction, a melancholy sense of humor) but whose much closer connection with the university and its attendant cultures of discourse shines through, I'd argue, in her much less wavering commitment to the language of explanation. Berssenbrugge was raised in a highly educated family ("I identify with my Chinese family," she has said, "a family of spirited academics"): her grandfather was a Harvard educated mathematician and her mother followed in those footsteps; her father has advanced degrees in Near Eastern Studies from Berkeley and, again, Harvard.[110] Berssenbrugge herself is a graduate of Columbia University's MFA program in creative writing and has taught at Brown and at the Institute of American Indian Art in Santa Fe. Her poetry is self-reading in the extreme: the characters in her poems (as in Ashbery, designated by "he"s, "she"s, and sometimes "I") do not "do" things so much as "have thoughts had about them," as Berssenbrugge uses the abstract form of the person to explore the kinds of expository writing she felt she could not do in prose.[111] In her active embrace of a poetics of auto-interpretation, Berssenbrugge allows us to see the very lively afterlife of Ashbery's explorations of poetry as a process of critical reading.

After her first few books, published in the 1970s, Berssenbrugge developed an increasingly long line with correspondingly long sentences, lending much of her poetry the jargony, conceptually dense feel of philosophically inflected literary criticism:

> The fog of the way we feel our way into this focus, seeking by feeling, lies in the indefiniteness of the concept of continuing focus, or distance and closeness, that is, of our methods of comparing densities between human beings.

Or:

> The first solution which occurs to us for the problem of the appearance of another person is that ideas of actual feeling instead of the appearance of feeling refer to points of tiny intervals or patches in the other person.[112]

Both of these sentences occur in the long poem "Fog," from her 1989 collection *Empathy*, and it's clear from these passages that the book is aptly titled. There is very little trace, here, of Ashbery's tendency to write poems that are both abstract and lack an immediate sense of "about"ness or subject matter. Instead, the abstractness has an almost startling focus, as it eschews traditionally poetic notions of metaphoric evocation in favor of a head-on definitional grammar. If one were not looking too closely, one might mistake these sentences for excerpts from a new Sianne Ngai project.[113]

But we are, here, in the business of looking closely, and upon doing so, it becomes clear that Berssenbrugge's mode of intellection is not simply identical to that of the literary analyst or theorist. For one thing, it is even less clear: a "solution" which is "ideas of actual feeling instead of the appearance of feeling refer to points of tiny intervals or patches in the other person" could more accurately be called an exacerbation of the original problem (of how one might recognize empathy). What is the difference between "ideas of actual feeling" and "the appearance of feeling"? The fact that the poem makes the distinction is telling; Berssenbrugge seems to want to say that ideas are the only things that allow us to move past appearances, even if the only way to move past them is to admit that everything is made up of them. Nearly ten years later, in *Four Year Old Girl* (1998), little has changed:

> If I dream I see light on a new bud in the woods, this is feeling used as thought, beautiful because of my attempt to contain it.[114]

The potential image—"light on a new bud in the woods"—is doubly removed from the poem; once by being in a dream, and again by the propositional "If" that renders the sentence a thought exercise. And it is in the thinking through of "feeling," turning it into an idea, that unleashes the aesthetic: the "beautiful," that is, that comes from the always unfinished processes of perception.

Such faith in the artistically generative power of cogitation is at once predictable, given Berssenbrugge's upbringing amongst professional thinkers (and her love of Derrida, Deleuze, and Spivak), and surprising, given the most common prescription of the creative writing workshop: "show, don't tell."[115] While that particular line of instruction—to evoke or describe with images, rather than with abstractions—is no longer seen as the cure-all it once was, it remains the case (as we have seen with early Ashbery criticism) that "extended pointmaking" is not generally regarded as a primary poetic task. But in those spaces where poetry is a discipline and poets encounter their disciplinary "neighbors"—philosophy, literary criticism, history; for Berssenbrugge also math—we can see the extent to which these encounters form the basis for an innovative poetics, one that undoes the certainty of sense perception and transforms it instead into a phenomenon in need of examination.

What was an unease about sidling too close to expository abstraction in Ashbery, then, becomes a way of embracing the progressive possibilities of a "philosophical frame of mind."[116] For Berssenbrugge, such an embrace is tightly connected to issues of race and gender, as women of color have historically been severely underrepresented in discourses about both intellectuality and avant-garde poetry. To combine the two is one way for Berssenbrugge to make her presence felt in both modes at once: as a woman of "theoretical inclination," as she has put it, and as an artist who can push on the boundaries of her genre while still being attentive to her embodiment in and relation to the world.[117] The feminine pronoun, in this connection, is wielded in her poetry with a knowing force:

> Such emotions are interruptions in landscape and in logic
> brought on by a longing for direct experience, as if her memory of experience were the trace of herself. Especially now, when things have been flying apart in all directions,
> she will consider the hotel lobby the inert state of a form.[118]

This passage, from the poem "Texas" in *Empathy*, finds the "she" experiencing "the trace of a desire" (for a "he") before breaking the stanza and beating the emotion back by *reading* it. The analytic tendency here is an obvious bid for control, a way to affirm the solidity of the woman's presence even "when things have been flying apart in all directions." It is destined to fail: the poem itself, which describes light striking a hand lingering on a surface as "a gold wing on the table," evokes a profound and rich sense of melancholy. But *as method*, critical reading functions in Berssenbrugge as a bulwark against a personal sense of dissolution. Abstraction, in this instance, works as a solidifying force.

Reading practices, as ways of confronting the essential uncertainties of the world, are thus indeed a way of "showing": rather than reflecting the picture that the mind's eye puts together, however, Berssenbrugge's work shows us a picture of the eye at work. But because her eye is so focused on the work of phenomenological explanation, the resulting poetry appeals only obliquely to sense perception (so not the eye at all, in fact). Instead, the words coalesce into something like a picture of mental labor as struggle:

> Lack of clarity within your environment is tormenting. It is felt as shameful.
> We feel we do not know how to even out a place for ourselves, where we should know our way about.[119]

Berssenbrugge is not interested in demonstrating what the "torment" of a "lack of clarity" looks like, but rather in what it feels like to the mind: like shame, and like not knowing "how to even out a place" for oneself. The irony of the line is that it itself is quite clear: it reads like explanatory prose. By itself, it would be hard to recognize *as* poetry, which is probably one of the intended effects. But something has to distinguish what Berssenbrugge is doing from essay-writing, and one of the things that does so is the poems' tendency to snap back into a type of qualified particularity: "there is such a thing as 'feeling something as luminous,' // thinking of him as the color of polished silver or nickel, or a scratch in these metals."[120]

The sudden visual specificity of silver and nickel heightens both the strange beauty and the metaphorical richness of the line: it's not immediately obvious what it might mean to think of someone as being "the color of polished silver," but such an image isn't designed to be obvious; it is designed to spark the imagination. The play between such provocation and the dry, nearly pedantic passages that rely heavily on the copula (lack of clarity *is* shameful and *is* tormenting; "feminizing an art of presence . . . *is* akin to those collages that verge on trompe l'oeil") emphasizes the means by which such images come into existence, which I'd argue strengthens their effect.[121] Indeed, this moment of particularly isn't even posited as an external given: the gerund "thinking" makes the comparison always already one of mental gymnastics. All poems are products thereof, of course, but the extent to which Berssenbrugge draws attention to those gymnastics, and the closeness with which those exercises hew to the literary philosophical and theoretical readings that have influenced her *Weltanschauung*, reveal how fundamentally the culture of critical discourse can weave itself into the fabric of experimental poetry in its academic age.

To return to an earlier point, while such a culture can be (and has been) exclusionary and/or protectionist, its reclamation by a woman poet of color signals several important things. Beyond being a way for minority voices to gain some control over a still-powerful form of cultural discourse (which, again, explains some of Ashbery's reticence about using it), poetry such as Berssenbrugge's evinces not simply control for control's sake, but a type of faith in the discourse being wielded. That is, passages such as the ones I've been quoting are not disingenuous uses of academese's sentence structures. Rather, they are a way of enacting an optimism about pessimism expressed succinctly by Robert Hass in *Time and Materials*: "it is good, sometimes, for poetry to disenchant us."[122] The removal, by poetry, of poetry's own aura is one way to enhance its ability to direct the reception of the beautiful; for

Berssenbrugge, the critical-evaluative mode allows her to form an impression of her mental and cultural identities that is irreducible to either one of those things individually.

The description of reading one's surroundings, of "feeling [one]'s way through the fog," places real value on that reading as a site of openness and possibility: a recollection, one might say, of the ways in which critical reading strives to inhabit a space of indeterminacy, even though we all of course want our readings to be "solid" and "right." To admit that the edges of experience or analysis are always already blurred can be difficult, but it is also a necessary step in the direction of what Berssenbrugge, in her poetry, imagines to be a deeply consequential form of aestheticized thinking. A short line tucked away near the beginning of "Fog" quietly encapsulates her project: "what ignorance," she writes, "can her description eliminate?"[123] It would be hard to think of a more succinct way to invoke the goals of scholarship in a perfect world: a utopian vision, to be sure, but one without which it would be too easy to lose sight of that long and important view. Certain forms of disenchantment, as it turns out, can pave the way for a renewed appreciation of our shared humanity, of the ways in which "other people exist in subtler forms than the body in daylight."[124] In her reading of her writing in the world, Berssenbrugge realizes the potential for elegance and reach contained within our most recondite inquisitive tendencies.

3

Poetry in the Teaching Machine

In a 1996 interview with the poet Mark Wunderlich, Jorie Graham admits that while teaching the craft of poetry "puts one into contact with an incredibly wide swath of reality" (a net positive, for a writer), the vocation in which many contemporary poets find themselves is also the source of an intractable, almost existential tension:

> [S]ometimes teaching feels like an extraordinary price to pay for the freedom to write poems. I find myself increasingly unable to write—to make contact with my work—while I'm "talking out" so much, burning a hole in my silence . . . I've taken to not writing at all when that starts to happen. I need certain things to remain secret from my own conceptual intellect for a poem to actually "happen."[1]

It is an articulate formulation of a not uncommon sentiment. Academically positioned writers of all stripes find themselves constantly navigating the balance between teaching and research work (to say nothing of administrative duties). Teaching, as a form of academic labor, occupies a somewhat embarrassing position in the profession: its importance is obvious, and a great many professors across disciplines take great care in their classrooms, but the rhetoric that upholds this work as a noble duty is tempered by a common professional mood that Vladimir Nabokov has evoked succinctly: "I am sick of teaching, I am sick of teaching, I am sick of teaching."[2]

Mark McGurl uses this quote as the very first line of *The Program Era* for good reason. Nabokov, who was working on *Lolita* at the time, was "sick of teaching" because teaching, a notoriously time-consuming activity, robbed him of time to do his "real" work—the work of writing fiction. *Lolita*'s success, McGurl goes on to note, in fact did allow him to steal that time back (he quit his job at Cornell). But no poet can hope for such a financial fate. Poets cannot in the main dream about agents or advances, or hope for livable royalties. Neither, indeed, can most literary critics. In their cases, the day job is simply *the* job, one not tempered by the possibility (however distant) of a salary produced solely from publishing. And now, as we know, a sizable portion of this job is a form of Althusserian reproduction: the teaching, that is, of one's form of writing (critical or creative) to undergraduate and graduate students.[3] Prose writers have a tendency to satirize this pursuit and its environs: books such as Nabokov's own *Pale Fire*, Elif Batuman's *The Possessed*, and John Barth's *Giles Goat-Boy* all turn the university into a kind of tragicomic theater of the absurd, full of characters pitiable for their own solipsistic obliviousness, pettiness, or strangeness.[4]

There is a similar tendency in the relatively small (but presumably growing) collection of poems written explicitly *about* teaching, but there is also an attendant seriousness that speaks to the inextricability of the poem's writer from its subject. In "The Obscure Room & My Inexplicable Weeping," Lyn Emanuel begins by lambasting her students:

> Kimber Lester, my student, while you cannot actually write
> a poem at least write a sentence to tell me why
> in the eighth stanza of this *text* the image of a bloody
> dagger hangs before me?[5]

It is not a very generous opening. That said, it is also funny to anyone who has ever led a creative writing workshop. The overwrought image of a "bloody dagger" is, after all, familiar territory for teachers of bathos-prone undergraduates. From there, however, the poem slowly transforms into a much more earnest examination of the relationship between this sentimental darkness and the real darkness that underlies it (Kimber, as it turns out, self-mutilates; "Jennifer," another student, has the face "of a wall guarding a moat"). It is a darkness, Emanuel admits, that she shares: "luckily looking out at you I can recall Finland, / that endless supple supply of night sky like black leather."[6] The ironized distance between Emanuel and her students collapses into an earnest shared unfamiliarity: each in their own world, student and teacher both are "swallowed in obscurity."

Kenneth Koch, a poet best known for his gleeful irreverence, is anything but when it comes to pedagogical work. In "The Art of Poetry," a long poem originally published in *Poetry* magazine in 1975, he begins on a slightly sardonic note—"to write a poem, perfect physical condition / Is desirable but not necessary"—but in the main, he calls for a striking degree of artistic sobriety. The poem wends its way through concerns about "friends who write as well as you do, who know what you are doing"[7] (a founding principle of the creative writing workshop), "find[ing] your own style" (another one), "the fear that one has 'lost one's talent'"[8] and writing "beyond your experience."[9] The effect is almost startlingly moving in its earnestness: Koch rejects the idea that poetry must be a byproduct of life lived by other means and recommends instead cultivating dedicated "environments for your poems and also people"; he implores his reader-student to "let your compassion guide you / And your excitement" and to remember "that what you do / Is immensely valuable, and difficult."[10] One imagines Koch's professing work at Columbia to have been not entirely dissimilar to Emanuel's at the University of Pittsburgh: sometimes exasperating, but also done with a keen awareness of the connection (even in isolation) between teacher-poet and student-poet.

Poems that treat the subject of pedagogy directly—"leaving our sullen classroom," Ellen Bryant Voigt writes, "I postponed my satchel of your poems / and wondered who am I to teach the young"[11]—are by necessity relatively clear. (Elizabeth Alexander's counter—"poetry, I tell my students / is idiosyncratic"[12]—true but notwithstanding.) To focus exclusively on such narratively straightforward pieces, however, would obscure the ways in which the concerns expressed within them also appear in more immediately challenging work. The argument of this chapter is that the difficult position of the creative writing professor—half tour guide, half guru—is in fact most thoroughly expressed in poetry which is not, ostensibly, "about" teaching. Indeed, the effect that it has on poetry that is itself difficult to parse is in a sense especially urgent, as the experimental writer in the academy must attempt to reconcile a penchant for opacity with the explicatory demands of pedagogy. Jorie Graham's work in *The End of Beauty* (1987) exemplifies this dialectic, and as such it will be this chapter's main case study. I want to suggest that the book's strong emphasis on the pleasures and dangers of the circulation of knowledge reflect the solidification of Graham's career, interrogating in particular the position of the artistic innovator as teacher. In the aggregate, the poems insistently ask: what does it look like to transmit poetically a real critical pedagogy? What does it mean to be the provider of information, on the one hand, and on the other the critical intellect that radically asserts that information cannot be taken as given?

To return for a moment to Emanuel's work above, we can see this tension poignantly exhibited, as her poems have a tendency to be otherwise highly elliptical. Making a five-point list that begins with the line "consider that," she writes a series of workshop comments, none of which are really workshop comments. "In this image of the bloody dagger," she writes as one comment, "in this densely botched moment of your personal life," she writes (unhelpfully) in another, "your life has gotten itself swallowed in an obscurity as deep / as the locked suitcase."[13] The bloody dagger, as cliché, covers up the transmission of anything about Kimber's life, leaving her in "obscurity"—but again, it's an obscurity that Emanuel intimately understands. Even if the poem is bad, she seems to argue, there are some things that ought to be kept secret.

The interplay of secrecy and revelation is in many cases also that of the personal and the generalizable. The title of this chapter recalls Gayatri Spivak's *Outside in the Teaching Machine*, in which Spivak, among many other things, examines the impossibility of "universalist claims in the human sciences," an assertion which makes the work of pedagogy a field in which the teacher will constantly feel "the ground shifting under her feet."[14] Spivak's work is, in the main, concerned with the pedagogy of racial and cultural identity—the deeply personal, that is, embedded within a culture geared toward essentialisms. As such, the content of her work fits more appropriately in the next chapter, where it will make a more extended appearance. But the title, and the recurrent outside-insiderness that it invokes, is also functional as a descriptor for the work of teaching performed by writers whose *writing* work might fare poorly under the examining eyes of the workshop.

Jorie Graham seems by all lights to have done just fine as a student in the MFA program at the University of Iowa. But as in the previous chapter, I am interested in the writer in a position of (relative) authority. *The End of Beauty* was written during Graham's return to Iowa as professor rather than student: a time in which, as she has put it, she "began learning to be the teacher that [she] became."[15] And so while one might struggle to call Ashbery an "academic poet," for Jorie Graham, there is no such problem. This chapter thus moves us from a general focus on conditions of reception to one on sites of production, and this is where the book shall remain.

The poems in *The End of Beauty* look and feel decidedly different from those in Graham's first two volumes, *Hybrids of Plants and of Ghosts* and *Erosion*, featuring a much longer, analytical line, heavily abstract diction, and a series of blanks, gaps, and variables that both ask and refuse filling in. Critics have pointed out that the narrative of stylistic progression that posits *The End of Beauty* as some kind of sudden breakthrough ignore, in the long view, the thematic consistencies (which usually center on her emphasis of metaphysical "betweenness") across her body of work. Bonnie Costello's description of *Erosion*, for example, as concerned chiefly with "the beautiful, the centering of images into an order where mystery is held and glimpsed" corroborates this observation.[16] I would note, however, that it is important not to let continuities of theme eclipse originality of form—and that to point out the stylistic and grammatical shifts that take place in *The End of Beauty* as being at least in part socially determined is particularly useful in charting the relationship between innovations in aesthetics and institutional situationality.[17]

My overarching analysis rests on the fact that the teaching of creative writing is fundamentally characterized by a contradiction: one that asserts that it cannot be taught even as it is *being* taught. This definitional doublespeak complicates its status as labor, the nature of the workshop leader's authority, and the nature of "craft" as pedagogical keyword. *The End of Beauty*, with its insistent focus on the giving and taking away of apposite language and knowledge, illuminates and is illuminated by these complications. The second poem in the book is entitled "On Difficulty," and it imagines, very obliquely, the journey of Adam and Eve out of Eden:

And in their temples a thrumming like
what-have-I-done?—but not yet a question, really, not
yet what slips free of the voice to float like a brackish foam
on emptiness—[18]

The lines are hard to hold on to: "what slips free of the voice" does precisely that, hovering in an ineffable space in which language and knowledge exist at an ungraspable threshold. Learning to know, as the poem's characters are doing, is figured as a process that a "you" can witness ("reaching each other for you to see, for you to see by, the long sleep/beginning, the sleep of resemblance"): a process that is strenuous and melancholy, resulting in the awareness that language is only "resemblance," but it is all that is left after the fall. The original knowledge of the nature of things—which is also an irretrievable loss—suffuses *The End of Beauty* with both a deep curiosity and a deep ambivalence about the authority of that curiosity. In dealing with these problems, Graham's poetry shuttles constantly between the thematics of secret and disclosure, and asks particularly where contradictory notions of freedom—as untransmissible artistic autonomy (the teaching-free "silence," to return to Graham's quote which opens this chapter, that many writers guard as a professional necessity) versus the transmissible capacity for something we might, however uneasily, call critical thinking—might lie in this continuum. The workshop, with its strangely authoritarian-egalitarian dual structure (professor as exemplar and leader, students as peer reviewers), carries with it an attendant uneasiness surrounding the relationship between notions of innate artistic talent and what could be called its talking cure.

In a half-snide, half-admiring review of Graham's 2005 collection *Overlord*, the *New York Times* poetry critic David Orr tries to put his finger on what, exactly, has made the poet such a "superstar" (as the review's title has it) in the world of her chosen genre. In context, it's an apt descriptor: Graham's rise to prominence is what MFA dreams are made of. After graduating from the Iowa Writer's Workshop in 1978, she took a tenure-track position there in 1983, accumulating awards and accolades (including a Pulitzer, a MacArthur grant, and the chairmanship of the Workshop) before moving to Harvard in 1998 to become the first woman to hold the Boylston Professorship of Rhetoric and Oratory, a position first occupied by John Quincy Adams and immediately prior to Graham held by Seamus Heaney.[19] Graham has thus spent the last couple of decades teaching creative writing outside the MFA circuit. I do not want to make overly much of this choice: while Harvard does not have a traditional graduate writing program (though it offers one through its Extension School), it offers exclusive workshops to its undergraduates and offers a "creative thesis" option for English majors. It is a job that offers tremendous amounts of "freedom to write poems," and its teaching retains basically the same structure as that of an MFA program. Why someone takes a job at Harvard may, in the end, simply be because it is a job at Harvard.

I will have more to say about the particularities of teaching creative writing below. But for now, back to the causes of superstardom. Orr runs through a list of incidental factors—Graham is "nice," she has extremely catholic tastes in poetry and is thus a "uniter, not a divider," she loves her students (here he makes a pointed reference to the accusations that Graham had, at the time, a tendency to pick her own students as winners of contests for which she was the judge).[20] He even, as seems obligatory for male journalists writing about Graham, has something to say about her good looks. But ultimately, he concedes, "more than anything else, Graham has succeeded because of the kind of poetry she writes."[21] Orr, in his unusual position as a poetry critic outside of the academy (although he was about to become a Hodder Fellow at Princeton), asserts that it's the combination of "sumptuously poetic" and "ostentatiously thinky" diction that has made her so popular, with the latter in particular responsible for her position within American tertiary education.

This "thinkiness" is overdetermined—Orr chalks it up to her frequent citations of Heidegger and poem titles like "Notes on the Reality of the Self" and "What is Called Thinking"—but there is something very telling about what Orr doesn't like about Graham's cerebral qualities and how her academic critics respond to the same thing. Graham is at her worst, Orr writes, when "her penchant for abstraction" becomes a "fogginess" that attempts to airily analyze, rather than describe, the actual events to which she (obliquely) refers. This abstraction, perhaps unsurprisingly, is one of the things that is most appealing about her work to academics. Kirstin Hotelling Zona, for instance, has characterized Graham's work approvingly as "a network of redoublings that form a 'dynamic shapelessness,'"[22] constantly in motion. A recent collection of essays on Graham emphasizes "the increasingly-foregrounded stylistic means by which [she] replicates movements of consciousness"—a style, the editor argues, that has had a lasting impact on experimental American poetry.[23] Charles Molesworth has argued that Graham's "philosophical disposition" predisposes her toward an aesthetic "formulation that removes detail in order to reveal process."[24] The ostentatious intricacy of Graham's verse lies, as Zona notes, in its refusal to choose between the poles of "autonomous" personal-lyrical style and what Helen Vendler has called a "persistent use of philosophical diction"—an analytic and abstracted mode of address that sees the self as contextually contingent.[25]

Vendler has been one of Graham's most consistent champions, identifying in her poetry an obsession with taxonomy tempered by the recognition that a complete interpretation is always already an impossibility.[26] Unlike a critic like Marjorie Perloff, Vendler has not made her name anointing or advocating for avant-garde poets. Where they overlap, tellingly, is in their Eliotic insistence that poetry ought to be *difficult*. If it is the job of the critic to "explain some complex state of affairs," as Vendler has it, then it is the job of the poet to produce those complex states of affairs.[27] Even given this commonality, Graham's position at the vanguard of poetic innovation is, ironically, subtle: her poems are indeed difficult but they do not necessarily shock; they are formally adventurous but are still recognizable as verse. Unless one is a dogmatic New Formalist, Graham's work is not outrageous in the literal sense. But the work her poems do *as* interrogation stages resistance to several contradictory statuses quo simultaneously: to the professionalized preference for rhetorical clarity in service of the workshop model but also to the *mythos* of poetry as an unteachable space of production; to the notion that institutionalized poetry writing merely reinforces the hierarchical relationship between teacher and student but also to the workshop's self-conception of radical horizontality.

Graham's poetry is thus of particular interest because of what it can tell us about the nexus of criticism, or the labor of reading specified in the last chapter, and what has been called "craft," or the content of the pedagogical labor that is the focus of this one. Criticism—Orr's accusations of "fogginess" notwithstanding—seeks out the intricate and the ineffable, favoring in Graham's poetry those moments where she is "unable to resolve the poem into 'sense'".[28] This work of professional reading, with which Graham's insistently inquisitive poetry resonates, stands in contrapuntal relation to those same inquisitive tendencies when applied to the work carried out in workshop: while the critic takes it upon herself to answer or complicate the questions poetry poses, the workshop leader (and pupil participants) asks why the poem itself doesn't already supply the answers. Graham's impetus toward poetic communication is thus hampered, on the one hand, by her critical knowledge that her poems' "questions" will be "deflected again and again," but necessitated, on the other, by her pedagogical status as a craftsperson.[29]

In D. G. Myers's now-standard history of the creative writing program, the word "craft" is used only few times—and when it is, it is more often used to designate the institutional formation of composition. But by the time Graham began her MFA at Iowa in the mid-1970s, the discipline of creative writing as the teaching and learning of a more-or-less transmissible skill was both well-established and in the process of further separating itself from the practices of criticism that had spawned it as a discipline—a discipline, Myers takes pains to note, that was originally intended as a new way of *understanding* literature, not as a set of techniques to produce it—over half a century prior. This moment is the moment at which Myers's story ends, and it does so on a melancholy note: by separating creative writing into a discipline in which "technique had been divorced from theory," Myers laments, "the original intention behind creative writing had been lost sight of."[30] Craft, in this telling, winds up being a blunt type of toolbox: a set of things that can be systematically applied to writing to improve it, in whatever way "improve" might be defined by the person plying the craft.

By the time Tim Mayers updates this history in 2005, creative writing as craft was a ubiquitous enough concept that he uses it to try and bring the projects of criticism and creative writing back together again in the form of "craft criticism."[31] Mayers, in fact, completely inverts the premise of Myers's work; he goes so far as to say that hermeneutics "should be, at best, a peripheral part of the discipline, important only insofar as it helps students and teachers understand more about *writing*."[32] This stance, I imagine, comes from Mayers's position as a composition scholar and thus as a member of a discipline, like creative writing, that takes pains to distinguish itself from traditional literary study. Focus on craft—as *techne*, as pedagogy, as skills that help writers write more clearly, forcefully, gracefully, or what have you—has been perhaps the single most depended-upon way of making this distinction.

All of this is to say that Graham enters the professional creative writing milieu at a time when criticism was taking off in one direction and creative writing in another. And while Graham is not a critic, she was a long-time student of philosophy, and the form of her work has a tendency to vacillate between reflecting that educational history and the "philosophical diction" it inspires, and the professional requirement that she transmit a set of techniques to a group of listeners. Indeed, Vendler's note about "philosophical diction" is the opening gambit of her chapter on Graham in *The Given and the Made*, and that opening centers mainly on educational biography—Graham's formidable tour, prior to her formidable career, of the Rome Lycée Français, the Sorbonne, NYU, and Columbia. So while Graham's idea of her own persona, as Vendler goes on to argue, might indeed be at once deeply global and fragmented, one context that is a constant is her presence in school. The last poem in *The End of Beauty* reiterates the "what"s of "On Difficulty," signaling the ongoing search for knowledge as wholeness, even in the face of that project's impossibility:

> What I want to know, dear are-you-there,
>   is what it *is*, this life a shadow and a dust-road have,
>   the shape constantly laying herself down over the sparkling dust she cannot own—
> What can they touch of one another, and what is it for[33]

In a sense, this is idealized workshop commentary: inquiry, that is, into the nature of the "life" of imagery, and the purpose of grasping for it (the "sparkling dust she cannot own"). So while Lynn Emanuel writes a workshop commentary that is not one, Graham writes something that is not workshop commentary that could be. Her stance toward knowledge is both supplicatory and pedagogical: in framing the question rhetorically as prayer ("dear are-you-there" God? It's me, Jorie Graham), she creates a sense of smallness and fundamental unknowability. But in the particularities of the dust road and the shadow, the questions can be read as gently leading, instructional in their demonstration of *how* to ask questions. Authority and skill, here, exist in perpetual tension with the conviction that knowledge is never final; this tension fundamentally underlies teaching as a vocation and informs both how we imagine the teacher as authority and what counts as the teachable. Graham may not write when she is "talking out" intensively about writing—when she is performing her role as knowledge-conveyor—but upon sitting back down to compose poems, the residue of that persona is everywhere present.

Take, for example, an excerpt from the long multi-part poem "Pollock and Canvas," an ekphrasis that begins by imagining the painter's process as he "leaned down over / the undefeated soil," deciding "to no longer let the brushtip touch, / at any point, / the still ground": these lines in their descriptive concreteness unravel in the poem's second part into a 30-section series of single lines such as "Oh but we wanted to paint what is not beauty, how can one paint what is not beauty . . . ?"[34] Throughout, Graham constructs an intense admixture of particularity and abstract totality:

> The clouds *like transcripts* over the pond
>   (did not die), the grammar the deepwater which mutters

    long before the sentence (hissing, mid-air)
  begins
    and keeps on keeps on, under the caught fish, lifted, silvery,
  keeping the wound
    alive. The caught with its outline, promising, promising . . .
    It is the window that makes things difficult (but here

  there is no window)[35]

The circulation in these lines between the concrete and the conceptual is very rapid, moving almost without pause between "clouds" (removed immediately from their empirical particularity by the simile comparing them to second-order recording), "grammar," "the sentence," "fish," "the wound," "the caught," "the window," and "things." Graham's phenomenological curiosity serves as both barrier and model: it's a form of thinking that can seem inward-looking in its cogitations, but its urgency suggests a desire to explain something, to make something clearer rather than more obscure. But even here, complication: the window, a transparency, "makes things difficult," but "here there is no window," implying that there is something easier, in the end, about obscurity. This dialectic that recurs throughout *The End of Beauty* is the dialectic that inheres between poetic innovation and the pedagogy of craft.

In this model of thought, we can see some of the things that concerned John Ashbery—anxiety about language's communicability and ability to index the world outside of it, the privacy of thought that poetry must both inhabit and invade—at work in a landscape more thoroughly backgrounded by the role of the poet as educator. These concerns are not, as I will continue to reiterate, restricted to creative writers; Graham's ability to succeed both amongst academic literary critics and in the broader "economy of prestige" is due at least in part to the way in which she aestheticizes the struggle for balance between rigorous intellectual perception and explanatory guidance.[36] As facets of a single goal—the development and dissemination of nuanced takes on cultural phenomena—the combination, and competition, of writing and teaching as forms of academic labor raise persistent questions of what kinds of freedoms they offer, and what prices academic workers might pay in return.

A related set of questions fleshes out this narrative in terms of specific *topoi* and formal devices. One important and almost wholly overlooked point of examination is the role of the secret as a key recurring theme throughout the book, one which topologically emphasizes the "silence" Graham points to as necessary for poetic production, but which is constantly undercut by the functions of language itself. Another—more noticed, because more ostentatious—is the series of blanks and variables scattered throughout the book, a formal innovation that is perhaps the most obvious signal of a more radical style that began with *The End of Beauty*. The following passage from "To the Reader," for instance, draws attention to the activity implied in the title by actually confronting the reader with gaps that she must fill: "and then out of nowhere sun (as if to expose *what* of the hills—/ the white glare of x, the scathing splendor of y, / the wailing interminable _____?)"[37] Below, I'll argue that Graham's "blanks" (which come not only in the form of literal gaps in the text but also in the form of x's, y's, parentheses, questions, and persistent "*what*"s) also trace a struggle with access informed by class feeling. As a teacher in a position of authority, Graham writes the quizzes and questionnaires, but there is a very real sense that she might not have the answer key. Thus the multivocality that is literal in Ashbery becomes enthymematic in Graham, involving the reader pedagogically in various exercises in abstract thinking.

Graham's "philosophical diction," then, is another facet of academic avant-garde tonality which can register a set of institutional concerns without taking them as directly thematic, expanding our sense of how this poetic formation might "appear" both on the page and as lasting cultural influence. In reframing Graham's particular dialectic between autonomy and contingency as one that is fundamentally tied to poetry's professionalized economies of knowledge, we can see the impact of academic labor—sometimes extractive, sometimes unalienated; at times progressive, at times conservative—on poetry that radically tests the boundaries of its own capability. In framing her expertise at once as always precarious, difficult to master, and yet teachable and transmissible, Graham's work speaks to a broader social imaginary of what constitutes our duty, as workers in the humanities, to those that share our professional space—to our fellow scholars and artists, to our students. Her aesthetic, in other words, is also that of a class feeling, one that has a crucial source in the movement between the protection of relative autonomy through the development of advanced discourse modalities, and the simultaneous assertion that those modalities are both pedagogically transferable and socially necessary. The freedom, in other words, comes from speaking a private language. The pleasure comes from giving that language away.

But given away to whom?

In this study's introduction, I mentioned that it is, generally speaking, easier to define "teaching" than "reading"; this applies too to its status as labor. If reading as exchangeable work takes a little squinting to see, teaching is very obviously labor in the traditional sense: students ostensibly pay tuition in order to be taught, and the poverty wages now paid by universities to their legions of precarious professors is for teaching, not research. However convoluted it has become, there is clearly a market of exchange here. In a sense, this clarity explains what I called the "professional mood" about teaching in general: because it is a specific service done for a wage, it is the thing that *feels* the most like work. To be "sick of teaching" is to be sick of selling your labor power.

This general state of affairs applies equally to professors of literary studies and creative writing; the teaching of creative writing, however, heightens considerably the contradictions between pedagogical practice as vocational training and as a type of mystical leadership, the latter of which can obscure the obvious mechanisms of exchange just described. Because of the way in which "craft" has operated, as discussed above, creative writing courses do not tend to enjoy the kind of status that has traditionally accrued to, for example, the graduate seminar in literature. Creative writing degree-seekers are usually required to take literature classes; the reverse is basically never the case. But as I'll detail now, the position of the artist as teacher *also* carries a mysticism in which the very personhood of the teacher is itself a type of pedagogy. Competition for access to the creative writing teacher is sometimes fierce; at the undergraduate level, upper-level workshops frequently require a portfolio-based application process all their own (again, something basically unheard-of on the literature side of things). What is shared with students in this type of classroom is, as in any other classroom, what the teacher knows, but in this case, what the teacher knows is bound up fundamentally with who she is.

In this connection, I'd like to return for a moment to the interview snippet that opens this chapter. When Graham talks about teaching as an "extraordinary price to pay for the freedom to write poems," both her choice of economic metaphor and her categorization of writing as freedom speak volumes about the unlikely ties that now bind labor and aesthetics in the literary academy. The reversal at work here is striking: teaching, which ostensibly pays *Graham*, becomes the "price to pay." Writing poems, which also pays her—in some combination of royalties, reading fees, and whatever part of her salary comes from the "research" arm of the research/teaching/service trifecta—becomes the activity that the "price" of teaching buys. In teaching, the teacher makes herself *accessible* to students; the role of professor is the role, in many cases, of demystifier. In writing, however, "bought" through the access of teaching, the professor (now writer) can fashion a very different relationship to those notions of availability and audience. But these relationships of exchange are not as straightforwardly grudging as they appear. Unlike Nabokov, Graham openly "loved" the chance to teach at Iowa; "a moment came when I knew," she has said, "looking into [my students'] faces, that I was handling things crucial to life."[38] The price of teaching, then, becomes a noble sacrifice; as a labor of love, it becomes a kind of gift.

To frame paid labor as gift is a move that seems untenable from the off, but in the economy of the workshop, such a conceptual impossibility points up yet again the positionality of institutionalized art-making. While both literary and critical writers in the academy take part in the business of skill transferal—that is, the ins and outs of how to write—such transferals take different trajectories, intensifying in the case of creative writing as one moves from an undergraduate to a graduate degree and diffusing in the case of graduate degrees in English, where the skill of analytical writing (emphasized heavily in composition and in introductory surveys) tends to take a backseat to the complications of reading texts to and at the depth required for advanced study. As reading in this latter case (and as I've discussed) is in fact inextricable from writing, writing of course remains central to the work of graduate teaching in the analytical humanities. But the presence of the creative writer as workshop leader in particular retains a persistent aura of the guru, offering up not just expertise but the promise of proximity to artistic talent. It is this presence, as performance of the self, that the writer in the academy makes available in the classroom.

To be available as an exemplar of artistic practice is to offer the self as gift, and to frame it in those terms brings the practice of artistic pedagogy into contact with the theories of the gift developed by thinkers such as Derrida and Lewis Hyde. Lee Konstantinou has offered a thorough analysis of the latter's grappling with the former's insistence that the gift as relation is always already an impossibility; in a global economic system bent on subjecting all transactions to the rules of the market, Derrida's argument goes, the recognition of gift as gift immediately contaminates it with the baggage of exchange.[39] Hyde, on the other hand, argues for the possibility of the artwork as gift even within modes of commodity exchange; according to Konstantinou, he "hopes to show that although the gift's unconditionality is necessarily circumscribed, the gift can nonetheless be distinguished from the commodity."[40] Interestingly, Konstantinou argues that such optimism appeals in particular to writers looking to unburden themselves from the weight of postmodernism's insistence upon reflexivity: Hyde, then, becomes a "palliative" to Derrida's deconstruction. Such a palliative might be a fantasy, but it nevertheless has "real consequences for how artistic and creative work more generally is undertaken."[41] To love the work of teaching, as Graham professes to do, softens the exchange relationship between that work and the work of writing poems; each becomes a foil for the other in her negotiations with artistic giving-away.

For indeed, "the freedom to write poems" registers as itself a kind of gift, even though it is already entered into a reciprocal relationship with the teaching and administrative work of the academic profession. Freedom from what? It cannot be the freedom from work—the university, after all, demands the labors just mentioned, as well as demanding the poetry writing. Graham's formulation, in which the freedom or even unalienation of artistic labor is knowingly, I'd argue, imagined *within* rather than *against* the umbrella of academic work, is inextricable from the narratives of access, comprehensibility, and seriousness that have involved her poetry for years. That the chance to write poetry is both given and taken away by teaching underscores the university as a place that can, in theory, furnish the autonomous silence necessary for poetic production and the scholarly frameworks designed for its reception, but one that would simultaneously cease to function if those knowledge producers, literary and critical, kept the means of their production wholly secret. Graham's availability as teacher and exemplar finds its counterpart in the ways in which her work operates on a critical level; if teaching is a "speaking out" framed as the opposite of the "silence" required to write, the freedom of writing is thus the freedom of an odd kind of privacy.[42] Odd, because of course nothing about the end product is private:

Graham's poetry is (comparatively) very widely read, and very widely written about, particularly for a living poet. What Graham "gives away" to students is very different from what she "gives away" to readers that would interpret her work: in the latter case, the giving manifests as a withholding.

This withholding has appealed to academic literary critics because, yet again, it proffers an invitation to do the work they were trained to do.[43] More importantly here, however, is the way in which Graham's invitation as withholding also manages to play into the double requirement of the poet as pedagogue. The doubleness inheres in the twinned expectation of disclosure and ineffable aura; the poet as academic figure is tasked at once with teaching students the tricks of the trade, as it were, and with embodying the faintly mysterious persona of someone who manages to make a living from their art. In Graham's case, this living is made because, rather than in spite of, her work's experimentalism; the density and ellipticality of her poems' conceptual frameworks reveal that desire to "recomplicate the oversimplified thing" that is also in many cases the desire of the academic humanities.[44] In the end, Graham registers possibilities for the creative writing program that move beyond the demand for rhetorical clarity and easily parsed choices of "craft" that are the natural pedagogical pitfalls of such programs: in the process, her restlessness asks us to imagine a more human humanities.[45]

To read Graham as an intellectual and pedagogical worker, then, is to look more closely at the forms of work that are being done as well as asked for in her poems. I would be remiss here not to acknowledge the other form of labor that drives *The End of Beauty* and which both complements and complicates its cerebral qualities: that of pregnancy and motherhood. Writing while pregnant with her daughter Emily, Graham's self is doubled not only metaphorically—as teacher and writer—but also literally, as she goes through the process of bringing another life into the world. The work of mothering—which is borne by the woman's body and then, as *parenting*, still disproportionately feminized—is overwhelmingly characterized as a type of radical selflessness.[46] It is no coincidence that the work of teaching, also done disproportionately by women, is often seen as a type of mothering, particularly at the primary and secondary levels (*in loco parentis*). This is also now the case at the tertiary level, with the lion's share of humanities teaching performed by the legions of adjunct instructors responsible for the bulk of introductory writing courses at colleges and universities across the country. These instructors are, by some estimates, over 60 percent female.[47]

Teaching and motherhood, while obviously not identical, reconfigure the self as a self "in service to," while the work of writing, while ostensibly (and, if one is a professional writer, actually) for other people, retains a sense of being *for* the self. *The End of Beauty*, written at the beginning of two journeys in which the self moves "out," retains an especially strong sense not only of the pressure that that "speaking out" (to use Graham's words again) puts on the work of writing but also of the odd space in which that journey takes place. This space is simultaneously intensely embodied and restlessly ethereal; a passage from the relevantly named "Self-Portrait as Both Parties" is illustrative:

> through the weeds, the weeds cannot hold her
> who is all rancor, all valves now, all destination,
> dizzy with wanting to sink back in,
> thinning terribly in the holy separateness.
> And though he would hold her up, this light all open hands,
> seeking her edges, seeking to make her palpable again,
> curling around her to find crevices by which to carry her up,
> flaws by which to be himself arrested and made,
> made whole, made sharp and limbed, a shape,
> she cannot, the drowning is too kind,
> the becoming of everything which each pore opens to again,
> the possible which each momentary outline blurs into again[48]

The motion outwards ("all destination") is accompanied by terror and two types of desire: on the one hand, there is the fear of the "holy separateness" and the accompanying need to "sink back in" to the singular body; on the other, there is the desire for precisely "the becoming of everything" and the "possible" which the evacuation of the self opens up. As a woman, the "she" in the poem takes a form (for the passage also has a Biblical undercurrent) that the "he" literally cannot grasp: the work of being a woman as both unknowable but fundamentally for another.

In this out-of-body experience, the poem hovers in a placeless mental space, which is both true of the majority of the poems in *The End of Beauty* as well as a bit unusual for Graham generally speaking: Vendler isn't wrong when she describes Graham's multilingual cosmopolitanism as one of her données. In *Region of Unlikeness*, for instance, she returns to Paris and Rome, and the majority of the poems are clearly and narratively rooted in Europe, as if to give anchor to the raw politicality of subjects such as the assassination of John F. Kennedy and the afterlives of Holocaust victims.[49] In contrast, the airy space of *The End of Beauty*, its immediate predecessor, feels transitional. This "roving consciousness"—marked grammatically in the passage above by the proliferation of small clauses separated by commas, like a series of small but urgent revisions—reflect the simultaneous and interrelated processes of becoming mother and becoming teacher.[50]

That all of this is happening at the University of Iowa is also significant. Located away from the country's major metropolitan areas (a "far-removed hamlet," as Graham has put it), the Writers' Workshop exemplifies in many ways the historical figure of the university as *atopia*—an institution that exists, in the monastic tradition, to take people out of places.[51] Of course, writers still wind up in Iowa City, which is very much a place, and recent bird's-eye level scholarship out of the University of Iowa itself seems to show that the writing of Iowa graduates and faculty locates itself disproportionately in the state, creating a "squatter regionalism" that underlies a surprising amount of twentieth-century fiction and nonfiction.[52] As is typical with such studies, no data was collected for poetry, so it's unclear if such a tendency obtains for students or faculty with degrees in that genre. Graham's work would seem to flout it: as just mentioned, *The End of Beauty* is essentially anti-regional, and when she does pick up definitive locales again in *Regions of Unlikeness*, she searches for the density of Europe. Iowa City's comparative smallness made her feel like she had to "learn how to be a citizen of a *place*"; one "where everyone is your neighbor," including your students. Living in Iowa was a particular kind of outward motion: citizenship, teaching, parenting. *The End of Beauty* was the escape inward, the thinking done while waiting "to get whatever group of kids [she] was responsible for to their next activity."[53]

Learning to "be the teacher [she] became," then, involved creating one kind of community through pedagogical labor—getting "the right group of people in a room," being responsible for them, giving them literal and figurative gifts—while creating another within her poetry that contains much of the same desire for togetherness and unified experience while thematizing the fundamental unknowability of experience itself.[54] The authoritative yet destructive modality of abstract pronunciation, the generalized "rip in the fabric where the action begins, the opening of the narrow passage" (from the very opening of the book) expresses neatly the painful gap in the self through which knowledge can be pushed toward the reader-student or pulled back away.[55] This line—and the book is full of torn veils—is also, more viscerally, an evocation of birth and the labor of navigating that passage, the violence of the "rip" suggesting something given up only reluctantly. But of course, without that violence, or the breaking of silence, nothing really begins, either: there is no "action" to propel the poem toward its reader.

Graham has spent a lot of time thinking about her work's relationship with the figure of the reader, and the way that she describes that encounter is very similar to the way in which she talks about the work that her students produce. On her readers:

> I wanted to create an energy field that would be able to carry sensation over to the reader without the reader having to intervene too early on with what you call "thought." In other words, I wanted the reader to look and feel and see and then, obviously, think—but very late in the particular process of these poems.[56]

On the production of poetry:

> Somewhere between the "I" that takes its authority from an apparent act of confessional "sincerity," and the "I" that takes its authority from seeing through to its own socially constructed nature, there is still the "I" that falls in love, falls out of love, gives birth, loses loved ones, inhales when passing by a fragrant rosebush—the "I" that has no choice but mortality. That "I" (Eliot would say personal yet collective) is emerging from the great philosophical fray of the last decade with a new respect for the mystery of personhood, and a more sophisticated understanding of its simultaneously illusory and essential nature.[57]

On teaching:

> Sometimes you can get yourself into conversation with that mystery, which will take you off course, which will take you in a direction you don't intend to go, which will force you to confront yourself [. . .] I often say to my students little phrases I use, "A poem isn't what you feel. It's how you feel about what you feel."[58]

"Mystery" (or "sensation") and "sophisticated understanding" (or "thought" or "confront[ing] yourself") jostle against one another in these passages and throughout Graham's interviews, with her obvious commitment to the former running up against her admission that the latter is necessary to process it successfully. In the search for some reconciliation between them, Graham's work speaks all at once to the persistence of creative writing's auratic mythologies, the scholar's desire for complexity and intricate nuance, and also to the teacher's sense of the larger purpose and transmissibility of that desire. These things, and the structures of authority that they either put in place or resist, are severely tangled up with one another: in a socially reproductive system, what do you do with the notion that knowledge transference is always already incomplete, that language never fully communicates, and that the origins of art are, according to art's own self-conception, fundamentally mysterious and thus inextricably individual? Is school, is *teaching* and *being taught*, worth anything at all in this context?

We know by this point that I'm going to say "yes" to that question, despite the significant barriers thrown up by the insistence that creative writing "cannot be taught" and, to use a shorthand, the semiotic turn. One way to think about the project of poetry-making, or indeed criticism-making, in an academic age is that while it is almost certainly harmed by the individualist *mythos* of "talent," it is enhanced by certain institutional activities that persist in spite of that *mythos*. Teaching, in its better instantiations, is perhaps the most important of these activities.

In Paulo Freire's landmark treatise on emancipatory educational techniques, the ideal dialogic mode of communication, which in its balance of reflexivity and being-for-another is posited as the only way of realizing a true humanism, depends for its actualization upon the idea of *critical thinking*.[59] In this study's introduction, I addressed the hollowing out of this phrase while suggesting that it is possible to fill it back in; Freire provides one account that remains forceful because of the way in which it ties theory to practice. Action, in Freire's formulation, is unthinkable without thinking—particularly thinking that turns back upon the subject in order to re-place itself in the world.[60] To bring together a treatise on revolutionary pedagogy and the quiet, only subtly political poetry in *The End of Beauty* may seem like an affront to both texts. And it is true that there is almost no way to read Graham's work as somehow advocating for the revolutionary liberation of a global class of the oppressed, no matter her actual politics.[61] But Graham's position on the status of knowledge—particularly the freedom that comes only from exposing and confronting the false consciousness of freedom—demonstrates quite well the difficulties that beset the class of educators tasked with cultivating "critical thinking" at its higher levels.[62] Freire's primary struggle in *Pedagogy of the Oppressed* lies in finding a way to confront the nagging question of cultural class that the book ostensibly takes as its subject: a way, in other words, to posit a relationship between educator and educated that does not reify a hierarchy between them.

Freire attempts to do this by way of a theory of radical dialogic communication: a speaking *with*, rather than a speaking *to*. But even this kind of solidarity cannot completely erase the traces of difference that separate the theorist from those about whom she theorizes.[63] To teach someone how to think puts one in the position of having already known how to do so, and the undoing of that presupposed security is never complete, only grappled with in the process of critical reflection. The restlessness that is the natural product of this grappling, which is linked by its nature to the contradictions inherent in the fundamental poetic enterprise, *contra* Wittgenstein, to "utter the unutterable," produce in poetry such as Graham's not a thematic oppositionality but instead a series of philosophically informed arguments about the transmission of knowledge.[64] The systematicity of institutional production, which is to say the preordained complicity of artistic production with the institutions that house it, is not circumnavigated but strenuously questioned by the play of enclosure and disclosure that mimics in its grammar a dreaming outside the system. Graham's dialogic imagination is both the reason why it often seems that the subject matter of her work is deliberately shrouded in a vital and abstract secrecy, and the means by which that same secrecy opens itself up to demonstrate, counterintuitively, how it can be an effective means to stage a "critique of the given."

The quote above is from "Self-Portrait as the Gesture Between Them [Adam and Eve]," the opening poem of *The End of Beauty*, and it establishes at the outset the abstract grammar that accompanies the poems' thematics of disclosure:

> But a secret grows, a secret wants to be given away.
> For a long time it swells and stains its bearer with beauty.
> It is what we see swelling forth making the shape we know a thing by.
> The thing inside, the critique of the given.[65]

The critique, posited as the growing fruit from the Biblical tree of knowledge, becomes in the process of its metaphorization a remarkably complicated series of conceptual paradigms: the paradisal bliss of ignorance versus the immanent knowledge of infinitely receding truth; the necessity of originality (even as a sin) versus sharing originality with others, thus negating it; the inaccessibility of experiential interiority versus the dialogic process that, in poetry, must in its communication open up that interiority to necessary scrutiny. The particularity of the apple, which is barely mentioned in the course of the poem (presumably to avoid the direct invocation of its symbolic burden, a burden that robs it of its particularity) gives way to conceptual meditation; "beauty" is invoked in its wholeness and the object of epistemology becomes simply "a thing." The naming of the thing as the "critique of the given" while simultaneously placing it in an unspecified interior (inside the body? Inside the mind? Inside the poem?) turns the object in upon the subject, making it inherent to subjectivity itself. Thus does the critique become immanent, an ever-present exteriority that in its nonidentity reinforces the notion that subjectivity is a continual process of cognition, one that cannot hypostatize into an authoritative or total identity.[66]

Graham's insistence on a deracinated grammar allows for readings such as this while circumscribing, due to the relative absence of particularity, a potential symbolism that would reduce the play of objects to a set of easily identifiable concepts. This heightened abstraction, in its insistence on a second, and third, look, and in its concealment of the relationship between the general concept and the particularity of experience that it tries to communicate, conveys an essential *difficulty* that restricts access to its own experience. It is this resistance to which the critic responds, for the economy in which the literary intellectual operates depends upon the dialectic between the graspability of the object and the recognition that this graspability is always a falsehood, that, to put it bluntly, there must always be more to say. Graham's poetry modulates between thought and world in such a way as to reveal both the necessity and limitations of such conceptual intellection: if hers is, as the critics quoted near the outset of this chapter indicate, a poetry of process, that process is one which does not settle upon objects for fear that they will, once held, cease to really exist. The nebulousness of the resulting language is in actuality incredibly particular as regards experience and as regards the nature of the conceptual, but the only way to get to this particularity is through an immanent critique of it, one that mirrors and indeed advocates for the kind of "critical thinking" that is so indispensable to literary critical practice.

Thus it is that Graham's poetry can enact a kind of critical pedagogy without slipping into a didacticism that would simply reinforce the hierarchical relationship between author and reader. Graham's ready admission of the fraught relationship between knowledge and the notion of truth appears in "Self-Portrait as the Gesture Between Them" as the nonidentity of objectivity in cognition that intractably contradicts the creational impulse:

10

So that she turned the thought of him in her narrow mind,
turned him slowly in the shallows, like a thin bird she'd found,
turned him in this place which was her own, as if to plant him but never
    letting go,

keeping the thought of him keen and simple in a kind of winter,
keeping him in this shadowlessness in which he needn't breathe,
him turning to touch her as a thing turns towards its thief,
owned but not seizable, resembling, resembling . . .

11

Meanwhile the heights of things were true. Meanwhile the distance of
the fields was true. Meanwhile the fretting of the light against
    the backs of them

as they walked through the fields naming things, true,[67]

The "truth" of paradise, which recalls in a way Benjamin's yearnings toward a radical identification of subject and object via the discovery of an Adamic language in "On Language as Such and On the Language of Man" ("*Über Sprache überhaupt und über die Sprache des Menschens*"), is figured here not as a totality, nor even something toward which to strive, but rather as a state in which humanity thinks of itself as free but is in reality only free from the aforementioned "critique of the given."[68]

The experience of thought, in which objects are "turned" but never fully set down, is the recognition of the fundamental and necessary ineffability of experience, one that does not capitulate to the easy hypostatization of objects. Even to hold something in the mind, as happens above, is in a sense to steal it, even if one recognizes that it is not "seizable" in its totality but is always "resembling." The false consciousness of received truth is framed in the poem as "freedom" that must be "taken from her" and replaced by the (self-)consciousness that the fruit from the tree of knowledge gives. The reflexivity that enters the poem as this happens mirrors the breaking up of the poem into single-line stanzas, a gesture which pulls the genre apart into its disparate pieces as a way to signal the radical break with identity that hearkens back to the dual character of the poem's title. It is a bittersweet and necessarily incomplete breakage: if we can read the "truth" of paradise as a form of authority, the releasing of that authority is not simply its disavowal but a recognition of the contradictory essence of knowledge and experience. What replaces positivistic knowledge is the sense that one is an "error" and, indeed, "liking that error, a feeling of being capable *because* an error," a sentiment that repeats a few line-stanzas later as "loving that error, loving that filial form, that break from perfection."[69] The embrace of the wrong turns the ever-incomplete process of thinking, which proceeds dialectically between the creative force of naming and the realization that the truth of that naming is always in error, into the most accurate way to represent experience.

Thinking as experience, or experience as thinking, validates the potential of intellectual labor as a liberating practice, but also foregrounds the problem of transmission and access: Graham's poetry, in its refusal to come to rest on a given set of graspable objects, remains elusive, still full of the "secret" even through its wanting "to be given away." As a form of knowledge, a secret is only half negative—it is not the unknown, it is the kept-hidden. As concealment, it is also negotiation, and with negotiation comes a form of power: the holder of a secret has the authority to decide when, how much of, and to whom to give information. The difference between a *secret* and more quotidian information imbalance (of the type typically posited, for instance, between teachers and students) is the nature of the knowledge undisclosed. Secret knowledge, because of the injunction against disclosure, assumes a special kind of importance, and at the same time attaches itself to the bearer of the secret in such a way as to render her vulnerable—for secrets, as anyone who has had to keep one could attest, are less about concealment than about the consequences (positive and negative) of telling.[70] These consequences are always being negotiated in Graham's work, because the secrets are never kept:

> But a secret grows, a secret wants to be given away. ("Self-Portrait as the Gesture Between Them [Adam and Eve]")

> What they want to know—the icons silent in the shut church . . . is how to give themselves *away* ("On Difficulty")
>
> The secret cannot be kept. ("Noli Me Tangere")
>
> the secret nobody knows like a rapture through his limbs, / the secret, *the robot-like succession of joint isolations* . . . This is how it tells itself: ("Breakdancing")
>
> Here is the secret: the end is an animal. / Here is the secret: the end is an animal growing by / accretion, image by image, vote by vote. ("Breakdancing") (all emphases in original)

This is a simple list of the actual occurrences of the word "secret" in the poems; not once is the secret referred to without an immediate reference to disclosure (or indeed the disclosure itself). But what does it mean to disclose the "secret" that "the end is an animal growing by accretion"? The revelation is not immediately personal, nor does it refer in any obvious way to a bit of information that would in fact need to be kept secret. The tension between a desire to divulge information—to *share* in the secrets of the trade, as it were—and a competing desire to retain a strong sense of enigma lies at the heart not only of Graham's work but also of the larger community of academic avant-garde poets. If the progressive and liberating practice of critical thinking is framed largely by the immanently critical idea that reality is to be, at all times, strenuously questioned, it follows that art can never fully disclose itself to the reader, as to do so would be to capitulate to the very notion of reified truth that both art and literary theory seek to trouble.

Full disclosure as complete intelligibility would also threaten the possibility (however problematic) of intellectual autonomy. Again, the concept is not meant to invoke ideas of radical individualism or libertarianism, but instead the recognition that certain forms of institutionality might in fact have autonomy as one of their primary virtues. In juxtaposing self-portraits framed as duality with tensions inherent to much larger structures of thinking and communicating, the idea of self-portraiture moves out from the literal "Self-Portrait" poems and into the rest of *The End of Beauty*, forming a matrix of self-reflexivity (the self as abstracted from itself, as dual) and commentary on the modes of thinking and speaking that form the self and give it purchase in the world.[71] This method of subject formation, because fragmentary and steeped in dialectical movement, is figured not as a totality to be conveyed but as a series of relationships both between competing desires within the subject and between subject and object: self and reader, self and structures of thinking, self and artistic-professional calling. Self-portraiture as *thought process* is crucial not only for understanding the continuities between poets such as Ashbery and Graham, but also for understanding how the intimate relationship between self and thinking affirms these poets as important and serious in the eyes of academics.

In the knowledge economy into which Graham enters in this book, the maintenance of a specialized, "philosophical" mode of communication is necessary not only for legibility among a certain kind of arbiter of cultural capital (the literary critic), but also and more idealistically in order to remain true to the idea that linguistic representationalism, following poststructuralism, is always in error. In this way, the function of the "secret" in Graham reflects the sophistication of Frank Kermode's framing of this very topic in terms of the positionality of the "interpreter" (a group that, I would argue, includes both poets and their critics): "Interpreters usually belong to an institution . . . and as members they enjoy certain privileges and constraints. Perhaps the most important of these are the right to affirm, and the obligation to accept, the superiority of latent over manifest sense."[72] Matei Calinescu takes up this idea in order to posit the literary critical reader as an interpreter whose task is to first find possible puzzles in a text, and then, ideally, to solve them in such a way that the puzzle opens up, rather than closes down, possible sites of meaning.[73]

Both of these critics work in fiction; in poetry such as Graham's, these kinds of propositions carry even stronger resonance. Even though she is a committed educator, Graham subscribes quite clearly to a theory of poetic production that values and relies upon the intuition—"the body," as she calls it, rather than "the conceptual intellect."[74] She refers, in this instance, to the pitfalls (as she sees them) of trying to interpret a poem as one is writing it. The secret, then, is another instance of the ways in which the poem enacts its quality of being for-another *as* a form of withholding; secrecy in a public medium is both protection and promise. What Graham wants to keep for herself is simultaneously that which she offers her reader and, in what follows, her reader as participant and student. In this connection, I turn to those more obviously experimental formal features of Graham's poetry—the blank and the variable—to show how they, too, serve a dual function as a concealment that protects the interests of the intellectual class as vanguard, and as a form of invitation that offers entree into that class, in accordance with its pedagogical aims.

For it is a strange reality, in the academy, that disciplines survive both by cultivating specialized and difficult-to-acquire sets of skills and forms of discourse while at the same time teaching those skills and discursive modes to as many people as possible. *The End of Beauty* evinces a preoccupation with this disciplinary conundrum in the forms of the blank and the variable, devices which maintain a sense of ineffability, distance, and abstract multiplicity in their erasure of a key grammatical term in a given phrase but can be simultaneously read as invitations or pedagogical tools. Thomas J. Otten, who to my knowledge is the only scholar to have written specifically on these blanks in Graham, notes in his first sentence on the subject that they are "like the kind meant to be filled in on a questionnaire or a grammar school quiz."[75] For Otten, the blank serves metonymically as a kind of marker for generic fluctuations that are imposed by historical materialism; consequentially, Graham registers in these blanks the "grammatical analogue of the slippages that constitute our contemporary sense of the material and the interpersonal."[76] His own insight in that first sentence—that the blanks might register also on the level of the *educational*—falls by the wayside. Otten rightly identifies the blank as a visual representation of the distance between writer and reader, and material reality and poetic reality, that is a thematic preoccupation of the book as a whole (pun unintended): a "perceptual tool" by which to paradoxically materialize absence.[77] In focusing so heavily on the fact of the *nothingness* in the blank, however, he does not address its status as something waiting to be filled in, as a complicated calculus that also includes variables such as x and y which serve similar functions in the poems but do not receive the same kind of attention due to the fact that their visual impact does not so neatly accord with a thesis about material particulates.

Otten's is a cogent reading, finely attuned to the philosophical weight that the gap or hole brings to bear on Graham's poetry. I do not, thus, refute it so much as refocus the scope of the devices' possibility. Both the blank and the variable, I argue, tend to crop up in instances where the voice in the poem turns very directly toward its reader; they ask to be filled in as an exercise in craft. Two particularly rich examples, the first from "To the Reader" and the second from "The Veil":

> I swear to you this begins with that girl on a day after sudden rain
> and then out of nowhere sun (as if to expose *what* of the hills—
> the white glare of x, the scathing splendor of y,
> the wailing interminable _____?)[78]

> In the Tabernacle the veil hangs which is (choose one):
> the dress dividing us from _____; the sky; the real,
> through which the x ascends (His feet still showing through on this side)[79]

Like Otten and Vendler—the former of whom identifies "To the Reader" as one of Graham's clearest (which is not to say accessible) examples of *ars poetica* and the latter of whom remarks that it is "neither the most successful nor the most moving of the poems in the book, but it is the most ominous"—I am drawn to "To the Reader" because of the way it communicates a theory of itself while refusing to give up the idea that said communication is always and necessarily incomplete.[80] In particular, I want to show how the imperative to fill in the blank, or to replace the variable with something *invariable*, is a professional and pedagogical imperative (in which the answer key is authoritatively held) that is immanently pressured by another, equal and opposite, to assert that there is no correct answer, that it is instead the process of thinking through no-answer that is the generative force of poetry. "The Veil," a much less-discussed poem, adds in an element of the divine mysticism that so preoccupies Graham, opening up the question of the role that mystical "creativity" has played in the (de)formations of creative writing pedagogy. As permanent gap and as something endlessly being filled, the formal moments of complete ineffability in Graham's poetry metonymically register the risks and rewards of vanguardist artistic production in a setting that requires its transmission to students.

In many ways, the questions of authority and of authorship that are raised by the gaps in the text mirror the tensions surrounding authority that beset the intellectual class more broadly. The title "To the Reader" from the outset forces the address of the poem outward, turning the potentially ruminative "as if to expose *what*" in the passage above into an exhortation. The *"what"* is itself a blank, of sorts: one could fill it with phrases such as *the light* or, if one is feeling sentimental, something like *the beauty*. But no variable after it, neither the x nor the y nor the blank, can grammatically answer the question. In fact, the genitive clauses would seem to imply that x and y can simply be replaced with two more instances of "the hills," turning the "*what*" into an answer already given: either "the white glare" or "the scathing splendor." Both are eminently plausible ways of describing a hillside with sun on it, and so the lines take on the feel of a leading question, or an aesthetic suggestion. Variable as they are, however, the possibility that x and y could be anything at all remains immanently open, refusing the authorial suggestions and remaining steadfast in their commitment to inaccessibility. In this way the hills remain radically nondescript; the inability of the poem even to settle on the relatively quotidian "white glare" or the heavily romantic "scathing splendor" only reinforces the sense that descriptive accuracy is always and already a failed project, though one that poetry always has before it.

It is this attention to the near-impossibility of truth in description—and the constant movement of thought required both to keep this fact in mind and to continue at any rate to strive toward greater and greater accuracy—that drives poetry such as Graham's forward, and lends to it the philosophical trappings that align it closely with the more speculative aims of literary criticism and theory. As pedagogy, it attempts to formalize the difficult process of teaching an art: it proffers aesthetic suggestion and invites participation, but is at all times haunted by the specter of radical individuality—the closed space of autonomy that is signaled by the very openness of aesthetic possibility. What it communicates is *thinking subjectivity*: a process that cannot be hypostatized (for it then cancels itself out) but must somehow be conveyed, or demonstrated. The "wailing interminable _____," then, is a remarkably efficient line in which the exhausting infinitude of thought is thematized as well as grammaticized, the missing noun invoking both the potential universality of its discourse by way of its invitation (you could fill the blank with anything) and the inaccessible nebulousness of that discourse's goal, which must as a process recede infinitely in front of the reader/student.

And indeed, Graham's characterization of herself (the "girl on her knees who is me") is not as an object, nor as a subject, but as a process that shuttles between them: "up over the fence not like an animal / but like a thinking, link by link, and over / into the allotted earth—for Science Fair—into the *everything*."[81] The unattached gerund—not "a thinking *being*" or "a thinking *person*" but just "a thinking"—defines the subject *as* the moment of its becoming, aligning existence not with a state but with perpetual motion. The experience of being, then, is placeless, difficult to pin down, made of endless discourse, and strenuously resistant to hypostatized meaning. If these characteristics also describe with more or less precision the version of intellectual reality experienced by academic humanists, I argue that this is no coincidence. The immanent critique that poetry such as Graham's performs, in which the pedagogical aim of modeling a thinking or writing process is constantly pressured by the self-reflexive destabilization of authoritative and/or authorial practices, aestheticizes the disciplinary anxieties of those literary critical intellectuals whose professional charge is to create and transmit forms of knowledge while remaining self-critically aware (in theory, if not always in practice) of the dangers inherent in reifying hierarchical forms of knowledge transmission. The struggle for intellectual autonomy, in other words, depends upon a measure of cultivated unintelligibility that confirms its place within the field of restricted production; the larger existential or political struggle depends upon the belief that "intellectuality" (to use Guillory's phrase) is a universalizable trait.[82] A subject formation that reflects the tension between enclosure and disclosure, of radical innovation and pedagogical self-reflexivity and explanation, is, then, that which forms the aesthetic imprint of the academic avant-garde.

In "The Veil," the thematic of disclosure and its opposite is even more straightforward: we are asked to choose between options that will serve to complete a sentence that begins "In the Tabernacle the veil hangs which is." The invitation to completion is also more straightforward: the poem turns into a multiple-choice question, giving us the options of "the dress dividing us from _____," "the sky" or "the real" as answers. The choice doubles in on itself as well: "the sky" and "the real" could both fill in the blank in the first option. The teaching of creative writing does not, of course, tend to involve multiple choice questions or fill-in-the-blanks. But there is much more here than the suggestion of quiz fodder; the idea of *word choice* is itself fundamental to the craft of writing, perhaps especially so when one is trying to teach the craft of poetry. There is no implication that any option is correct, or more correct than the other—and in fact, given Graham's preoccupation with the *"everything"* that poetry attempts to encompass, the difference between "the sky" and "the real" is relatively minor. The latter is already an emphatic abstraction; the former is pulled into the realm of the abstract not only by dint of its referential vastness but also by Graham's insistence, as in

"Self-Portrait as the Gesture Between Them," on "the critique of the given," which in this case is framed as "dividing": the separation of the subject from the object, the mourning that results, and the insistence that the result of the mourning (of the error, of "being an error") is not an end but merely an endless beginning. If the paradisal "freedom" of the Garden is an illusion worth shedding, it is so worthy because the very expression of "unfreedom" is itself a mark of liberation—and that expression is precisely thinking.[83]

If we read the blank as also being fillable by the options that follow it, "the sky," as a sign whose referent falls under the umbrella of "the real," becomes less choice (a) of choices (a) and (b), but rather the choice of metonymy over the greater totality of metaphor. Again, neither choice is posited as "correct"; indeed, as with the blanks in "To the Reader," there is a sense in which anything could fill the space, regardless of the possibility that the answer key is sitting right there. The aesthetic gestured toward in the suggestion of the blank, "the sky," and "the real," however—the veil could either *be* the sky or *divide* us from the sky, *be* the real or *separate* us from it—is one that prizes the grand philosophical gesture over the minutiae of private life, and with that priority comes extreme difficulty in the teaching of craft. If poetry is that which makes itself "resistant to its meanings," then the veil in the Tabernacle is also, in addition to the choices given, the resistance to disclosure "through which the x ascends (His feet still showing through on this side.)"[84] The variable in this case can really only be filled in with "savior" or something similar, the mystical force which can be glimpsed but will not suffer full explanation, residing as he does in "the realm of uncreated things." The invocation of a numinous ether during a stanza that reads a bit like a craft exercise throws into relief the problematics of the transmission of the means of cultural production, a problematics that I will attempt to divide, by way of conclusion, into three interrelated parts.

First: to be somewhat discrete-mathematical about it, assume that hermeneutics and poetic production as strenuous processes of thinking are regarded as important and as pedagogically transmissible. I am venturing to suggest that most academic literary critics and teachers of creative writing would so regard them; if the latter is still undecided about the enterprise, the proliferation of academic creative writing nevertheless continues apace, and something must be on the syllabus. If this first assumption is the case, a second assumption tempers and resists it: artworks that can operate as objects for hermeneutic study must operate at a level of difficulty that is complemented (even completed) by that project, and criticism must also *itself* operate at a level of difficulty that preserves it (and by extension the objects of its study) from the systematizing rationality of instrumentalist administrative forces. What follows from these premises as a third factor is an ideological desire and a professional need to *teach* which finds itself in confrontation with a desire for intellectual autonomy that is preserved at least in part by a reliance on opacity.[85] In Graham's poetry, the insistence on the presence of the veil, whose function is to shield, or hide, is consistently disrupted by its being torn: "there is / a rip in the veil / which is the storyline," the storyline being the communicable, that which can "shine / through" the impenetrability of the poem's abstract grammar:

> On the one side the tearing (the story)
> on the other the torn (what it lets shine
> through) and in between the veil being rent (*for all
> eternity*) by this place made of words,
> the gap her calling
> would extinguish,
> the mother of this story[86]

The "place made of words" is also "the gap" which is also the veil in the Tabernacle, a holy site of divine presence that we are literally prevented from seeing by the blocking presence of an object. The duality of Graham's self-portraiture resurfaces here as the confrontation of the emphatic assertion that the abstract word-place can see through to the object (rending the veil) with the incredibly difficult, because heavily de-particularized, grammar of the poetic act itself. What "story" is communicated through the tear in the veil? It remains a secret.

But the secret discloses itself, or strives to do so, in full knowledge that full disclosure would "extinguish" the essential "gap" that allows the duality of the subject (here writer, author, mother thus creator) to assert its resistance to totality. What it discloses thus becomes not precisely itself but rather the *process of its disclosure*, the act of thinking that pulls away from the pursuit of the identity of the real—lets it ascend "into the realm of uncreated things"—in order to preserve the open space of nonidentical possibility that is a major generative force of philosophical inquiry. The irrational space of this possibility, which Adorno recognized as immanently susceptible to the categorizations and neutralizations of the culture industry, cannot retreat into itself as total ineffability, but neither can it disavow itself; it must disclose the process by which it grapples with its own necessities.[87] The subjective focus of poetry such as Graham's brings into view, even in its formal abstraction, the processes of systematic formation and resistance to systematicity that forms the social imaginary of the humanist and poet in the academy. The container that we are in is one of the only containers that allows us to really think through the possibility of being container-free.

4

Citational Coding

In an analysis of Percival Everett's novel *Erasure*, Lavelle Porter draws our attention to a passage that encapsulates the general state of cultural expectation for Black art and literature: Everett's protagonist, an academic and fiction writer nicknamed Monk, is desperately trying to figure out a way to succeed in publishing, whereupon his editor "pushes him to consider writing more commercially viable fiction, which in Monk's case means fiction with immediately legible blackness as its subject matter."[1] In a fit of pique, Monk dons a pseudonym and dashes off a thinly veiled satire of *Native Son* called *Ma Pafology*—but no one gets the joke, and the book goes on to win a major award for its realism and candor, despite the fact that Monk is both on the award committee and argues vociferously against his own work. There are some ways of writing, *Erasure* acidly reminds us, that seem to be the only legible ones for Black authors.

Porter's book, *The Blackademic Life*, exists in part to make other kinds of Black narrative legible, specifically those narratives that take academia as a focal point. Everett's novel is perhaps the most formally adventurous of the books in Porter's study, and I would argue that it is telling that it is also the book that most explicitly takes on the subject of the charismatic dominance of "experiential authenticity" in literature by racialized or minoritized writers. *Erasure* was published in 2001 and rereleased in 2021, pointing up the pressure that the integrationist period in American higher education continues to exert upon Black writing that grapples with it. The introduction of Black and ethnic studies departments into predominantly white institutions in the latter half of the twentieth century (often alongside departments of women's and gender studies) has been a bit of a double-edged sword: on the one hand, it has clearly expanded educational and scholarly opportunity for minoritized intellectuals and writers. On the other, and as Rinaldo Walcott reminds us, integration, as a type of juridical emancipation, cannot be synonymous with Black freedom—nor can it simply replace the spaces created by historically black colleges and universities.[2] For Black academic creative writers (like Everett and his protagonist), navigating the space of the post-'60s university has also involved the diversification—limited, gradual, still seriously flawed—of professionalized creative writing programs, and the integrationist logics (market and otherwise) that beset them.

What I am interested in is how Black avant-garde poets trained in and operating out of universities have signaled their awareness of their positions vis-à-vis these concurrent movements and their legacies. If the previous two chapters of this book have focused on poetic responses to the fact of academic labor, this one and the one after it are concerned chiefly with academically inflected *ways* of working—how form is affected by method. This chapter thus argues that a full account of vanguardist African American poetry requires sustained attention to the ways in which Black poets theorize. The particular complexity and significance of integrationist history as it affects both Black literary studies and creative writing necessitates, I think, its own space in this larger story of poetry and literary studies, and in what follows, I hope to add another node to the already rich and continually growing body of scholarship that has pointed out the difference race makes in conceptualizations of cutting-edge artistic production.[3]

The poets that I look at in this chapter—primarily John Keene and Claudia Rankine, by way of Melvin B. Tolson, Lorenzo Thomas, and others—signal their relationship to the academy by explicitly invoking a scholarly network and deploying discipline-specific terminology in discipline-specific ways. They do this to the near-exclusion of personal or autobiographical narrative, preferring instead a poetic "thinking through" that interrogates and subverts the expectation of personal revelation or experiential mimesis in creative writing by persons of color. The overarching assertion of this chapter is that the move from a poetry of racialized experience to one of racial analysis is one that has been catalyzed by the university's role as a predominant site of poetic production and consumption. The double-edged sword obtains here too: for the university has provided both the disciplinary structures that have standardized a poetics of mimetic experience, as well as the structures that have provided the critical and theoretical tools to challenge and subvert those standards. Indeed, the historical development of Black studies as a field encompasses both, as we'll see. And increasingly so does creative writing, creating a dialectical space of production in which method really can be meaning.

Of course, Black poetry of Black studies, as it were, does not even begin to cover the huge range of experimental styles to be found in the African American avant-garde. Indeed, the kinds of citational practice that I am looking at in this chapter are themselves specific, a single scholarly node in a much larger web of poetic citation that encompasses entire literary, musical, and mythical traditions. But while the intertextual connections that tie African American poetic writing to histories of, for example, jazz and African mythology have been productively explored, the relationship between the university's role in the production and study of Black literature and the aesthetics *of* that literature remains much less trodden territory.[4] This can in part be explained by the fact that the academy has a much longer history of racial exclusion than inclusion, but in recent decades, it is indisputable that the formation and expansion of African American literary studies has had a huge impact on the formation and expansion of African American literature as a category. The contours of this category, in turn, have impacted the discipline of creative writing insofar as they provide the exemplars from which students of creative writing draw their notions of craft and form.

Ronald A. T. Judy's excellent and complex survey of the development of African American theories of literature, particularly his reading of the "tropology of the literal African American experience"[5] in Dexter Fischer and Robert Stepto's *The Reconstruction of Instruction* and Charles T. Davis and Henry Louis Gates Jr.'s edited collection *The Slave's Narrative*, demonstrates clearly that the actualizing potential involved in literary writing is in the case of African American literature inextricably and tightly bound up with "a certain preoccupation with mimetic representation, and with discovering in that representation the basis for a cultural canon."[6] Judy's historiography focuses on the role of the slave narrative in building these frameworks of representation and experience, and he argues that the delineation of the object field for African American literary studies has problematically rested on a specific invocation of Black experience—namely, the "writing into being" that accompanies the emancipatory motions of post-slavery literacy. Keeping the Black avant-garde in view is to keep in view evocations of Black experience and community that do not fit well within these paradigms of representation. The specific "bad fit" that I want to examine is one that is in some senses tightly circular: rather than eschewing the academic structures that privilege a certain kind of subject formation in Black writing, these authors turn the terms and frames of analysis back upon the reader in virtuosic performances of interrogation. By keeping their methods of tradition-breaking within the university's purview, as it were, Keene and Rankine remind us that there are surprisingly scholarly ways to be program poets who, in Mark McGurl's words, "will not get with the program."[7]

McGurl's account of non-white creative writing is, unsurprisingly, to be found in the section of *The Program Era* entitled "Finding Your Voice." Like Gates (indeed, citing Gates), and bearing out Judy's assertions regarding the history and development of African American literary history, McGurl turns to the slave narrative as both the form from which contemporary Black literature springs and as the form that essentially separates Black writing from "modernist" writing:

> First person [narration] may have been suspect in the eyes of Henry James and the New Critics for its seemingly inherent lack of impersonality—or, rather, its difficulty in producing the literary effect of impersonality—but the appeal of *speaking for oneself*, or of *having one's voice heard*, is obvious when it is considered as an act primarily of political self-representation.[8]

He goes on to say that "through the medium of progressive education, this model of self-expressive liberation . . . would be distributed throughout the American educational system,"[9] including to white suburban youth increasingly alienated from their own senses of self. In this sense, the slave narrative is made to bear the entire affective weight of the creative writing "I," and Black identity writing, in which marginality is central, becomes a singularly important (and perhaps the only acceptable) form of Black literary expression in the modern era. The foregrounding of this subgenre in the history of creative writing's obsession with "finding your voice" is allowed, I would argue—and here I bring Judy's historiography to bear on McGurl's—by the delineation of the subject field of African American literature as that of "the Generic and Authenticating Narratives" begun in earnest in the mid-nineteenth century by Fredrick Douglass.[10] The separation between Black forms of literary expression and so-called modernist (Eliotic, white) forms of the same is thus a result not, of course, of some natural or naturalizable difference in how Black and white people "do" literature, but rather the result of a complex series of negotiations regarding the disciplinary status of both the study of minoritized literature and of creative writing.

This is synchronic history. McGurl's characterization of voice-finding over the Cold War period and beyond as a trajectory from slave narrative, to broader forms of Black "self-representation,"[11] to the fictionalization of that self and finally its reinsertion as a liberated voice within larger narratives of both collectivity and autonomy, interlocks closely with Judy's excavation of the rationales behind and consequences of the 1977 Afro-American literature seminar at Yale, a seminar that transformed the discipline of African American studies. Judy's reading of that moment in literary history is worth quoting at some length. Analyzing the ways in which Henry Louis Gates and Robert Stepto approached the reading of Frederick Douglass, he writes:

> "[B]oth their readings are exemplary of three central ideas that issued out of the Yale school of Afro-American literary theory. First, they are demonstrations that Afro-American literature can withstand critical scrutiny. Second, they are demonstrations that close readings of Afro-American texts yield their linguistic (and cultural) wealth. And third, they suggest that through such sustained critical reading it becomes possible to delineate an Afro-American literary history as a field of substantial scholarship, to engage in a project of canon formation. The Yale school begins that delineation of its canon with the slave narratives, maintaining that the slave narrative was the archetype for all subsequent Afro-American literary forms.[12]

The foregrounding of "subjectively grounded narrative writing"[13] in which Blackness's very heterology is itself central was absolutely essential to the establishment and growth of a recognizable and distinct field of African American studies, one that could defend heterology against the assimilating tendencies of centralist authority in the academy. But the focus on and consequent canonization of this lineage of identity writing render other kinds of Black writing illegible to the very disciplines designed to make them legible and transmissible, as Judy goes on to argue about such texts as the African-Arabic Ben Ali slave manuscript. Nathaniel Mackey puts it another way, stressing the centrality of marginality: "African American writing," he notes, "is most likely to be recognized and valorized for . . . the provision of an otherwise absent or underrepresented (thus new) perspective, conveniently known as the Black perspective" that goes hand in hand with "canons of accessibility and disclosure" inimical to difficult or complicated aesthetic choices.[14] Writing oneself into being, in other words, looks less like freedom when the terms of that being have been set for one in advance.

In *Renegade Poetics*, her landmark study of innovative African American poetry, Evie Shockley also highlights the degree to which attempts to theorize Black literature—as form, as discourse formation, as cultural aesthetic—have served (to use Gates's own formulations, perhaps, against him) to *in*scribe new hegemonies even as they attempt to *de*scribe that which has been hitherto denied discursive authority.[15] Analyzing the ways in which Gates and Houston Baker Jr., in contrasting ways, theorized the militant rhetorics of the Black Arts Movement, Shockley concludes that despite their resistance to "racial essentialism," both theorists "still purport to identify that which is *Black* about these textual structures and, therefore, the texts that employ them."[16] Shockley's critical angle is different from Judy's and Mackey's insofar as she is interested in finding moments of aesthetic innovation from within poetry often read as more "traditionally" oriented; nevertheless, the problematics of field delineation remain: she draws our attention to this moment not to undercut the project of delineation itself (she goes on to do her own, in feminist counter-formation to Gates and Baker), but rather to underscore the deep difficulties inherent in the designation of objecthood necessary for disciplinary formation. But these very difficulties are of course also themselves objects around which disciplines and critical (and, as we shall yet again see, creative) practices coalesce. In this case, I want to distinguish between the projects of African American literary studies and the more "interdisciplinary" realm of Black studies writ large, even as the former is obviously a subset of the latter. The distinction is thus somewhat artificial: both are, as the sociologist Fabio Rojas has put it, the result of "a social movement targeting [a] bureaucracy,"[17] or what Hortense Spillers has called "a movement becom[ing] a curricular object."[18] And both have heterogeneous roots in the various factions of the civil rights movement, university administrative structures, student activism, and intellectual coteries. But as a formation that touches a huge number of "preexisting" areas of specialization, from political science to art history, Black studies also has endlessly proliferating object fields, while African American literary studies necessarily has a more delimited one—one that corresponds, roughly, to that of literary studies in general. Academics who work on African American literature are thus a distinct "occupational group," again to use Rojas's phrasing, with terminologies built upon or in counter-formation to those used to discuss other kinds of literature.[19] These discourses serve a twofold function: to define the qualities of the discipline's objects and to establish some kind of protocol for analyzing them. And so while it is doubtless true that the scholarship of Gates, Stepto, and even Baker helped to establish the "writing into being" paradigm that would later become a type of de facto mode or expectation for creative writers of color, it is also indisputable that the *critical language* they used to do that work forms an enormously rich literature in its own right. In a sense, then, the discursive lineage I am tracing runs from Du Bois's ceaseless pursuit of a sociohistorical theory of the "concept of race" through Gates's reworking of the play of signification and Spillers's excavations of an "American grammar" inseparable from the logics of enslavement directly to the poetry itself: the vocabularies of Black theorization used to build an alternative literary mode.[20]

This mode, I want to suggest, relies on a particular lexical code: a way of "sharing, repeating, critiquing, and revising" the core concepts of a discipline.[21] These codes can be used, as Gates notes, to form specific kinds of collective identities, asserting a form of agency over and against other pre-established codes. In response to the fully developed systematicity of creative writing and the pressures that canonicity brings to bear on those systems, this sort of citational practice can now be looked at as part and parcel of the serious play that can radically revise received notions of subjectivity. The foundational figures of African American literary studies, in other words, may have had the slave narrative in mind as they outlined the contours of African American literature and its responsiveness to the semiotic-theoretical paradigms also gaining traction during the period, but they left the door open for those theoretical discourses to be reused and re-presented in contemporary literature as a new form of aesthetic subject formation. That subject formation uses a form of lexical coding (and, by extension, affective coding) previously relegated to academic literary criticism in order to explode the notions of Black literary identity perpetuated by creative writing's insistence on narrative clarity and affective transparency—an insistence undergirded by the history of African American literary canonicity.

So although I am examining but one small slice of Black creative practice, I think it's one that is particularly illustrative of the specific circumstances these writers continue to negotiate within predominantly white institutions. These circumstances involve, among other things, navigating the disciplinary terrain that determines how, with what/whom, and where the space for Blackness can be carved out. As has been well documented, the creation of such terrain, which involves the creation of the conditions for legibility and reception in hostile environments, entails an enormous amount of labor, most of it uncompensated. What I am looking at here is the perhaps less bleak picture painted by the work produced: ways of being in language, and of valuing that being, that will endure in difficult spaces without merely capitulating to those spaces' logics. I will let Hortense Spillers do the talking here, from an interview with Keith D. Leonard: "the first thing was to learn how to say, symbolically, 'Get your finger out of my face. I am going to sit right here and we are gonna talk.' We had to put down some stakes as *serious scholars*."[22]

While there are risks involved, as Judy, Shockley, Mackey and others remind us, in the establishment of such stakes under the conditions to which Spillers refers, those same reminders are themselves attempts to shift (rather than do away with) said stakes by challenging the reification of African American literature's object fields. For Black poets working in proximity to these debates, who are in effect *producing* those object fields, there has been a clear opportunity to move the ground of poetic value from the authenticating personal-individual narrative to one more obviously entangled in conversations about that very source of value. They are, in effect, creating a true poetics of *bricolage*, "reconstellat[ing] cultural items by wrenching them out of their assigned function."[23] These constellations form a new disciplinary nexus for the practice of Black creative writing in the American academy, the writers themselves the "nomadic pedagogues" teaching us how wide the discursive and referential range for that practice can be.

The quoted phrase above comes from Melvin B. Tolson's *Libretto for the Republic of Liberia*, published in 1953. It was followed in 1965 by the first (and only completed) volume of *Harlem Gallery*, a verse epic that, like *Libretto*, has only relatively recently received sustained critical attention. Though markedly different in style, Tolson's work is in many ways the most obvious precursor to that of the authors who are the main focus of this chapter: with its dense allusive networks spanning hundreds of years and multiple continents, and its clear love of the ruminative tone even through its often raucous cast of characters, Tolson's poetry creates a sense of race that feels almost more scrutinized than narrated, though of course it does both. His work also prefigures its own reception, which itself prefigures the tense situationality of African American writers in an increasingly integrated higher ed environment. That is to say: Tolson spent his career in and around historically black colleges and universities, but his graduate degree (and much of the inspiration for his epic) was from Columbia, and the mode of his poetry often provoked a predictable skepticism in which he was seen as "the white critics' flunky."[24] He has since been rescued from this charge multiple times, but its leveling in the first place points up how hard it is to disentangle whiteness from the displays of erudition—put bluntly, the academicity—that Tolson favored.

In this connection, the implications of Tolson's heavily citational practice in poems such as *Libretto for the Republic of Liberia* and *Harlem Gallery* have been teased out perhaps most convincingly by Lorenzo Thomas when he writes:

> As with the references and citations in Pound's *Cantos*, the text and footnotes of *Libretto* constitute Tolson's own indispensable curriculum . . . [i]ndeed, what is offered here can be seen as an Afro-centric alternative to Pound's syllabus—not because the poets chose different sources, but because Tolson offers a quite different perspective for reading them.[25]

The invocation of an "indispensable curriculum" is particularly apt coming from Thomas, a noted poet-scholar in his own right and a member of the Umbra group, a collective that was an important predecessor to the Black Arts Movement and that constituted, along with groups like that which formed around the magazine *Dasein* (founded at Howard University but never formally recognized by it), a type of academy-within-the-academy in which the Black literati flourished.[26] Aldon Nielsen's analysis of Thomas's poetry demonstrates, perhaps unintentionally, the fraught connections between African American innovation in poetry and the institutional ideas of academic disciplinarity within and against which it is constantly working. Thomas, a creative writing instructor from 1973 until his death in 2005, sought throughout his career to "enter into English, and not just to qualify as a native speaker [his first language was Spanish] but to exceed the qualifications of the writing and speaking subjects surrounding him."[27] In very different ways, writers such as Tolson and Thomas worked within the disciplinary standards of their "surroundings" in such a way as to assume for the Black writer and intellectual in the mid-twentieth century a literary heritage that could draw with impunity from the allusiveness of both modernist literature and philosophy *and* the oral and musical stylings of the "genuine communal Afro-American tradition."[28] In Tolson's words: "*Mehr licht* for the Africa-to-Be!"[29]

Tolson's deployment of Goethe's last words in the second stanza of *Libretto for the Republic of Liberia* follows the line "[t]he rope across the abyss," appended to which there is the note "V. Nietzsche, *Thus Spake Zarathustra*." The diasporic reimagining of Nietzsche's eternal return fixes from the very beginning Tolson's idea that an independent republic for freed slaves can and should still have (and make use of) access to a scholarly philosophical tradition and its attendant languages, one that can seamlessly juxtapose the work of Nietzsche with the Ghanaian scholar and education advocate James Kwegyir Aggrey (who appears six notes down). This view of the intellectual landscape citationally re-places authors like Nietzsche and Dryden in a network of thinkers designed to form an alternative curriculum, one written expressly for the purposes of figuring, rather than "expressing," the Black literary subject position. Such figuration resists, as Anthony Reed has put it, the "impossible imperative" of Black expression to be "at once singular and exemplary": individually authentic and yet representative of *all* such expression, a paradoxical totality that all but proscribes the heterogeneous pastiche of Tolson's work.[30] The written citational note in poetry, which retains its slightly paradoxical and Derridean existence as a central supplement, borrows a form of scholarly authority-networking that is both attendant to the kinds of communal thinking emphasized by Thomas as well as to the possibilities for new and expansive horizons for that "Afro-American tradition."

Lorenzo Thomas's poetry does not itself contain footnotes. Instead, its scholarly affiliations are thematic and tonal—and troubled. In this, it is more in a lineage with Tolson's *Harlem Gallery*, though less epic in scale. In "Embarkation for Cythera," whose title evokes both the painting by the eighteenth-century French painter Jean-Antoine Watteau and Baudelaire's poem about it, Thomas writes:

> The idea of a written language
> when before
> the words in our

> mouths were enough.
> Not that it takes anything away
> from the people we are,
> "Education"[31]

Nielsen uses this passage to note how, in a way that echoes the pre-deconstructive moment, the supplement of the written mark comes to replace the originary-seeming nature of the spoken word.[32] I would point out the grammatical continuities between "written language," "it," and "Education," which establish an equivalency between the first and last terms, asserting that poetry that can be faithful to a written tradition of scholarly literacy and to the oral stylings of folkways and music is not an either/or proposition. The qualification comes a few lines later, as he writes: "[a]ll the fine mommas walking inside . . . / Can hardly read / this paper without stumbling over 'embarkation' / What someone has done to us, that / my words become unintelligible."[33] The difficulties of Thomas's position here are clear: he finds himself confronting the systemic factors that have made him "unintelligible" to members of his own community in the very language that he acknowledges as being beyond them. This frustration is palpable throughout his work; as he puts it in "Better Physics," "there is something I don't like about theories of moving things . . . something I also dislike about figures / Of speech that tempt you to misunderstand."[34] The reflexive antagonism between Thomas's desire for legibility within his community and these other literacies in which he also participates can help, in part, explain his sensitive and generous reading of Tolson's work even as Tolson failed to gain the kind of traction that one might have expected in the heady early years of the Black Arts Movement.

Indeed, by 1966, David Llorens could already remark in a review of Fisk University's First Black Writers' Conference that Tolson, who was a major participant *at that very conference*, was "a man whose works were unjustly buried."[35] This sense of antecedence makes generational sense—Tolson was 46 years older than Thomas, and 1966 would be the last year of his life—but it is I think important to note that *Harlem Gallery* was not yet published when "Embarkation for Cythera" was written. This overlap underscores both the deep heterogeneity of the moment in general—as A. B. Spellman has put it, an "array of art that ranged from abstraction to social realism, revolutionary screed to diasporan idealism to historical reflection . . . with all of the stops in between"—but also in particular just how important the cultural moment of the mid-1960s was and is for our understandings of the links between the academy and the avant-garde.[36]

On this point, and on Tolson specifically, Michael Bérubé has put it succinctly:

> The academy . . . gets pictured, and pictures itself, as both the destruction and the fruition of the modernist revolution: as conservative antagonist of the margin and as institutional guarantor of its existence and survival. And in Melvin Tolson's magnum opus we find this cultural [contradiction] at its most acute.[37]

This tension plays itself out on various levels, heightening its complexity: we can tease out versions of it in the links between literary criticism and creative writing, and within literary studies itself as it struggles to delineate its own contours. What connects Tolson to later writers like Claudia Rankine and John Keene is how he poeticizes a certain kind of scholastic disciplinary formalism, without (despite some readings to the contrary) allowing it to become white-aspirational. But here, too, the poetics of immanent critique are at work. Tolson uses a bewildering array of literary citations in his greatest poems not only to rewrite the terms of Black experience to include a broader range of reference than its containing disciplines had heretofore imagined, but also and relatedly to assert his position that the academy and its languages could, with sufficient effort, become the kind of cultural "guarantor" that could assure the continued existence and dissemination of Black intellectual culture.[38]

This rewriting and assertion is precisely what puts Tolson's work in such an odd critical position: Black Arts–era scholars like Thomas claim him for staunch Afrocentricity, and play down his relations to the white literary establishment, to try and rescue him from his contemporaneous white critics that praised him for his "transcendence" of race and mastery of the modernist style. Tolson, as Thomas indicates, was certainly not an anomalous figure in the history of "Afromodernism," but Thomas also has nothing to say in *Extraordinary Measures* about *Harlem Gallery*, possibly because Tolson's Afrocentricity in *Libretto for the Republic of Liberia* is (for several reasons) a bit more even and significantly less self-reflexive. As a poem about the place of art in Black society—in particular, the tensions between "high" and "low" culture that play themselves out in this art—the first-person, "high" culture (and PhD-holding ex–art professor) Curator in *Harlem Gallery* personifies the tensions that Bérubé points out above. He feels distinctly uncomfortable both in the presence of the snobbish Regents of the Harlem Gallery, Black aspirants to the upper middle class, but also in the Zulu Club, stomping grounds of *"vox populi"* poet Hideho Heights. "The Zulu Club Wits," Tolson writes, "(dusky vestiges of the University Wits) / screech like a fanfare of hunting horns / when Hideho flourishes his hip-pocket bottle."[39] The Gallery is aiming for a very difficult middle ground: one that can "chronicle," as the last lines of the poem go, "a people's New World odyssey / from chattel to Esquire!"[40]

That the odyssey ends at Esquire—either the juridical qualification, or, less probably, the magazine—might be enough for a critic to complain that Tolson's no better than Guy Delaporte III, the Regents' figurehead voice. But the entire point of the Harlem Gallery (and *Harlem Gallery*) is to reframe the terms of Black literary subjectivity such that the question of assimilation or resistance to hegemonic discourse becomes moot, giving way instead to the shifting "textuality" of race as a concept.[41] And as Bérubé has already discussed at length, Tolson's heavily reflexive performance relies just as much on discussions of the institutional possibility of an avant-garde as it does on the question of race.[42] Tolson's academy, and his modernism, allowed him to be deeply supportive of the definitional projects of the Black Arts Movement, but his very academicity—his use of its formal registers and its rhetorics of searching, his appeals to a type of literary tradition more critical than expressive—means that his work has been relatively slow to gain purchase in African American literary studies, and has been virtually absent from creative writing programs. It is some products of these latter programs to which I now turn; in them, it is evident that even if "unjustly buried," the strength of Tolson's radical textual reworking has found a way forward.

"In the mark event, you enter your signature." So begins *Seismosis*, John Keene's first book of poetry, published as a collaboration with the African American abstract artist Christopher Stackhouse. The quoted line is the first poem, entitled "Process," in its entirety. For a reader familiar with capital-T Theory, the sentence should sound weirdly familiar. While it's not a quote pulled directly from another source, it uses three major keywords, two titular, that appear in Jacques Derrida's well-known essay "Signature Event Context." The "mark event," in *Seismosis*'s case, shuttles between being both the act of writing or drawing (the event in which a mark is made) and an identifying moment (the event in which one is marked). In both cases, a "signature" is entered: itself a paradoxical form of mark that is at once absolutely original and, like all other forms of communication, infinitely iterable.[43] The entering of the signature is the "Process" that defines the event, making the "mark event" itself—as identifying or as writing process—also at once highly individual and beholden to the iterability of language, the latter of which asserts itself in the break of its formation as impersonal and endlessly moveable.

Seismosis is a book of poetry that uses these and many other keywords drawn from the broad canon of literary theory to form an authorial subjectivity that appeals directly to the formal trappings of academic mastery. In particular, Keene, marked and marking, lays claim to a disciplinary formalism that uses some of the same tools that allowed African American literature to stake out its territory. What results is a literary subjectivity illegible to the "find your voice" mandate of creative writing, one foisted particularly on people of color. Instead, we find an avant-garde Black poetry of analytical and philosophical scholarship that finds a very different kind of individual-communal voice in the pastiche of academic keywording. This is not to say that Keene's use of academic terminology is somehow meant to suppress, surpass, or obviate the kinds of writing more closely aligned with the literary history that programs of African American literary studies have spent so long defining. Indeed, writing such as Keene's would not be possible without the whole history of that struggle, on the parts of both scholars and writers of literature—a struggle that continues and in which Keene himself, as a professor of creative writing, African American studies, and African studies, is deeply involved. It is instead to point out the continuing complexities of the university's position regarding discourses of centrality and marginality, and to try and articulate a theory of Black writing that can foreground these complexities not simply as appeals to Euro-descended authority but as expressions of expanded intellectual agency.

One of Keene's admitted poetic influences was Norman Pritchard, and I'm going to detour into his work briefly because it creates another useful layer, on top of those of Tolson and Thomas, in the geology of the poetic methods described here.[44] Pritchard's work suffered from an illegibility that will sound extremely familiar: Langston Hughes couldn't find any use for it in 1966 while revising the *New Negro Poets* anthology, a book that had already come under a bit of fire for containing poets who "write too much like white folks."[45] Pritchard's influence on Keene is extremely clear, even when their typographical methods do not match up (which they often, in fact, do). A representative example: first Pritchard, "Autumnal" from *Matrix*, in its entirety:

> august falling
> leaves
> grounded thoughts
> a montage over-exposed
> a collage
> of
> bucolic silences[46]

And second, two lines from Keene's "Analysis I":

> the urban skyline by dawn. Shapes: an umbrella arrowing along a hip, the tracery
> {inchoate} {gaze} {reduction} {series} {shear} {concept} {journey} {by} {experimental} {signals}[47]

Keene's second line is a literal montage/collage of keywords that undergird the quiet observation of the line before it, much in the same way that Pritchard undergirds his own observation about leaves with the notion that for the poet, the leaves are in the first place "grounded thoughts." Here, in Pritchard, is a poetic of abstract thinking that is both contemporaneous with and similar to Ashbery's, with none of the laudatory legacy. (Pritchard's fate, much like Tolson's and I suspect for some of the same reasons, was to be published by mainstream presses like Doubleday and then promptly to fall into obscurity.) In Pritchard, much as in Keene, the overt subject of Blackness does not take center stage. What critics like Thomas and Nielsen have found instead is a "tampered English" that resonates with a larger lexical framework of African American speech, a "signifying glossolalia of Black language as intervention in the world" that demands that we expand our very conceptions of the term "Black language" beyond an authenticating personal narrativity.[48]

The parallels between Pritchard's form of tampering and Keene's, in the latter of which single keywords are listed almost like flashcards, stem from this resistance to mimesis. Where they differ, importantly, is in the vocabularies that register that resistance. Pritchard takes chunks of text and stretches them out ("the re is an own of m any col ours") or frantically repeats them: in "Gyre's Galax," the phrase "above beneath" with only slight modification (the addition of "in" or "lit") is repeated no fewer than 29 times in a row, taking up an entire page.[49] Keene performs a similar, if less extreme, kind of stretching and repeating, but with a lexicon that is geared toward a language of citation and theorization (toward which the title of the poem above points).

One reason for this difference is that the book is essentially an analytical project: the poems in *Seismosis* engage, at varying levels of obliqueness, with Christopher Stackhouse's drawings, themselves extremely abstract. The keywords toward which Keene gravitates—*subjectivity, sign/signify, margin, positionality, mark*—form a poetic "aboutness" that runs tangentially to the dominant stylistic expectations for African American literature, finding affiliation instead with the language used to analyze said literature and culture. There is thus a way in which this poetry both is and is not "about" Blackness, that insists on inhabiting a space in which the narration of subjectivity depends upon a thinking through of the concept of subjectivity itself, rather than a depiction of anything that could be called experientially mimetic.

And yet it *is* mimetic, in much the same way that Ashbery or Graham's poetry could be said to be mimetic—in its analytic explorations, it reflects quite clearly the process of *thinking* subjectivity. Keene's collaborator has similar investments even outside of *Seismosis*: in addition to being a visual artist, Stackhouse is also a poet with an MFA in writing and interdisciplinary studies from Bard's graduate division. He has served as an editor at both *Fence* and *BOMB* magazines, known for their publications of avant-garde art and writing, and he has done visiting stints as a critic and artist at the Maryland Institute College of Art, Naropa University, Bethel University, and Ohio State University. Stackhouse's 2012 poetry collection, *Plural*, contains poems entitled "Mark" and "After Alain Badiou." In *Seismosis*, only his visual art appears. Keene's version of ekphrasis is, as he puts it, "a gesture *against* ekphrasis, in spite of the work itself. So, it's ekphrasis that is trying to disentangle itself from ekphrasis. Which is sort of crudely Derridean."[50] What emerges is a mixture of analysis and meditation that renders Stackhouse's scribbly, nearly anxiety-producing drawings (reminiscent in many cases of Cy Twombly's work) as departure points for and accompaniments to Keene's processes of disentanglement and working-through.[51] In the discourse surrounding abstract art, Keene finds issues of marginality and access that are similar to the ones that plague literary work that falls outside the boundaries erected for it by disciplinary history. In response, he forms a kind of shadow canon in which the abstract language of critical analysis is not only appropriate in its application *to* Black literature, as we have seen, but is appropriate and generative *in* the literature itself.

This alternative conception of poetic method imagines a sustained engagement with the specialized vocabulary of semiotics, positing a reality in which what could be called hegemonic textual frameworks can be used to radical aesthetic ends. This radicality is redoubled in the case of African American poetry because of the way in which academic language has been positioned as somehow inherently or fundamentally opposed not only to Black but also to poetic language, rendering it always already inappropriate to talk about it as either one, let alone both. But this is precisely what Keene's work asks us to do, in the process arguing that analytic abstraction can possess just as much force as narrative pathos in the quest for the expression of Black agency over and against the forces of white supremacy. Returning, for elaboration, to "Process": "In the mark event, you enter your signature." The opening of the book is in its second-person address like the opening of a guest book, the event of which occasions the second event, and the second mark: that of signature, that which assures the presence of the source of an utterance even through its absence. What is Keene's signature? It is, if we are to use Derrida's formulation, both the singular mark attached to his presence in non-presence, and the infinitely iterable mark of writing that undoes the very concept of singularity by dint of its readability.[52] All entries of signature, in other words, fail to represent a singular presence. The Derridian definition of signature, then, is precisely a "mark event" which in fact *refuses* signature even as the event itself creates it. "Process" only records the process by which the signature is entered. For its refusal, I'll turn to a poem entitled "Self."

"Self" is the only poem in *Seismosis* that explicitly mentions race. It begins with the line, in text slightly larger than that in the rest of the collection, "Self, black self, is there another label?*"[53] The asterisk that follows the line precedes all the lines that follow it, making each subsequent line an annotation to the first inquiry—for example "*In the mark, how does one identify authenticity or its inverse?" The last annotation, which is linked to the first poem by a keyword that does not appear in the intervening text, reads "*In the end, refuse signature." It would be easy to read this line as falling into a kind of post-racial utopianism, carrying with it the idea that all one needs to do to find "another label" for a "Black self" is simply to refuse the "mark event" of skin color. And it's true, to state it another way, that "Self" alone in *Seismosis* firmly identifies the speaking voice as attached to a body of color. But if the signature is the mark of individuality destroyed in its emergence by the fact of iterability, it absolutely makes sense for a poetry such as Keene's to refuse it: for it is precisely the idea of the (related, because narrativized) iterability of a Black self that a work such as *Seismosis* puts under erasure.

It does so by appealing to a kind of language—itself susceptible to the Derridean charge of radical reproducibility—that is not normally associated with the "signature" of the "Black self," but that is instead associated with the *critical analysis* of that self. There is nothing less (or more) "real" about this language, nor is there anything less (or more) realistic, but there is no appeal to rea*lism*. The first two notations to the first line of "Self" are illustrative:

> *Raised to itself as a global agent, figure and ground impel representation.
> *Does selving assign or resignify?[54]

These lines, combined with the seventh ("*Subjectivity: or is there another label?") form a neat packet of identity studies keywords: *agent* (and its relation, "agency"), *representation, selving, (re)signify, subjectivity*. There are more in other lines: "identity," "Other," "positionality." Words such as these often function in academic discourse as assemblages of syllabic building blocks, around which whole vocabularies of analysis are built. Take, for example, a passage that appears on the second page of Fred Moten's *In the Break*, on radical Black performance and performativity. Bringing together Saidiya Hartman and Judith Butler's work on alterity, he writes:

> [a] critique of the subject animates Hartman's work. It bears the trace, therefore, of a movement . . . wherein the call to subjectivity is understood also as a call to subjection and subjugation and appeals for redress or protection . . . are always already embedded in the structure they would escape.[55]

The repetition of the prefix "sub-" forms a rhythmic alliteration, connecting the keywords "subject," "subjectivity," "subjection," and "subjugation," and stretching them over as well to "structure," forming a poetic rhythm of vocabulary that is not unlike the sibilant music of "does selving assign or resignify?" This is not to say (unfortunately) that all criticism is somehow also poetic. It is, however, to point out that there is nothing less "authentic" about a poetry of analytical keywords than one of mimetic or experiential narrativity.

If Keene shares Norman Pritchard's predilection toward "tampering" with the language expected of the Black poet in the age of the slave narrative's canonical presence, but does so by using the language of deconstruction and identity studies, it might come as no surprise that he would find intellectual resonance in the work of Gayatri Spivak. After attending a talk of hers at NYU in September of 2013, Keene writes:

> One aspect of her talk that I found most compelling was her discussion of her efforts toward what she called "supplementing vanguardism," which is to say, helping to create a *subaltern intellectual*, in terms that Antonio Gramsci articulated a century ago. As she noted, she has aimed for "intellectual labor conversations," viewing her work in part as "using intellectual labor to produce intellectual labor in students," moreso than merely imparting information. This, one might say, is part of the new epistemology she was trying to fashion. She went on to talk about this work as "epistemological performance," and, against the obsession with STEM, talked about the necessity for a "training of the imagination," an "aesthetic imagination," which she correlated with "the humanities at work."[56]

Even from this concise description it is clear that Spivak's remarks are part and parcel—or perhaps more accurately, a summation—of the work that forms the bulk of *Outside in the Teaching Machine*, a book whose stated purpose is to stake out, in both broad and dense theoretical terms, the "responsibility of the academic/intellectual/artistic hybrid."[57] The responsibility alluded to cuts both ways: both of the thinker who occupies hegemonic corporeal or discursive space, and for (and to) those that occupy a subaltern or marginal place in the institutional spheres of intellectuality.

Spivak's most important theoretical touchstone is almost certainly Derrida, and while it is coincidental, I think it significant that one of the more prominent Derridean texts in *Outside in the Teaching Machine* is *Limited, Inc*, in which a reprint of "Signature Event Context" appears before the title essay. Indeed, it is featured as a way into the recuperation (or productive perversion, as Spivak would surely admit) of Derrida for a radical politics of language, which in Spivak's view *is* action. From "Limits and Openings of Marx in Derrida":

> I should first like to indicate the most important "political" lesson that I have learned, the habit that I have acquired, from my own (mis)-interpretation of Derrida: the awareness that *theory is a practice* . . . [e]ven the provisional establishment of such a binary opposition is the condition and/or effect of certain norms by way of strategic exclusions. This special care not to exclude the other term of a polarity or the margins of a center has carried us also to a questioning of the normative character of institutions and of the disciplines in and by which we live. Derrida has repeatedly warned us . . . that we cannot allow our practice, even of deconstructive critique, to become a continuation of business as usual after the appropriate apologies. It is thus with a strong feeling of the political potential of Derrida's work that I shall make certain suggestions today.[58]

Recognizing that Derrida is not specifically attacking the "overdetermined management of language" that is her particular concern, Spivak nevertheless is very clear about the ability of *deconstruction*'s language(s), properly applied, not only to be appropriate to but indeed to amplify the voice of the marginalized.[59] The idea of normative language, in which binaries like theory/practice are taken as a given, breaks down under a deconstructive gaze. That said (and this is one of poststructuralism's more frustrating tenets, one that Spivak nevertheless deftly handles), the breaking-down of language by deconstructive language does not then put deconstructive language into the place of a structure. All it can do—but it is a significant "all"—is to add *"another* . . . fictional structure—what elsewhere I call 'supplement of the code,'" with which supplementary recognition "everything is possible against the language police."[60] Thus the elaborate dance of keywords continues: "supplementing vanguardism," a key phrase for Keene in Spivak's lecture on intellectualism and pedagogy, can also be thought of as the Derridean *supplément de code*, where the "code" in question is the rationalist structure of language which reinforces extant relations of power. To supplement vanguardism *with* code, then, is to add these semiotic challenges to extant narratives of vanguardist action.

To transpose this discussion of social, political, and intellectual labor onto the aesthetics of poetic form and language, which is to say onto poetic work, is to look at the codes that a supplementary vanguardism, as it were, might stand to destabilize. In Keene's case, he puts on an "epistemological performance" designed to showcase precisely the kind of intellectual labor that takes in and adds itself onto, as expansion and rupture, the extant semiological frameworks of the discourse mode(s) into which he is entering. These modes include African American poetry writ large, African American experimental poetry, and experimental poetry writ large. The middle mode is formed, roughly, by the Venn diagram–like overlap of the first and third, though it would be wrong to say that that overlap is simple, or that it is even widely recognized *as* an overlapping category. What Keene's work moves toward is an analytical excavation of that category, in abstract terms:

> J: aura, or the lyrical-contemplative tendency
> S: beyond its window, its shadow I am recoding[61]

In "Aura," of which these are the opening two lines, the poetic voice is presented dialogically, as a semi-exchange between S and J (these letters could stand for "Stackhouse" and "John" respectively, though it's unclear why the artist would be referred to by his surname and Keene by his first). In the grammatical formulation of the first line, "aura" would seem to be defined by the phrase "the lyrical-contemplative tendency." Again, as academics, it is difficult to read the word "aura" and not immediately be transported into theory, this time that of Walter Benjamin and his ambivalent stance toward the "destruction" of art's aura by the processes of mechanical reproduction. And it is this term, which is also "the lyrical-contemplative tendency," that Keene is explicitly "recoding" in the opening lines of this poem. To recode aura is, to transpose a definition from Benjamin back onto the poem, to recode "authenticity" and "the ritual function" that adheres to received notions both of art's uniqueness and of its social purpose.[62] To recode, importantly, is not to destroy but instead to repurpose, or (with apologies to actual programmers) to reprogram for use in another operating system. Keene recodes the "contemplative tendency"—which has resonances both with creative and with intellectual labor-practices, e.g. Wordsworth's craft advice that poetry should only be written after its potential author had "thought long and deeply" about his powerful overflow of feelings.[63] Even more aphoristically, one might think of the term "the life of the mind," here in an application that blurs the boundaries between "poetic" and "academic" contemplation, and further, that claims new territories of "authenticity" for the Black poet working on the margins.

In his work, then, Keene codes and recodes the "subaltern intellectual" whose practice roots itself firmly at the intersection of margin and center. The dialogic form of "Aura," in which the lines do not so much answer one

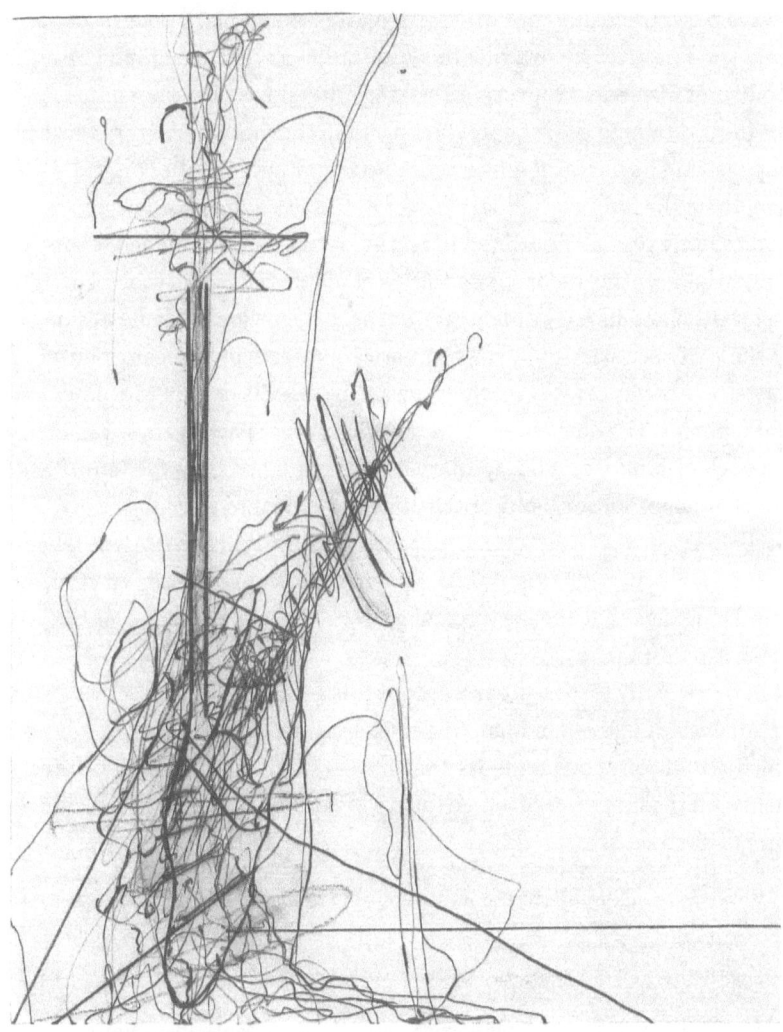

Christopher Stackhouse, *Untitled*, from John Keene and Christopher Stackhouse's *Seismosis* (1913 Press, 2006). The piece, which appears on page 57, faces the poem "Analysis II." Reprinted courtesy of the artist.

another as form an accumulation—much like Ashbery's "Fantasia"—moves between these poles, as in the lines "S: transaction—what emerges from the unseen streaming into / J: (out of) margins / S: leaking contact (origins)."[64] The first two lines tip toward and then away from marginality, recognizing that the margin of a center is often the center of a margin. "Into" is thus always parenthetically "out of," particularly for the Black poet in the academy. The line after it confirms this motion-in-place while emphasizing the product of dialectical rupture: a "leaking" that flows out of a "contact" with "origins," retaining that contact but, again in the motion of the parenthesis, emphasizing its outward movement. We might imagine the "origin," in this case, to be the long disciplinary history of African American literature and studies, only partially outlined here: the narrative that, indeed, takes "origins" to be a central and irrepressible facet of its existence, a tool for affective exploration and literary emancipation, be it the origin of slavery as posited by the early scholars of African American studies or the continental and diasporic African origins reached toward by the Black Arts Movement and Black studies. The narratives of "authenticity" that have been woven around just such originary and disciplinary histories are precisely the "aura" which Keene aims to "recode": out of the affective appeal to the subject matter of Blackness (while retaining some measure of "contact"), and into the "shadow geometries, synthetic origins" (the poem's last line) of an abstracted, analytical language that speaks forcefully to the challenges that beset the "subaltern intellectual."

A particularly forthright example of this aesthetic recoding can be found in "Analysis II." The poem is written in long couplets, the second lines of which are disjointed fragments that have a distinctly hard-science feel to them, and the first lines of which form a breathless treatise on the historical place of abstract art:

> So we were talking about the idea and utility of distance, you know, and we got onto
> the theory that the crust and upper mantle are broken between successive
>
> how just before you perceive something as an identifiable object, indexed by the reality
> felt as a rolling or rocking motion, more or less fluid, but constantly moving
>
> in which you regularly live and function, your rods and cones capture it as something
> retrograde, surface motion similar to the eyes at an approaching storm[65]

Almost all of the couplets work grammatically as units ("onto" goes into "the theory that," and "the reality" in the second stanza makes sense as a grammatical antecedent for "felt"), but break with each other as the reader moves down the page. What ties the poem together are those first lines of each couplet which, strung together, constitute a sort of run-on essay. Made (however heretically) into prose, these lines form a paragraph from which the following is excerpted:

> Lyotard of course describes this in a slightly different but salient way, and it's this, I think, that abstract art really embodies, points to, approaches, not exactly the kind of ideal shape or form that Plato is talking about so much as another, anticipatory and shifting version the Dogon have described, though Kant's version is in there too [. . .][66]

The "this" in question is pre-rational perception, the formless shapes and colors that we process in the instant before they congeal into "an identifiable object." Ultimately and collectively, the lines form a justification of sorts, one that explores the paradox of abstract art (and, by extension, abstract thought): on the one hand, "we conceive // . . . of abstract art as reductive," while on the other, we find it difficult to understand, difficult to find where the pleasure lies in observing it. What we have trouble doing, according to Keene, is "experiencing a more immediate pleasure beyond or outside instant mimetic // . . . recognition," a thought which explicitly draws upon Lyotard drawing upon Kant drawing upon Plato, but also and crucially adds in the perceptual philosophy of the Dogon peoples of Mali, rupturing and then recoding the history of thought on the sublime, the abstract, and the "postmodern."[67] The history of non- or anti-mimetic expression is reformulated as a total history, one that begins in "our earliest images, the kinds we find in the caves // . . . near Lusaka" and "through the Americas, Africa, and Asia."[68] The language and art of abstraction, in other words, is framed as essentially part and parcel of the global aesthetic experience, one that has been subsumed under the need for mimetic narration as liberatory practice. The "idea and utility of distance" returns in this reframing as there for the taking all along in the poetic formulation of Black subjectivity.

Abstraction and analysis are linked in Keene's poetic practice by way of his experimental ("crudely Derridean") ekphrasis, one that uses a critical distance not usually associated with the "poetic"—much less associated with racialized poetics—to explore the limits of its own capacities.[69] (Claudia Rankine will explore some of the same limits using a different kind of distance, as I will show below.) In the language and practice of citational coding, Keene finds a way to assert a radical poetics of Black subjectivity in which that subjectivity lays irrepressible claim to a mode of discourse typically considered to be outside the boundaries of its literary expression. Testing the limits of ekphrasis, and indeed of poetic expression more broadly, then, has less to do with what it can and cannot do than with who it has and has not typically contained. Keene's academic sensibilities, deeply ingrained by a life spent in and around universities and drawing from the para-academic structures that informed Black intellectual production in the sixties, seventies, and eighties, frame literary analytical vocabulary and grammars ("describe the means by which each concept aims to affect representation," from "Azimuth") as a radical means of expression capable of creating just as legitimate a form of Black poetic language as those languages more fully in line with canonical histories.[70]

But the break, as with all avant-garde sensibilities, is never full. In other, and in Keene's, words: "the design event begins in subjectivity."[71] In "Metaphysics"—the title itself placing the poem within a long tradition of philosophical thought—Keene explores Stackhouse's work in the context of other Black artists whose work lies along a spectrum of abstraction. The lines, isolated, are as follows:

> As in Driskell, the small metaphorical forms, ecstatic without boundary.
> As in Gilliam, outlined forms of landscape or escape which depart from calligraphic strategy.
> As in White, where an artist elects and then exaggerates the influences of a metaphysics, signifying message or passage as pure gesture or space.[72]

The artists referred to are David Driskell (who received his MFA from Catholic University), Sam Gilliam (MFA Louisville), and Charles W. White (student at the Art Institute of Chicago and an instructor at Otis College of Art and Design until his death in 1979). The first two are, broadly, abstractionists (Driskell was also a noted art historian), while White was a renowned socialist realist. Together with Stackhouse, they form a small canon of Black artistic production with which Keene's language thinks: there is no attempt to interact with a specific work by any of the artists (save perhaps the Stackhouse drawing that faces the poem in the book); instead, Keene muses broadly and abstractly on the production of all four, echoing in his poem a collective aesthetic: both deracinated but concerned with racial identities, both "without boundaries" and full of "ruptures" but keenly aware of "connection within disconnection." The addition of White seems curious at first—why include

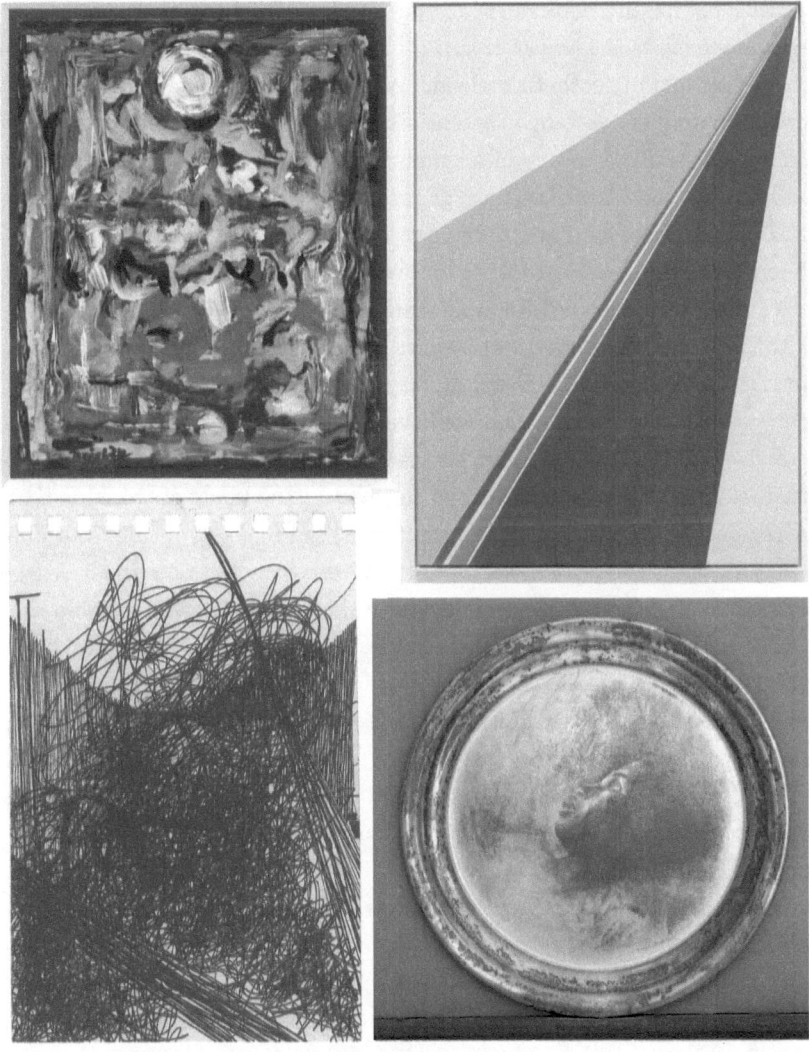

Clockwise, from top left: David C. Driskell, *The Sunset* (2011) © Estate of David C. Driskell, courtesy of DC Moore Gallery, New York. Sam Gilliam, *Ionesque* (1965) © 2022 Sam Gilliam/Artists Rights Society (ARS), New York. Photographed by Fredrik Nilsen Studio, courtesy of David Kordansky Gallery, Los Angeles. Charles White, *Vision* (1963), etched silver plate, diameter: 5 3/4 in. (14.6 cm) © The Charles White Archives, photograph courtesy of the Blanton Museum of Art, The University of Texas at Austin, gift of Susan G. and Edmund W. Gordon. Christopher Stackhouse, *Untitled* (2006), reprinted courtesy of the artist.

a realist painter in a book full of abstract art and conceptual abstractions, one that emphasizes the power of anti-mimetic expression?—but makes sense in this context of aesthetic dialectic. What the poems in *Seismosis* strive to do, ultimately, is to retain an essential connection to the "subject," narrowly conceived, of Blackness, while simultaneously forcing a widening of that subject that speaks the language of academic disciplinarity back to both African American studies and to creative writing, both of which have rendered Keene's mode of poetic thinking more or less historically illegible.

Driskell, Gilliam, White, and Stackhouse, framed by Keene by Plato, Kant, Derrida, Benjamin, and Lyotard (who themselves are thus reframed in turn): this is a very different literary expression of "identity's landscape, concise or layered" from what we have been taught to expect out of Black creative writing in the program era, as it were.[73] But the same institutionality that fosters those expectations also fosters the kinds of thinking that, when pushed to the edge of its own forms, can make us rethink not only what it means to speak Black identity in literature, but how the language of critical analysis can be made to serve those ends in radical fashion. In "Axioms," Keene writes: "What is visible: the sign enigma that punctures the tried idioms."[74] He speaks here of his own work, of Stackhouse's enigmatic drawings, and of the theories of language—in which the sign is an endlessly receding enigma—that have helped him formulate this avant-garde poetry of thinking. *Seismosis* is made possible by a whole host of previous struggles and disciplinary developments that saw the rise, and then the establishment, both of creative writing and of ethnic and cultural studies in the American academy. Its break from the dominant aesthetic(s) espoused by both disciplines is performed in light of this fact, and talks back to it via methods of signification that Gates might well recognize as seriously playful reterritorialization. As in the phrase, woven through "Axioms" like the song refrain it is: "*enigmatic signifier.*" The words do double duty: they both speak to the ways in which the poststructural signifier remains persistently mysterious, refusing to settle into the transcendental sign, and identify Keene himself *as signifier*. As signifier, Keene is both the one who signifies, and also the one who refuses to settle: and there's a lesson in that, for those of us who also depend upon the possibilities contained in the communities and codes (and recodes, and decodes) of academic critical analysis.

"My dream MFA program would have a philosopher, an eco-poetics person, and a political analyst on staff with the poets."[75] Claudia Rankine's MFA program at Columbia University, perhaps predictably, did not have her dream faculty. Instead, like all well-established MFA programs in creative writing, it had a stable of high-profile poets, including at the time J. D. McClatchy (Rankine's advisor), Henri Cole, and Dan Halpern. The writing faculty today includes the poets Shane McCrae, Dorothea Lasky, and Timothy Donnelly. Provided that they are also good teachers, these are good names to have on the roster when one is learning to write poetry; Rankine acknowledges as much, even as she wishes for some disciplinary expansion. She was, as she puts it, "guided well" through to the completion of her manuscript, which later became her first book, *Nothing in Nature is Private* (1995).

And yet it is also true that *Nothing in Nature* is a product of a program in which Rankine felt mildly uncomfortable; she behaved, she says, "a bit like a tennis player—trying to hit poems over the net back to a roomful of people. There's that constant struggle between satisfying the expectation of the program and what your unconscious wants to investigate."[76] When she received her first box of author's copies, she says, she was "mortified." It is both difficult and easy to see why: difficult, because the poems in *Nothing in Nature is Private* are clear and elegant, personal and family-oriented. The imagery is striking:

> *The way I look mirrors my father.*
> *I am everywhere in the faces of Black men.*
> *Imagine the concern I feel for myself.*[77]

But easy, because Rankine's work has since developed in explosive and decidedly genre-bending directions, ones that render lines such as "to understand, to feel the obvious held / up in the history trafficking my heart" dangerously sentimental, inward-facing, *obvious*.[78] These are not the lines of a poet whose work is featured in anthologies of conceptual poetry. Then again, it's unclear why anyone would think of Rankine as a conceptual poet in the current, "uncreative writing" sense of the word: if anything, Rankine has in her more experimental work burrowed even deeper into the personal, to the point where it becomes strange, monstrous, and sometimes wildly fictional. In the process, it foregrounds more and more starkly the project of critical analysis—particularly, as in Keene, those analyses inflected by poststructuralism and its relations—and argues for its centrality to innovative creative thought.

Rankine's books follow a relatively neat trajectory in which each book becomes more recognizably "experimental" than the last; by the time we get to 2004's *Don't Let Me Be Lonely: An American Lyric*, the poetry is half-essay, half-fiction, half–multimedia art book. That's three halves and no poetry; the poetry fits in precisely insofar as the book overflows its own generic boundaries. This same trajectory is also one from less to more analytical: while the poems in *Nothing in Nature is Private* are broadly descriptive, presenting series of images with little to no commentary, *Don't Let Me Be Lonely* is almost more commentary than image—the images, instead, are "actual" images, taken from television stills or photographs. In the decade that separates the books (and which produced two more, *The End of the Alphabet* in 1998 and *PLOT* in 2001), Rankine moves very firmly away from the kinds of expectations of narrative clarity and clarity of subjectivity that she encountered during her own experience in an MFA program—and yet she continues to teach creative writing, encouraging her students toward the kinds of "messiness" that she felt she could not pursue during the course of her own degree.[79]

A longtime professor at Pomona College, briefly the Isenman Professor of Poetry at Yale, and now a professor at NYU, Rankine has also taught at both the Iowa Writers' Workshop and at the University of Houston, the latter of which offers the (still relatively rare) PhD in creative writing, billed as a degree in "creative writing and literature." Rankine wrote much of *Don't Let Me Be Lonely* while on sabbatical from Barnard College, and finished the book while teaching at Iowa. Not unlike Graham, the university has been a constant in Rankine's career. Unlike *Seismosis*, there is no question of whether or not this book is "about" Black bodies and Black experience, though it is also in some senses a maximalist work that attempts to capture an entire hypermediated zeitgeist. The foregrounding of raced subjectivity in *Don't Let Me Be Lonely* is in fact a complicated return to Rankine's MFA thesis. Her second and third books move rather sharply away from the overt subject of race, instead focusing on themes of woman- and motherhood. Both display the kinds of pronounced fictionality that will both characterize but also be complicated and subverted by *Don't Let Me Be Lonely*: the entirety of *The End of the Alphabet* is addressed to an imaginary woman named "Jane"; *PLOT*'s plot, as it were, follows two characters—Liv and Erland—and their child, Ersatz, in their pre- and post-familial struggles. Rankine's work on these books coincides with her work on a popular anthology, *Women Poets in the*

21st Century, coedited with Juliana Spahr. *The End of the Alphabet* and *PLOT* contain the kinds of experiments in tone and form that will characterize *Lonely*, but the subject of race remains largely suppressed. Rankine's return to a poetics of racial politics was not, as we now know, an isolated incident: her most famous book by far, *Citizen*, is a relentless compilation of racist micro- and macroagressions (and, in the case of a long exploration of both Serena Williams's career and the infamous Zinedine Zidane headbutt, their larger-than-life retaliations).[80]

In the years since its publication, *Citizen* has provoked an extremely rare kind of public conversation about literature, one that is widespread in a way almost unheard of for a book of poetry (or criticism: it was nominated for the National Book Critics' Circle Award in both categories, a first for the organization). I focus here on *Don't Let Me Be Lonely* to the relative exclusion of this newer book for several reasons. One is that *Lonely* is, in both content and form, *Citizen*'s necessary prologue. (They share a subtitle: *An American Lyric*.) Another is that *Lonely* was the first product of Rankine's "return" to Blackness as subject matter—it shares with *Nothing in Nature* an epigraph from Aimé Césaire, and as she began the later book, Rankine has said that she felt as if she "finally had the tools to address race and the space around what it means to be human."[81] This notion raises the question of what tools allow a poet to "address race." In Rankine's case, those tools appear to be, as they are in Keene, very far removed from the poetic tennis balls, as it were, that Rankine attempted to hit over the net of the workshop classroom. Instead, Rankine uses a combination of ironized fictionality and analytical impersonality or distance (both of which are also fundamental characteristics of *Citizen*) to form a poetics of intellectual ethics—a program, in other words, for the ethical consumption of the cultural products of the twenty-first century, particularly televised media.

Don't Let Me Be Lonely ranges hugely in subject matter but considerably more narrowly in theme: the prose snippets (there are no traditionally lineated stanzas) begin with a consideration of the experience of death—"there was a time I could say no one I knew well had died"—and move through a friend's breast cancer, several hate crimes, a sister's loss of her husband and children, ads for antidepressants, the withholding of pharmaceuticals from HIV-infected South Africans, considerations of the liver, and the security state that the United States became after 9/11. The predominant pronoun is "I," though the things that the "I" relates tend not to be strictly auto-

Untitled image of television static that appears repeatedly throughout Claudia Rankine's *Don't Let Me Be Lonely: An American Lyric* (Graywolf Press, 2004). Courtesy of the author.

biographical (Rankine does not, for instance, have a sister whose husband and children were killed in a car crash). In its candid confrontation of the ubiquitous fact of death and loss, the book is harrowing. Scattered in amongst the text is a series of images, many of which are set into the frame of an old vacuum-tube TV set. This TV, its face filled with static and within which one can barely perceive the outline of George W. Bush's head and torso, is also used as a section-break marker, giving the reader the sense that she is flipping through channels as the book progresses.

 The overall feel of *Don't Let Me Be Lonely* is one of a paradoxically disjointed connectedness, a sense that the disparate channels on Rankine's poetic TV are all showing the same, bleak program. Rankine's prose, which intensifies this sense, is somehow both coolly analytical and deeply intimate:

"I am not exactly a crying person, though my eyes tear up frequently because of my allergies. In any case, the other tears, the ones that express emotions, the ones that recognize and take responsibility for the soul don't come."[82] Throughout, Rankine positions herself among a scholarly network of writers (creative and philosophical): Emmanuel Levinas, Jacques Derrida, Georg Wilhelm Friedrich Hegel, Cornel West, Wallace Stevens, Gertrude Stein, J. M. Coetzee, Paul Celan, Joseph Brodsky, Myung Mi Kim, and others. Rankine's use of this community of thinkers forms a large-scale argument about the layered functionality of the arts and humanities in the face of structural injustice: poetry and criticism, in other words, are both what attune us to the contours and injustices of the world, and a potential key, used correctly, to working through the implications of what they force one to notice.

By paying particular attention to the analytical function of art, Rankine's work in *Don't Let Me Be Lonely* puts forth notions of Black subjectivity and Black creative writing that are, like Keene's work, based on something other than the transmission of specific personal experiences. But Rankine, unlike Keene, simultaneously faces head-on the subject of the Black experience in America, which is intricately and inextricably connected to violence and death at the hands of white people. Yet critics tend, again, to obscure this fact in favor of discussing Rankine's formal innovations and difficulties, which is to say that there seems to be a missing connection between the deployment of those innovations and the renegotiation of what counts as appropriate ways of forming Black poetic subjectivities.[83] Rankine spent nearly a decade between *Nothing in Nature is Private* and *Don't Let Me Be Lonely* doing just such a renegotiation, a fact that it is important to highlight not only because of what it can tell us about the capabilities of avant-garde poetry more generally but also because of the institutional and disciplinary contexts in which it can take place. These contexts—the university, philosophy, African American studies, Black scholarship—are the contexts in which Rankine has developed both her notions of poetic thinking and the poetic task, and in turn their responsibilities toward what it means to "find your voice."

I'll return, in this connection, to the epigraph that connects the two books. It comes from Césaire's celebrated *Cahier d'un Retour au Pays Natal* (*Notebook of a Return to the Native Land*), and has taken on the status of a generalized aphorism. The quote appears, interestingly, in two different translations. I reprint them both: the first is the epigraph to *Nothing in Nature is Private*; the second, to *Don't Let Me Be Lonely*.

> I would go to this land of mine and I would say to it:
> "Embrace me without fear . . . And if all I can do is speak, it is for you I shall speak."
> And again I would say:
> "My mouth shall be the mouth of those calamities that have no mouth, my voice the freedom of those who break down in the solitary confinement of despair."
> And on the way I would say to myself:
> "And more than anything, my body, as well as my soul beware of assuming the sterile attitude of a spectator, for life is not a spectacle, a sea of miseries is not a proscenium, a man screaming is not a dancing bear . . . "[84]

And most of all beware, even in thought, of assuming the sterile attitude of the spectator, for life is not a spectacle, a sea of grief is not a proscenium, a man who wails is not a dancing bear . . .

The first epigraph is taken directly from the English translation of Césaire's poetry by Clayton Eshleman and Annette Smith, published in 1983. The second version does not appear to be from any published collection of Césaire's works in English, but does happen to be the epigraph to a 1998 article by David Levi-Strauss in *Nka: Journal of Contemporary African Art*. The article details the horrors of the Rwandan genocide, and the Chilean-American artist Alfredo Jaar's attempts to document them through the well-known installations called the *Rwanda Project*.[85] Levi-Strauss writes: "Alfredo Jaar's Rwanda works attempt to throw light on an occluded history and to act as an indictment of the world's silence and inaction . . . [i]s this something that art can or should attempt to do? . . . Jaar refuses to make a choice between politics or ethics and aesthetics."[86] In one of his installations, Jaar places photographs that he took in Rwanda into black boxes, gridded and laid on the gallery floor, and overlays each photo with a written description of the photo itself, obscuring the image with text. The viewer is thus placed at a triple remove from the image (from the actual site where the image was taken, to the photograph, to the text overlaid on the photograph that the viewer must read in lieu of witnessing either of the former two things), forcing a consideration of what, exactly, it means to spectate suffering and death.

To pile epigraph upon epigraph, the quote that greets you upon visiting Alfredo Jaar's website is (currently) from William Carlos Williams, namely the famous quip "it is difficult to get the news from poems, yet men die miserably every day for lack of what is found there." In *Don't Let Me Be Lonely*, Rankine embarks on a project specifically designed to bring the news and poetry crashing together. Jaar's work has no direct bearing on Rankine's that I'm aware of, but the deep networks concerning ethics, aesthetics, and "thinking art" that connect them are nonetheless striking. (Jaar has said of his own process, "my work is 99% thinking and 1% making," and he has been known to tell his students to "stop making stuff.")[87] The Césaire epigraph to Levi-Strauss's article on Jaar, which is also the epigraph to *Don't Let Me Be Lonely*, turns Césaire's musings to himself into a much stronger imperative, one directed outward. In this way Césaire's stricture to himself as a Black intellectual becomes an ethical directive toward all intellectuals, and the shift from the longer quote in *Nothing in Nature is Private* to the shorter, more declarative version in *Don't Let Me Be Lonely* signals a similar move on Rankine's part toward an affective poetry of racial/raced subjectivity that does not rely on the transcendent "I" to do its emotional work.

To this end, the techniques that Rankine has utilized increasingly between writing her MFA thesis and writing *Don't Let Me Be Lonely* are based upon this ethical movement outward, from the "I" that contemplates paternal resemblance to a far-ranging "I" that sees itself as part of a vast network of thinking agents. I want to suggest that *Don't Let Me Be Lonely*'s particular way of situating itself among these networks is only fully legible upon taking into account some of the structures of thinking developed and propagated/promoted by the academic humanities—structures that include methodological practices like the development of large and diverse citational apparatuses, and more abstract modes of theoretical and theorizing discourse developed precisely to define and analyze textuality and subjectivity.

In so doing, I wish to put a finer contextual point on some of the excellent work already done on Rankine's poetic modes. In a recent article on *Citizen*, Kamran Javadizadeh points up Rankine's "reconfigurations of the lyric subject" performed along and against the backdrop of Robert Lowell's (and thus whiteness's) historical domination of the category. He describes *Citizen*, tellingly, as a "critical intervention," and *Don't Let Me Be Lonely*'s

"I" as a "critical exploration." Rebecca Macmillan, in a similar vein, analyzes *Don't Let Me Be Lonely's* "archival poetics" along a continuum of experimental modes, including "unconventional scholarship" and "autotheory," but does not go so far as to recognize the book itself precisely *as* a type of scholarship.[88] Anthony Reed, in one of the most sustained and richly complex treatments of the book, details Rankine's "strategies of impersonality and citation," arguing that such strategies, which he dubs "postlyric," fundamentally disrupt *both* the atomized individualism and the essentializing universalism of the Black first-person address, leaving the reader suspended instead in a documentation of "the textual nature of blackness as a social encoding of difference."[89] His argument is an essential piece in the larger puzzle of contemporary poetic anticipations of racialized reading; my analysis draws our attention both to the role of systematized creative writing in the development of such reading modes, and to the ways in which those poetic anticipations stage their encounters with and resistances to the "mirror of representation" in specifically scholarly terms.[90]

Don't Let Me Be Lonely, in this connection, contains over 30 pages of notes. These notes were, in large part, compiled by a graduate student assistant at the University of Iowa, a fact that nudges the book (or, at the very least, its relations to the means of production) in the direction of a scholarly monograph. But it remains a long way from the kind of writing that, say, you are encountering right now. The notes exist, according to Rankine, in order to "take away the 'literal truth' authority from the text"—leaving the body of the book, ostensibly, to depart from "facts" where necessary.[91] But the book is not fictional so much as it is hyper-truthful, exploiting both the expectation that poetry (particularly poetry by minoritized writers) will contain some kind of transcendent truth-content and, less ironically, the claims that critical and philosophical inquiry have on the realm of knowledge. It consistently subverts the assumption that poetry's truthfulness is contained within its subject formations and in the relaying of experiences; Rankine's "I" is also sometimes a "you," and it attempts to do the work of a whole population experiencing grief, death, and other forms of loss. The truth toward which the poetry speaks is the truth of the structural formations of subjectivity, formations that in Rankine's view can only be properly attended to with a wide critical lens trained upon perceptual complexity—a commitment, in other words, to the ethics of criticality fostered, even if not always successfully, by humanistic inquiry.

The first scholarly figure to appear in *Don't Let Me Be Lonely* is Cornel West, and the essay referenced is "Black Strivings in a Twilight Civilization," the only essay that West has written specifically on W. E. B. Du Bois. Rankine writes:

> Cornel West makes the point that hope is different from American optimism. After the initial presidential election results come in, I stop watching the news ... [a]ll the non-reporting is a distraction from Bush himself, the same Bush who can't remember if two or three people were convicted for dragging a Black man to death in his home state of Texas.[92]

West's essay, in many ways, is a version of *Don't Let Me Be Lonely*—an extended effort to come to grips with what he calls the "tragicomedy" of twentieth-century American life, a life full of unprecedented systemic violence and inequality. "A central preoccupation of Black culture," West writes, "is that of confronting candidly the ontological wounds, psychic scars and existential bruises of Black people while fending off insanity and self-annihilation."[93] This sentence could be on the back of Rankine's book, if one substituted the book's title for the phrase "Black culture."[94] West, a prominent Harvard (and Yale, and Princeton) intellectual himself, sharply critiques Du Bois for his brand of Enlightenment rationalism: a rationalism that famously led him to a kind of minority elitism, one that West disavows even as he occupies a very similar cultural space to the one Du Bois did a century prior. Du Bois, West argues, possessed an "American optimism" that "screened him" from the existential crises of nationalism and belonging that both plagued Black America generally and drove the Black nationalist movement.[95] This naive optimism is different, as Rankine points out, from the heavily tempered "hope" to be found in "Black harmonies of spiritual camaraderie" (West's words) that recognizes and faces Black invisibility and namelessness.[96]

West's is certainly not an anti-intellectual or even anti-Western argument (though it is the latter to a degree): "Black Strivings" proudly displays a formidable command of the Western intellectual and literary canon, making note of everyone from Emerson to Kurt Tucholsky, and insists upon the necessity of an intellectual culture that sustains a "deep commitment to the life of the mind."[97] West's deep admiration for Du Bois (visible even through his critique) stems from his own version of that commitment, one that struggles as Du Bois's did with the lived realities of African Americans and the Black intellectual's responsibility, as both invisible and hypervisible, toward that reality. Rankine's invocation of West in the opening pages of *Don't Let Me Be Lonely*, in other words, signals early on the book's preoccupation with the troubled relationship between the analyzed and the analyzing. Poetry's ability to conflate them in acts of self-reflexiveness allows Rankine to interrogate that conflation by thematizing it as thinking subjectivity: not the personal, but the conditionality of that quality; not the "authentic," but the precariousness of that possibility given the violence of whiteness.

An ethical creative practice, under these circumstances, foregrounds the deeply complex networks that make such thinking subjectivity possible. Insofar as Rankine, as self or author, appears in *Don't Let Me Be Lonely*, she appears as a record of her reading; in this and throughout the book, what appears as most traditionally "personal" is fictionalized, and that which appears dryly discursive is in fact the most intimate glance. The intellectual milieu in which Rankine situates her work thus surrounds, and is indeed part and parcel of, the recent history of "the poststructuralist critique of ethics and the ethical critique of poststructuralism."[98] This is a critique that revolves at least in part around the concept of the subject and its duties toward its other; in this way, it fits in well with Rankine's reimagining of the African American poetic "voice." *Don't Let Me Be Lonely* argues that that voice can, and perhaps even should, take its cues from the aesthetics of critical analysis, which is to say the form of a discourse that ranges over its subject matter(s) and insistently asks *can this be explained*?

The answer is often *only partially*, and as much as we like to think that we in the business of literary criticism are in the business of providing explanations, we are also in the business of providing a never-ending series of questions. This state of affairs is, perhaps, why the deconstructive movement in the late twentieth century struck such a chord: on the one hand, its insistence that the only answer to be had in textual scrutiny was the fact that there are no answers was a powerful philosophical provocation, one that in some senses promised a task for literary scholars in perpetuity. On the other, its staunch disavowal of capital-T Truth raised questions not only of its so-called practical relevance but also, and more importantly, of its possible ethical myopia or dangerous relativism. I call attention to this tension because the second scholarly figure that Rankine cites directly in *Don't Let Me Be Lonely* is the seemingly inescapable Jacques Derrida.

Musing on the media coverage of the execution of Timothy McVeigh (coverage that, Rankine asserts, attempted to "immunize him from his actions" because he was "visually the boy next door," i.e. clean-cut, clean-shaven, and *white*), Rankine writes:

> What does it mean to forgive and how does forgiveness show itself? "Forgiveness forgives only the unforgivable," Jacques Derrida claims. Timothy McVeigh never asked to be forgiven. He managed to suggest that both condemnation and forgiveness were irrelevant by quoting William Earnest Henley's poem "Invictus": "It matters not how strait the gate, How charged with punishments the scroll, I am the master of my fate: I am the captain of my soul."[99]

The passage is accompanied by a photograph of a gurney used for lethal injections. Continuing in the theme of deep networks, "Invictus" is almost certainly more famous for being a poem that inspired an incarcerated Nelson Mandela (and, indeed, is the title of a 2009 movie about him) rather than for being the last words of an incarcerated Timothy McVeigh. The politics of forgiveness are at work in this case, too, as some of the most contested points of Mandela's legacy remain those surrounding his stance toward forgiveness and reconciliation after violence. Perhaps unsurprisingly, Derrida uses the case of South African apartheid as a case study in *On Cosmopolitanism and Forgiveness*, which is the work to which Rankine refers. Rankine, too, turns to South Africa in *Don't Let Me Be Lonely*—late in the book, we find a picture of Mandela, hands outstretched, wearing a T-shirt with the words "HIV POSITIVE" printed in block letters upon it.[100] I will return shortly to this image, and the text surrounding it.

Derrida posits two contradictory, irreconcilable, and mutually dependent versions of forgiveness—the contingent "political" version, in which forgiveness is offered upon its asking and on condition of repentance, and the unconditional, religiously valenced "pure" version, which is offered freely and is intelligible only in the face of that which cannot be forgiven. Nelson Mandela, Derrida insinuates, decided upon reconciliation while in prison, but at no point upon a politics of unpolitical forgiveness, as it were—despite the fact that Desmond Tutu, as the president of the Truth and Reconciliation Commission, mobilized the christianized rhetoric of "repentance and forgiveness" in the wake of apartheid.[101] McVeigh never asked to be forgiven, and Mandela never really forgave: as historically unrelated as these two things may be, Rankine forces them together (provided that one is the kind of reader that has read, or will consult, the Derrida in question) in a consideration of the role of raced agency in a global system of violence. Being "the captain of [one's] soul" has very different implications for McVeigh, who gets at least some forgiveness without asking for it even as he is put to death, than it does for Mandela, whose functioning in the post-apartheid system was contingent upon his acceptance of the asking for "forgiveness" that would allow South Africa to (re)assimilate into the global order.

Rankine continues on the next page with the following assertion: "Forgiveness, I finally decide, is not the death of amnesia, nor it is a form of madness, as Derrida claims. For the one who forgives, it is simply a death."[102] Forgiveness, Rankine goes on to argue, involves a completed living-through, an understanding so complete that it cannot be anything other than the total vacancy of death. This is a complicated reading of and reaction to Derrida's analysis. On the one hand, it is a diametric opposition: Rankine's argument that forgiveness requires the full admission of a thing's happening—"it is in the end the living through, the understanding that this has happened"— runs directly counter to Derrida's claim that true forgiveness deals only in the "unintelligible," the total "incomprehension" of the criminal by the victim. "As soon as the victim 'understands' . . . the scene of reconciliation has commenced, and with it this ordinary forgiveness which is anything but forgiveness."[103] On the other hand, by identifying forgiveness-as-understanding with death's terrible vacancy, Rankine reinforces a dedication to an ethics of *not*-understanding, to a "willingness to be complex" that looks quite a bit like the very unintelligibility that Derrida puts forth as so essential to the pure concept of forgiveness. (The full sentence from which that phrase comes reads as follows: "It strikes me that what the attack on the World Trade Center stole from us is our willingness to be complex.")[104] Confronting the impossible or the utterly illogical remains central to her project—but she does not name this confrontation "forgiveness," as Derrida does. Pure forgiveness, in Rankine's view, is neither sacred nor desirable; it is instead the total absence of feeling ("beyond all that is hated or loved") that forms a parallel to the discussions of depression and its accompanying pharmaceuticals that also runs through the book.[105]

Having failed to find in Derrida's concept of forgiveness the kind of truly ethical confrontation with the abyss that he says is there, and in the pharmaceuticals connection, Rankine turns back toward Cornel West's conception of hope. (Bear with me: the deep networks of this book tend to force one to write sentences like the one I've just written.) Immediately preceding the aforementioned picture of Nelson Mandela in the "HIV POSITIVE" shirt are the names of the 39 pharmaceutical companies that sued to prevent generic antiretrovirals from becoming available in South Africa, causing untold numbers of deaths. (The lawsuit was eventually withdrawn following public pressure.) Immediately following, the book's narrator recounts the day when Thabo Mbeki changed his stance on AIDS (admitting that it was caused by a virus, and not by poverty and malnourishment), allowing the distribution of the generic drugs. The time it took him to reach this decision resulted in the deaths of some third of a million people more, the vast majority of whom were Black South Africans.[106]

Rankine writes: "My body relaxes. My shoulders fall back. I had not known that my distress at Mbeki's previous position . . . had physically lodged itself like a virus within me."[107] This distress, she goes on, was ineffable in its depth: "It is not possible to communicate how useless, how much like a skin-sack of uselessness I felt. [. . .] One opens the paper. One turns on the television. Nothing changes. My distress grows into nothing."[108] Out of the nothing, however (which looks at first like the vacancy-death that she identifies with forgiveness), emerges hope: "Such distress moved in with muscle and bone. Its entrance by necessity slowly translated my already grief into a tremendously exhausted hope. [. . .] Then life, which seems so full of waiting, awakes suddenly into a life of hope."[109] There are echoes here not only of her earlier citation of West, in which he differentiates hope from American optimism, but also to his claim that "despair and hope are inseparable."[110]

For Rankine, digesting the news—which is essentially the digestion of the ongoing deaths of nonwhite peoples around the world—requires not only an ethical confrontation of the positionality of uselessness but also the careful intellectual consideration of how to react to that condition. How are we to operate in a world that rewards careful scrutiny with a constant despair? The answer, for Rankine, is to take some of the principles that Derrida puts forth—the confrontation with the incomprehensible, the admission of the impossibility of a signifier's purity—and to port them over into West's assertion that since the base condition of the African American is a kind of facing-nothingness (invisibility, namelessness, despair), the only hope to be had must be pulled precisely from this nothingness. And out of this nothingness emerges an ever-expanding network of people who are also confronting it; they form a more abstract version of the community that West argues is a prerequisite for any kind of hope in the face of existential despair. This is the widest possible angle from which to view the book: in her media-centric maximalism, Rankine loops together 9/11 and the epidemic in South Africa; systematic state violence and the continuation of hate crime. But Rankine also forms a much smaller, secondary community within this sprawling global framework, a "thinking-with" cohort of scholars that offer ways of *processing* experience as an alternative to its narration. Her reflexive renegotiation of what it means to write "about" the Black experience involves a deep attention to affective poignancy tempered with a remarkably academic insistence on detailing the causes and stakes of that poignancy. As is hopefully clear by this point, Rankine's affiliations with the academic humanities are closely bound to her sense that a dense complex of difficult intellectual connections is precisely the "tool" that she found she needed in order to "address race" in her poetry.

This is not to say that these connections have only ever been made by academics, nor that they can only be made in academia. But the truth of the matter is that in the twenty-first century, relatively few people that are not somehow involved in university learning will be familiar with West or Derrida or Julia Kristeva or Hegel—the latter of whom first appears in *Don't Let Me Be Lonely* precisely in this kind of context: "In college, when I studied Hegel, I was struck by his explanation of the use of death by the state."[111] Hegel is framed, understandably, as someone who is studied in college. There is a level on which Rankine's work speaks to anyone who might pick up the book—there are plenty of pages that do not rely on late Derrida, or on an understanding of Wallace Stevens's politics—but there is also a level on which the book is written expressly *to* readers who also studied Hegel in college (or in graduate school). Familiarity with the "Coercion and Crime" and the "Ethical Life" sections of *Outlines of the Philosophy of Right* is not strictly essential to the reading of *Don't Let Me Be Lonely*, but it is extremely helpful when trying to get a picture both of the specific lens(es) through which Rankine is processing her experience of contemporary culture, and more generally the kinds of intellectualism that she finds important.[112] That is to say, to recognize these figures in Rankine's poetry is also to recognize that *Don't Let Me Be Lonely* is not only an exquisite lament but also a powerful methodological demonstration, one that shows academic humanists *in particular* the importance of the ethical turns of some of the figures on whom they have come to rely so heavily.

"Education is the art of making people ethical": a bold statement in today's educational climate, and perhaps a bold one even in Hegel's.[113] Nevertheless, he makes it, though he tempers it heavily with the sobering observation that the kinds of habits that education can instill—the habit of thinking of oneself as a spiritual, rational animal, "trained against capricious fancies"—can also kill us out of sheer airtightness.[114] Rankine does not reference this particular passage in *Don't Let Me Be Lonely*, but her juggling of intellectual acuity and affective depth displays a similar dialectical tension, one that is acutely aware that to intellectualize a systemic problem is not *a priori* an ethical good. The aforementioned reference to Hegel appears in the context of the US's manhunt for Osama bin Laden after 9/11, but it applies also to the acts of domestic terrorism, as it were, committed by the state against its own (Black) people in the cases of Abner Louima and Amadou Diallo. The former was sexually assaulted by NYPD officers in 1997, the latter, unarmed, shot 41 times in 1999 by members of the same police force. Rankine's narrator reacts to both events physically: "I get a sharp pain in my gut . . . I have had it all my life. Not quite a caving in, just a feeling of bits of my inside twisting away from flesh in the form of a blow to the body."[115]

Even this transmission of an affective state has an analytical ring to it, an ironized distance from the fact of physical pain, the image of the flesh retreating from itself described as "just a feeling." But Rankine is quick to point out that no number of references to Hegel or anyone else can rationalize away that feeling: "Sometimes I think it is sentimental, or excessive, certainly not intellectual, or perhaps too naïve, too self-wounded to value each life like that, to feel loss to the point of being bent over each time."[116] The desire to *be* intellectual (it is the only thing in the sentence that is negated, rather than in excess) comes up against the physicality of empathy and the necessity of that physicality for the writing of poetry: "[t]hough Myung Mi Kim did say that the poem is really a responsibility to everyone in a social space . . . [s]he did say, in so many words, that what alerts, alters."[117] The key, to my mind, is that word *alerts*: an action that can be both physical (waving your hands at someone, say) *or* intellectual (the entire project of critical analysis could easily be said to be an extended project in alerting people to things). The practice of poetic alerting/altering in *Don't Let Me Be Lonely* intellectualizes the physical, not to rationalize it away but instead to startle us out of our preconceptions about what it looks like to speak the language of racialized violence and, more broadly, racial experience in poetry.

This startling, in the end, is the most fundamental form of Rankine's aestheticized intellectual ethics: the media ought to startle us; death and violence and systemic racism ought to startle us out of despair or numbness and cause us to take stock of our cultural moment. In attending to the heaviest subjects of poetry and politics with the analytic assistance of an academic citational network, Rankine does the double-edged work of re-forming Black poetic subjectivity in the service of a radical aesthetics while also demonstrating the ethical imperatives of what is usually assumed to be the deeply abstract project of critique and analysis. "Addressing race," in this case, means paying close attention to the Black experience in a wide, structural sense, rather than using the assumed transparency of the Black narrativized self as metonymic for that experience. The language of theorization fundamental to this address is an artifact of Rankine's continuing situatedness within the university—*Don't Let Me Be Lonely* cannot really be read without this contextual framework, and some of its most powerful messages are expressly directed to those who also work within it. It should perhaps be unsurprising, then, that one of the book's closing gestures comes from Emmanuel Levinas, to whom Derrida turned late in his career, helping the ethicist into the critical spotlight:

> Then all life is a form of waiting, but it is the waiting of loneliness. One waits to recognize the other, to see the other as one sees the self. Levinas writes, "The subject who speaks is situated in relation to the other. This privilege of the other ceases to be incomprehensible once we admit that the first fact of existence is neither being in itself nor being for itself but being for the other, in other words, that human existence is a creature. By offering a word, the subject putting himself forward lays himself open and, in a sense, prays."[118]

With its echoes of Hegel, this passage binds the essence of existence together with the linguistic faculty. We may never "see the other" precisely as we see ourselves, but the effort is paramount whenever we affirm our existence through language.

In this chapter, we've seen how African American poets have used the theoretical and citational practices of Black literary and cultural studies to rewrite the terms on which they engage with the subject of "the Black experience." It is often, as Rankine (and Tolson) reminds us, lonely work. But in the citational network as method, these poets dialectically re-place a sense of community, creating something with the expressive qualities that make creative writing so appealing while refusing the false communality-in-individualism of an assumed generalized experience. The injunction in Rankine's title is also an invitation into this work; she is creating with her American lyrics the very "dream MFA program" envisioned at the start of this section, in which disciplines like literary studies and philosophy bear equal responsibility for the training of poets. This expansion of the available methodologies for producing literary work expands also the horizon of possibility for creating and theorizing the poetic subject, perhaps paradoxically allowing Black writers a broader sense of control over their own heterogeneity. We may be past the point where we can take seriously any claim that one can write oneself to freedom. Such claims recapitulate the logics of "burdened individuality" that themselves burden the creative writing program.[119] But one may, perhaps, offer up a theory of freedom, one that others may take up, learn, and then begin to practice. And in this moment of word-offering as prayer, where the expressive goals of creative writing and the problematics of semiotics converge, we can see the melancholy hope of the academic avant-garde.

5

Archival Authorizations

It is no secret that Susan Howe loves libraries. They form, for her, a "second Nature," a phrase that evinces both her Romantic sensibilities and her abiding sense of the inviolable vitality of reading. She has put it perhaps most forcefully in her 2011 Blaney Lecture, sponsored by the Academy of American Poets:

> I believe this currently exiled spirit—Keats's "beauty is truth, truth beauty," Walter Benjamin's "the beautiful is neither the veil, nor the veiled object, but rather the object in its veil," William Carlos Williams's "beautiful thing! aflame," then "beauty is a defiance of authority"—I believe this spirit—a deposit from a future yet to come—is gathered and guarded in the domain of research libraries and special collections.[1]

The cause and conditions of this spirit's exiling go unsaid. What *is* clear is that the spirit "gathered and guarded" in the educational/institutional spaces of research libraries is intimately connected to those most poetic of abstractions, Truth and Beauty. In particular, the power of the research institution to acquire and preserve the objects of history such that they may be exhumed, inspected, and given new literary life makes these institutions indispensable for Howe's poetic practice.

This deep connection was, on the one hand, not always so obvious: while Howe's poetics have always been heavily dependent upon the frequent consultation of outside sources, it is her later poetry that really wears its archival heart on its sleeve.[2] On the other hand, Howe's career as an avant-garde historian and "magpie" archivist began long before she accepted a professorship at SUNY Buffalo in 1991. The offer itself almost certainly had something to do with the success of *My Emily Dickinson* (1985), a book inspired by Charles Olson's *Call Me Ishmael*. Together, these volumes form the foundation of a sub-genre of "creative criticism" that remains underpopulated.[3] When the book was published, Howe was working as a clerk in a bookstore in Guilford, Connecticut. Three years later, she was offered $12,000 to teach a class at Buffalo, and the rest, as they say, is history.[4]

Howe's relationship to the American university makes her central to this book's story, but in a way that is somewhat idiosyncratic: with a bachelor's degree from the Boston Museum School of Fine Arts, she is perhaps the least traditionally "credentialed" of the figures in this study, and certainly the least professionalized. This perceived status disparity would dog her throughout her career, exacerbated by her familial and spousal proximity to elite institutions: her father, Mark DeWolfe Howe, was a professor of law at Harvard; her husband, the artist David von Schlegell, taught at Yale. When she did secure a permanent academic post, it was as a founding faculty member of what would become one of the country's most well-known but also non-traditional academic programs: the Poetics Program at Buffalo, a single-genre doctoral program in which students are actively encouraged to straddle the divide between critical and creative writing. The program's self-description, like that of Iowa's, is deeply revealing: of its history, the program's website declares that "the Poetics Program developed out of the vision . . . that poetry and poetics could be taught in a doctoral program by non-academic poets." What could it possibly mean for professors—which is the rank that Susan Howe, Charles Bernstein, Robert Creeley, and the other founders all held—teaching in a doctoral program to be "non-academic"? One assumes that this designation indicates that the poets in question did not have MFAs, but the label still sits deeply askew in this context. These sorts of linguistic gymnastics often accompany any insistence upon the mutual exclusivity of academia and innovative poetry, despite the obvious fact that in the case of the Poetics Program, they're mutually sustaining.

Susan Howe embodies this contradiction in many ways. For the past several decades, she has been just as academically situated as Jorie Graham or Claudia Rankine—indeed, one reading of the Poetics Program's history statement is that the program was developed to bring "non-academic poets" *into* the academy, thus making them academic poets. A less generous reading is that it is a form of denial, of the "'in' but not 'of'" variety. The very beginning of *My Emily Dickinson* presages this uncomfortable affective complex in both philosophy and setting: "In the college library I use there are two writers whose work refuses to conform to the Anglo-American literary traditions these institutions perpetuate."[5] The writers she refers to are Dickinson and Gertrude Stein; both of these authors are to be found in nearly every library, collegiate or not, in the United States. And they are both firmly part of the "Anglo-American literary tradition" fostered in American universities. This is not to say that they are somehow less radical than they were at the time of their writing, or indeed than they still are now. It is instead to say yet again that what "institutions perpetuate" can take many forms.

It is, after all, the university library that held the resources Howe needed to complete *My Emily Dickinson*, an unabashedly avant-garde act of critical writing. But while the book draws upon sources that range from the facsimile edition of Mary Rowlandson's narration of her captivity by Native Americans to Richard Ellman's biography of James Joyce, there was one thing which Howe had no access to as she wrote the book: Dickinson's manuscripts, housed at the Houghton Library at Harvard. She worked instead from R. W. Franklin's two-volume edition, and the reprinted poems in *My Emily Dickinson* come from Thomas H. Johnson's three-volume edition, a work whose editorial influence on and subsequent distortion of Dickinson scholarship has been well noted.[6] That Howe emphasizes Dickinson's refusal to "conform" to the literary standards not of her day but of the institutions that would later determine the makeup of the American literary canon says less about Dickinson than it does about Howe's view of herself at work: an outsider—a woman, a faculty wife—on the institutional inside, angry and desirous.

To make *My Emily Dickinson* about Susan Howe, however, and not about Emily Dickinson (or Mary Rowlandson or Jonathan Edwards) would be at once dully obvious and a critical exercise beside the point: biography informs all kinds of literary writing, creative and critical, and in Howe's case, there is plenty of work in which autobiography shows up uncloaked. But that opening moment of connection between a library-ensconced yet extra-institutional Howe, her library card afforded to her by the chance of marriage rather than scholarly validation, and the equally ensconced yet critically neglected objects of her study serves as a hint of things to come. In this chapter I argue that in Howe's later works, the autobiographical self appears as the self at work in historical research, authorized to appear precisely because of its access to worlds of origins in academic archives. Howe shows us one important version of what it is like to become an academic avant-garde poet: to begin as an outsider to the traditional lineage of expertise, but to be determined to assert a subjectivity equal to it. Predictably, this uncloaking of the self—of the "lyric I," to put it more controversially—bears on its surface little resemblance to the kinds of "confessional" work more commonly associated with the first-person point of view. But its persistent presence testifies to the enormous importance that, despite many and well-documented avant-garde claims to the contrary, the authorial subject still holds in conceptions of poetry of all stripes.[7]

In Howe's case, and the cases of poets who follow in her wake like Jena Osman, Myung Mi Kim, and Catherine Taylor (to all of whom I will return and all of whom have MFAs or PhDs), this self gains purchase primarily *as an academic self*: the authorization to speak autobiographically emerges from a methodological commitment to historicism and a concomitant access to the archival materials that universities offer to their faculty and students. To the extent that Susan Howe has been portrayed as one of poetry's great rebels, such a characterization might seem surprising. But it remains the case that the astonishing breadth of her historical knowledge and the use to which she puts historical materials has been significantly augmented by her ability to do research in special collections. She needed the Sterling Memorial Library to write *My Emily Dickinson*, Yale professor or, as was the case, no. Moreover, a position in the academy was something that Howe did actually desire for years, even though (or perhaps precisely because) she felt as though she did not belong there. Predictably, however, this sense of nonbelonging failed to dissipate upon Howe's landing in the collegiate classroom. Her position and identification as an artist, a figure whose cultural place and ethos has historically been one of freedom and independence (however mythical), precluded any sense of real comfort in her new job security.

But in the archive, Howe could discover "outsiders"—from Edwards to Dickinson to Peirce—and reconstruct their histories as her own. In so doing, Howe's authorial self takes its present as seriously as the past. Her matter-of-fact historical narratives are never far from an image or narrative of the conditions of that material's discovery: a reading room and its problems of access, the image of the author as a "grave robber" doing her work in the middle of the afternoon, the work done on trains, in graduate seminars, and at various library desks. The conditions of possibility, in other words, are strenuously foregrounded in a way that makes the works' institutional contextuality unavoidable—and in the process, she reimagines the neo-confessional self as the disclosure of those conditions. While an erudite historicism has seen Howe through a great many book projects, it arguably culminates in *The Midnight*, published in 2003, as she brings her archival sensibilities to bear on her own family. It will thus serve as this chapter's main case study. Its fusion of documentary, autobiography, and highly experimental poetics starkly illustrates the uneasy points of contact between these methodologies and thus between the critical and creative traditions from which they arise.

The very opening of the book evinces a version of this split allegiance, framed explicitly in discipline-specific terms: "There was a time when bookbinders placed a tissue interleaf between frontispiece and title page in order to prevent illustration and text from rubbing together. Although a sign is understood to be consubstantial with the thing or being it represents, word and picture are essentially rivals."[8] Deftly, the book becomes a symbol for the methodological boundary that Howe, the frontispiece, finds herself delineating: rubbing on one side against the poststructural impulse to separate signifier from signified—to be abstract, to deny the possibility of a fixed truth indicated by language—and on the other against the historicist tendency toward just that truth, fixed in material evidence. The sudden swing in subject material mirrors the swings in style and form that characterize the book (and Howe's later work more generally); in the case of *The Midnight* the dialectic is further complicated by subject matter. For where, exactly, does the familial-introspective impulse fit on this spectrum, defined as that spectrum is by "critical" rather than "creative" practice? Certainly it concerns itself with the kind of truth-in-origins and clarity of purpose that would align itself with historical narration, but there is mysticism there as well, couched in terms of the irreducible subjectivity of experience. Confessional poetry in the more traditional sense has gained such huge purchase in American creative writing because of the amenability of this dual character to the workshop model: the cultivation of individual creativities tempered by the pedagogical imperative to craft something that can be improved by group discussion. The insistence on the extra-institutional source of artistic inspiration, in other words, shares very close quarters with the institutional space of that inspiration's refinement.

Howe's version of the introspective narrative reads as anything but traditional, but it is born of a deep concern with what lurks within the thematics of this most common of poetic subjects and, perhaps even more obviously and importantly, the spaces of traditional literary-historical scholarship. It would be easy to say that because Howe's archival work in *The Midnight* comes, unusually, not from a university library but from her own inherited collection of books, that the book represents an institutional break, a declaration of independence from the colonizers of knowledge (as it were). The more difficult position, but I think the correct one, asserts nearly the reverse: that in *The Midnight*, Howe brings her past into the institutional fold of the archive and its research methods, ultimately overriding her own tendency to position herself as an inveterate academic outsider, excluded from the places that house the written and unwritten histories of literary cultures. The strength and even purposefulness of this tendency in Howe has been overstated. Much stronger, in the end, is her insistence that to go into the library as a vanguardist is to destroy neither the place nor the title. Instead, it is to create a richly contextual and deeply complicated image of authorial presence, one that recognizes, as Howe implicitly does in the quote at the beginning of this chapter, that the academy can be the guardian of obscure and even radical things as well as the upholder of "tradition," and that these functions need not be mutually exclusive.

I am making an intervention into a line of criticism on Howe that has circled around my subject without landing upon it, which is to say that a number of writers have taken up the subject of Howe's authorities and authorizations and her explorations in the archive without directly addressing these subjects' connections to Howe's institutional situationality after *My Emily Dickinson*. Stephen Collis's *Through Words of Others: Susan Howe and Anarcho-Scholasticism* would seem from its title to have taken the wind out of my argumentative sails, but Collis is far too invested in portraying Howe as a radical destroyer of all things hierarchical, an "invisible searcher" who "sees *form* as potentially *anarchic* . . . and the institutional structures of publication and interpretation . . . as an affront to the eternal permissions of poetic license."[9] The valuation of precisely the kind of mystical freedom ("eternal permissions") so often attached to the visual and literary arts stems from the fact that Collis is himself a poet interested in defending his own "anarcho-scholastic" practice; *Through Words of Others* takes obvious stylistic cues from *My Emily Dickinson* and *The Birth-Mark* but lacks their immense scope of reference. The "institutional structures" to which Collis refers are structures within which Howe works quite well; her project is to find new configurations of material institutionalized and institutionalizable rather than to do away with the institution altogether. Collis rightly diagnoses the twin tendencies that his book's title describes, but his own argument refuses to see it as any kind of real dialectic.[10]

Susan M. Schultz, another poet and admirer of Howe, takes a more nuanced view in "The Stutter in the Text: Editing and Historical Authority in the Work of Susan Howe," writing that "she doesn't attempt to step outside tradition, but to redescribe and reframe an existing one in such a way that it admits women."[11] This is exactly correct, as is Schultz's sense that "what is most radical about [Howe's] work is her sense that the tradition is wild and that entry into the wilderness makes the poet into a scout or a captive." Part of my argument takes up where Schultz leaves off, particularly on the subject of what "tradition" in her view might mean when it comes to the authority vested in the curatorial act of what Schultz identifies as "editorship." That Howe was a product of her specifically *disciplinary* time (a time that saw the overlap of New Critical, deconstructive, and New Historicist ways of reading and writing) is Schultz's conclusion, and it will be my starting point for an examination of how this disciplinary matrix has affected the aesthetic of that important and vexing poetic construct, the authorial subject.[12]

The subject of autobiography in Howe is one that appears as well, albeit less frequently, but this work too tends to take Howe's predilection toward palimpsestic and paratactical historiography as a kind of artistic given without seeing it as professionally symptomatic. Marjorie Perloff denies the presence of the "lyric I" in Howe altogether, though that denial comes in 1989, well before Howe turns to historical explorations of the familial variety.[13] Taking the opposite view, namely that Susan Howe's poetry is highly and thoroughly autobiographical, Kathy-Ann Tan has devoted a large part of a book to the subject, arguing in *The Nonconformist's Poem* that Howe's "dominant representation of self is characterized by a certain quality of authorial liminality which undermines the hegemonic structures of language."[14] Howe's historical autobiography, in this account, serves to further accentuate the defining abstract features of Howe's work: linguistic fragmentation, interrogation of fixed meaning, and vanguardist iconoclasm. On the whole, critics have spent nearly all of their time going over various ways in which Howe's work is unlike all other poetic work; very little has been said about Howe's status on the inside, as it were, and how *that* makes its presence felt.

This observation is in no way meant to take away from the fact of Howe's striking originality: as Perloff has noted, Howe "seems to have had no apprentice period during which she wrote derivatively, 'in the style' of X or Y"; this is almost certainly the case not only because she transitioned from being a visual artist to a poet in her late thirties, as Perloff also observes, but also and consequently because her education took place outside the system of creative writing, in which workshops naturally (if sometimes unintentionally) produce apprentice mentalities and styles.[15] Having nevertheless gone on to teach creative writing and to found a program that is equal parts creative and critical, Howe is thus not a product of creative writing culture so much as an unlikely but definitive propagator of it.

An outsider on the inside in many senses—a point on which the most cogent voice thus far has been that of Oren Izenberg, who writes in "Poems In and Out of School: Allen Grossman and Susan Howe" that in Howe's poetry we find "an elaborate allegory of freedom, and yet, even by her own account, it is a curious sort of freedom only achievable—or legible—within institutions."[16] Izenberg identifies the cultural situation of both Howe and Grossman as products of a time when the transition from a starker inside-outside divide between innovative artistry and the academic institution to a situation in which said innovators reside "fully and without alternative within an 'administered world'" was nearing completion.[17] Izenberg's chief interest is how this cultural situation affects each poet's conception of "representation," and his focus lies in large part on Grossman. Using Izenberg's observations about Howe's cultural position to examine how traces of the autobiographical-confessional make themselves felt within structures of avant-garde aesthetics will demonstrate that there exists a striking kind of optimism about Howe's archival iconoclasm—one that posits the multigeneric, academic subject position as authorized by, and authorizing, the historiographical and archival work that can shape whole scholarly disciplines.

Here, I aim to augment Srikanth Reddy's compelling work on explanation and archival historicism in Marianne Moore, a poet whose versified anatomies, he argues, contain a "metadidactic" quality that "questions the entrenchment of institutionalized disciplines" by recreating whole systems of knowledge illegible to the norms of, for example, library cataloguing systems.[18] It would be very easy to describe Howe's work in nearly identical terms, and the oppositional pull of vanguardist rhetoric would make it tempting indeed. Like Moore, Howe is interested in the question of "how one field of knowledge [can] illuminate another," and like Moore, Howe brings together a remarkable array of subject matters into contact within single texts.[19] But while Reddy argues that Moore's work privileges these leaps as "distraction over concentration," I would argue that the opposite is true for Howe.[20] Far from evincing an anarchic desire to do away with disciplinary specificity, Howe pieces together a self *from* such specificity, negotiating her way through methodological quandaries particular to those interested in history and hermeneutics.

Early in *The Midnight*, for example, the reader encounters this set-up: "Upon the interpreter this ambush / Theory at war with phenomena" followed by "Tinsel hope I intersect linen silk."[21] The "interpreter," in a style of address faintly reminiscent of Ashbery, could be the literary critic, or it could be Howe herself, ambushed by her own intellectual fealties ("theory" and "phenomena"). In the last line, there is the desire: "hope I intersect." If "theory" and "phenomena" are at war in this stanza, then the intersection desired cuts between them, not necessarily with the promise of peace but at least with the hope that allegiances to both does not result in annihilation. Again, there is very little true anarchism here: while critics such as Collis and Susan Barbour insist that Howe's methodology "presupposes no origins" and is therefore anarchic in the Derridian sense, it would be more exact to say that Howe searches for origins that she fears may not be there, taking refuge in the (occasionally fetish-)character of archival material as positive remains of the past's facticity.[22]

In this way, the autobiographical impulse in her work becomes something akin to an affective mapping of her relationship to her professional conditions—her family becoming subject to her archival training, and her whole self a self in motion amongst the academy's materials and spaces. Her work's status as important and pioneering not only does not suffer because of its concerns with these traditional and/or institutional sites of poetic production, but is in fact enhanced by them. And attention to the ways in which Howe radically reframes and remakes both historicist scholarship and "confessional" poetics also helps to categorize and contextualize her work in a way that does much more than identify her as a sometimes-Language poet or as a figure who stands entirely on her own, as if that could ever be the case for any writer, creative or critical. Origins and originality, as it turns out and as Howe has long recognized, are the products of all kinds of unexpected collectivities.

In a 1995 interview with Lynn Keller, Howe is blunt about her stylistic preferences:

> I do not like confessional poetry. These days, in America, confession is on every TV program, let alone in most poems. Just today as I was eating breakfast in your college dining hall, there was a TV suspended from the ceiling blaring out a program called *True Confessions*—where people come on and say, "My father molested me when I was three," or "My mother was an alcoholic," et cetera. By now it's totally boring, or maybe it's my Yankee sense of decorum.[23]

This moment is yet another reminder of how deep-seated the mode of poetic-critical perception that Gillian White has called "lyric shame" really is; part of the difficulty in writing about the first-person subject in avant-garde poetry is the way in which so many claims about the latter are predicated upon a repudiation of the former.[24] As we have seen in the last chapter, the predication (and its concomitant negative affects) needn't always be the case even in those instances when it is in fact something like "the lyric subject" that is the object under scrutiny. But Howe's sense that her "Yankee decorum" and the confessional mode are irreconcilable does evince something like the type of shame that White identifies; I am interested in the ways in which Howe, like White's "avant-garde readers," nevertheless finds herself unable to circumscribe herself.[25] This is not to say that her poetics of confession are somehow accidental; on the contrary, she is hyper self-aware. That very awareness, I suggest, leads her to lean heavily on both the contextualizing powers of historical research and the authorizing image of the authorial self performing said research activities. The self that appears is thus literally self-as-author, in both the poetic and critical sense, as Howe candidly (even when metaphorically) addresses the ways in which the institutional structures in which she does her work allow and resist her, and in the end—paradoxically—create her.

This change over time is most strikingly apparent in *Frame Structures*, the 1996 reissue of several of Howe's earliest published works. Juxtaposed in this book are four short collections from the 1970s and a long eponymous poetic-prose introduction written specifically for the reissue that bears some significant resemblances, as Perloff has observed, to Robert Lowell's "91 Revere Street." (Lowell: "I was a churlish, disloyal, romantic boy, and quite without hero worship for my father." Howe, on going to the zoo with her own father: "I was a deep and nervous child with the north wind of the fairy story ringing in my ears.")[26] The cover of the book is illustrated with a black-and-white photograph, taken by Howe, of her first husband David von Schlegell's sculpture *Untitled Landscape* in a phase of early construction. The steel framing undergirding the massive aluminum panels is all that is visible, making the sculpture look more like the side of a yet-to-be-raised barn than the abstract sail or hull that the finished piece evokes. The title of the book and its cover art stand in heavy-handed concert, with the nakedness of unfinished art mirroring the familial and historical framing materials that undergird Howe's early work.

The major and telling difference between a poet like Howe and one like Lowell is that while Lowell turns his family into the world, Howe is more interested in turning the world into her family, hauling together China and Cape Cod in the service of a global-historical ancestry. The creation of Susan Howe, in this account, requires the careful reading and researching skills that attend a scholarly life; the creation of Robert Lowell relies more heavily on the poignant anecdotes of personality that highlight the inner brokenness of a seemingly charmed American *Bildung*. Lowell's aesthetic has, of course, found its place in the American academy—but Howe's mode is much more clearly *of* it. In the space of just under 30 pages, Howe covers her family's history and its relation to American academia and British colonialism, the dealings of John Adams (she is related to John Quincy) in transatlantic Netherlandish trade, the history of Buffalo, New York, the semi-tragic life story of Henry Wadsworth Longfellow, and a small treatise on antiquarianism and the archive. The effect is one both of intense learnedness and of intense introspection, a combination that fuses the learnedness *to* the introspection and marks them as mutually dependent. It is also an effect that will become a trademark of Howe's work in books such as *Pierce-Arrow* and especially *The Midnight*, as she settles into her position as a professional writer, researcher, and teacher.

"Frame Structures," as an introduction, makes almost no mention of the poems that follow it; it is instead a trove of what reads as "pure" information, shot through with lyricized fragments as afterthoughts or enigmatic addenda. Sentences like "in the nineteenth century *Weetamoe* was a working farm owned by gentleman farmers," for example, are immediately followed by lines such as "just think of your ear as eyes of very mirrors Weetamoo. Cinder of the lexical drift."[27] The musical fragments lend a sense of continuity between the later addition and the earlier work, but the overwhelming sense one gets from "Frame Structures" is that of careful explanation. But explanation of what? Let's take a look at "Chanting at the Crystal Sea," a long poem in which the speaker is both mythical and clinical:

> I built a house
> that faced the east
> I never ventured west
> for fear of murder.
>
> Eternity dawned.
>
> Solitary watcher
> of what rose
> and set
> I saw only
> a Golgotha
> of corpses.[28]

Clearly, the "I" in this excerpt (and from the verses surrounding it) points not back toward Howe as a person, but out toward an unnamed, almost Biblical figure (later: "I stopped my children's eyes with wool / as the angel did with Jacob") who journeys through time and space, tracing a blurred outline of the world in a surreal picture of a complete history. But the poem ends its fifteen-page run thusly:

> I see my father approaching
> from the narrow corner of some lost empire
> where the name of some great king still survives.
> He has explored other lost sites of great cities
> but that vital condition—
> the glorious success of his grand enterprise
> still eludes him.[29]

The tone softens here as the lines lengthen, and even without the preface, it might not be difficult to read this father figure as an "actual" father, the "my" in the line becoming the possessive of Howe herself. *With* the preface, however, the reader is inevitably reminded of the anecdote in which Howe's father is cornered into being the intellectual caretaker of the archive of Supreme Court Justice Oliver Wendell Holmes, the work being "a biography he may not have had time nor inclination to write."[30]

The paternal Howe died suddenly at age sixty, an early end for an academic career, and in Susan Howe's remembrance of him there is a sense that despite his immense connections—"when my father was a graduate student at Harvard Law School, he was one of a special group Professor Felix Frankfurter referred to as 'my boys'"—Mark DeWolfe Howe was nevertheless relegated to oblivion by the institution that produced him.[31] In the spring of 1985, Susan Howe's son, also named Mark, was rejected from Harvard (though he was admitted to, and subsequently attended, Yale). The decision is an ancestral slight. Writing about it in her journals, Howe laments: "massive hurt and a fear that I failed my father—or that Harvard simply forgot his life—his work—that on February 28 at 60 he was swallowed up and vanished into nothing and no-one REMEMBERS."[32] DeWolfe Howe, in this account, was both authorized and eaten by the academy, and her wish is not for her father never to have involved himself with Harvard, but rather to have won its recognition, the "glorious success" that she felt he deserved but never had.

Indeed, Howe's papers from the years before her establishment at Buffalo reveal the extent to which her emotional states were tied to her (and her loved ones') perceived success or failure within the academic system. In April of 1984, she writes "My ED [Emily Dickinson] piece was of course rejected by New Directions 'too academic' I love that. Me academic! No academic press would touch that book."[33] It's an exemplary quote: she knows she's not an academic, so the rejection is amusing (if still devastating) in its inaccuracy. At the same time, there's more than a hint of desire—desire for *My Emily Dickinson* to be in fact touchable by the academic press, desire for the New Directions rejection to be factually accurate—that lurks behind the sarcasm. (New Directions, of course, would in fact wind up publishing not only *My Emily Dickinson*, but also, to date, twelve more of her titles.) Later, as she struggles to find a permanent post at Buffalo or elsewhere, she is passed up for a time in favor of her friend and colleague Charles Bernstein, who is offered the Grey Chair in English in the spring of 1989. She writes: "I spent two long winters up there. Charles has been there and only commuting three weeks and he has the future job. Creeley's post. A great honor and well deserved—Charles will be wonderful. I would not have been nearly so good still it would have been nice to be asked."[34] The work is described as toil—long winters spent in a kind of exile, away from her husband (still at Yale). And Howe is, as ever, bitingly self-deprecating. But there is no question that Howe can also see herself in this moment being named the Grey Chair, and that if it had been offered to her, she would have accepted it not merely out of financial necessity (though money was always a part of her calculations at this time) but also because the university was the home of many of those whom she held in highest esteem—Bernstein and Creeley among them. It makes sense, in this context, to look at her work and its formulations of autobiography in terms of how they negotiate a cultural situation in which the avant-garde stays in school.

The Midnight examines the life and mourns the death of Susan Howe's mother, the Irish actress and playwright Mary Manning. Typically, however, the volume ranges through a slew of topics, including the history of bed curtains, frontispieces, and a bit of biographical material on the landscape architect Frederick Law Olmsted, wedding archival work and its various positivisms to subject matter (personal anxieties, family heirlooms, childhood memories) more often dealt with in the introspective-confessional mode. The personal, for Howe, looks something like this:

> One Sunday afternoon in the gift shop at Hartford's Wadsworth Athenaeum, wandering among the postcards, notepapers, ties, scarves, necklaces, key chains, calendars, magic markers, pens, pencils, posters, children's games, paperweights, and art books, displayed to be worshipped or acquired, my attention came to rest on a pedestrian gray paperback. I was preparing to teach a graduate seminar on what has been called "The Great Awakening" of the 1740s. This intercolonial religious revival, with its growth of an itinerant ministry and field sermons, swept through the Connecticut River Valley, then considered back country, in the wake of the arrival of the English evangelist George Whitefield in 1739 . . . and Jonathan Edwards' restrained but furious eloquence.[35]

I quote at length to draw attention to the seamlessness with which Howe moves from a musical list of objects to a course description. It's a transition that repeats itself in the sections entitled "Bed Hangings," comprised of the compact, often enigmatic rectangles of verse planted squarely in the center of the page for which Howe is known.[36] The poems in these sections generally stay well away from anything that could be called personal narrative; instead, they are presented as the fruit of academic labor, snapping quickly in tone from this:

> One of the perplexing questions
> on which the members of the Bed
> Curtain Seminar were able to
> shed very little light was that of
> how early valences attached
> to the tester frame **Technical Note**
> Other rubbish a bottomless chair[37]

To this:

> Research project the 1960
> Bed Hangings Symposium
>
> Scholar student participant
> Published papers remain
> Say flowing forces haunt
> leaving no shade patters
> Why huntress why pattern[38]

To say that a given poetic work is the product of laborious research and study is not to say much of anything; what's generically definitional about Howe's work in this connection is how the Lowell-esque moments of intimate, familial narration become another academic archive, one that is not (yet) housed under the auspices of a university but is subject to much the same technical treatment and artifactual reverence that accompanies encounters with rare books and manuscripts. Howe authorizes her own family, and thus herself, to occupy what she considers the sacred space of historical research through this transformation.

Howe's sense of self in *The Midnight* is in this way built primarily upon a kind of professional identity, one that confesses its troubled relationship to the conditions of its production and the disciplinary boundaries that contain it. In these tonal movements from "matter-of-fact"ness to a more surreal lyricism, Howe-as-archivist/theorist and Howe-as-poet meet in a clash of authoritative affects. For example: in the first "Bed Hangings" section, after a few lines in which the practicalities of nonconformist-Protestant theology are discussed—"the denomination admits no / correlative save Christ and his / apostles for the rote of ethic"—Howe begins the next rectangle of text with the lines "I am going to confine myself / beneath disguises a catalogue / of categories."[39] The facts, this juxtaposition seems to tell us, serve as the "disguises" under which the self hides, separate and inscrutable. "I come to / you," she writes, "with neither crook nor shoe / nor scrip a Presbyterian cloak though admittedly eyelet holes."[40] No shepherd of men, as it were, Howe peeks at the reader through "eyelet holes" that she has made during her study of complicated and intricately woven textiles—study that results in lyrics like the following:

> Penelope is presented as
> working a shroud for Laertes
> the father of Ulysses
>
> Cobweb gossamer ephemera
> miscellaneous bundle 34
>
> The shirt worn by William
> the Silent when he fell by
> an assassin is still preserved
> at the Hague[41]

The first stanza reads like an art analysis, the second as a fragmentary musing on an archival box, and the third a dry factual statement that masks a commentary upon what kinds of material artifacts we deem worthy of preservation in museums and other official chambers of historical memory. The "miscellaneous bundle 34," upon which the entire verse hinges, lends the lines that surround it a sense of the tempting disorganization of the archive, the sense of wading through "ephemera" that can lead to empirical, biographical, or critical discovery.

This wading is the activity that Howe shares in common with her counterparts in the academic humanities, particularly as the sense that archival work can right historical wrongs increases and broadens.[42] As she dredges up intimate details of the life of Frederick Law Olmsted and continues her recovery of the neglected (as she sees it) American pragmatist Charles Sanders Peirce, she firmly places her familial archive into the annals of bibliographic history. In the process, she treats her origins as she would the frayed manuscripts that are so precious to her, the "categories" and "catalogues" of historical research that the reader must untangle and decipher becoming the tissue of lace in which the authorial presence wraps itself. It would be an unlikely cloak for a writer truly at odds with any kind of scholarly methodology, but a much likelier one for a writer whose faith in those methodologies is made strong by persistent critique. Why bother trying to alter the face of scholarly study and poetry writing unless you think both things worthwhile enough to change?

As we've seen, while the poems that make up "Bed Hangings" give up little to no directly autobiographical detail, what they do outline is the process by which they are transformed by research performed by a situated "I":

> Surviving fragment of
> New England original
> bed hanging handsome
> cambleteen red curtain
> (1746) "a sort of fine
> worsted cambels" Camlet
> Imitation camlet scrap
> To describe Camlet I will
> look into Chambers and
> Postlethwayt[43]

Lyric play, in this selection, meshes finely with citation and dry assertion: the music of "hanging handsome / cambleteen red curtain" and the repetitive nearly to nonsense tumbling of "c" words in *cambleteen/curtain/cambels/ Camlet/camlet/Camlet/Chambers* is offset by the flatness of the author's bibliographic intentions in the last three lines. But those intentions, dry though they may be, are also telling. *The Chambers Dictionary* is a well-known and widely available text, the OED for Scrabble aficionados, but Malachy Postlethwayt's *Universal Dictionary of Trade and Commerce*, published in 1766, is a decidedly more obscure book, available nearly exclusively in university libraries. Postlethwayt's definition of "camlet" is also much longer and more detailed, and contemporaneous with the scrap of curtain that Howe describes.[44] The kind of exacting historical detail with which Howe is obsessed (and which finds its symbolic counterpart in the book's preoccupation with fine laces and fabrics) is made possible by specialist textual archiving. Her access to Postlethwayt enhances her relationship to the material object of the lace fragment. This relation and enhancement, I would argue, is metonymic of that between her familial archive and the structures of knowledge determined and delineated by academic disciplinarity.

Howe's archival explorations, then, serve as a kind of foil for the type of "rawness" that Lowell describes in his famous differentiation of "raw" and "cooked" verse.[45] The scandal of a life confessed is replaced by the authority of a life researched, or a life spent research*ing*. In this connection, Howe's exaggeration of facticity, in particular the foregrounding of fact-finding missions and the studiously dry, almost pedantic tonality so offset by lyric musings and the occasional disclosure of authorial anxiety, largely replaces the truth-claims of experiential "authenticity"—but the replacement serves not at all in this case to efface Howe's writerly subjectivity, because she relays the missions *as well as* the facts. Even when Howe's maternal line isn't under discussion (and oftentimes it isn't), the motions of research activity—"I will look into Chambers and Postlethwayt"—remain in clear view. When it is under discussion, these motions are redoubled by Howe's quest to incorporate the ephemera and marginalia of her inherited books into the larger historical networks she has spent so much time and energy studying. Autobiographical poetry in the style of Lowell or Plath depends upon the affective weight of circumstances made monstrous; in Howe's reinterpretation it relies upon the methodical exposure of the links between the individual subject and the labyrinth of historicity.

What makes *The Midnight* so compelling for a study of poetic autobiography-in-the-academy is that occasionally the fact-finding missions and the experiential rawness that they usually supplant crash into one another. This occurs on two occasions, broadly defined: during Howe's encounter with some of the research library's barriers to access, and during the long illustrative process of turning her family's bibliographic materials into an archive. These moments form especially evocative versions of the tonal shifts that mark the poles of poet and scholar in the "Bed Hangings" sections. To begin with the first: while Howe seems generally to both revere and fear major university special collections, these feelings come to a head in a section of the book entitled "*Ovaltine*," the title making an at-first bizarre connection between the malted drink and the ovalness of the "reception antechamber" at the Houghton Library's rare books collection at Harvard.[46] The significance of the title is never made clear, but Ovaltine is usually thought of as a child's drink, and if Howe feels like anything in this episode in the library, she feels like a child. Coming in at about nine pages (excluding a brief interlude on Olmsted), the section is remarkably long, given Howe's propensity to shift from topic to topic. She spends a long time, in other words, contemplating her own affective reactions to the spaces in which she works. And it is in this contemplation that Howe's poem-essay becomes most overtly confessional, revealing awkward anxieties about class position and institutional belonging that stand in sharp contrast to the authoritative statements of fact that liberally pepper the volume.

In a twist that aligns her in a way with "Program Era" creative writing, Howe uses experiential rawness and its associated authenticities to distance herself from the sites of institutionalized control to which she (nevertheless) attempts to gain access. Put shortly, she insists that she doesn't belong: the Houghton has too many doors ("two single wooden doors . . . concealing too modernist plate glass doors . . . I enter an oval vestibule, about 10 feet wide and 5-6 feet deep, before me double doors again; again plate glass"), too many guards, is too saturated with "the Institutional Gaze."[47] The entire episode revolves around a 1991 visit to view the manuscript copy of Emily Dickinson's "My Life had stood—a Loaded Gun" as well as other poems. Howe was at the time a newly minted professor, having finally secured that permanent post at Buffalo. Between her observations about the grandiosity of the building with its "ponderous glass chandeliers," her fretting about her wardrobe and her new Coach briefcase ("I wonder if I am more worried about my appearance than any of the scholars who have already made it into the Reading Room"), and finally her inability first even to open the door to the reading room and then to produce the proper credentials (a curator's note) for the librarians, "Ovaltine" seethes with a panicky self-consciousness that is sometimes difficult to read.[48]

Upon being asked by a guard (clad, improbably, in "what could be a J. Press tweed sports jacket") to produce her identification—to produce, in other words, some document that authorizes her claim to herself—she realizes that the name she goes by (*Susan Howe*) is not the name on her driver's license (*Susan von Schlegell*). She writes:

> I feel the acne rosacea on the Irish half of my nose getting worse. I am blushing, defensive, desperate, and this is only the public sector. "I am a professor at the State University of New York at Buffalo," I hastily add, hoping the word "profes-

sor" will stop him from wondering about the questionable status of SUNY Buffalo to the ivied upper ranks.[49]

This is anything but an authoritative self. She wields her credentials nervously and clumsily, repeatedly hammering home the fact that she is in but not *of* the world of Harvard's libraries and their associated class privileges. In this connection, Howe's startling forthrightness about her feelings toward her literal and figurative structural surroundings exposes the institutional ribs that undergird not only garden-variety (as it were) educational hierarchy, but also much of the historical antagonism between creative writing and literary criticism.[50]

But access to the Houghton's reading room nevertheless remains a professional necessity; between the Dickinson and the Charles Peirce manuscripts, the library contains the archival source material that will see Howe through several important books of poems. Moreover, we never learn whether or not she does get to see the Dickinson manuscript for which she came—it's possible she didn't on that trip, but readers of Howe will know for a fact that she has spent considerable time in the bowels of the library, poring over manuscripts with other archival workers. Indeed, in the time we see Howe struggling to do her work, she is recognized by one of the scholars in the reading room: "'Are you Susan Howe?' Someone at the oak table behind my back whispers my real name."[51] The woman turns out to be working on Elizabeth Prescott Spofford, an obscure "protégée of Thomas Wentworth Higginson," Dickinson's most famous correspondent. So even in this forbidding space, Howe finds colleagues, despite her emotional states' constant registering of her as an outsider.

The episode highlights the tragic absurdity of the contradictory authorizations at war in Howe's subject position: one the one hand, outsiderness is a credential in and of itself. To be pushed out of Harvard has a type of cultural capital all its own (think, for example, of the kind of mythology that attaches to a figure like Bill Gates precisely *for* dropping out of it). On the other, there is the vulnerability and loneliness: the feeling of not-belonging has no joy in it for Howe. There is no gleeful shattering of all the plate glass—she leaves that, tellingly, to Steuben glass executive and library namesake Arthur A. Houghton himself. "Houghton showed he was serious about producing a quality product by smashing every piece of glass . . . in the Steuben warehouse about one month after he assumed control."[52] The last sentence of the paragraph reads: "Emily Dickinson's heavily marked copy of Emerson's *Poems* is in the Emily Dickinson Room on the second floor in a bookcase behind locked glass."[53] Smashing glass to put up new and better glass: it protects, but it also restricts, and Howe's relationship to the institutional archive sees itself doubly reflected in this dual function.

In the end, Howe breaks the glass of the poignant familial narrative in order to put up the protective glass of archival disciplinarity, moving from the study of Dickinson to the study of her family's own bibliographic history. The vast majority of the illustrations in the book come from the books owned by her aunt, uncle, and mother, and all of the photographs are of family as well. There is plenty of poignancy in this choice of subject matter, and in the stories with which Howe chooses to enhance them, but together they do not form the tightly experiential version of subjectivity that one might expect from confessional poetry. Instead, Howe surveys her inherited materials with the contextualizing eye of the historian, allowing her uncle John Manning's copy of Robert Louis Stevenson's *The Master of Ballantrae* to become a study of Stevenson's correspondence, transforming a petty critique of her mother by one Micheál Mac Liammóir into a brief career sketch of the latter. A childhood in New England becomes indistinguishable from that of Frederick Law Olmsted. As Howe writes herself into the archive, she rewrites poetic methodologies as historicist ones, transforming both in the spirit of creative-critical interrogation that is a hallmark both of her own work and of the program she helped to establish.

This methodological crosshatching places Howe-as-author in two separate positions that are at times codependent and at times contradictory: as researcher/observer, and as owner/participant. Her handling of her aunt Louie Bennett, noted suffragette and union activist, exhibits both polarities. Some of her work on Bennett reads like a Wikipedia entry:

> After WWI she was intensely involved in the Irish labor movement and served as General Secretary of the Irish Women Workers' Union (IWWU). In 1932 she became the first woman President of the Irish Trade Union Congress (ITUC), a position she held until 1955. She died in 1956. Recently her face appeared on a 32p Irish stamp, and there is a bench dedicated to her memory in Stephen's Green.[54]

The passage is accompanied by a photo of the stamp in question, as if to add empiricism to empiricism. But Howe also fiercely defends her right to meddle with the objects she holds dear, thereby putting her own mark on the course of bibliographic history in a way that no archival scholar would dare do with materials that he or she did not own: she duct-tapes, for example, the spine of one of Bennett's childhood books. "Damage control—" she writes. "Its cover was broken. So your edict flashes daggers—so what."[55] It's an explanation and a defense that wouldn't be necessary unless the book's readers did in fact have an "edict" forbidding such tampering. As with her panicked inner monologue in the Houghton, Howe's act of rebellion takes shape under the gaze of normative institutional practices, a gaze under which Howe feels both intensely uncomfortable but also, at times, safe.

This safety stems less from the normativity of historical methodology than it does from the possibilities contained within it—that is to say, what ends empiricism can be made to serve. Howe is a firm believer in the possibility of historical truth, "naive enough," as she puts it, "to hope that the truth will out."[56] The work that she does to recover the truth of suppressed narratives, be it that of Dickinson or Peirce or Olmsted, all takes place under the auspices of the university library, the "guardian" in her mind of much of the material evidence of these figures' historical selves. To insert her own self into that archive, with duct-tape or poetry, is both blasphemous and sacred: it challenges the idea that anything can or indeed should be perfectly preserved in a past state, and it challenges the idea (eroding in this day and age) that archives are made by third parties, the arbiters of culture, long after the makers of cultural materials are gone. But it also upholds the unavoidable truth of change over time, that is, the very thing that makes the study of history possible. In Howe's mother's family, she writes, books were objects "to be held, loved, carried around, meddled with, abandoned, sometimes mutilated."[57] For Howe to avoid doing any of these things with the books in her possession would be to absent herself from the making of her own history—would erase her, as it were, from her own archive.

And so for Howe to become part of the archive, noting in careful and dry detail who inscribed her mother's copy of Yeats's *Later Poems* and then following it up with "we loved to read that one together," is both to submit to the truth of time's passing and to make a grab for timelessness. What's more, by authorizing herself (despite her misgivings) via the empirical authority of literary-historical scholarship, she adds herself, her strong-willed mother, and her activist aunt to the books—books that have, has Howe has emphasized time and again, been dominated in writing and reading by men.[58] Beneath a picture of her mother's house from an old family album, she writes, "I am assembling materials for a recurrent return somewhere."[59] Despite the lingering sense that she is some kind of uncouth archival intruder (and despite the fact that elite institutions often do very little to reassure researchers that they are not intruding), Howe sees the act of material preservation and documentation as one of the best ways to prevent the twin erosions of time and hegemony.

The marks and leavings inside her family's books—the articles pasted into her uncle John's copies of *Alice's Adventures in Wonderland* and *The Master of Ballantrae*, the homemade bookmarks still pressed inside her mother's book of Yeats—serve as a record of authentic possession, material proof of the fact of care and attention. In *The Midnight*, they share equal space with Howe's efforts to make similar records of more well-known figures: connecting Stevenson with Yeats, as if to reinforce the relation between her mother and her uncle, Howe reprints one of Yeats's editorials in *The Boston Pilot* in which he balks at Stevenson's portrayal in *Ballantrae* of a "blackguard adventurer" as an Irishman. "Mr. Stevenson is certainly wrong," Yeats writes, "in displaying him for a typical Irishman. He is really a broken-down Normal gentleman, a type found only among the gentry who make up what is called 'The English Garrison.'"[60] Yeats the poet becomes Yeats the adventure-story reader, defensive of his national heritage and what he sees as its essential character. In these moments, Howe taps into a deep desire to humanize "figures" into something more like "family." It's a desire that the archive (and its use by biographers) helps enormously to unlock and then fulfill. Frederick Law Olmsted in this account is both the designer of Central Park and a man who wrote "[m]y mother died while I was so young that I have but a tradition of memory rather than the faintest recollection of her."[61]

But this movement cuts both ways, and Howe is perhaps even more interested in making family into figures. *The Midnight* is not a book that settles for the banality of reiterating everyone's essential or quotidian humanity: instead, it thinks deeply about the authority vested in the discursive practices of academic disciplines (in this case history and literary criticism), and what kind of transformative power that authority might make available to the subjective experience of connectivity. The Manning family library, as an archive, rearranges the *extant* archive into a network of new traceable relations—between Yeats and Stevenson, Stevenson and his portraitist Girolamo Nerli, Dickinson and Spofford—and less tangible, more implied networks between Howe's self and its surroundings: Olmsted to Hartford and his mother's early death, his mother's death to Mary Manning's death, John Manning's dying to Emerson's memory loss (as told by Thomas Hardy).[62]

It also points up the strangeness of the archival researcher's obsession with marginalia, even as it defends and participates in it: at the end of the "*Ovaltine*" episode, we encounter a note from Roger E. Stoddard, former curator of the Houghton Library. We learn that at some point, the volumes in the Emily Dickinson Library were "closed . . . for further examination" due to scholars' fruitless and book-damaging searching for scribbles or notes that could be traced back to the poet. Underneath is a picture of John Manning's copy of *Alice's Adventures*, open, a single passage toward the bottom of the page noted by a vertical line in the margin. There is both no way to know for sure that that line was made by Howe's uncle, but there's also very little doubt that it was. The mark exists in a perpetual limbo, a historical Schrödinger's cat—and it is marks like these that send scholars again and again into the libraries. Hundreds of people have searched for Dickinson marginalia, and no one but Howe has searched for John Manning's—but the juxtaposition of that penciled line with the fact of all of those dogged literary historians turns the page from *Alice's Adventures* into an artifact in its own right, and implies that it shares in the sense of mystery and its promises that drive archival desire.

Through and because of all of this, Howe remains nearly constantly at work: musing on her work with Charles Peirce's microfilmed manuscripts, she writes "I am a detective, an editor, a director, a watching eye. I work in a zone of colorless absence. The original is untouchable, what I see before me, incorporeal."[63] The sentences are a pithy summation of Howe's affective relationship toward her work, work which often, to hear her tell it, consumes her.[64] On the one hand, Howe consistently positions herself as somehow kept apart from the source material that she needs; on the other, the terms with which she describes herself—detective, editor, director—are all positions of power. In the archive, Howe confronts a kind of trauma that is perhaps even more painful to confess than that involving loved ones: that is, the existential wobbling that accompanies identifying oneself with one's work. Nowhere is the link between work and self in Howe's oeuvre more present than in *The Midnight*; consequently, nowhere are the tonal swings between the discourse of historicism and of lyricism more pronounced. Both are sources of power—one holds a kind of sway over literary scholarship, the other over creative writing—but they do not rest easy when being made to share the same space.⁶⁵

For indeed, they exist as one another's controls: analytical rigor against the sentimental manipulations of memory, the empathy of experience against the depersonalizing chill of historical facts. In *The Archaeology of Knowledge*, Foucault insists upon one of the broadest but to my mind most compelling definitions of the archive: the abstract, disciplinary and terminological function that renders statements intelligible as belonging to this or that generalized field of knowledge. There exists a *"historical a priori,"* in his account, that is "not a condition of validity for judgements, but a condition of reality for statements."⁶⁶ That enunciations can be pitted against one another at all is thus a function of the archive. That we can think of ourselves as being in any sense delimited or connected—and how we register the difference between the two—is also a function of the archive. To inhabit the archive in this way, which is what she strives to do in her later works, Howe positions herself in the deep time of what might be called "geofamilial" history. What she does there, Foucault expresses as well:

> [. . .] not to awaken texts from their present sleep, and, by reciting the marks still legible on their surface, to rediscover the flash of their birth; on the contrary, its function is to follow them through their sleep, or rather to take up the related themes of sleep, oblivion, and lost origin, and to discover what mode of existence may characterize statements . . . in the density of time in which they are preserved, in which they are reactivated, and used, in which they are also—but this was not their original destiny—forgotten, and possibly even destroyed.⁶⁷

The Midnight affirms by its very title its movement through the insomniac spaces of strong affect and insatiable curiosity, gathering the lost and obscure together in a scholarly-poetic project of re-navigating the past in the present. The authority and authorization of Howe's neo-confessional self, sometimes tenuous and sometimes triumphant, emerges out of the confrontation of these academic and personal histories.

Susan Howe's work in *The Midnight* may be deeply original, but it is also in many ways archetypal, and her legacy is broad. Other writers who marry historicist with poetic work do so in ways that exhibit the markings of their particular educational milieus; their writing forms a kind of mini-network in which we can see the nuanced effects of various archival "turns" in scholarship making their way into avant-garde poetics. The following expansion into the poetry of Myung Mi Kim, Jena Osman, Christian Hawkey, and Catherine Taylor is meant to be a generous sampling of some of that network, rather than a comprehensive examination. These poets each find and then, importantly, frame themselves as participants in and producers of a documentary process involving an examination of the conditions of the work's production. From the theoretical and abstract to the magically real to the quotidian, these writers explore the work of history in a way that makes it patchwork, the seams and stitching there for the taking. Although Osman and Taylor in particular are often grouped into the category of "documentary poetics," I am making a distinction here between the form of research-based poetry that tangles with autobiography and authors such as, for an excellent and important example, M. NourbeSe Philip, whose 2008 book *Zong!* is a harrowing and insistently non-narrative retelling of the story of the eponymous slave ship, in which 150 enslaved Africans were thrown overboard in a grotesque act of insurance fraud. *Zong!*, like many works of poetry both experimental and non, is obviously a product of years of research, but Philip confines her own first-person narration to an addendum at the end that accompanies the notes. Her primary concern is not the personal labor, academic or otherwise, that went into the writing of the text. This more "impersonal" (for lack of a better term) style of documentary poetry, from Muriel Rukeyser to Mark Nowak to C. D. Wright, has of course a rich presence in the contemporary poetic landscape, but its relationship to its own modes of production is different from what we see in Howe and in the poets that follow here.

Perhaps the most subtle version of the tendency I've been describing in this chapter infuses the work of Myung Mi Kim, a writer whose career has currently come to rest at Buffalo but whose educational history includes an MA from Johns Hopkins University and an MFA in poetry from Iowa. Her time at Iowa overlapped with that of Jorie Graham; the latter secured a tenure-track position there just before Kim began her MFA in 1984. Kim's first book, *Under Flag*, was published in 1991. Her first four full-length books—*Under Flag*, *The Bounty* (1996), *Dura* (1998), and the book that will be my focus, *Commons* (2002)—all deal in a fundamental way with Kim's identity as a Korean American (she immigrated with her parents at the age of nine). They are all expressly political, and they all studiously avoid the narrative disclosure of authorial-personal detail. But *Commons* stems most obviously from the compilation of a long-standing poetic project and a dedicated "reading project," as Kim herself has put it.[68] "Those which are of foreign origin," she writes. "Those which are of forgotten sources."[69] In this meshing, questions of knowledge production and archival memory draw out a version of the personal that contains, in addition to the wavering alienation of cross-cultural identity, a sense of the work required to fully articulate that identity. That work, for Kim, involves a careful study of multiple strains of history, and *Commons* collects this work in a testament to the tenuous whole contained within the empirical fragment.

With its detached and fragmentary style, Kim's work is in many ways reminiscent of Howe's, but it is not simply this old chestnut of postmodern poetics that makes Kim a logical-seeming successor to Howe at Buffalo.[70] Like Howe, Kim moves in and out of declarative and elliptical tonalities, highlighting the tension between history's facticity and the visionary leaps of poetic speech. And like Howe, Kim uses the former as a springboard toward the latter. Kim does not share Howe's preoccupation with libraries, and so the poetic persona that develops out of these foci and topoi is a more muted version of Howe's reading-into-writing—but this lack of overt academic presence, as it were, does not diminish the sense upon reading that *Commons* builds the authority of identity out of identity's placement within (and near disappearance into) a Foucauldian version of the archive. Kim puts it thusly toward the very beginning of the book, setting the tone from the start: "The transition from the stability and absoluteness of the world's contents / to their dissolution into motions and relations."[71] The lines don't form a sentence; instead they leave "the transition" as an object of definition or scrutiny to stand on its own, without a controlling verb to tell us what its function might be. There is the distinct sense, however, that its function might be to dictate how the book is read. The book itself, in other words, details the dissolution of historical stability into "motions and relations"— a move that does not negate historicity so much as change its essential character.

The clutter of texts, quotation fragments, and fictions that follow give one the sense that the book is almost more curation than creation. In several sections entitled "Vocalise," Kim reprints bits of material from her reading project involving anatomy and dissection, particularly that of the female body. These selections range from the notes of fourteenth-century anatomist Mondino di Lucci to an anonymous account of the death of a girl from massive internal injury during the Second World War. They are arranged in chronological order, which is a kind of stability, but they are surrounded by text that contains a much more inscrutable principle of organization, even as it often shares the anatomists' dry tone: "In southwest and south-central Kansas the worst condition is plants stunted or killed off by extremely dry soil. Adding to farmers' woes are infestations of green bugs and brown wheat mites."[72] The destruction of bodies by war and natural disaster, and of female bodies by science, are brought together in *Commons* under the auspices of an ecological retelling (broadly conceived) of the history of violence and imperialism, and about the perils of viewing history as a series of discrete events. The fractured nature of Kim's poetic compilations is meant to undermine "the central organizing myth of comprehensive knowledge" even as it attempts, in its "desire for the encyclopedic," to read through to the sources of her identity as Korean, displaced, linguistically liminal, female.[73]

The concept of the self as an immutable part of "the world's contents" is in many ways the primary subject of Kim's poetic renegotiation, though it is couched in abstract terms that thwart conventional expectations of "identity writing." (In this way, her work is part of the milieu into and out of which the subjects of my fourth chapter are working.) There's no sense at all, really, of autobiographical narrative in *Commons*—what shows up is a much more generalized sense of "Koreanness," as well as the precarity of that identification in the face of the conditionality of all statements, poetic or historical. This is a feature of the vast majority of her poetry, but *Commons* has a relentless, multi-sourced feel to it that distinguishes it from her earlier work and signals a different, if still related, set of concerns about the link between personal experience and the experience of history. Experience, transmitted through statement, becomes subject to the disciplinary-archival conditions of all historical statements, and enters into their ranks on a level plane. "This is the leveling of the ground," Kim writes, in reference both to writing and to war.[74] Because of its increased overt engagement with "documentation," *Commons* shifts the frame of the personal in a slight but significant way, such that it includes the intimate anxiety surrounding the work of writing itself: "Mapping needles. Minerals and gems. Furs and lumber. Alterations through the loss or transposition of even a single syllable."[75] The imperative to "get it right," as it were, come up against the very unclear category of "right" itself. Whose history? Whose politics? Written by whom, for whom?

In a sense, *Commons* rewrites and reframes Kim's first book, *Under Flag*. War dominates both works thematically, but while *Under Flag* relies on a more face-value or semi-transparent version of experiential memory, *Commons* interrogates the concept of historical transparency itself. It is telling that one of the more popular poems from *Under Flag* is "Into Such Assembly," a poem that very directly details the alienating process of immigrating to the United States. The lines "Over there, we had a slateblue house with a flat roof where / I made many snowmen, over there" jostle against the stanza that follows it: "No, 'th,' 'th,' put your tongue against the roof of your mouth, / lean slightly against the back of the top teeth" it begins, continuing this way for a couple more lines before ending with the poignant "look in the mirror, / that's better."[76] The poem conveys the vaguely humiliating ritual of learning to speak English (and the implication that one is a "better" person after having done so) via an appeal to the *ethos* of experience and personal narrative. The experiences conveyed in *Commons* are very different, and are raw in a different way: the jumble of voices that vie for attention throughout the book give testament both to themselves but also to the authorial presence collecting, collating, and occasionally creating them whole cloth. This procedural focus shifts our attention to a slightly different facet of Kim's identity, one that is a compilation of reading and research: one that is, in her own words, an active agent in the "perpetually incomplete task of tracking what enters into the field of perception."[77]

Kim's work in *Commons* thus relies less on experience of identity than it does on the experience of *encounter*.[78] It is a slight but important distinction. The self, in this reformulation, is just as much a historian as the subject of history, a position that parallels the kind of creator/critic persona favored by institutions such as Buffalo. When the more traditionally personal enters into the work, it serves not as a window into truth so much as an occasion to turn the work back outwards toward the wide community of statements that make up any given archive. An entire page in *Commons* contains nothing but the following: "[when my father died and left me nothing] // [this is how I speak]."[79] Kim's father died suddenly when she was a teenager. Normally this is the kind of subject matter that carries deep confessional *pathos*, but Kim uses it to reiterate the inextricability of the personal from the sociopolitical ("this," i.e. *Commons,* is how she speaks about her father's death). In a move that is really only thinkable from the perspective of academic poetic experiment, *Commons* contains its own thesis statement: "*COMMONS* elides multiple sites: reading and text making, discourses and disciplines, documents and documenting. Fluctuating. Proceeding by fragment, by increment. [. . .] The meaning of becoming a historical subject."[80] It cannot be described much better than that, and it is abundantly clear that the process of becoming a historical subject, for Kim, involves the "discourses and disciplines" tasked with keeping, revising, and rewriting the history books.

Kim's use of the archive as the engine for a new kind of autobiography—rooted in academically recognizable research practices and empirical discourse—aims toward a political aesthetics of resistance to monolithic historical narrative. The work of Jena Osman, a Buffalo graduate rather than faculty member, shares some of these characteristics, while being more overtly focused on the image of the self at work. The influence of Howe in this respect is very clear. Osman graduated with her PhD in poetics from Buffalo in 1998, four years before Kim was brought on but eight years before Howe retired. Insofar as one can have avant-garde academic credentials, Osman has them: her MA is in creative writing from Brown, another hotbed of experimental literary practice.[81] Osman, as an actual student in two programs that mesh creative and critical production, is a very good example of what the system can produce when its teachers are pulled from the poetic vanguard.

Osman's work, unlike Kim's or Howe's or even Graham's, has been academically inflected from the beginning. Her first full length collection, *The Character* (1999), contains footnotes which themselves have footnotes. They're not a parody of academic style (they range from quotes by Emerson and Barthes to semi-sardonic asides such as "can we really fault the Russian director Meyerhold for not mentioning the Russian fairground, but instead placing all of his attention on French and Italian models?"[82]) so much as they are a way of reappropriating a formal trope from one genre and applying it to another, with the resulting work being recognizably poetry with distinct academic monograph undertones. Now a professor of English and creative writing at Temple, Osman's work has settled somewhere in the gap between poetry and lyric essay with hints of performance art—her latest work, *Public Figures*, involved taking pictures from the point of view of some of Philadelphia's more well-known statuary.[83] (It turns out they are often looking at trees.) In her 2010 collection *The Network*, we can see the development of an authorial persona who, in lieu of divulging details about family or heritage or childhood trauma, reveals the trace-lines of intellectual curiosity and its attendant emotional states.

The Network, like *The Midnight* and *Commons*, is about a huge range of things—as Siobhan Phillips put it in a review, "Osman uses prose, stanzas, drawings, photographs, maps, and diagrams; she cites references from history, literature, science, law, and popular culture. In the breadth of her juxtaposed investigations . . . she extends an avant-garde lineage that includes Susan Howe, Leslie Scalapino, and Lyn Hejinian."[84] It would be easy to bury the personal under heaps of information about Arctic exploring, the sugar trade, and the history of New York's financial district. But again, this is not the aim of this poetry, despite its seeming affinities with Language-based, antisubjective theory-praxes of radical collectivity. Osman's subjects are by and large separate from her personal identity: a white woman, she writes about race relations in the Philadelphia Mummers' parade, and about the intimate relationship between slavery and (disaster) capitalism. But if she "stays out" of these subjects to let her sources speak instead, she nevertheless reinscribes herself as the collector and curator of these sources, an insistent human behind the history.

The opening of *The Network* is a scene of work substitution: "A magazine asks me to invent a world. Ambivalent about my assignment, I try to skip out."[85] And skip out she does, by means of a retreat into the disciplines of etymology and philology. One of the more striking visual aspects of the book is the smattering of word trees that populate the volume, ranging from "landscape" and the Latin "paciscere" (from the infinitive *paciscor* and progenitor of, oddly, both *peace* and *propaganda*) to, in the "Financial District" section, "credit," "money," and "panic." Osman, like Howe, is interested in the relationship between the aesthetics of empiricism and of lyricism, their juxtaposition throwing each into relief as a discursive or rhetorical construct. The story that Osman is interested in telling about herself is primarily one of her role as investigator, one who, like all good researchers, returns again and again to her subject on a mission to come to some new understanding of it. The role of poet, in this connection, serves as a kind of elliptical argumentative glue: in lieu of thesis statements, transitions, and easily delineated logic, Osman strings her research findings together with lines such as:

> what's at stake in parallels
> of water below and ice above

> the private idea, the public object
> the sail and mast
> the wind and lash[86]

"What's at stake in parallels" is never stated outright, though it's made abundantly clear by the book's side-by-side arrangement of, most prominently, racism and commerce. "The public object" is both the poem/poetry and in some sense the archival record as a record of public events. It also contains the idea of "the public" as a political term. "The private idea" is thus not only a metaphor for late capitalistic privatization of the public sphere, but also the transformation that an archive undergoes when touched by a human intellect.

In the short middle section of *The Network*, entitled "The Franklin Party," Osman suddenly becomes very visible as the intellect doing the transforming. Writing about the disastrous 1845 expedition by Sir John Franklin and 129 crewmembers to the Arctic, Osman's "I" pops into the frame: "I return to the mystery of Franklin, researching the details. I meet with a dancer and a puppeteer about a possible collaboration. I outline a script . . . the project never gets off the ground."[87] The confessional, for Osman, shows up in her affective relationship to her research: the curiosity that engenders it, the frustration (as she calls it, "the lively failure") that results when it does not go as planned, the authority contained within it that is both solid and fleeting. There is a moment of colliding worlds: "After a reading I have a conversation with poet Ron Silliman. He tells me that he may be related to Sir John Franklin."[88] Silliman, he tells her in an email that she reprints, has "been mucking around in the archives . . . in an attempt to either prove or disprove the connection."[89] There isn't one, as it turns out. Osman muses on the lack:

> I dig out the notes I took years ago on the Franklin party. I think, perhaps this story is more about the empty space on which parataxis relies, rather than about facts and timelines. I know the beginning, I know the end: How do I choose to fill in the blank of the in-between? Is that choice really a free choice?[90]

The last question is in some sense rhetorical, but Osman's grappling with her own authority as a writer and scholar is very much in earnest. She maintains her love of timelines (the book is full of them, particularly in "Financial District," where each street is accompanied by a version of its history presented in linear form), but is keenly aware that no timeline can ever be complete. She tries again:

> 2003. While the U.S. makes its case for invading Iraq in the newspapers, I find myself making another attempt. I hardly touch the analogy: the brute force of the expedition, its naivete. Franklin and his men had no plans to hunt for food, no sleds, too many mouths to feed, giant ships that almost instantly locked in the ice, and particular opinions about the locals."[91]

Of course, she *has* touched the analogy, as it sits before us on the page, drawing a bright red line between seemingly disparate histories of Western imperialism. Forging these types of connections is a crucial part of the historian's task, indeed the humanist's task, and it too is never complete. Programs like Buffalo's Poetics Program are in many ways designed to make this task an inextricable part of poetic production, and its experimentations are rooted in the pushing of disciplinary boundaries. Osman's poetry, like Howe's and Kim's, stages this pushing specifically *as* one within and against the work of academic research, and her reformulation of what it means to write "personal" poetry focuses our attention on the ways in which we are implicated in and intimately entangled with proliferating historical narratives.

At the intersection of a great many characteristics that I've discussed here is the work of Catherine Taylor in *Apart* (2012), a "lyric prose" meditation on the history of South Africa and Taylor's place in it. Taylor, who is white, was born in South Africa, though she has spent most of her life (and has received nearly all of her education) in the United States. She does not have an MFA—instead, she has a PhD in English from Duke, where she wrote a dissertation entitled "Authorship On the Line: Electronic Writing and the Construction of the Author." (*Apart* is, in many ways, also a treatise on the construction of the author.) She now teaches at Ithaca College, almost exclusively in a creative writing capacity: her courses include seminars entitled Poetics, Writing Nonfiction, and Autobiography, although she used to teach classes in literature at Drake and Ohio Universities.

Apart straddles a few genres; it is like Howe's work in *The Birth-Mark* and *My Emily Dickinson* insofar as it contains and mixes elements of poetry, critical essay, and autobiography. Ugly Duckling, *Apart*'s publisher, classifies it as "Poetry/Essay." (The book is also a part of UDP's "Dossier" series, which focuses on works with "an investigative impulse.") The book is in some ways a cross between Kim's work and Osman's: like Osman, Taylor focuses her critical attention on the subject of imperialism and race relations, but like Kim, the impetus for her focus on a foreign country is her own sense of national (non-)belonging. *Apart* is the most adamantly and "traditionally" personal of all the work in this chapter; as such, it intensifies the tension between the aesthetics of individual sensibility or identity and radical collectivity that is their most prominent shared characteristic.

The epigraphs that pepper *Apart* could themselves form a small essay on the book's intellectual goals and concerns. One opening quote from Gramsci's *Prison Notebooks* reads: "The starting point of critical elaboration is the consciousness of what one really is, and is 'knowing thyself' as a product of the historical process to date which has deposited you in an infinity of traces, without leaving an inventory. Therefore, it is imperative at the outset to compile an inventory." Another, from Fredric Jameson: "The telling of the individual story and the individual experience cannot but ultimately involve the whole laborious telling of the collectivity itself." A third, from Édouard Glissant's *Poetics of Relation*: "If, thus, we allow that an aesthetics is an art of conceiving, imagining, and acting, the other of Thought [as opposed to one's thought of the Other] is the aesthetics implemented by me and by you to join the dynamics to which we are to contribute."[92] These quotes serve, as epigraphs often do, as distillations of the project of the book as a whole. In Taylor's case, as with Howe and Kim and Osman, it's a project that requires the kind of inventory that Gramsci exhorts us to make—then and only then can one fully relate one's experiences, as it is only then that one recognizes them in their utter contingency.

What makes *Apart* legible as poetry (and this is not an open and shut case; for me, the term "lyric essay" simply shifts the burden of description from the word "poetry" to the word "lyric," which I find to be a less helpful category) are in large part the juxtapositions of an immediate sensibility about "what one is," and the empirical reportage of "the historical process to date which has deposited you" into that sensibility. Those juxtapositions jar, and the associative leaps required to move between them are, bluntly, poetic: rather than telling a story or making an explicit argument, the book arranges stories and arguments such that they become an impressionistic picture of something larger than the sum of its parts.

A long section entitled "Duffer's Drift" contains, on the top half of each page, a personal narrative of Taylor's half-horrified, half-fascinated viewing of a reverse minstrel show (black dancers in whiteface) in a Cape Town club.

On the bottom half, in smaller type reminiscent of footnotes, quotes and facts such as "In *The Future of the Image*, Jacques Rancière writes of what he terms dialectical montage and symbolic montage" implicitly insert the personal narrative into a history of statements about minstrelsy, spectacle, and violence.[93] Taylor addresses the section to her partner, "A," and names it "a piece that perversely insists on keeping worlds apart."[94] Of course it does no such thing—by the end of the section, the text exhorts itself: "*make the sequence of the whole intelligible.*"[95] It doesn't quite do that either; instead, it rests somewhere in between, in the gap that poetry occupies between unknowability and positivism.

Through it all, Taylor develops an image of the authorial self in the process of creating the picture:

> I am in the Manuscripts and Archives Division of the University of Cape Town's Special Collections, reading through files documenting the work of a women's anti apartheid group, the Black Sash, whose rallies my mother attended as a student. I have been here every day for several days. I am not sure what I'm doing. I seem to be enjoying myself.[96]

The passage makes explicit the connection between archival and personal narrative that, when combined, create a dynamic and radically contextualized version of the individual in history. It also allows us to see the affective state of the person doing the research, and it's a state with which anyone who has done academic research in an archive will be familiar: the exploration is fun, but (perhaps because) we're all a little lost all the time. Interweaving the emotional matrix of intellectual curiosity with the affects of disclosure that accompany confessional poetry makes for an intense reading experience, one that is actually amplified rather than dulled by the insertion of "impersonal" factuality and empirical statement. In an important sense, the facts speak for themselves—Taylor includes whole sections of victim lists from Black Sash's records, horrifying with or without context—but in a more important one, they are illegible without sustained attention to the systemic factors implicit in their existence. What *Apart* says is that this state of affairs is also true for *persons*, and that the (re-)contextualizing work that historians, archivists, and literary critics are trained to do can radically alter the way in which we think of the speaking subject in first-person poetry.

Taylor's white South African heritage makes an apolitical look at her familial history nearly impossible (or, if not impossible, irresponsible), and so

Apart uses the discourse modes of confession and historiography toward explicitly political ends. The book candidly examines the shame, guilt, and relief of white privilege and the desperate searching among white progressives for something that will exculpate them from the sins of their race. Searching through the boxes of photos that make up part of the Black Sash archival record, Taylor writes: "I find myself looking for evidence that [my mother] did something in the face of state-based terror, looking to pull her out from the crowd, looking to excuse her from her history, and maybe me from mine. But no one is excused."[97] Shifting tone slightly into the abstract, she continues: "the archives are layered with evidence of many lives—the documented and the documenters. Sometimes, the documents are covered with disturbing personal eruptions in the margins."[98] As a documenter, Taylor focuses our (and her) attention upon the responsibility of the humanistic disciplines to orient themselves toward a self-reflexivity that itself orients toward global justice.

If that sounds hyperbolic, it may be because of the assumption that current experimental literature (particularly that produced within an academic setting, with academic methodologies) cannot in good faith speak about having a role to play in the quest for something as distant and idealistic as a kind of global egalitarianism. The historicity of the avant-garde rests on this line of thought. *Apart* challenges its readers to conceive of archival study and highly crafted autobiography as tools that can be made to serve these kinds of political ends, and if it does not aim directly at practical efficacy, it makes a forceful argument for the necessity of careful study in the creation of art with a conscience. This argument is not undialectical: for every authoritative statement of historical fact that Taylor makes, she exposes the uncertainties, contradictions, and vulnerabilities that compel her to find those facts and yet stubbornly remain after she has found them.[99] The last page of the book contains the lines "maybe nothing can be said and there's no way to say it, maybe words are to be resisted, but silence can also mean a *simple and crass morality* [shh, shh, doesn't matter, doesn't matter.]"[100] Silence, for Taylor, is (of course) not an option, but neither history nor poetry is the last word: it can merely alert us to our situatedness, and at its best, it can alter the way that we conceive of ourselves in social space.

Each of the writers discussed thus far cultivates a sense of unreality in the face of facticity through various forms of fragmentation, be they tonal or content-based or even simply grammatical. Christian Hawkey's *Ventrakl*

(2010), which will be my last because possibly strangest case study, does not share this trait. *Ventrakl* is a remarkably *un*fragmented book due to its particular strain of monomania: the book takes a long and surreal look at the life, poetry, and death of the early-twentieth-century Austrian poet Georg Trakl. *Ventrakl*'s version of elliptical styling and poetic sensibility stems from its semi-conceptual, semi-procedural backbone: it began as a translation project, à la Pound, in which the translator (Hawkey) knew none of the language (German) he was to be translating.[101] What results is a book whose 150 pages contain only 30 titled poems, only one of which is a "traditional" translation (Hawkey learned German over the course of his writing) and none of which, following Trakl, is much more than a page long. They are scattered throughout the book in ones and twos, followed always by a piece of what is best called "metatextual" material: a photograph with explanation, an "interview," or biographical or literary-critical commentary. These latter texts point to Hawkey's sources and archival research and, as with Howe and Kim and Osman and Taylor, they foreground the image of the authorial self at work.

The aim, according to Hawkey's preface, was to create something that "occur[s] at some site between our languages, texts, names, as well as between our (ghostly) bodies redoubled by the erotics of collaboration and translation."[102] The effect is less a seamless blending than an admixture full of seams, an attempted collaboration that is always already failed because of the barrier of death. Hawkey's work, too, foregrounds the affective complexity of historical research, and much of the "voice" of *Ventrakl* relies on a kind of professional earnestness (frustration, excitement, reliance on and suspicion of empiricism). But then there are the poems/"translations":

> Of course: a word, a bombed-out hut, a hut-hole
> Fluorescent gowns, emptied of fullness rise from. Vertical
>
>   birds
>   suffer
>   wind
>   less
>   ness and
>
> A bent vernacular, a hand washing a photograph
> As if water's softness alters
> Anything in time.[103]

Many are very loosely homophonic (the phrase "a bent" appears several times, presumably the result of Hawkey's encounter with *Abend*, German for "evening"), and some are procedural in a gimmicky way. Hawkey actually does shoot a book of Trakl's poems with a shotgun, for instance, and then creates a poem (most probably "Ten Holes") by dictionary-translating bits of remaining text. There is more than a bit of performative vanguardism in procedures like these, of the kind that makes many critics impulsively roll their eyes. But while *Ventrakl* might rely somewhat on the any-publicity-is-good-publicity model of experimental art, in the end the book relies relatively little on its procedural tricks and twists. Instead, *Ventrakl* is more aptly an exploration of what it might mean to document a learning process—one that is substantially different than that of the other authors in this chapter, but one that also bases its aesthetics of personal disclosure on the accumulation and dissolution of personal authority through the process of research work.

As Marjorie Perloff has noted in a review of Hawkey's work, Trakl's poems are a stark reflection of his deeply troubled and foreshortened life:

> Mystery, lyric intensity, strangeness, animism: no poet embodied these qualities more than did the early twentieth-century Austrian poet Georg Trakl. Poor, drug-addicted from an early age, and possibly involved in an incestuous union with his sister Margarete, Trakl enlisted in the army in World War I and participated in the bloody battle of Grodek on the Eastern Front.[104]

This battle would, eventually, kill him: unable to process the horror of war, Trakl took an overdose of cocaine and died at the age of twenty-seven. Hawkey's obsession with Trakl stems from the movement between closeness and distance: on the one hand, both Trakl's life and his poetry reside at an enormous remove from Hawkey's (the latter of whom graduated from the University of Massachusetts at Amherst's MFA program in poetry and now teaches at the Pratt Institute in Brooklyn). On the other, the historical and affective parallels (however inexact) between "the first machine-based war of the twentieth century" and the United States' perpetual being-at-war— "the ongoing wars in Iraq and Afghanistan"—draw Hawkey toward Trakl and add a sense of political urgency to what is otherwise a distinctly surreal aesthetic.[105] But to be able to connect himself to Trakl through a chasm of history, circumstance, and language, Hawkey needs to do some serious work. It is the work itself, rather than its fruits, that make up the meat of *Ventrakl*.

Throughout the book, Hawkey imagines multiple and repeated sites of physical confrontation between himself and Trakl, meditates extensively upon photographs and biographical information, and worries increasingly over whether any of his efforts (not the least of which include learning Trakl's language) have brought him any closer to his mysterious, troubled interlocutor:

> I could quote other writers, other biographers, such as Francis Sharp, who was, perfectly, the passive construction of biographic reportage . . .
>
> I could provide dates about [Margarethe Trakl's] life, I could provide facts.
>
> I could present these to you in a form that conveys authority, certitude:[106]

He *could* do these things, and indeed he does do them (the next page is a chronology). The subjunctive implication that he won't do them hangs over the work like a strange white lie, or an implication that "authority" and "certitude" are not what he is after—though the book would be substantially diminished in both size and scope if he had abandoned the quest for various kinds of authority (linguistic, disciplinary) at the outset. Hawkey's "more actively explanatory" mode (as Bruce Andrews has put it) of American poetic vanguardism involves this confessional vacillation between desire for and abdication of expertise.[107]

At one point, over three unbroken pages, Hawkey provides a litany of facts he has learned about Trakl over the course of his reading and archival research, prefacing each with a particularly loaded "I know":

> I know Wittgenstein professed to understand nothing of your poems. I know he also observed that their tone delighted him, that it was "the tone of true genius." I know you died in a military hospital in Krakow. I know the day you died, the month you died, the year.[108]

Toward the end of this passage, Hawkey begins to repeat the phrase "I am repeating, reinscribing the myths," emphasizing the incantatory feel of the piece and also drawing our attention to the way in which facts are pressed into the service of myth, and the way in which knowledge itself metastasizes into a mythology of legitimation.[109] What Hawkey is "reinscribing," here and in other passages that draw on translation theory, literary critical discourse ("[this line] evokes the entire tradition of 19th century European lyric poetry") and biography ("Margarethe was the last of six children in the Trakl family, born when Georg was five, and they were close friends during childhood"), is the reification (and deification) of expertise, and of the cultural currency of facts.[110] This form of the critique of positivism is unwilling to deny the necessity of an empirical grounding; Hawkey obsessively explores the details of Trakl's life not in spite of his commitment to highly oblique poetry but in fact in order to set it within a context that includes an ethics of learning.

The urgency of this contextualization is redoubled by the ethics of translation. For Hawkey to ignore Trakl's German entirely, in this post-Poundian moment, is out of the question. What remains to be asked is what purpose the German could serve that moves its place in the text beyond one of instrumentality, both in the Benjaminian sense as a fallen "*mere* sign" and as another demonstration of academic legitimacy.[111] In *Ventrakl*, the German language serves a parallel function to that of the historical and biographical information—an unfurling of the process of coming-to-know in which instrumental knowledge becomes both the goal and the byproduct. On the one hand, experimental translation writ large aims to level the ground between source and target by producing text that cannot be read as purely derivative. On the other, the deeply personal framework of *Ventrakl* disallows the tendency of that leveling to become ahistorical and abstract. It also shines a painful spotlight on the global hegemony of English, and the monoglot arrogance that it so easily inculcates among its native speakers. So despite his searching for something beyond "traditional" translation, Hawkey's monolingualism is not a proud ignorance. Foregrounding the self at work is his way of forestalling any notion that poetry, however elliptical, bears no responsibility to the contexts of its production. These contexts are multiple and overdetermined; for *Ventrakl*, they involve the ability to perform, and the authority gained by, historical research, as well as the political gesture of learning a foreign language as an Anglophone adult.

Ventrakl's final gesture—a traditional, *en face* translation of Trakl's last and arguably greatest poem, "Grodek"—reads both as a kind of triumphant signing-off and as a very odd thing for such a staunchly experimental book to do. The translation stands as a testament to the pleasures and the pitfalls of expertise's primacy on the global market of knowledge:

> [Grodek] is also a poem of witness, a poem written by a poet who experienced one of the first battles of WWI. It is a poem that only indirectly bears witness to

the poet. This witnessing takes place in the language. In fact, it is this language, the German language. It is also an event, a specific historical event. Maybe this is why the poem resists, resists translation, any form of translation. Or perhaps it demands a specific category of translation: a faithful one. It demands an attempt to be true to its truths, their traces.[112]

Like Howe, Hawkey places some amount of faith in the idea that there exists something that could be called objective truth, and that moreover, "the truth will out." Framing that possibility in terms of the personal requires a frank confrontation with the mechanisms by which truth is arbitrated. For the creative writer in the academy, the a priori truth of the personal-experiential that is a kind of disciplinary mandate for poetry writing jostles against the mandates of the humanistic disciplines (history, literature, et cetera) that require the kind of contextualization of subject matter made possible by the archive. To make these contextualizations *of* the personal, then, situates oneself as an active agent both *in* and *as* the rewriting of history. When the avant-garde stays in school, we do not simply get a watered-down experimentalism. Instead, at the crossroads of flourishing programs in creative writing and struggling but vibrant programs in literature, history, cultural studies, and more, we have an academic avant-garde: one frontier of many, perhaps, but one that is indispensable to our understanding of the ongoing conversation between poetry and the university.

Coda

Toward an Aesthetics of Disciplinarity

Optimism, as Lauren Berlant has shown us, is cruel.[1] I have tried in the preceding to make sure that my optimism regarding both poetry and the pursuit of literary studies won't be mistaken for an apologia for the university as a whole, but there is a blurriness there that is perhaps unavoidable. After all, it is the university—a structure that was built on and continues to perpetuate social and economic inequality, a structure whose response to our era of disaster capitalism has generally been to throw gasoline on the fire—that has been the longstanding home in the United States for the study of literature, history, and philosophy, and the more recent but increasingly dominant patron of literature's production. To defend a house's occupants is not to defend the house itself, of course, but neither am I persuaded by what Anna Kornbluh might call a "destituent" response to the current state of American tertiary education. That is to say that I, *with* Kornbluh, believe that the "social spaces" at the heart of any life called human need formal supports, and that the project of sustained literary inquiry is one of those spaces in need.[2] Does it need the university as such? Perhaps not. But failure to imagine a home for what we desire does a disservice to what poets and critics and poet-critics and writers and readers do best: build other worlds that test other cases, other conditions for possibility, other forms of life.

But if the problem of social and state support looms over nearly every area of basic research, the problem in some spheres is also doubly formal. What, in other words, is the form of inquiry to which this book has been pointing for all of these pages? If the university is a structure, so are disciplines, much to seemingly everyone's chagrin. I began this book with one bowdlerized keyword—"critical thinking"—and I will end it with another:

interdisciplinarity. If "critical thinking" is a term I hope to recuperate, "interdisciplinary," as the adjectival form of a phenomenon at once idealistic and cynical, is one that I don't. Jonathan Kramnick, both on his own and with Anahid Nersessian, has already effectively covered this terrain; I will briefly reprise their cogent arguments here. In short: the mistake of the idealists, which is to say those who (justly) believe that the future of knowledge production should be a communal one, is in thinking that that communality must necessarily involve a communal epistemological object—the Truth, the nature of things, etc. This way of thinking about the target of inquiry leaves them vulnerable to the cynics, usually university administrators, who think about disciplines primarily in terms of their efficiency or inefficiency in relation to satisfying market demand. (Not, it should be noted, in relation to actual resource-intensiveness: as is well known, humanistic disciplines such as English and modern languages and musicology are some of the most resource-efficient departments on campus.) Because this vulnerability will persist as long as the university remains a structure in thrall to capital, the best way to think about the relationships between disciplines is to respect their radical plurality of explanation—their form, that is, as always already contingent upon an object of inquiry irreducible to any other object.[3]

As a type of destituent thinking, then, interdisciplinarity in its current instantiation as an administrative keyword winds up privileging radical shapelessness and contingency (moving always towards that most nebulous but profitable of non-shapes, "innovation"). As dis-organization, it privileges management. To reorganize requires the articulation not of non-form but precisely of other or more forms. It also requires more cogent articulations of current forms. Although it might be said to "blur the boundaries" between creative and critical work—and this is in fact how I had framed it, narcissistically, when I began research for this project—the work examined in *The Academic Avant-Garde* does not articulate a new discipline so much as it does a newly committed sensibility regarding the study of literature. So while Kramnick and Nersessian (and, for that matter, Kornbluh), responding to a reemergent formalism in literary studies, have focused on form itself as the thing that needs, well, form, I want to spend some time here in this most speculative part of any book thinking about a smaller but to my mind no less important slice of that larger pie: the form, which is to say the constructed legibility, or indeed aesthetics, of the discipline itself.

I am as much a believer in the explanatory power of Foucault as the next critic, but he has done no favors for the idea of discipline and disciplinarity. In the place of those two words, we now read hierarchy, oppression, imprisonment. We also read power and constraint, but always with a negative valence. As microcosms of the larger educational apparatus of which they are a part, there's no doubt that to be trained in disciplines such as English or history has meant and can currently mean any of these things—to be disciplined, in other words, to uphold cultural imperialism or white supremacy. But there is no reason this must continue to be so, as myriad works of scholarship prove year on year.[4] What does any of this have to do with poetry? Poetry writing, as a discipline often thought to not be one (in keeping with the logic of individualism discussed at this study's outset), turns around and retorts to such thinking in inescapable form, in its highly concentrated constructedness. An obvious but nevertheless interesting and central paradox of the genre is its dialectical movement between freedom and constraint; this shifting duality is a fundamental reason why poetry dominates the discourse on literary form in general.[5] What I have argued in this study is that various facets of academic inquiry (and the working conditions, unevenly distributed, of that inquiry's possibility) can be widely and radically generative for poetry; what I want to reflect further upon now is the form that poetry, in reciprocal gesture, might provide to literary analysis.

I want to suggest, in other words, that considered in the aggregate, academic avant-garde poetry crystallizes the form of literary studies in a way that literary studies itself cannot. Which is not to say that the discipline doesn't already have things that everyone would agree to be formal entities. What else is the scholarly book or article? The conference presentation is a form, as is the keynote lecture. These in turn share other formal (this time largely rhetorical) qualities, cross-generically, that are often most clearly explicated in our classrooms: methodological frameworks, citation formats, argumentative signposting, lists of evidence such as the one I'm making right now. But what I think poetic explorations of reading, teaching, theorizing, and historicizing do is to render out from these other structures something like a procedural aesthetic—a sense, that is, of a sensibility or disposition towards literary studies' objects of inquiry, one even more fundamental than method and indeed out of which methodological specificity and plurality can grow.

I am returning here, in a way, to the discussion in this book's first chapter of Alvin Ward Gouldner's "culture of critical discourse"—to put it somewhat reductively, that reflexive tendency to argue that things are not as they seem. In the professional reader, this analytic impulse needn't always be "paranoid," as Eve Sedgwick would famously (rather not) have it, but it is almost always searching, questioning, building endless edifices of answers that lead to yet more questions.[6] What academic avant-garde poetry shows us is a distilled version of that culture: the form, as Louis Menand has put it, of the "hermeneutic" disciplines.[7] While this is an umbrella that includes multiple discrete disciplines defined departmentally (e.g., English, comparative literature, most of philosophy), I (unlike Menand) would define hermeneutics *itself* as a discipline, one with a plurality of objects but fundamentally different in relation to those objects than the "empirical" or "behavioral" disciplines.[8] This way of thinking about disciplinarity stretches, but only slightly, Kramnick's conception of epistemological plurality. The specific habits of mind that undergird the analysis, the "what does it mean?", of cultural production: this is the form that academic avant-garde poetry delineates.

But that delineation is not merely *reflective* or mimetic. While I have been arguing for the duration of this book that poetry such as, for example, Susan Howe's uses a type of methodology familiar to the literary critic or historian, and further that it also contains some of the deep and abiding contradictions of purpose and positionality that also characterize the work of the academic humanist, the way in which it both utilizes those methodologies and expresses those contradictions gives us an articulation of something that lies beyond any individual instantiation of either poetry or literary criticism. Projecting queries about metaphoricity, reading, knowledge transmission, and subjectivity in its theoretical and historiographical instantiations into poetic form, the academic avant-garde creates spaces in which those queries build forms of life and ways of being; it is the discipline of literary study made literature, made speculative and thoroughgoing and potentially unconfined, in the end, to current institutional forms.

In this reciprocal movement between criticism-into-literature and literature-into-criticism, we see the work of thinking—the "work[ing] of the given," the alteration or reconceptualization of extant relations—as work, precisely *in* its skepticism, that is irreducibly iterative and repetitive, inefficient, non-teleological, anti-utilitarian, endless but unalienated, communal but uncompromising in its dissatisfaction with current communalities.[9] This is work that is hard to appropriate, hard exactly to commodify, a fact that I will elaborate upon below. At least in part because of this difficulty, the conditions under which such work can be done are increasingly inaccessible and, when accessed, increasingly constrained. Insofar as it persists, however, this work of thinking in or through poetry precisely *in terms of* its disciplinary nexus, and in or through thinking's instantiations as labors of reading and writing and teaching, provides both an alternative to the scientism that sometimes inflects "experimental" art as well as a more forceful articulation of what disciplinarity in the humanities might have to offer a broader theory of post-capitalistic modes of production. The aestheticization of the literary-analytical impulse, informed by and informing other disciplines but still integral to itself, looks towards what Natalia Cecire has called a "future without modernity."[10]

One way to insist upon a different futurity is to insist upon a type of epistemological dialectics: clarity only in complication, knowledge only in unknowing. I have been suggesting that this movement becomes most visible in the convolutions of poetries that take up humanistic epistemologies as their analytic objects. As we have seen, these movements are not untroubled, the utopia is not total, the world would not be perfect if it were populated with billions of poets and English professors, or, indeed, poets who are English professors. It almost pains me to add a "but" here, so total is the general sensibility that the category "professor," in particular, is an irredeemable one. But (there it is, sorry) if the contradictions that beset academic avant-garde poetry—the tensions, evinced in its very name, between center and margin, protectedness and vulnerability, social reproduction and social transformation, preservation and revolution, what to keep and what to burn—are an important interlocutor or even analogue for the contradictions of the modern humanities, that aforementioned visibility of form will be useful for both a reckoning with these contrasting positionalities as well as a basis for locating reasons for confidence.

In this connection, take the poet and professor Nathaniel Mackey, whose book *Splay Anthem* (2006) is one of the more radically difficult works of poetry to have won the National Book Award. The two "serial poems" that make up the book are a continuation of a much longer project on the creation mythologies of the Dogon people of Mali, and according to the book's helpful explanatory introduction, "each [serial poem] is the other's twin or contagion, each entwines the other's crabbed advance. They have . . . shadowed each other from the outset, having a number of things in common, most obviously music."[11] This introduction, somewhat unusually, is written by Mackey himself. Occupying an endowed professorship of creative writing at Duke University and possessor of a PhD in English literature, Mackey is trained—one might argue predisposed—to explicate his own work in critical prose, reflexively exploring its functions of seriality, multiplicity, and importantly, that "crabbed advance": a sideways-forward, sidelong glancing, never direct, never the quickest way through. What does such a progression look like? In "Song of the Andoumboulou: 40," a figure out of the creational miasma appears. "Asked his name, he said, / 'Stra, short for Stranger.' / Sang it. Semisaid, semisung. / 'Stronjer?' I asked, semisang, / half in jest. 'Stronger,' / he / whatsaid back."[12] The transformation of "Stranger" into "Stronger" rests upon dialogic incomprehension, upon the originary figure's refusal to make himself familiar to the other. All the same, myths live in their telling, and so this portion of "Song of the Andoumboulou" goes on to admit, "Lore made of / less-than, more than he'd admit, / muse / made of wished-it-so . . . Ubiquitous / whiff had hold of our noses, / nostrils flared wide as the sky."[13] Dependent upon an ethics of both "less-than" and "more," this retelling of the Dogon story of rebirth revels in the fact that it can be "ubiquitous" and cloaked at once, a "whiff" of something that derives its strength ("stronger") in our desire, unmet, to know it.

As a repudiation of transparency that is nevertheless an engagement in dialogue, as a text whose narrative folds endlessly in on itself, refusing standard temporalities, but that nevertheless contains its own contextualizing paratext, Mackey's work in *Splay Anthem* is a creation myth on a constant search for itself. The multimodal delving into and bringing to light of "a tale told many times over, / muttered under one's breath unintended"[14] is also the recursivity of literary analysis, a production of readings. To do these things endlessly takes great effort—witness the "nostrils flared," taking in as much air as possible—but it is effort that does not look like the makework of what Jasper Bernes has called "the 24/7 of the inescapable job."[15] It is also not work that the speaker feels the need to repudiate or to feel abashed about: the anxiety surrounding the "unintended" muttering of songs sung too many times does not stem from a fear that their meaning is exhausted by all of this reading, but rather that finding the next song to sing, "braid[ing] what we'd / read and what we'd heard and what / stayed sayless," is difficult and urgent.[16] The carving out, in this case, of a diasporic Black episto-ontology is presented procedurally, as a literal journey that ends at the beginning of the next process of naming: "wanting our want to be / so / named, kept at bay as we were, / what / the matter was wasn't a question, no / ques- / tion what / it was."[17] The radically enjambed lines assert that the problem isn't "a question, no"—being "kept at bay," marginalized, is "the matter." What to do? Question everything, and take up space and time doing it. Such an inhabitation of the "center," unlike in poets such as Ashbery and Howe, is a victory, rather than a potential defeat.

We can return to Bernes in this context: if the resistant discourse of countercultural arts movements—notions of "play, fun, de-repression, intimacy, and affective intensity"—have been all-too-successfully coopted into managerial practices designed to make work endless, then we must take seriously what the aforementioned sense of endless search could entail that isn't yet another version of speedup.[18] After all, academic labor feels like an "inescapable job," just like millions of other jobs, because it exists in a system wherein any scrap of a worker's time can still somehow be used to extract value. Unlike, say, driving for Uber, academic work is indexed to a general bureaucratic sense of "productivity" that has *no object other than itself* that can be bought or sold. This has its own insidious effects in that it creates a type of market economy where one might not otherwise exist: no one, for instance, makes real money off of poetry books (or scholarly ones, for that matter). But a creative writing job's requirement that you have two published collections to even apply for an entry-level academic position (as seems increasingly to be the case at elite programs) is the grotesque re-commodification of something that has been, in the traditional economic marketplace and to come back to Leigh Claire La Berge's terminology, decommodified. It may thus seem as if we are between a rock and a hard place, that the quotidian particulars of social reproduction in the university context simply eliminate the possibility that the work done under their auspices could escape the logics of capital. Maybe this is simply true. But it doesn't help us think about what the work itself actually is or how it functions (or indeed if it can function) in itself.

Although it may seem irresponsibly ahistorical to do so, attempting to consider activities like making poetry, thinking about texts, performing humanistic research, and so on independently of their re-commodification at the hands of productivity regimes is vitally important for any vision of a democratized future both for these activities and for analogously "useless" ones. For that is the charge: that this work has no immediate utility. It is, of course, utilized within the institution for sloganeering (the "advancement of knowledge") and rankings ("high research output"), but otherwise, it doesn't do a very good job of advancing the interests of, say, global finance. Perhaps predictably at this point, I argue that this is both what is most important about it and also what characterizes it as a form. I am attempting here to "reclaim from corporate application terms integral to our disciplines' own histories," as Sarah Brouillette has argued that we must.[19] In her account, one of the most important aspects of such a reclamation rests precisely on reaffirming the "non-purposive" nature of study and art-making—not for a "study without ends, but rather study premised upon the knowledge that not all ends are capitalist ends." I'd add further that the actual struggle to articulate such an alternative set of goals can itself run counter to the instrumentalization/commodification of knowledge and creativity by institutions beholden to the demands of the marketplace.

The building and maintenance of a humanistic discipline, I am suggesting, is an activity whose constituent processes tend to resist the subsumption of time to capital. In this, as La Berge would argue, it can be said to be aesthetic.[20] Poetry's participation in these processes can enrich our understanding of poetic *and* critical labor; it brings our attention precisely to that aesthetic dimension of critical work. After all, and as I have been demonstrating throughout this study, the complex disciplinarity of academic avant-garde poetry relies quite heavily on the notion of work—but it is, crucially, work that is deeply *inefficient*. For a recent example, we can turn to the 36-poem section in Jennifer S. Cheng's *House A* (2016) wherein each poem is entitled "How to Build an American Home." The titles promise product, or at least the way to productivity (by way, not coincidentally, of immigration), but the poems deliver only the promise that such a guide can never be forthcoming: "if we could trace such a system of invisible directions," she writes in the very last fragment, "unearth an inheritance of fractures and cracks, we would know once and for all how decades have no margins, oceans do not stop."[21] The endlessness at play here is an altogether different form of circulation. The motion of the tides does not wear the ocean down but instead erodes and alters the face of the land, changing (or erasing) its "margins." The building of an American home has transformed, in a deep and knowing irony, into the slow and inexorable wearing away of solid ground.

What gets built in its place? The vast and anti-proprietary ocean of analytic language itself: the process of "trace[ing]" or "unearth[ing]" that is always, in its conditional, on the horizon. These procedures may in and of themselves be productive, in the same way that nearly any human activity can be said to be productive, but in a way that necessarily departs from the ever-increasing pace of modernity—a pace that precludes, for all but a few of us, any sustained time to think. One way to claw that time back is to insist upon a refusal to take things, especially language, at face value. In an essay entitled simply and wonderfully "No," the poet and critic Anne Boyer puts it thusly:

> "[Poetry's] flights into a wide-ranged interior are, in the world of fervid external motion, sometimes a method of standing still. Poetry is semi-popular with teenagers and revolutionaries and good at going against, saying whatever is the opposite of something else, providing nonsense for sense and sense despite the world's alarming nonsense."[22]

This description is attitudinal and procedural; it describes one of poetry's potential *habits*. The title *House A*, in this habit, is the reversal of the proprietary and individualized notion of "a house." Christian Hawkey's translation theories, as discussed in the last chapter, make nonsense out of the "sense" of traditional translation and analytical sense, in a way, out of the nonsense of the United States' endless wars. Not all poetry—certainly not even all of the poetry treated in this book—is oppositional in precisely this way. But all of what I've discussed in this study relies upon an analytical rigor derived from the study of language *as a textured, formed, and friction-forming thing*. That friction has always been produced by literary writers; indeed, it has since Shklovsky been a defining characteristic of the literary in general.[23] But in a world wherein "creative" work has been defanged in any number of ways, it is I would argue not the form of the writing (the "finding of one's voice") but the form of the reading (the interrogation of voice as such) that still maintains the frisson required to "go against," as Boyer puts it, the slick marketization of everything existing. In its rigorous reading of itself, then, academic avant-garde poetry formalizes the disciplinarity of literary inquiry as a re-formation of poetic texturality, creating a basis for poetic life that is fundamentally grounded in critical sensibilities.

Perhaps, in this final analysis, we might have a notion of "the critical" that would not sit comfortably on university homepages, or on the lips of corporate recruiters. The sensibility just mentioned, this "aesthetic of disciplinarity," involves constant and recursive questioning (often without answer), a repudiation of the hierarchy that places action above intellection, an insistence on the value, to alter and repurpose a risky phrase, of searching for searching's sake. These activities *produce* poetry and intellection, to be sure, but they continue somewhat remarkably to exist as production relatively free from direct capture by capital. It doesn't work on Instagram; it can't be put on a card, or an advertisement; it is uninteresting to mass media and not amenable to Taylorized assembly. The price of this freedom, in our current moment and system, is a sense of doom: the sense, in a world that has pressed the notion of criticality into the service of a toothless centrism, that a life of artistic or humanistic intellection will never be broadly available as a form of life, as a pursuit that allows one to live.

And for all of the things that I have just said about what academic avant-garde poetry *does* do, I want to make it clear that in the end, it does not show us a definitive way out of this conundrum. To invoke Gouldner a final time, it must be remembered that the intellectual class formation is both unsteady and contradictory, "emancipatory and elitist."[24] The freedom invoked above, and as I have suggested throughout the course of this study, is available to a vanishing few, and that scarcity is fostered not only by capital but also by class interest. Poetry cannot singlehandedly democratize that freedom. But I would be remiss if I did not end on a note that reinforces constituent potential. If this poetry does not show us a way "forward," it is because its way is circuitous, "crabbed"; it takes its time. In this laborious time-taking, academic avant-garde poetry constitutes a powerful reminder: that disciplined hermeneutics is and has a form, that the clarification of that form is a useful organizational tool. To critique a thing, from oneself to entire expressions of historiography, is to throw oneself upon the gears of language-as-usual. How many people would it take to get those gears to stop? What else, in that silence, might start to move, or to sing?

Notes

Introduction: The 500 Pound Gorilla

1. Charles Bernstein, ed., *The Politics of Poetic Form: Poetry and Public Policy* (New York: Roof Books, 1990), 157.

2. I refer here to Arnold's prescient and often very funny dissection of the merits of English vs. French literature in "The Literary Influence of Academies," in which he finds French literature (particularly poetry) lacking in the "genius" he ascribes to the English poetic tradition, but concedes that the tendency of the French to form academies dedicated to the passing on of intellectual skill and tradition concentrates "the mental aptitudes and demands which an open mind and a flexible intelligence naturally engender." Matthew Arnold, *Essays in Criticism* (London and New York: Macmillan and Co., 1906), 56.

3. Mark McGurl, *The Program Era: Postwar Fiction and the Rise of Creative Writing* (Cambridge, MA: Harvard University Press, 2009), 24.

4. Chad Harbach, ed., *MFA vs NYC: The Two Cultures of American Fiction* (New York: n + 1, 2014); see also Leslie Jamison, "'MFA vs NYC' Is Most Useful as an Explanation of How Writers Get Paid," *The New Republic*, February 27, 2014, http://www.newrepublic.com/article/116778/mfa-vs-nyc-most-useful-explanation-how-writers-get-paid. In 2016, Loren Glass edited a collection in response to McGurl's work; in the main more considered than the pieces in *n+1*, the collection contains many fine essays, a number of which take on poetry. As a series of relatively short and self-contained pieces, however, it cannot maintain a sustained analysis of any one phenomenon, even as it stands as a useful overview of possible analytic focal points. The essays most closely adjacent to my argument are Stephen Voyce's and Simon During's. Loren Glass, ed., *After the Program Era: The Past, Present, and Future of Creative Writing in the University* (Iowa City: University of Iowa Press, 2016).

5. See Christopher Kempf, *Craft Class: The Writing Workshop in American Culture* (Baltimore: Johns Hopkins University Press, 2022).

6. Anthony Reed, *Freedom Time: The Poetics and Politics of Black Experimental Writing* (Baltimore: Johns Hopkins University Press, 2014), 6.

7. Leigh Claire La Berge, *Wages Against Artwork: Decommodified Labor and the Claims of Socially Engaged Art* (Durham, NC: Duke University Press, 2019), 3.

8. There has been a recent proliferation of books that have taken up this subject, most of which owe a debt (acknowledged or otherwise) to Miya Tokumitsu's book *Do What You Love: And Other Lies About Success and Happiness*. In it, she charts the transformation of "having a job" as a concept that came tied to ideas about material security to one that has come to signify much more abstract (and much more precarious) ideas about "self-actualization" and "self-worth." Further, as she notes in a *Jacobin* article previewing the book, the "DWYL" paradigm "distracts us from the working conditions of others while validating our own choices and relieving us from obligations to all who labor, whether or not they love it."

Miya Tokumitsu, *Do What You Love: And Other Lies About Success and Happiness* (New York: Regan Arts, 2015); Miya Tokumitsu, "In the Name of Love," *Jacobin*, January 2014, https://www.jacobinmag.com/2014/01/in-the-name-of-love/. See also Sarah Jaffe, *Work Won't Love You Back: How Devotion to Our Jobs Keeps Us Exploited, Exhausted, and Alone* (New York: Bold Type Books, 2021), and Amelia Horgan, *Lost in Work: Escaping Capitalism* (London: Pluto Press, 2021).

9. La Berge, *Wages Against Artwork*, 22.

10. See La Berge, 202.

11. La Berge, 8.

12. Alan Golding is cogent on this point: "criticism of Language writing's assimilation into the academy," he writes, "rests on an impossible, ahistorical wish for an ideologically pure, uncontaminated avant-garde." In this connection, see also the preface to the collection of essays, edited by Charles Bernstein, entitled *The Politics of Poetic Form* (1989). Bernstein notes that "with no more than a couple of happy exceptions, the poets presented here are not affiliated with any university and their investigation of poetics and politics continue to be conducted without much institutional support. I find this encouraging." In 1989, Bernstein was about to take up the Gray Professorship of Poetry at SUNY Buffalo. Of the list of contributors, fully half have held university appointments. Bernstein, *The Politics of Poetic Form*, viii; Alan C. Golding, *From Outlaw to Classic: Canons in American Poetry* (Madison, WI: University of Wisconsin Press, 1995), 147.

13. Paul Mann, *Theory-Death of the Avant-Garde* (Bloomington, IN: Indiana University Press, 1991), 62.

14. Mann, 29.

15. McGurl, *The Program Era*, 12.

16. Theodore Martin, *Contemporary Drift: Genre, Historicism, and the Problem of the Present* (New York: Columbia University Press, 2017), 23.

17. Kenneth Goldsmith, *Day* (Berkeley: The Figures, 2003).

18. See Craig Dworkin and Kenneth Goldsmith, eds., *Against Expression: An Anthology of Conceptual Writing* (Evanston, IL: Northwestern University Press, 2011), xxix.

19. Kenneth Goldsmith, *Fidget* (Toronto: Coach House Books, 1994).

20. To be fair, there is no shortage of manifestoes on the part of conceptual poetry. The introduction to the anthology *Against Expression*, edited by Goldsmith and Craig Dworkin, is perhaps the most carefully thought-through statement of the movement (if it can be so called) and its attendant poetics. But to conflate criticism and manifesto would be to make a rather grave category error. In her historicization of "experimental" as terminology for poetry, Natalia Cecire has pointed up the ways in which Language poets were "heavily preoccupied ... with knowledge and knowledge-production in its dual poetic and critical projects"; this legacy of epistemological preoccupation would be to my mind what really ties Language poetry to systems of academic thought and what separates a poet like Charles Bernstein (about whom more below) from a colleague in his own department (Goldsmith). Dworkin and Goldsmith, *Against Expression*; Natalia Cecire, "Experimentalism by Contact," *Diacritics* 43, no. 1 (2015): 11, https://doi.org/10.1353/dia.2015.0003.

21. A strange and interesting exception to this characterization of conceptual poetry would be the Canadian Christian Bök's use of *scientific* methodologies to produce *The Xeno-*

text, an ongoing series of works in which Bök manipulates bacteria to produce strings of proteins "readable" as poetry—poetry that will reproduce *ad infinitum*, potentially outlasting the human race. Christian Bök, *The Xenotext: Book 1* (Toronto: Coach House Books, 2015).

22. In her book *Experimental*, Natalia Cecire does an analogous type of historicizing, arguing that writers in the late twentieth century "re-narrated" the literary forms of the modernist period in order to shape contemporary definitions of "experimental writing." Natalia Cecire, *Experimental: American Literature and the Aesthetics of Knowledge* (Baltimore: Johns Hopkins University Press, 2019).

23. Sarah Brouillette, *Literature and the Creative Economy* (Palo Alto, CA: Stanford University Press, 2014), 8.

24. Brouillette, 9.

25. A notable exception to this general rule would be Andrew Epstein's brisk essay on Language poetry in and around the academy, which was published in 2000 in *Lingua Franca*. In his mapping of the terrain, Epstein asks bluntly "what's so bad about the academy? Is it really so dangerous for poetry?"—but he is asking the question with the aim of getting a generally biographical answer. His sketch of the criticism and spats that accompanied Language poetry's settling into the academy is indispensable; my aim here, given the much larger space that I have, is both to broaden the scope of the poets under consideration and to look closely at the poetry itself. Andrew Epstein, "Verse vs. Verse," *Lingua Franca*, September 2000, 50.

26. On this latter phenomenon and its related economies, see Timothy Yu, "Instagram Poetry and Our Poetry Worlds," Poetry Foundation, April 15, 2019, https://www.poetryfoundation.org/harriet/2019/04/instagram-poetry-and-our-poetry-worlds. These forms of poetry have, in certain cases, carried over to the physical-book bestseller list: as Yu notes, in 2017, Rupi Kaur's *Milk and Honey* outsold the next most popular poetry book by a factor of 27.

27. McGurl, *The Program Era*, 49.

28. Gillian White, *Lyric Shame: The "Lyric" Subject of Contemporary American Poetry* (Cambridge, MA: Harvard University Press, 2014), 271. These are some of the last words of her book; in many ways, this volume is meant to answer her implicit call for an examination of this "hyperaware" poetry.

29. John Ashbery, *Collected Poems, 1956-1987*, ed. Mark Ford (New York: Library of America, 2008), 549.

30. I adapt the quoted phrase from John McPeck's *Critical Thinking and Education*, quoted in Tim John Moore's broadly sociological *Critical Thinking and Language*. The phrase also echoes John Dewey's "reflective thinking," by which he meant the ability to "consider in a thoughtful way the subjects that do come within the range of experience." Tim John Moore, *Critical Thinking and Language: The Challenge of Generic Skills and Disciplinary Discourses* (London; New York: Continuum, 2011), 9, 16.

31. Gayatri Chakravorty Spivak, "Thinking About the Humanities," *The St. John's Humanities Review* 6, no. 1 (2007): 102.

32. Spivak, 105.

33. Spivak, 106.

34. The most comprehensive treatment of this phenomenon, and our tendency to read a contemporary sense of the "I" backwards into older poetry, is Virginia Jackson's *Dickinson's Misery: A Theory of Lyric Reading* (Princeton, NJ: Princeton University Press, 2005).

35. Stanley Fish, *Is There a Text in This Class?* (Cambridge, MA: Harvard University Press, 1980), 335.

36. John Guillory, *Cultural Capital: The Problem of Literary Canon Formation* (Chicago: University of Chicago Press, 1993), 340.

37. Bernstein, *The Politics of Poetic Form*, 163.

38. Stuart Hall, "Cultural Studies and Its Theoretical Legacies," in *Cultural Studies*, ed. Lawrence Grossberg, Cary Nelson, and Paula Treichler (New York: Routledge, 1992), 284.

39. Hall, 286.

40. Robert Cashin Ryan, "Academy Fight Song: My University in Ruins," *Avidly*, May 8, 2019, https://avidly.lareviewofbooks.org/2019/05/08/academy-fight-song-my-university-in-ruins/.

Chapter 1. The Dream and the Deed

1. Wallace Stevens, *Letters of Wallace Stevens*, ed. Holly Stevens (Berkeley: University of California Press, 1966), 33.

2. Stevens, 26.

3. Holly Stevens, *Souvenirs and Prophecies: The Young Wallace Stevens* (New York: Knopf, 1977), 71.

4. Stevens, 71.

5. Stevens, 74.

6. Alan Filreis, "Wallace Stevens and the Strength of the Harvard Reaction," *The New England Quarterly* 58, no. 1 (1985): 32, https://doi.org/10.2307/365261. Stevens's entire curriculum is enumerated in the second chapter of *The Collected Letters*.

7. Stevens, *Letters of Wallace Stevens*, 20.

8. Frank Lentricchia, *Modernist Quartet* (Cambridge: Cambridge University Press, 1994), 5–9.

9. Lentricchia, 13.

10. There is in fact a small cottage industry dedicated to finding points of resistance in Stevens's verse. Janet McCann states it bluntly in the opening of her study of Stevens and Christianity: "Wallace Steven's poetry is about resistance." Malcolm Woodland asserts that Stevens opposes the status quo via a complicated and sometimes contradictory apocalyptic rhetoric; in the process, he runs through a list of critics who have also found the poet to be one who took surprising stances against the going political order. He does not, however, include Melita Schaum, whose essay on resistant politics in Stevens and HD makes an appearance in Bart Eeckhout's book that examines Stevens's (resistant) critical reading practices. Bart Eeckhout, *Wallace Stevens and the Limits of Reading and Writing* (Columbia, MO: University of Missouri Press, 2002), 29; Janet McCann, *Wallace Stevens Revisited: "The Celestial Possible"* (Woodbridge, CT: Twayne Publishers, 1995), ix; Malcolm Woodland, *Wallace Stevens and the Apocalyptic Mode* (Iowa City: University of Iowa Press, 2005), 6.

11. Wallace Stevens, *The Collected Poems of Wallace Stevens* (New York: Vintage, 1990), 350.

12. Eeckhout, *Wallace Stevens and the Limits of Reading and Writing*, 28.

13. Siobhan Phillips has made an argument to the contrary; regarding Stevens, she emphasizes that the routines of his "daily life support continual creative expectation." While it may be true that Stevens, like his father, appreciated the stability his job afforded, and while Phillips does recognize Stevens's own grapplings with futurity, she understates both the distance between Stevens's desire for the real and his belief that he can get to it, and the degree to which his quotidian comforts came consistently with work-related melancholy, with the wish "to read more and think more and be myself more" instead of worrying about "saving money." Siobhan Phillips, *The Poetics of the Everyday: Creative Repetition in Modern American Verse* (New York: Columbia University Press, 2009), 73; Stevens, *Letters of Wallace Stevens*, 763.

14. Srikanth Reddy, *Changing Subjects: Digressions in Modern American Poetry* (Oxford: Oxford University Press, 2012), 8–9.

15. Stevens, *The Collected Poems of Wallace Stevens*, 120.

16. Alvin Ward Gouldner, *The Future of Intellectuals and the Rise of the New Class: A Frame of Reference, Theses, Conjectures, Arguments, and an Historical Perspective on the Role of Intellectuals and Intelligentsia in the International Class Contest of the Modern Era* (New York: Seabury Press, 1979), 20. Gouldner splits this "New Class" into two main factions: humanistic intellectuals (to which faction professors belong) and the intelligentsia (whom he envisions as a kind of technocratic elite, well before Silicon Valley had anything to say about the ways in which we should live our lives). It is beyond the scope of this study to go into much detail about the ways in which Gouldner's vision of the intelligentsia in particular has or has not held up; suffice it to say that his predictions about the humanistic intellectual have been more or less accurate, particularly as regards to it eventually being (in Bourdieuian parlance) the "dominated" faction of this class field as Gouldner imagines it.

17. Gouldner, 29.

18. See Evan Kindley's work, discussed below, for an account of this phenomenon in historical (rather than discursive) terms during the somewhat understudied period of about 1930-1950. And as John Guillory has put it in an essay he wrote very shortly after the publication of *Cultural Capital*, "the 'crisis in the humanities' represents not the deliberate self-immolation of these disciplines through a process of politicization but rather the effect of their marginalization over the long term in relation to other disciplines" that better serve the needs of the extra-academic managerial class. Evan Kindley, *Poet-Critics and the Administration of Culture* (Cambridge, MA: Harvard University Press, 2017); John Guillory, "Literary Critics as Intellectuals," in *Rethinking Class: Literary Studies and Social Formations*, eds. Wai Chee Dimock and Michael T. Gilmore (New York: Columbia University Press, 1994), 114.

19. See, of course, Barbara Ehrenreich and John Ehrenreich, "The Professional-Managerial Class," *Radical America* 11, no. 2 (1977): 7–32. For a brisk, recent overview of the fate of the term, see Gabriel Winant, "Professional-Managerial Chasm," *N+1*, October 10, 2019, https://nplusonemag.com/online-only/online-only/professional-managerial-chasm/. Gouldner and the Ehrenreichs were writing almost concurrently; it is clear which theory of professionalism won out in general usage. My own sense of why this is so is that "the PMC," as it were, sticks more closely to traditional materialist theories of class formation.

20. Gouldner, *The Future of Intellectuals and the Rise of the New Class*, 48.

21. Gouldner, 45.

22. Jerome J. McGann, *The Scholar's Art: Literary Studies in a Managed World* (Chicago: University of Chicago Press, 2006), 214.

23. Charles Bernstein, *Attack of the Difficult Poems: Essays and Inventions* (Chicago: University of Chicago Press, 2011), 14; Gouldner, *The Future of Intellectuals and the Rise of the New Class*, 60.

24. Gouldner, *The Future of Intellectuals and the Rise of the New Class*, 60.

25. Marjorie Perloff, "Pound/Stevens: Whose Era?," *New Literary History* 13, no. 3 (1982): 487, 503, https://doi.org/10.2307/468795.

26. See the first chapter of Helen Vendler, *On Extended Wings: Wallace Stevens' Longer Poems* (Cambridge, MA: Harvard University Press, 1969).

27. Edward Ragg, *Wallace Stevens and the Aesthetics of Abstraction* (Cambridge: Cambridge University Press, 2010), 29.

28. Stevens, *The Collected Poems of Wallace Stevens*, 61.

29. Eeckhout, *Wallace Stevens and the Limits of Reading and Writing*, 13. See also Melita C. Schaum's earlier overview of Stevens and literary criticism, *Wallace Stevens and the Critical Schools* (Tuscaloosa, AL: University of Alabama Press, 1988).

30. Eeckhout, *Wallace Stevens and the Limits of Reading and Writing*, 20. Newcomb's study of modernism and canonicity, Eeckhout argues, favors the "extrinsic" at the expense of the "intrinsic." For better or worse a believer in dialectics, I will be attempting a synthesis of the two approaches.

31. Simon Critchley, *Things Merely Are: Philosophy in the Poetry of Wallace Stevens* (New York: Routledge, 2005), 15.

32. Stevens, *The Collected Poems of Wallace Stevens*, 94.

33. Gerald Graff emphasizes the uneasy and eventually hierarchical coexistence, particularly at older-guard schools such as Harvard, of vernacular philologists and "generalists," the latter of whom wound up teaching composition while the former produced the majority of the new "scholarship" ushered in by Daniel Coit Gilman's model at Johns Hopkins University in the late nineteenth century. Gerald Graff, *Professing Literature: An Institutional History* (Chicago: University of Chicago Press, 1987), 65–74.

34. Stevens, *The Collected Poems of Wallace Stevens*, 144.

35. Stevens, 176.

36. Stevens, 350.

37. Over the course of several letters to the editor Henry Church in the early 1940s, Stevens wrote lengthy suggestions for setting up a "Chair of Poetry" at Harvard, "to study the theory of poetry in relation to what poetry has been and in relation to what it ought to be." One of his models, albeit flawed, for who might fill such a chair was none other than George Santayana. See Stevens, *Letters of Wallace Stevens*, 376–78.

38. McDonald's *Learning to be Modern*, in addition to being an indispensable history of the relationship of Pound and Eliot to their respective collegiate years, delineates the ways in which modernism's pluralities (so, the many "modernisms" we can speak of as coexisting) stem from a refusal to choose between models of education as literally conservative or as innovative. "The recurrent problem," she notes, "has been to determine whether the

academy is, as it were, inside the culture and responsible for the maintenance of the *status quo* or outside and responsible for change." Gail McDonald, *Learning to Be Modern: Pound, Eliot, and the American University* (Oxford: Oxford University Press, 1993), 184; William Carlos Williams, *Selected Poems* (New York: New Directions Publishing, 1985), 74.

39. Perloff spends the most time outlining her version of this taxonomy in *Unoriginal Genius*. She loops Howe's work into this history by paying close attention to referential pastiche in *The Midnight*; my own analysis later in this book emphasizes the ways in which this style does not and cannot operate without the university as a scaffold. Marjorie Perloff, *Unoriginal Genius: Poetry by Other Means in the New Century* (Chicago: University of Chicago Press, 2010).

40. Susan Howe, "Vagrancy in the Park," *The Nation*, October 15, 2015, https://www.thenation.com/article/archive/vagrancy-in-the-park/.

41. Stevens, *Letters of Wallace Stevens*, 18. See also Alan Filreis, "Wallace Stevens and the Crisis of Authority," *American Literature* 56, no. 4 (December 1984): 560–78, https://doi.org/10.2307/2926156; Filreis, "Wallace Stevens and the Strength of the Harvard Reaction."

42. When it comes to writers of color, the situation is obviously different, due to exclusionary structures in higher education. Harvard, for instance, took a good 200 years to admit Black students, and nearly another century before it permitted them to reside on campus. (For an overview, see the introduction and first chapter of Werner Sollors et al., *Blacks at Harvard: A Documentary History of African-American Experience at Harvard and Radcliffe* [New York: NYU Press, 1993].) Thus, the modernism of the Harlem Renaissance, for instance, was filtered very differently through the educational apparatus. I return to this topic in the fourth chapter.

43. See Hugh Hawkins, "Charles W. Eliot, Daniel C. Gilman and the Nurture of American Scholarship," *The New England Quarterly* 39.3 (1966), 291–308, and Kipton D. Smilie, "Humanitarian and Humanistic Ideals: Charles W. Eliot, Irving Babbitt, and the American Curriculum at the Turn of the 20th Century," *Journal of Thought* 47, no. 2 (2012), 63–84: 67. Recently, Chad Wellmon and Paul Reitter have pointed out that in fact, this reform movement took its cues from similar changes underway in German universities. No less influential a figure than Friedrich Nietzsche lamented the transformation in terms strikingly similar to Santayana's, "decry[ing] an educational system given over to skills training and mock[ing] philologists as 'etymological roman candles.'" Paul Reitter and Chad Wellmon, "Permanent Crisis: The Humanities in an Age of Disenchantment," *Times Literary Supplement*, no. 5904 (May 27, 2016): 16–18.

44. Filreis, "Wallace Stevens and the Strength of the Harvard Reaction," 38.

45. Filreis, 39.

46. Taking their cue from advocates of radical pedagogy such as Paulo Freire, scholars such as Marc Bousquet, Martha Nussbaum, and Christopher Newfield have mounted monograph-length critiques against what they see as the increasing influence of free market capitalism and neoliberalism on universities, particularly ones that are nominally "public." A representative quote from Bousquet finds him describing the modern academy as a "labor system that runs primarily on a disposable faculty, and which increasingly devalues the cultural and critical work of the humanities in favor of the profitable applied research and job-training services provided to corporate capital by a technical intelligentsia." In such

an environment, it follows, students along with humanities professors become (wittingly on the part of the professors, perhaps unwittingly on the part of students) a kind of embattled underclass. Marc Bousquet, "Academic Labor and the Reflexive Turn in Literature and Cultural Studies," *College Literature* 31, no. 4 (2004): 174, https://doi.org/10.1353/lit.2004 .0051. See also Marc Bousquet, *How the University Works: Higher Education and the Low-Wage Nation* (New York: NYU Press, 2008); Christopher Newfield, *Unmaking the Public University: The Forty-Year Assault on the Middle Class* (Cambridge, MA: Harvard University Press, 2011); and Martha C. Nussbaum, *Not for Profit: Why Democracy Needs the Humanities* (Princeton, NJ: Princeton University Press, 2012).

47. Louis Menand, in *The Marketplace of Ideas*, details things differently: in his account, Eliot's liberalization of the curriculum was the harbinger of the modern general education system. Eliot, he argues, was trying to preserve the credentialing authority of the professional schools (of law and medicine) by making a bachelor's degree a prerequisite thereto, but remained committed to the bachelor's as a degree wherein students could "study subjects for the love of them." One might argue that "the system we have inherited," as Menand puts it, may be "liberalization first, then professionalization" in theory, but hardly in practice. Louis Menand, *The Marketplace of Ideas: Reform and Resistance in the American University* (New York: W. W. Norton & Company, 2010), 97.

48. See Paul Mariani, *The Whole Harmonium: The Life of Wallace Stevens* (New York: Simon and Schuster, 2016), 22–23.

49. Filreis, "Wallace Stevens and the Strength of the Harvard Reaction," 29.

50. Stevens, *The Collected Poems of Wallace Stevens*, 64.

51. From "Martial Cadenza," Stevens, 238.

52. George Santayana, ed., *The Last Puritan: A Memoir in the Form of a Novel* (Cambridge, MA: MIT Press, 1995), 187.

53. My formulation here is based on the now-classic Bourdieuian conception of culture as a space or field of positions, in which neither the field nor the positions are fixed but rather perform a kind of elaborate dance in relation to one another, shifting according to which fields the positions find themselves in. Pierre Bourdieu, *The Field of Cultural Production* (New York: Columbia University Press, 1993).

54. In an exploration of Steven's predilection for tautology and that predilection's implications for the idea of poetic autonomy, Andrew Goldstone touches upon the "boundary" that Stevens treads between more traditional linguistic sense and the radical freedom of non-referentiality. Goldstone's focus lies mostly on the ways in which Stevens's and Paul de Man's conceptions of linguistic freedom necessarily and paradoxically rest in their "relation to [their] social context"; here I am concerned with putting a finer point on that context by expanding upon the afterlife of Stevens's desire for "the autonomy of poetry within the university." Andrew Goldstone, *Fictions of Autonomy: Modernism from Wilde to de Man* (New York: Oxford University Press, 2013), 154–67.

55. Stevens, *Souvenirs and Prophecies*, 41.

56. Stevens, *The Collected Poems of Wallace Stevens*, 41.

57. Stevens, 39.

58. Stevens, 130.

59. Stevens, 130. On Ramon Fernandez's relationship to Stevens, see James Longen-

bach, *Wallace Stevens: The Plain Sense of Things* (New York: Oxford University Press, 1991), 161–62.

60. See Juliana Spahr, *Du Bois's Telegram: Literary Resistance and State Containment* (Cambridge, MA: Harvard University Press, 2018). I am trying, in general, to resist the siren song of Spahr's nihilism, persuasive as it is.

61. *Pace* David Lehman, who insists in *The Last Avant-Garde* that Language poetry cannot be avant-garde precisely because it "cannot exist outside of the university." This view, I think, is the easier one to take, as it absolves its holder of having to examine the assumptions necessarily made in choosing to view the academy as incapable of being anything other than a bastion of tradition. David Lehman, *The Last Avant-Garde: The Making of the New York School of Poets* (New York: Anchor, 1999), 370.

62. John Guillory, *Cultural Capital: The Problem of Literary Canon Formation* (Chicago: University of Chicago Press, 1993), 340.

63. Charles Bernstein, *All the Whiskey in Heaven: Selected Poems* (New York: Farrar, Straus and Giroux, 2010), 213.

64. Brian McHale, "Making (Non)Sense of Postmodernist Poetry," in *Language, Text and Context: Essays in Stylistics*, ed. Michael J. Toolan (London; New York: Routledge, 1992), 6–35.

65. The clearest account of the transition of many of the Language poets to posts at some of the nation's most elite universities is Alan Golding's *From Outlaw to Classic*. Golding slightly overstates the degree to which the academy has transformed as a result of this absorption, obscuring some of the ways in which mitigating circumstances surrounding the academic economy paved the way for such poetry's inclusion, rather than the other way around. Alan C. Golding, *From Outlaw to Classic: Canons in American Poetry* (Madison, WI: University of Wisconsin Press, 1995).

66. Bernstein, *Attack of the Difficult Poems*, 11.

67. Bernstein, 16–19, 8.

68. Andrew Epstein's summary of the relationship between Language poetry and the academy describes this culture, fittingly, as an "amorphous blob" consisting of "the academic creative writing establishment and its presses, prizes, and professors." He notes that in the 1980s, poets such as Bernstein "still prided themselves on their marginal status," but by the end of the decade, their transition into the academy (both as workers in the system and as objects of analytical work) was well underway. Andrew Epstein, "Verse vs. Verse," *Lingua Franca*, September 2000, 46, 48.

69. Tellingly, Bernstein does not link this culture *directly* to creative writing graduate programs, preferring instead to leave it as a vague formation that is aided and abetted by certain kinds of institutionalized creative practices but not necessarily the sole product thereof. In a 2003 interview with Marjorie Perloff, he even goes so far as to say that while "the problem of 'official verse culture'" remains, "creative writing programs, taken in aggregate, are more open now to alternative approaches to poetic composition." Bernstein, *Attack of the Difficult Poems*, 240.

70. See Hank Lazer's sober(ing) treatment of this subject in "American Poetry and Its Institutions," in *The Cambridge Companion to American Poetry since 1945*, ed. Jennifer Ashton (New York: Cambridge University Press, 2013), 158–72. Timothy Yu has also recently

examined this claim in light of "Instagram poetry"; he argues that such poetry—which does have mass-market appeal—exists in an almost entirely separate economy from poetry produced outside the social media platform. Timothy Yu, "Instagram Poetry and Our Poetry Worlds," Poetry Foundation, April 24, 2019, https://www.poetryfoundation.org/harriet/2019/04/instagram-poetry-and-our-poetry-worlds.

71. Marjorie Perloff, "Poetry on the Brink," *Boston Review*, June 2012, http://www.bostonreview.net/BR37.3/marjorie_perloff_poetry_lyric_reinvention.php. She then, with less concision, sketches out the formal qualities of such a poem: "[T]he poems you will read in *American Poetry Review* or similar publications will, with rare exceptions, exhibit the following characteristics: 1) irregular lines of free verse, with little or no emphasis on the construction of the line itself or on what the Russian Formalists called 'the word as such'; 2) prose syntax with lots of prepositional and parenthetical phrases, laced with graphic imagery or even extravagant metaphor (the sign of 'poeticity'); 3) the expression of a profound thought or small epiphany, usually based on a particular memory, designating the lyric speaker as a particularly sensitive person who really *feels* the pain."

72. D. G. Myers, *The Elephants Teach: Creative Writing since 1880* (Englewood Cliffs, NJ: Prentice Hall, 1996), 168.

73. See in particular his reading of Eliot's relationship to Oxbridge, a fascinating transatlantic addendum to Myers's history: "[T]he fact remains that much crucial early support for modernist literature ... did come from universities; it just didn't come from professors. In fact, it was university students who responded most avidly to modernism in its formative years. Notably it was not simply, or even primarily, modernist poetry or fiction that excited the undergraduates of the 1920s; it was modernist criticism." Kindley, *Poet-Critics and the Administration of Culture*, 56.

74. Kindley, 142.

75. Kelly Ritter and Stephanie Vanderslice, "Teaching Lore: Creative Writers and the University," *Profession*, 2005, 110.

76. Kindley, *Poet-Critics and the Administration of Culture*, 112.

77. Langdon Hammer's study of Crane, Tate, and Lowell in *Hart Crane and Allen Tate: Janus-Faced Modernism*, as well as his exploration of the contexts of Plath's writing in "Plath's Lives," are the full-fledged accounts from which my remarks here are all too quickly drawn and condensed. In particular, he emphasizes the ways in which these mid-century figures were shaped by the educational-professional systems in which they either participated (in Tate's case, later in Lowell's and Plath's), or against which they rebelled (Crane's case, but also, curiously, Lowell's—the latter's dialectical performance of the role Tate had given him as a student-mentee portrayed as the force which, paradoxically, reinforced Lowell's cultural authority). Langdon Hammer, *Hart Crane and Allen Tate: Janus-Faced Modernism* (Princeton, NJ: Princeton University Press, 1993); and Langdon Hammer, "Plath's Lives," *Representations* 75, no. 1 (August 1, 2001): 61–88, https://doi.org/10.1525/rep.2001.75.1.61.

78. Robert Lowell, *Life Studies and For the Union Dead* (New York: Farrar, Straus and Giroux, 2007), 75.

79. Frederick Seidel, "Robert Lowell, The Art of Poetry No. 3," *Paris Review*, Winter–Spring 1961, http://www.theparisreview.org/interviews/4664/the-art-of-poetry-no-3-robert-lowell.

80. See Hammer, *Hart Crane and Allen Tate*, 212–13.

81. Mark McGurl, *The Program Era: Postwar Fiction and the Rise of Creative Writing* (Cambridge, MA: Harvard University Press, 2009), 21.

82. Seidel, "Robert Lowell, The Art of Poetry No. 3."

83. Lowell, *Life Studies and For the Union Dead*, 84.

84. Indeed, Hall invokes Lowell multiple times over his long invective against "Hamburger University" and its creative issue. More generously, Kamran Javadizadeh has detailed the ways in which Lowell's sense of interiority has remained a crucial touchstone even for some of our most important experimental poets (in his case, and indeed mine, Claudia Rankine). Donald Hall, "Poetry and Ambition," Poets.org, March 9, 2005, https://www.poets.org/poetsorg/text/poetry-and-ambition; Kamran Javadizadeh, "The Atlantic Ocean Breaking on Our Heads: Claudia Rankine, Robert Lowell, and the Whiteness of the Lyric Subject," *PMLA* 134, no. 3 (May 2019): 475.

85. This position, I think, works toward addressing what Christopher Kempf has pointed out as an over-reliance on the notion of "progressive education" as the sole driver of creative writing's success. While the shift toward "personal expression" in educational contexts was doubtless integral to the development of the modern conception of the student, it's important to remember, as Kempf lucidly argues, that the notion of *workshop* (my emphasis) is driven by the notion that the "tempering of expression is the hallmark of craft practice." Christopher Kempf, *Craft Class: The Writing Workshop in American Culture* (Baltimore: Johns Hopkins University Press, 2022), 9.

86. I take this phrase from the title of Goldstone's aforementioned study; he describes the phrase as "granting the problematic status of ideas of autonomy" while "steer[ing] clear of treating those ideas as mere deceptions or delusions." Goldstone, *Fictions of Autonomy*, 8.

87. In 2015, Jon Goodwin used a range of data available from the Modern Language Association to track various trends within the academic job market in English over the course of the twentieth century; in the results, he notes unequivocally that "by the early 1970s, the job market [for tenure-track positions] had collapsed." There were seven separate panels during the 1974 MLA Convention dedicated to discussion of said collapse; department chairs had begun posting job notifications for the fact that there were no jobs (so please, they said, stop sending us your materials unrequested). Jonathan Goodwin, "Jobs of the MLA," *Jonathan Goodwin* (blog), January 10, 2015, http://jgoodwin.net/blog/jobs-of-the-mla/.

88. Paul Reitter and Chad Wellmon, *Permanent Crisis: The Humanities in a Disenchanted Age* (Chicago: University of Chicago Press, 2021).

89. "That the modern humanities have been in permanent crisis, then, stands to reason," Reitter and Wellmon argue. "They have repeatedly failed to do what has been promised of them." In this case, "what has been promised" is nothing less than "to maintain the human." On a separate note, Louis Menand makes an argument that places the demographic widening of American universities (and, by some proxy, their faculties) and the transformation of English as a discipline side by side; he does not, however, think of them as causally linked, nor does he fully develop any theory of causality between that transformation and the rhetoric of "collapse." Reitter and Wellmon, 17–18; Menand, *The Marketplace of Ideas*, 72–73.

90. Kempf, *Craft Class*, 9. Kempf wants to argue that the workshop both resists and produces these economies; I am less sanguine about the first part of that claim. Wellmon describes the notion of the humanities as threat neutralization in an interview with Len Gutkin and Merve Emre for *The Chronicle of Higher Education*: "The humanities in their modern, institutional forms function as release valves, or a safe institutional space, for talk about values, meaning-making, or ethical concerns generally within a capital-driven system [. . .] 'the humanities' aren't just a 'miracle of irrationality'; they serve a distinct institutional and social function—to keep certain kinds of questions cordoned off from the *real* knowledge work of other domains, like the natural sciences and technology." Merve Emre et al., "The Groves of Academe Are Always on Fire," *The Chronicle of Higher Education*, August 17, 2021, https://www.chronicle.com/article/the-groves-of-academe-are-always-on-fire.

91. Reitter and Wellmon, *Permanent Crisis*, 16.

92. Guillory, *Cultural Capital*, 340; Nick Mitchell and Zach Schwartz-Weinstein, "The Fantasy and Fate of Ethnic Studies in an Age of Uprisings: An Interview with Nick Mitchell," *Undercommoning*, July 13, 2016, https://undercommoning.org/nick-mitchell-interview/.

93. For an extensive history of "the instrumental university," see Ethan Schrum's eponymous book. In particular, Schrum covers the complex situation of the American university around midcentury, arguing that while the upheavals of the seventies were certainly real, "the federal research economy and the Cold War merely nourished an instrumental bent initially built on a decades-long quest for rational ordering of the modern world." Ethan Schrum, *The Instrumental University: Education in Service of the National Agenda after World War II* (Ithaca, NY: Cornell University Press, 2019).

94. Abigail Boggs and Nick Mitchell, "Critical University Studies and the Crisis Consensus," *Feminist Studies* 44, no. 2 (2018), https://doi.org/10.15767/feministstudies.44.2.0432.

95. For a brisk overview of this story, as well as a slightly contrarian take on it, see Joseph North, *Literary Criticism: A Concise Political History* (Cambridge, MA: Harvard University Press, 2017), 6–12.

96. Emre et al., "The Groves of Academe Are Always on Fire." In the conclusion to *Permanent Crisis*, Reitter and Wellmon point out that "the humanities" as a concept is also very young—"primarily an invention of American higher education between 1930 and 1950." But the study of literature and philosophy, different as it of course was, far predates "the humanities" as a concept. Reitter and Wellmon, *Permanent Crisis* (2021), 224.

97. See North, *Literary Criticism*.

98. Stevens, *The Collected Poems of Wallace Stevens*, 355.

99. Stevens, *Letters of Wallace Stevens*, 123.

100. Stevens, *The Collected Poems of Wallace Stevens*, 429.

101. Stevens, 383.

Chapter 2. Reading Ashbery Reading Ashbery

1. I borrow this chapter title formulation from David Nowell Smith's chapter entitled "Reading Heidegger Reading" in *Sounding/Silence: Martin Heidegger at the Limits of Poetics* (New York: Fordham University Press, 2013). Smith's interests in embedded theories of reading and the relationship between poetry and thinking mirror my own.

In 1976, *Self-Portrait in a Convex Mirror* won three of the most prestigious awards that can be bestowed upon a book of poetry: the Pulitzer Prize, the National Book Award, and the National Book Critic's Circle Award. *Houseboat Days* was a finalist for the NBCC award in poetry.

2. John Ashbery, *Collected Poems, 1956-1987*, ed. Mark Ford (New York: Library of America, 2008), 499–500.

3. Susan Schultz, in her introduction to *The Tribe of John*, calls it the "Ashbery industry." Susan M. Schultz, ed., *The Tribe of John: Ashbery and Contemporary Poetry* (Tuscaloosa, AL: University of Alabama Press, 1995).

4. John Ashbery, *Other Traditions*, Charles Eliot Norton Lectures (Cambridge, MA: Harvard University Press, 2000), 1.

5. Ashbery, 1–2.

6. Theodor W. Adorno, *Aesthetic Theory*, ed. Gretel Adorno and Rolf Tiedemann, trans. Robert Hullot-Kentor (Minneapolis, MN: University of Minnesota Press, 1997), 2.

7. Andrew Epstein, *Beautiful Enemies: Friendship and Postwar American Poetry* (Oxford: Oxford University Press, 2006), 129.

8. Epstein, 162. See also Vernon Shetley, who posits Ashbery's "image of the authentic artist" as "not so much one who is on the outside or the margin but one who is *between*, who resists the dogmatisms of both the vanguard and the establishment." Vernon Lionel Shetley, *After the Death of Poetry: Poet and Audience in Contemporary America* (Durham, NC: Duke University Press, 1993), 106.

9. Nick Lolordo, "Charting the Flow: Positioning John Ashbery," *Contemporary Literature* 42, no. 4 (December 2001): 772, https://doi.org/10.2307/1209052.

10. Karin Roffman, *The Songs We Know Best: John Ashbery's Early Life* (Farrar, Straus and Giroux, 2017), 100, 121; and Jesse Zuba, *The First Book: Twentieth-Century Poetic Careers in America* (Princeton University Press, 2015), 108–9. See also Karin Roffman, "The Art of Self-Education in John Ashbery's Childhood Diaries," *Raritan* 30, no. 4 (Spring 2011): 94–116.

11. John Ashbery, *Reported Sightings: Art Chronicles, 1957-1987*, ed. David Bergman (New York: Knopf, 1989), xvii, http://archive.org/details/reportedsighting00ashb.

12. Ashbery, xvii.

13. Ashbery, xvii.

14. Ashbery, *Other Traditions*, 11.

15. Bonnie Costello, "John Ashbery and the Idea of the Reader," *Contemporary Literature* 23, no. 4 (1982): 493, https://doi.org/10.2307/1207945.

16. Daniel Cottom, "'Getting It': Ashbery and the Avant-Garde of Everyday Language," *SubStance* 23, no. 1 (January 1994): 14–16, https://doi.org/10.2307/3684790. Cottom's reading is a slightly cynical precursor to Christopher Nealon's excellent study of Ashbery's tendency to "wander away" from politics and spectacle—Nealon reads this apoliticality as an active and deliberate attempt to locate poetry in a haven-like space away from capitalist accumulation. Christopher S. Nealon, *The Matter of Capital: Poetry and Crisis in the American Century* (Cambridge, MA: Harvard University Press, 2011), 73–106.

17. Zuba, *The First Book*, 110.

18. Vernon Shetley qtd. in Zuba, *The First Book*.

19. Cf. Marjorie Perloff, "Normalizing John Ashbery," Electronic Poetry Center, 1998, http://epc.buffalo.edu/authors/perloff/ashbery.html.

20. Mei-mei Berssenbrugge, *I Love Artists: New and Selected Poems* (Berkeley, CA: University of California Press, 2006), 54.

21. Alvin Ward Gouldner, *The Future of Intellectuals and the Rise of the New Class: A Frame of Reference, Theses, Conjectures, Arguments, and an Historical Perspective on the Role of Intellectuals and Intelligentsia in the International Class Contest of the Modern Era* (New York: Seabury Press, 1979), 28, 59. See also his performance of his own call for a "sociology of sociology," particularly his discussion of "Academic Sociology" in *The Coming Crisis*. His description of its ability to maintain "genuine openness to intellectual novelty and . . . amnesia about its own heritage" presages, in a way, what he will say nine years later about intellectuals writ large. Alvin Ward Gouldner, *The Coming Crisis of Western Sociology* (New York: Basic Books, 1970), 160.

22. See Larson's *The Rise of Professionalism*, which effectively traces the development of the meritocratic social imaginary of the school—her analysis strongly echoes Bourdieu's in *The Field of Cultural Production* in its identification of an economic world (albeit slowly) reversed. Larson's is a broader and more America-centric analysis of the cultural position of the educated, particularly the struggle of the new professional class to balance contrary desires: that of preserving an elite status and that of democratizing the access to "social status" that education suddenly afforded. Magali Sarfatti Larson, *The Rise of Professionalism: A Sociological Analysis* (Berkeley: University of California Press, 1977), 149; Pierre Bourdieu, *The Field of Cultural Production: Essays on Art and Literature* (Cambridge, England: Polity Press, 1993). For a particularly elegant account of close reading's "genealogy," see Julie Orlemanski, "Hermeneutic Construction," Stanford ARCADE, March 16, 2015, http://arcade.stanford.edu/content/hermeneutic-construction.

23. Gouldner, *The Future of Intellectuals and the Rise of the New Class*, 65.

24. Ashbery, *Other Traditions*, 6.

25. Jasper Bernes, "John Ashbery's Free Indirect Labor," *Modern Language Quarterly* 74, no. 4 (December 2013): 519, https://doi.org/10.1215/00267929-2345154.

26. John Ashbery and Jarrett Earnest, "JOHN ASHBERY with Jarrett Earnest," *The Brooklyn Rail*, May 3, 2016, http://www.brooklynrail.org/2016/05/art/john-ashbery-with-jarrett-earnest.

27. Ashbery and Earnest. There's a way in which Ashbery's nonchalance about literary critics—which he emphasizes enough in interviews to make it seem like a kind of effort—is related to his poetics of walking or wandering away, as Christopher Nealon has described it in "John Ashbery's Optional Apocalypse." Nealon, *The Matter of Capital*.

28. See, of course, Bruno Latour, "Why Has Critique Run out of Steam? From Matters of Fact to Matters of Concern," *Critical Inquiry* 30, no. 2 (2004): 225–48, https://doi.org/10.1086/421123, and also Rita Felski, *The Limits of Critique* (Chicago: University of Chicago Press, 2015); Rita Felski, "After Suspicion," *Profession*, 2009, 28–34.

29. Mitchum Huehls, *After Critique: Twenty-First-Century Fiction in a Neoliberal Age* (Oxford: Oxford University Press, 2016), 8.

30. Elaine Auyoung, "What We Mean by Reading," *New Literary History* 51, no. 1 (2020): 111.

31. Auyoung, 94; Jonathan Kramnick, "Criticism and Truth," *Critical Inquiry* 47, no. 2 (December 22, 2020): 218–40, https://doi.org/10.1086/712118.

32. Cf. Paul Grimstad's claim that "discourse" can be defined as "just those interpretive mental acts that are the end and object of scholarship in the humanities" and then (or thus) that "human persons [are] *constituently* discursive." Paul Grimstad, "Against Research: Literary Studies and the Trouble with Discourse," *American Literary History* 26, no. 4 (2014): 650.

33. Roffman, *The Songs We Know Best*, 182–84.

34. See Susan M. Schultz, "'Returning to Bloom': John Ashbery's Critique of Harold Bloom," *Contemporary Literature* 37, no. 1 (1996): 35, https://doi.org/10.2307/1208749. Schultz is eager to separate Bloom and Ashbery, reading *Flow Chart* as a sustained attempt to get out from under Bloom's reading of him.

35. For this notion, my gratitude goes to Evan Kindley.

36. John Ashbery and Vasilis Papageorgiou, "Interview with John Ashbery," *Chromata*, October 22, 2006, https://chromatachromata.com/interview-with-john-ashbery/.

37. Ashbery, *Reported Sightings*, 392–93.

38. Paul Breslin, "Warpless and Woofless Subtleties," *Poetry* 137, no. 1 (1980): 50, https://doi.org/10.2307/20594000.

39. Claude Rawson, "A Poet in the Postmodern Playground," *Times Literary Supplement*, July 4, 1986, 723.

40. David Shapiro, *John Ashbery: An Introduction to the Poetry* (New York: Columbia University Press, 1979), 10–11.

41. Cf. Paul Grimstad, "Is 'Against Theory' a Pragmatism?," *The Minnesota Review* 70 (2008), http://www.theminnesotareview.org/journal/ns70/grimstad.shtml.

42. Schultz makes a similar point regarding Ashbery's concerns about his relationship to tradition and the canon. Namely, she argues that in the very discursive *Three Poems*, "the speaker . . . places himself inside and outside of the game, participating in a spectacle in which he also plays a central role. It becomes impossible to fetishize a self that cannot be extricated from its situation either as participant/poet or spectator/critic, or so Ashbery seems to hope." Schultz, "Returning to Bloom," 36.

43. Ashbery, *Collected Poems*, 503.

44. Cf. Bernes on Ashbery's "identifi[cation] with a pastoral poetry of leisure, refusal, and distancing" Bernes, "John Ashbery's Free Indirect Labor," 537.

45. Ashbery, *Collected Poems*, 497.

46. Ashbery, 505.

47. Its first reprinting seems to have appeared in the June 1707 issue of *Muses Mercury*, a short-lived but popular magazine. It was later anthologized in Thomas Percy's *Reliques of Ancient English Poetry*. "The Nut-Brown Maid," *The Muses Mercury, or, Monthly Miscellany* 1, no. 6 (June 1707): 134–39; Thomas Percy, *Reliques of Ancient English Poetry: Consisting of Old Heroic Ballads, Songs, and Other Pieces of Our Earlier Poets, (Chiefly of the Lyric Kind): Together with Some Few of Later Date* (London: Printed for J. Dodsley in Pall-Mall, 1765).

48. Ashbery, *Collected Poems*, 537.

49. Ashbery, 538, 540.

50. David Herd, *John Ashbery and American Poetry* (Manchester: Manchester University Press, 2000), 173–74.

51. JP O'Malley and John Ashbery, "Interview with Poet John Ashbery," *Christian Sci-*

ence Monitor, April 15, 2013, http://www.csmonitor.com/Books/chapter-and-verse/2013/0415/Interview-with-poet-John-Ashbery.

52. See also Walter Benjamin, *Selected Writings*, ed. Marcus Paul Bullock and Michael William Jennings, vol. 1, 4 vols. (Cambridge, MA: Belknap Press, 1996).

53. O'Malley and Ashbery, "Interview with Poet John Ashbery."

54. As the poet Michael Robbins has put it, "form grounds us in a community, however attenuated or virtual." Michael Robbins, "Equipment for Living," The Poetry Foundation, April 1, 2015, //www.poetryfoundation.org/poetrymagazine/articles/detail/70208.

55. Whether or not poets such as Pound, Eliot, and Stevens managed to actually accomplish this break is another question. Altieri, for his part, thinks that they do; Modernist abstractions in his view "jettison" the Romantic vision of "how the individual psyche finds itself empowered to proclaim its freedom" precisely *through* a "richer self-consciousness" that is capable, as in Stevens, of disclosing the most "fundamental and *transpersonal* properties" of the intellect (my emphasis). In his discussion of the pervasive and dialectical power of abstract techniques in Modernist poetry, Altieri also breaks down the division between aesthetic legacies in Ashbery: by foregrounding various strains of abstract self-reflexivity, we can see how Vendler's claim for a romantic, Stevensian lineage and Perloff's claim for a more strenuously formal and oppositional Poundian one are, ultimately, merely two pieces of a larger puzzle. Charles Altieri, *Painterly Abstraction in Modernist American Poetry: The Contemporaneity of Modernism* (Cambridge: Cambridge University Press, 1989), 57–128; Marjorie Perloff, *The Poetics of Indeterminacy: Rimbaud to Cage* (Evanston, IL: Northwestern University Press, 1999); and Helen Vendler, *The Music of What Happens: Poems, Poets, Critics* (Cambridge, MA: Harvard University Press, 1988). For an overview of the critical history of the Pound/Stevens debates, albeit one that stops in 1982 and tips heavily in Pound's favor, see Marjorie Perloff, "Pound/Stevens: Whose Era?," *New Literary History* 13, no. 3 (1982): 485–514, https://doi.org/10.2307/468795.

56. Ashbery, *Collected Poems*, 543.

57. Ashbery, 547.

58. Ashbery, 545.

59. Ashbery, 547.

60. Ashbery, 547.

61. Evan Kindley, "Big Criticism," *Critical Inquiry* 38, no. 1 (2011): 92, https://doi.org/10.1086/661644.

62. See Kindley's references to Terry Eagleton, Luc Boltanski, and Laurent Thévenot in notes 44 and 45, particularly his summation of the relationship between justification's social "embeddedness" (as an activity) and its intellectualism (in its tone). Kindley, 94–95.

63. In "Society," the long and final complete section of *Aesthetic Theory*, Adorno offers a generalized analysis of this situation that is broadly applicable. The artwork, in accordance with the broader frame of the entire book, navigates the difficult channel between its "social production" (and thus its immanent commodification) and the rejection of "every semblance of existing for society," recognizing always that its autonomy is itself socially produced. *Aesthetic Theory*, 236–38.

64. Ashbery, *Collected Poems*, 538.

65. The actual beginning of the poem "Litany" stars with an even stronger declaration

of the dialectic between the accessible and the inaccessible: one column could not be plainer, enjoying "toast" and "going to church" and "having wine and cheese," while the other muses that *"this must be a hole/Of cloud/Mandate or trap,"* a *"haze"* that covers over *"whatever/ Could be happening/Behind tall hedges/Of dark, lissome knowledge."* Ashbery, 555.

66. Ashbery, 538.

67. Graff uses this term in his discussion of the mechanisms of the literary humanities' self-perpetuation, first by New Criticism and then by Theory: he is critical of the "routinization" spiral in which these reading methodologies participate, but goes on to say that "if this account seems too pessimistic, it should also be noted that . . . these very tendencies have generated their own self-critique, a theoretical awareness of themselves," an awareness which he deems "promising." Gerald Graff, *Professing Literature: An Institutional History* (Chicago: University of Chicago Press, 1987), 242.

68. One of the best explanations of this phenomenon can be found in Keston Sutherland's *Stupefaction*, particularly in Chapter 2, "Wrong Poetry." Sutherland's argument, made mostly via Adorno's *Minima Moralia*, is that radical poetry insists on creating a feeling of "being wrong" in order to first identify the bourgeois philistine and then to disabuse him of any lingering effects of *das Rechtbehaltenwollen*. This stance does not precisely define the kind of poetry that the poets in this study write (indeed, their poetry is relatively non-confrontational in this regard) but their poetics of deflection and self-interrogation certainly make it difficult for a non-specialist reader to feel as if she is "getting it right." Keston Sutherland, *Stupefaction: A Radical Anatomy of Phantoms* (London: Seagull Books, 2011).

69. Adorno, *Aesthetic Theory*, 1.

70. Adorno, 35.

71. Adorno, 121–24.

72. Adorno is here actually quoting Benjamin, in one of the many palpably tense overlaps between their theories and worldviews. Adorno, 205.

73. Ashbery, *Collected Poems*, 540.

74. Shapiro, *John Ashbery*, 1.

75. Adorno, *Aesthetic Theory*, 229.

76. Ashbery, *Collected Poems*, 570.

77. Cf. Shetley, *After the Death of Poetry*, 111–17.

78. Ashbery, *Collected Poems*, 543.

79. I do not mean here to conflate the directionality of this statement with some notion, necessarily, of "progress," particularly given Ashbery's modernist lineage. Though as Charles Altieri points out, modernism's antihistoricism can be usefully reread precisely in terms of its abstraction, as a turn toward the delineation of the more general labor practices that constitute the broader field of creative (and here I would add intellectual) activity. The generality on display here, then, becomes as in Stevens a "experimental means of freeing individual expressive energies from the temptation to cast that individuality in specular autobiographical terms." Altieri, *Painterly Abstraction in Modernist American Poetry*, 13–37, 388–89.

80. Breslin, "Warpless and Woofless Subtleties," 46; Dana Yeaton, "Compliments of A Friend: A Review of John Ashbery's *As We Know*," *The American Poetry Review* 10, no. 1 (January 1981): 34–36, https://doi.org/10.2307/27776637, 34.

81. See John Keeling's 1992 essay entitled "The Moment Unravels," in which he takes Ashbery's dialectic in stride, strangely, as something that can be neatly assimilated into the poem's various affective states, all of which come together to form a series of mementos: "at this point in section I it has become obvious that we have been following the poet (part of the time) as he has been flipping through a scrapbook or photo album." John Keeling, "The Moment Unravels: Reading John Ashbery's 'Litany,'" *Twentieth Century Literature* 38, no. 2 (1992): 133, https://doi.org/10.2307/441615.

82. Ann Lauterbach, "What We Know as We Know It: Reading 'Litany' with JA," *Conjunctions* 49 (2007), http://www.conjunctions.com/archive.htm.

83. Ashbery, *Collected Poems*, 550.

84. Ashbery, 565.

85. Ashbery, 564–65.

86. Ashbery, 579.

87. Ashbery, 556.

88. Ashbery, 599.

89. Writing in *The American Poetry Review* in 1979, Jonathan Holden summarizes this poetic strategy, linking it as many others have to the aesthetic ideals of Abstract Expressionism: it is "the assumption that a work of art can present to us a *gestalt* which is recognizable without reference to a specific context, which can be general yet feel specific." Jonathan Holden, "Syntax and the Poetry of John Ashbery," *The American Poetry Review* 8, no. 4 (1979): 38, https://doi.org/10.2307/27776249. See also Jonathan Holden, "The Abstract Image: The Return of Abstract Statement in Contemporary American Poetry," *New England Review (1978-1982)* 3, no. 3 (April 1981): 435–49, https://doi.org/10.2307/40355411.

90. Ashbery, *Collected Poems*, 598.

91. Ashbery, 601.

92. Ashbery, 601.

93. See again Christopher Nealon's theses on Ashbery's propensity to "wander away" from things. Nealon, *The Matter of Capital*.

94. Adorno, *Aesthetic Theory*, 340.

95. Ashbery, *Collected Poems*, 601.

96. See, in particular, Bourdieu's reading of Flaubert, in which Flaubert's relentless attention to the fact of mundaneness—his desire to "write well about mediocrity"—is framed as the product of a confluence of social and economic forces to which Flaubert was subject. The radical contextualization that Bourdieu practices in this reading is incredibly appealing, particularly to one's sense that modernist dreams of autonomy were simply that. But there are reasons to take dreams seriously, particularly in those analytical cases where the focus is on art's imprint on history, rather than the other way around. Bourdieu, *The Field of Cultural Production*, 204.

97. Ashbery, *Collected Poems*, 601.

98. Ashbery, 601.

99. Ashbery, 601–3.

100. Gouldner, *The Future of Intellectuals and the Rise of the New Class*, 39.

101. Gouldner, *The Coming Crisis of Western Sociology*, 488.

102. Ashbery, *Collected Poems*, 603.
103. Ashbery, 603.
104. Ashbery, 603.
105. See Adorno, *Aesthetic Theory*, 128.
106. Ashbery, *Collected Poems*, 605.
107. Ashbery, 605–7.
108. John Keats, "On the Grasshopper and Cricket." In *Poetical Works* (London: Macmillan, 1884). Ashbery, 607.
109. Ashbery, 607.
110. See Mei-mei Berssenbrugge and Laura Hinton, "Three Conversations with Mei-mei Berssenbrugge, 2003," *Jacket Magazine*, April 2005, http://jacketmagazine.com/27/hint-bers.html.
111. As an undergraduate at Reed College, Berssenbrugge was required to turn in an analytic senior thesis, but she "had a mental block against expository writing. So [she] submitted some poems to Michael Harper for a creative thesis." But her "block" against expository writing had nothing to do with exposition per se; she later developed an interest in a poetic style that is, as she says, "'like' expository" prose—though some might quibble with her further characterization of it as "direct and clear." Berssenbrugge and Hinton.
112. Berssenbrugge, *I Love Artists*, 45–46.
113. I refer, here, to Ngai's work in affect studies, where her accounts of various "ugly feelings"—anxiety, envy, paranoia, and others—have been hugely influential in literary studies. See Sianne Ngai, *Ugly Feelings* (Cambridge, MA: Harvard University Press, 2009).
114. Berssenbrugge, *I Love Artists*, 73.
115. For Berssenbrugge's reading habits (as well as the nature of Ashbery's influence on her), see Mei-mei Berssenbrugge and Zhou Xiaojing, "Blurring the Borders between Formal and Social Aesthetics: An Interview with Mei-mei Berssenbrugge," *MELUS* 27, no. 1 (2002): 199–212, https://doi.org/10.2307/3250643.
116. Berssenbrugge and Xiaojing, 209.
117. Berssenbrugge and Xiaojing, 209.
118. Berssenbrugge, *I Love Artists*, 26.
119. Berssenbrugge, 43.
120. Berssenbrugge, 43.
121. Berssenbrugge, 51.
122. Robert Hass, *Time and Materials: Poems 1997-2005* (New York: Ecco, 2008), 10.
123. Berssenbrugge, *I Love Artists*, 2006, 41.
124. Berssenbrugge, 42.

Chapter 3. Poetry in the Teaching Machine

1. Jorie Graham, "The Glorious Thing: Jorie Graham and Mark Wunderlich in Conversation," interview by Mark Wunderlich, 1996, http://www.poets.org/viewmedia.php/prmMID/15774.
2. Mark McGurl, *The Program Era: Postwar Fiction and the Rise of Creative Writing* (Cambridge, MA: Harvard University Press, 2009), 1.

3. I refer here, perhaps obviously, to Althusser's essay "Ideology and Ideological State Apparatus." Louis Althusser, *Lenin and Philosophy, and Other Essays* (New York: Monthly Review Press, 2001).

4. Vladimir Vladimirovich Nabokov, *Pale Fire: A Novel* (New York: G. P. Putnam's Sons, 1962); Elif Batuman, *The Possessed: Adventures with Russian Books and the People Who Read Them* (New York: Farrar, Straus and Giroux, 2010); and John Barth, *Giles Goat-Boy; or, The Revised New Syllabus* (Garden City, NY: Doubleday, 1966).

5. Cole Swensen and David St. John, eds., *American Hybrid: A Norton Anthology of New Poetry* (New York: W. W. Norton, 2009), 111.

6. Swensen and St. John, 112.

7. Kenneth Koch, "The Art of Poetry," *Poetry* 125, no. 4 (1975): 188.

8. Koch, 194.

9. Koch, 202.

10. Koch, 197–98.

11. Ellen Bryant Voigt, *The Lotus Flowers* (New York: W. W. Norton, 1987), 13.

12. Elizabeth Alexander, *American Sublime: Poems* (St. Paul, MN: Graywolf Press, 2005).

13. Swensen and St. John, *American Hybrid*, 112.

14. Gayatri Chakravorty Spivak, *Outside in the Teaching Machine*, 2nd ed. (New York: Routledge, 2009), 53.

15. Thomas Gardner, "Jorie Graham, The Art of Poetry No. 85," *Paris Review*, Spring 2003, http://www.theparisreview.org/interviews/263/the-art-of-poetry-no-85-jorie-graham.

16. Bonnie Costello, "Jorie Graham: Art and Erosion," *Contemporary Literature* 33, no. 2 (July 1, 1992): 374, https://doi.org/10.2307/1208675.

17. See also Kirstin Hotelling Zona, "Jorie Graham and American Poetry," *Contemporary Literature* 46, no. 4 (December 2005): 674, https://doi.org/10.2307/4489140; James Longenbach, "The Place of Jorie Graham," in *Jorie Graham: Essays on the Poetry*, ed. Thomas Gardner (Madison, WI: University of Wisconsin Press, 2005), 206–18; and Charles Molesworth, "Jorie Graham: Living in the World," *Salmagundi*, no. 120 (October 1998): 276–83, https://doi.org/10.2307/40549079. For a detailed formal analysis of Graham's earlier work, see Brian Henry, "Exquisite Disjunctions, Exquisite Arrangements: Jorie Graham's 'Strangeness of Strategy,'" *The Antioch Review* 56, no. 3 (July 1998): 281–93, https://doi.org/10.2307/4613707. Graham's reaction to the critical hoopla around *The End of Beauty* is telling. In her 2003 *Paris Review* interview, Graham expresses some exasperation with the success of the book: "Also, in a way, I wrote *Region [of Unlikeness]* to get something between me and *The End of Beauty*. I wanted to get out from under it. It's really nice when people like a book, but you feel, Christ, does that mean that's what I have to write now?" Graham acknowledges, here, the long shadow that literary critical attention can cast upon a body of work—there is something about *The End of Beauty*, aesthetically, that arbiters of poetic taste (almost all of whom, nowadays, are academics) have been unwilling to let go. Gardner, "Jorie Graham, The Art of Poetry No. 85."

18. Jorie Graham, *The End of Beauty* (New York: Ecco, 1987), 9.

19. One of the few profiles of Graham to actually disclose all of the listed dates is Craig Lambert, "Image and the Arc of Feeling," *Harvard Magazine*, February 2001, http://harvardmagazine.com/2001/01/image-and-the-arc-of-fee.html.

20. The quote itself is textbook snark: "'I love all of them,' she says [of her students], and it must be true, because they show up with remarkable frequency as winners of the many contests she judges." This allegation (not originally made by Orr) was the source of, relatively speaking, one of the contemporary poetry world's biggest scandals, involving not just Graham but the editors of several major poetry series, as well as other contest judges. It resulted in an almost complete elimination of major poetry prizes with "anonymous" judging. See John Sutherland, "American Foetry," *The Guardian*, July 4, 2005, sec. Books, https://www.theguardian.com/books/2005/jul/04/news.comment.

21. David Orr, "Jorie Graham, Superstar," *The New York Times*, April 24, 2005, sec. Books/Sunday Book Review, http://www.nytimes.com/2005/04/24/books/review/24ORRL.html.

22. Zona, "Jorie Graham and American Poetry," 670.

23. Thomas Gardner, ed., *Jorie Graham: Essays on the Poetry* (Madison, WI: University of Wisconsin Press, 2005), 4. Of further interest is the way in which Gardner characterizes the relationship between Graham's poetry and the criticism of it: he notes that the essays in the collection attempt to describe these "movements of consciousness" by "reenacting" them, positing a fundamental link between Graham's poetic discourse and literary critical discourse in which both are defined by intellectual reflexivity.

24. Molesworth, "Jorie Graham," 278.

25. Zona, "Jorie Graham and American Poetry," 669; Helen Vendler, *The Given and the Made: Strategies of Poetic Redefinition* (Cambridge, MA: Harvard University Press, 1995), 92.

26. Vendler, *The Given and the Made*, 106–11.

27. Helen Vendler, "The Function of Criticism," *Bulletin of the American Academy of Arts and Sciences* 36, no. 2 (November 1982): 15, https://doi.org/10.2307/3823075.

28. Thomas Gardner, *Regions of Unlikeness: Explaining Contemporary Poetry* (Lincoln: University of Nebraska Press, 1999), 168.

29. Gardner, 171.

30. D. G. Myers, *The Elephants Teach: Creative Writing since 1880* (Englewood Cliffs, NJ: Prentice Hall, 1996), 168.

31. Tim Mayers, *(Re)Writing Craft: Composition, Creative Writing, and the Future of English Studies* (Pittsburgh: University of Pittsburgh Press, 2005), passim.

32. Mayers, xv. Emphasis in original.

33. Graham, *The End of Beauty*, 94.

34. Graham, 81.

35. Graham, 87. Emphasis in original.

36. This phrase is taken from the title of James English's widely-cited book on the culture of literary awards; in it, English makes the argument that universities are essentially awards in and of themselves (and are ready-made for the proliferation of "cultural competition"), but that they are in the end not necessarily more important than the machinery of the non-academic, post-patron patron of art (e.g. the Nobels). James F. English, *The Economy of Prestige: Prizes, Awards, and the Circulation of Cultural Value* (Cambridge, MA: Harvard University Press, 2005), 256.

37. Jorie Graham, *The End of Beauty* (Hopewell, NJ: Ecco, 1987), 23.

38. Gardner, "Jorie Graham, The Art of Poetry No. 85."

39. Lee Konstantinou, "Lewis Hyde's Double Economy," *ASAP/Journal* 1, no. 1 (2016): 124–25, https://doi.org/10.1353/asa.2016.0007.

40. Konstantinou, 126.

41. Konstantinou, 129.

42. It should be noted that "availability" here is used in a limited sense; after all, the number of students that have "access" to Harvard, where Graham now teaches, is comparatively miniscule. Konstantinou addresses this issue in the conclusion of the essay discussed above; in it, he writes that "if what we care about is abolishing class, wholly dissolving the distinction between public and private, returning art to our life in common—the question of what art might be an emblem of (and whether or not it is a gift) dissolves into a more comprehensive political economic project (a project that contemporary artists and writers might serve in a variety of ways). In none of these cases, however, will we need to change our attitude toward art." Konstantinou, 145.

43. One could say that it "invites readerly participation," but I remain skeptical of this formulation, as it tends to function as a vague catchall for what poetry is doing when it withholds meaning. It may be true, but it doesn't tell us anything about who is being invited, or what they might be invited to do. Charles Altieri, responding to Jed Rasula and Linda Reinfeld's arguments about readerly agency, has formulated this skepticism thusly: "[d]oes the reader really need restoring? Are there any major traditional works that encourage readerly passivity, or demand readers reach any one predetermined conclusion by refusing to allow the reader space for engaging what the work has made available to them as a possible condition of the self or world?" Charles Altieri, "Some Problems about Agency in the Theories of Radical Poetics," *Contemporary Literature* 37, no. 2 (1996): 211, https://doi.org/10.2307/1208873.

44. Gardner, "Jorie Graham, The Art of Poetry No. 85."

45. In 1999, *College Composition and Communication* published a series of short pieces that examine these pitfalls and possibilities from the nexus of creative writing and composition studies: as Ted Lardner (quoting Lester Faigley) expresses it, "most of the pedagogical discourse in creative writing noticeably lacks a social perspective on composing, one in which 'human language (including writing) can be understood only from the perspective of a society rather than a single individual.' In traditional creative writing classrooms, little overt investigation goes on of writing poems or stories or plays as a practice of literacy, much less of literacy acquisition as a process of acquiring 'not only the words of language but the intentions carried by those words and the situations implied by them.'" Ted Lardner, "Locating the Boundaries of Composition and Creative Writing," *College Composition and Communication* 51, no. 1 (1999): 72–77, https://doi.org/10.2307/358962.

46. See for example a 2016 essay in the *Los Angeles Review of Books* which provides an interesting overview of the changing landscape of literature on and about motherhood, noting that recent work has tended "to describe motherhood in violent terms" that evoke "a disintegration or obliteration of the self." Lily Gurton-Wachter, "The Stranger Guest: The Literature of Pregnancy and New Motherhood," *Los Angeles Review of Books*, accessed August 2, 2016, https://lareviewofbooks.org/article/stranger-guest-literature-pregnancy-new-motherhood/.

47. Of course, *in loco parentis* has been a guiding principle at American universities for

a century; the shift, then, is not so much from "not parenting" to "parenting" as from the "fatherly" transmission of values and cultural capital to the feminized labor of basic skills transferal. A recent article in *The Nation* on adjunct labor sampled a handful of statistics: "official statistics from the 2009 National Center for Education Statistics analysis say women make up 51 percent of all adjunct faculty, but a smaller survey conducted by the adjunct group Coalition on the Academic Workforce, which asked faculty directly about their employment status, put the proportion of female adjunct faculty at 61 percent. By way of comparison, the American Association of University Professors estimates that full-time tenured faculty are 59 percent male." Kay Steiger, "The Pink Collar Workforce of Academia," *The Nation*, July 11, 2013, https://www.thenation.com/article/academias-pink-collar-workforce/.

48. Graham, *The End of Beauty*, 15.

49. Cf. James Longenbach's short essay "The Place of Jorie Graham," in which he argues that Graham's poems "simultaneously conjure and disperse locations," locating her dialectic in a philosophy of geospacial play—and again in this account, it is this shuttling between discursive modes of disclosure and mystery that forms the core of Graham's poetic difficulty. Longenbach, "The Place of Jorie Graham."

50. Gardner, "Jorie Graham, The Art of Poetry No. 85."

51. Gardner.

52. Nicholas M. Kelly, Nikki White, and Loren Glass, "Squatter Regionalism: Postwar Fiction, Geography, and the Program Era," *Post45*, no. 7 (April 2021), https://post45.org/2021/04/squatter-regionalism-postwar-fiction-geography-and-the-program-era/.

53. Gardner, "Jorie Graham, The Art of Poetry No. 85."

54. For the literal gifts, see Jorie Graham, "Between the Covers Jorie Graham Interview | Tin House," Between the Covers, accessed May 24, 2021, https://web.archive.org/web/20210422160146/https://tinhouse.com/transcript/between-the-covers-jorie-graham-interview/.

55. Graham, *The End of Beauty*, 3.

56. Gardner, "Jorie Graham, The Art of Poetry No. 85."

57. Graham, The Glorious Thing: Jorie Graham and Mark Wunderlich in Conversation.

58. Graham, "Between the Covers Jorie Graham Interview | Tin House."

59. Paulo Freire, *Pedagogy of the Oppressed*, A Continuum Book (New York: Seabury Press, 1970), 87–124.

60. Freire, 51–53.

61. Graham is outspoken about her dismay regarding the state of world affairs, and her later work takes on quite directly the thematics of climate change, about which she speaks with particular passion. See Deirdre Wengen and Jorie Graham, "Imagining the Unimaginable: Jorie Graham in Conversation," Academy of American Poets, February 21, 2014, https://www.poets.org/poetsorg/text/imagining-unimaginable-jorie-graham-conversation.

62. In a short op-ed for *Inside Higher Ed*, John Schlueter observes (as I have in this study's introduction) that the phrase "critical thinking" turns up somewhere in most universities' mission statements, but that it refers to a set of abilities that, despite a handful of researchers devoted to the subject, no one has truly defined, let alone figured out how to teach. He argues for an explicit treatment of "thinking skills" across disciplines. John

Schlueter, "Higher Ed's Biggest Gamble," *Inside Higher Ed*, June 7, 2016, https://www.inside highered.com/views/2016/06/07/can-colleges-truly-teach-critical-thinking-skills-essay.

63. The socioeconomic dimension of the relationship between teacher and student in Freire's formulation is anything but clear. In his analysis, socioeconomics takes a back seat to the idea of ideological oppression, in which the class demarcations fall less along material lines than they do along lines of a specific notion of self-awareness. The struggle, then, is not to recover lost materiality, but "to recover their lost humanity"—a condition which presumably includes socioeconomic security and justice, but only as side effects of the much more abstract and ultimate goal of something like necessity. Freire, *Pedagogy of the Oppressed*, 44.

64. Cf. Adorno's argument that a similar paradox regarding the ineffable is both what befalls and what constitutes the discipline of philosophy; the difference, for him, between it and art rests chiefly in its formal registers, and the processes by which those come to be. This is not to say that the thinking processes of art and philosophy are at odds, only that their rhetorical devices cannot be brought into contact; where they do join is in the dialectic, in which each "keep[s] faith with their own substance through their opposites: art by making itself resistant to its meanings; philosophy, by refusing to clutch at any immediate thing." Theodor W. Adorno, "Negative Dialectics and the Possibility of Philosophy," in *The Adorno Reader*, ed. Brian O'Connor, trans. E. B. Ashton (Oxford: Blackwell, 2000), 60–65.

65. Graham, *The End of Beauty*, 4.

66. The refusal of hypostatization is what constitutes the "negative" in Adorno's *Negative Dialectics*, and because this refusal is itself a thought process, negative dialectics and immanent critique become mutually constitutive. "Philosophy," in this formulation, is thus "obliged ruthlessly to criticize itself." Cf. Adorno's insistence on art's radical self-uncertainty in *Aesthetic Theory*. Adorno, "Negative Dialectics and the Possibility of Philosophy," 55; Theodor W. Adorno, *Aesthetic Theory*, ed. Gretel Adorno and Rolf Tiedemann, trans. Robert Hullot-Kentor (Minneapolis, MN: University of Minnesota Press, 1997), 2.

67. Graham, *The End of Beauty*, 5.

68. Benjamin's yearning toward the ultimate language of creation—naming language—is in a sense a remarkable feat of idealism, but it should not therefore be read as advocating for a transcendental theory of language. Language, for Benjamin, communicates not the thing in itself but rather the "mental being of man," which is inescapably linguistic and endlessly striving in its most authentic moments toward the "incommunicable." Walter Benjamin, "On Language as Such and on the Language of Man," in *Selected Writings, Volume 1: 1913-1926*, ed. Marcus Paul Bullock and Michael W. Jennings, trans. Edmund Jephcott (Cambridge, MA: Harvard University Press, 2004), 62–74.

69. Graham, *The End of Beauty*, 7.

70. Cf. Luise White's analysis of secrets and lying in historical narratives, particularly in terms of how the concealment or disavowal of information impacts the disciplinary formation of history in its search for truth. The keeping of secrets, she maintains, is fundamentally about "negotiating a social world" in which one must continually "reconstitute and renegotiate" the terms of said keeping that lies always on a continuum of disclosure. Luise White, "Telling More: Lies, Secrets, and History," *History and Theory* 39, no. 4 (December 2000): 22.

71. There are clear continuities here between Graham's style of self-portraiture and Ashbery's—there is no titling a poem "Self-Portrait" these days, especially when one has admitted Ashbery as an influence, without invoking "Self-Portrait in a Convex Mirror" (or the eponymous book in its entirety). And indeed, Graham's reflexive concern with epistemological dialectics and the effect/efficacy of such modes of thinking resonates with the motions of Ashbery's earlier poem as he moves back and forth between Parmigianino's painting and his veiled explanations of and conjectures about it (and, by extension, about himself). John Ashbery, *Self-Portrait in a Convex Mirror: Poems* (New York: Viking Press, 1975).

72. Frank Kermode, *The Genesis of Secrecy: On the Interpretations of Narrative* (Cambridge, MA: Harvard University Press, 1979), 4. The ecclesiastical focus of Kermode's argument—one of his primary touchstones is the Biblical parable—is relevant to Graham as well; while I have not focused on the strong spiritual tendency in her poetry, there is certainly a way in which the "secret" also functions as a mystical and semi-permeable barrier between the mortal and the divine.

73. Matei Calinescu, "Secrecy in Fiction: Textual and Intertextual Secrets in Hawthorne and Updike," *Poetics Today* 15, no. 3 (October 1994): 463, https://doi.org/10.2307/1773318.

74. Wengen and Graham, "Imagining the Unimaginable."

75. Thomas J. Otten, "Jorie Graham's _____s," *PMLA* 118, no. 2 (March 2003): 239, https://doi.org/10.2307/1261412.

76. Otten, 250.

77. Otten, 242.

78. Graham, *The End of Beauty*, 23.

79. Graham, 45.

80. Otten, "Jorie Graham's _____s," 241; Vendler, *The Given and the Made*, 107.

81. Graham, *The End of Beauty*, 23–24.

82. John Guillory, "Literary Critics as Intellectuals," in *Rethinking Class: Literary Studies and Social Formations*, ed. Wai Chee Dimock and Michael T. Gilmore (New York: Columbia University Press, 1994), 123.

83. Cf. Adorno, "Negative Dialectics and the Possibility of Philosophy," 67–68. Adorno's formulation of "thought as such," as "an act of negation, of resistance to that which is forced upon it," is extremely useful for thinking through the ways in which the emphatic separation of the poetic utterance from its object, an emphasis that in many ways is a primary feature of many of the poets under discussion in this study, can be framed as vanguardist resistance, even if it is not politically thematized. To consider oneself, as Graham does, as "a thinking" is thus to consider oneself a constant and strenuous resistance to "that which merely exists, is merely 'given.'" Negation in this sense is not restrictive but almost intolerably generative.

84. Adorno, 65; Graham, *The End of Beauty*, 45.

85. Cf. Guillory's application of Gramsci's distinction between "traditional" and "organic" intellectuals, in which the autonomy of the former—a category that includes academic humanists—is determined by their "investment in the *historical* rather than the contemporary conditions of their identity." In Gramsci's words, they reserve for themselves a "special qualification" not rooted in anything empirically measurable, but rather in a his-

torical resistance to systematicity that is at root idealist and/or utopic in its philosophy. Guillory, "Literary Critics as Intellectuals," 129–30.

86. Graham, *The End of Beauty*, 46–47.

87. See Adorno, *Aesthetic Theory*, 336.

Chapter 4. Citational Coding

1. Lavelle Porter, *The Blackademic Life: Academic Fiction, Higher Education, and the Black Intellectual* (Evanston, IL: Northwestern University Press, 2019), 142. See also the excellent and bracing analysis of the novel in Rolland Murray, "Not Being and Blackness: Percival Everett and the Uncanny Forms of Racial Incorporation," *American Literary History* 29, no. 4 (December 2017): 726–52, https://doi.org/10.1093/alh/ajx027.

2. Rinaldo Walcott, *The Long Emancipation: Moving toward Black Freedom* (Durham, NC: Duke University Press, 2021).

3. Some of the most prominent of these scholars include such figures as Aldon Nielsen, Lorenzo Thomas, Evie Shockley, Michael Bérubé, Nathaniel Mackey, Anthony Reed, and Kathy Lou Schultz, all of whom will make more specific appearances throughout this chapter. See in particular Michael Bérubé, *Marginal Forces/Cultural Centers: Tolson, Pynchon, and the Politics of the Canon* (Ithaca, NY: Cornell University Press, 1992); Aldon Lynn Nielsen, *Black Chant: Languages of African-American Postmodernism* (Cambridge: Cambridge University Press, 1997); Aldon Lynn Nielsen, *Integral Music: Languages of African-American Innovation* (Tuscaloosa, AL: University of Alabama Press, 2004); Evie Shockley, *Renegade Poetics: Black Aesthetics and Formal Innovation in African American Poetry* (Iowa City: University of Iowa Press, 2011); Anthony Reed, *Freedom Time: The Poetics and Politics of Black Experimental Writing* (Baltimore: Johns Hopkins University Press, 2014); Nathaniel Mackey, *Paracritical Hinge: Essays, Talks, Notes, Interviews* (Madison, WI: University of Wisconsin Press, 2005); and Kathy Lou Schultz, *The Afro-Modernist Epic and Literary History: Tolson, Hughes, Baraka* (New York: Palgrave Macmillan, 2013). The larger discussion surrounding race, intellectualism, and the avant-garde, meanwhile, has been led by writers such as Cathy Park Hong, Dorothy Wang, and Matthew Clair among many others shepherding it in articles and forums into literary journals and popular magazines alike. See in particular Dorothy J. Wang et al., "Race and the Poetic Avant-Garde," *Boston Review*, March 10, 2015, https://bostonreview.net/blog/boston-review-race-and-poetic-avant-garde, as well as Wang's scholarly book, *Thinking Its Presence: Form, Race, and Subjectivity in Contemporary Asian American Poetry* (Stanford, CA: Stanford University Press, 2013); Cathy Park Hong, "Delusions of Whiteness in the Avant-Garde," *Lana Turner*, no. 7 (2014), https://arcade.stanford.edu/content/delusions-whiteness-avant-garde; and Matthew Clair, "Black Intellectuals and White Audiences," *Public Books*, May 1, 2016, http://www.publicbooks.org/nonfiction/black-intellectuals-and-white-audiences.

4. Nathaniel Mackey's *Discrepant Engagement*, for example, deals chiefly with "dissonance" as a musical (or anti-musical) through-line connecting a canon of authors ranging from Robert Duncan to Wilson Harris. More recently, Anthony Reed has looked at Black experimentalism through the lens of lyric expectation, arguing (among other things) that radical Black poetry and music uses an "allusive postlyric voice" that refuses the totalizing "authenticity" of Black experiential narrative. My own argument runs, in this sense, paral-

lel to Reed's. Nathaniel Mackey, *Discrepant Engagement: Dissonance, Cross-Culturality and Experimental Writing* (Cambridge: Cambridge University Press, 1993); Reed, *Freedom Time*, 107.

5. Ronald A. T. Judy, *(Dis)Forming the American Canon: African-Arabic Slave Narratives and the Vernacular* (Minneapolis: University of Minnesota Press, 1993), 49.

6. Judy, 47.

7. Mark McGurl, *The Program Era: Postwar Fiction and the Rise of Creative Writing* (Cambridge, MA: Harvard University Press, 2009), 314.

8. McGurl, 260 (emphasis in original).

9. McGurl, 261.

10. Judy, *(Dis)Forming the American Canon*, 38.

11. McGurl, *The Program Era*, 264.

12. Judy, *(Dis)Forming the American Canon*, 18.

13. Judy, 24.

14. Mackey, *Paracritical Hinge*, 240. Mackey's own poetry—which I treat at some length in this study's conclusion—is a testament to the fact that difficult and complicated aesthetic choices in Black literature can garner quite a lot of attention. His work bears fewer overt markings of its author's scholarly leanings than that of the authors focused upon in this chapter; I instead refer readers to the long, dense explanatory preface that opens *Splay Anthem*: an essay which creates an alternate syllabus for poetic learning, one that places Duke Ellington in close proximity to H. D.

15. See Henry Louis Gates Jr., "Editor's Introduction: Writing 'Race' and the Difference It Makes," *Critical Inquiry* 12, no. 1 (1985): 5.

16. Shockley, *Renegade Poetics*, 6 (my emphasis). See also Anthony Reed's conceptualization of a "hermeneutic circle" of "Black genius," in which the metonymic creation of Black narrative is always already interpellated by the metaphoricity of "Blackness" itself, which attaches "spontaneously" to any such creation. Reed, *Freedom Time*, 12.

17. Fabio Rojas, *From Black Power to Black Studies: How a Radical Social Movement Became an Academic Discipline* (Baltimore: Johns Hopkins University Press, 2007), 8.

18. Keith D. Leonard and Hortense Spillers, "First Questions: The Mission of Africana Studies: An Interview with Hortense Spillers," *Callaloo* 30, no. 4 (2007): 1067.

19. Rojas, *From Black Power to Black Studies*, 14.

20. W. E. B. Du Bois, *Dusk of Dawn* (Oxford University Press, 2007); Henry Louis Gates Jr., *The Signifying Monkey: A Theory of Afro-American Literary Criticism* (New York: Oxford University Press, 1988); and Hortense J. Spillers, "Mama's Baby, Papa's Maybe: An American Grammar Book," *Diacritics* 17, no. 2 (1987): 65–81, https://doi.org/10.2307/464747.

21. I take those four verbs from Gates's definition of lexical procedures in Black American literature; see Gates, *The Signifying Monkey*, 121.

22. Leonard and Spillers, "First Questions," 1057.

23. Gayatri C. Spivak, "Scattered Speculations on the Question of Value," *Diacritics* 15, no. 4 (1985): 87, https://doi.org/10.7916/D8VM4B4F. It is significant that Spivak, in this essay on the concept of value, points to Derrida's conception of citationality as exemplary *bricolage*. See also, of course, Gates on signification and Signifyin(g); the citation of theory, thinkers, and other literary traditions by the poets in this chapter often contains a subtle critique, "signifyin(g)" upon the tradition even as it uses it.

24. This is the biting turn of phrase used by Rita Dove in her introduction to Tolson's work as she describes his early reception. Dove, of course, does not see Tolson as such a flunky. Melvin Beaunorus Tolson, *Harlem Gallery, and Other Poems of Melvin B. Tolson*, ed. Raymond Nelson (Charlottesville: University Press of Virginia, 1999), xvii–xix.

25. Lorenzo Thomas, *Extraordinary Measures: Afrocentric Modernism and Twentieth-Century American Poetry* (Tuscaloosa, AL: University of Alabama Press, 2000), 117.

26. In addition to Thomas himself, Aldon Nielsen, James Smethurst, and Michel Oren are all excellent chroniclers of this time period. Oren worked only on the Umbra group, but his history of that brief but influential gathering is generally seen to be definitive. See Michel Oren, "The Umbra Poets' Workshop, 1962-1965: Some Socio-Literary Puzzles," in *Belief vs. Theory in Black American Literary Criticism*, ed. Joseph Weixlmann (Penkeville Pub. Co., 1986), 177–223; Nielsen, *Black Chant*; and James Smethurst, "The Black Arts Movement and Historically Black Colleges and Universities," in *New Thoughts on the Black Arts Movement*, ed. Lisa Gail Collins and Margo Natalie Crawford (New Brunswick, NJ: Rutgers University Press, 2006).

27. Nielsen, *Black Chant*, 147.

28. Lorenzo Thomas, "The Shadow World: New York's Umbra Workshop & Origins of the Black Arts Movement," *Callaloo*, no. 4 (1978): 62, https://doi.org/10.2307/2930880.

29. Tolson, *Harlem Gallery, and Other Poems of Melvin B. Tolson*, 159.

30. Reed, *Freedom Time*, 17, 99.

31. Lorenzo Thomas, *The Bathers* (New York, NY: I. Reed Books, 1981), 23.

32. Nielsen, *Black Chant*, 154.

33. Thomas, *The Bathers*, 24.

34. Lorenzo Thomas, *The Collected Poems of Lorenzo Thomas*, ed. Aldon Lynn Nielsen and Laura Vrana (Middletown, CT: Wesleyan University Press, 2019), 103.

35. David Llorens, "Seeking a New Image: Black Writers Converge at Fisk University," *Negro Digest*, June 1966, 80.

36. John H. Bracey Jr., Sonia Sanchez, and James Smethurst, eds., *SOS—Calling All Black People: A Black Arts Movement Reader* (Boston, MA: University of Massachusetts Press, 2014), 23.

37. Bérubé, *Marginal Forces/Cultural Centers*, 71.

38. In other words, Tolson performed in verse a similar kind of cultural labor that Du Bois performed in prose. See Bérubé, 144, as well as Kathy Lou Schultz, "To Save and Destroy: Melvin B. Tolson, Langston Hughes, and Theories of the Archive," *Contemporary Literature* 52, no. 1 (2011): 108–45, https://doi.org/10.1353/cli.2011.0014. See also Spillers: "Fifty years from now, if young, apprentice scholars are of American culture and global culture, and if somehow they lose sight of Black Studies and civil rights movement and aftermath, that means something didn't happen right today." Leonard and Spillers, "First Questions," 1058.

39. Tolson, *Harlem Gallery, and Other Poems of Melvin B. Tolson*, 272.

40. Tolson, 363.

41. See Reed, *Freedom Time*, 21.

42. See in particular, beyond the block quote above, the entirety of the chapter entitled

"Tolson's Negativity," in which Bérubé carefully charts the thematized avant-garde throughout *Harlem Gallery*. The chapter is as thorough a proof as we have that while his feelings about canonicity were deeply conflicted, one of Tolson's fundamental conceptions of "poetic success" was "acceptance by the academy." Bérubé, *Marginal Forces / Cultural Centers*, 71.

43. Jacques Derrida, "Signature, Event, Context," in *Limited Inc* (Evanston, IL: Northwestern University Press, 1988), 20.

44. Keene makes note of this influence in a blog post entitled "Celebrating the Umbra Workshop @ CUNY," in which he documents both his presence and the happenings at a gathering of Umbra writers that was, by his account, an arresting combination of reading, memorial, and critical discussion about the group and its lasting influence. John Keene, "Celebrating the Umbra Workshop @ CUNY," *J's Theater* (blog), November 2, 2013, http://jstheater.blogspot.com/2013/11/celebrating-umbra-workshop-cuny.html.

45. Hughes qtd. in Nielsen, *Black Chant*, 42.

46. Norman H. Pritchard, *The Matrix, Poems: 1960-1970* (Garden City, NY: Doubleday, 1970), 35.

47. John Keene and Christopher Stackhouse, *Seismosis* (Roanoke, VA: 1913 Press, 2006), 49.

48. Nielsen, *Black Chant*, 134, 142.

49. Pritchard, *The Matrix, Poems*, 53.

50. John Keene, in discussion with the author, December 2013.

51. It is not insignificant, I think, that the only other text I can find that has these line drawings of Stackhouse's appended to them is an essay by the former University of Maryland English and comparative literature professor Keguro Macharia, in a moving piece on leaving the profession and returning to Kenya. One of the drawings in the essay is the same as the drawing that concludes *Seismosis*. Stackhouse's art, it seems, resonates deeply with thinkers trying to make sense of their status on the margins, without ever depicting anything that one might point to as "marginal." Keguro Macharia, "On Quitting," *The New Inquiry*, May 3, 2013, http://thenewinquiry.com/essays/on-quitting/.

52. Derrida, "Signature, Event, Context," 20.

53. Keene and Stackhouse, *Seismosis*, 19.

54. Keene and Stackhouse, 19.

55. Fred Moten, *In the Break: The Aesthetics of the Black Radical Tradition* (Minneapolis: University of Minnesota Press, 2003), 2.

56. John Keene, "Gayatri Spivak & Anne Carson @ NYU," *J'S THEATER* (blog), September 8, 2013, http://jstheater.blogspot.com/2013/09/gayatri-spivak-anne-carson-nyu.html (emphasis added).

57. Gayatri Chakravorty Spivak, *Outside in the Teaching Machine*, 2nd ed. (New York: Routledge, 2009), x.

58. Spivak, 109–10 (emphasis added).

59. Spivak, 116. The intellectual move that Spivak makes in this piece is subtle, almost perfectly deconstructive itself, and very intricate. The main task of "Limits and Openings of Marx in Derrida" is to demonstrate how little Marx there is in Derrida, but then to show precisely how much is contained in that littleness: in the gap between poetry and meta-

phors of political economy, Spivak finds in Derrida's thinking ample room to insert the proper name of Marx; to, as she puts it, "risk the trace-structure *at every step*" in the quest for a proper critique of universalization and essentialism.

60. Derrida qtd. in Spivak, 114.

61. Keene and Stackhouse, *Seismosis*, 9.

62. Walter Benjamin, *Illuminations*, ed. Hannah Arendt, trans. Harry Zohn (New York: Schocken Books, 2011), 221, 224.

63. William Wordsworth and Samuel Taylor Coleridge, *Lyrical Ballads*, ed. R. L Brett and Alun R Jones (London; New York: Routledge, 2005), 291.

64. Keene and Stackhouse, *Seismosis*, 9.

65. Keene and Stackhouse, 56.

66. Keene and Stackhouse, 56.

67. Lyotard's *Lessons on the Analytic of the Sublime* and "Answering the Question: What is Postmodernism?" both explore the possibilities that inhere in the pre-conceptual phase of cognition. Keene's writing in particular seems to reflect Lyotard's use of Kant in his description of "modern" art: "To make visible that there is something which can be conceived and which can neither be seen nor made visible: this is what is at stake in modern painting. But how to make visible that there is something which cannot be seen? Kant himself shows the way when he names 'formlessness, the absence of form,' as a possible index to the unpresentable. He also says of the empty 'abstraction' which the imagination experiences when in search for a presentation of the infinite (another unpresentable): this abstraction itself is like a presentation of the infinite." The project of criticism comes under similar treatment in *Lessons*, in which it is framed as a project that is constantly caught up in a violent dialectic of sublime feeling and reason: the "principle of thinking's getting carried away." Jean François Lyotard, *The Postmodern Condition: A Report on Knowledge*, trans. Geoffrey Bennington and Brian Massumi (Minneapolis: University of Minnesota Press, 1984), 78; Jean François Lyotard, *Lessons on the Analytic of the Sublime: Kant's Critique of Judgment* (Stanford, CA: Stanford University Press, 1994), 55.

On the specific invocation of the Dogon: this ethnic group is the primary focus of much of Nathaniel Mackey's work, in several serial poems (collectively entitled *Song of the Andoumboulou*) stretching out over multiple volumes of poetry, including *Whatsaid Serif* and the National Book Award–winning *Splay Anthem*. Keene's connection to Mackey is both personal and scholarly: before the publication of *Annotations* and his subsequent leaving of the PhD program at NYU, Keene considered writing a comparative dissertation on diasporic imaginings of "African spiritual systems," and one of his authors included Mackey. Like Keene, Mackey is interested in the Dogon's interest in "unfinished" or preconceptual perception: the Andoumboulou are, as he puts it, "rough drafts" of human beings, drawing attention to the necessity of abstraction in myth-making across cultural time and space. John Keene to Kimberly Andrews, "Followup Questions," December 16, 2013; Nathaniel Mackey, *Whatsaid Serif* (San Francisco: City Lights Books, 1998); and Nathaniel Mackey, *Splay Anthem* (New York: New Directions, 2006).

68. Keene and Stackhouse, *Seismosis*, 56.

69. See, again, Lyotard's analysis of Kant's *Analytic of the Sublime* and its vision for the project of criticism—a vision that sees critically analytical work as that which is perpetually

overstepping and then, capitulating to a state of conceptual reason or rationality, violently redrawing its boundaries.

70. Keene and Stackhouse, *Seismosis*, 13.

71. Keene and Stackhouse, 38.

72. Keene and Stackhouse, 22.

73. Keene and Stackhouse, 22.

74. Keene and Stackhouse, 94.

75. Claudia Rankine, Jennifer Flescher, and Robert N. Casper, "Interview with Claudia Rankine," *Jubilat*, no. 12 (2006), https://web.archive.org/web/20171127171140/http://poems.com/special_features/prose/essay_rankine.php.

76. Rankine, Flescher, and Casper.

77. Claudia Rankine, *Nothing in Nature Is Private* (Cleveland, OH: Cleveland State University Poetry Center, 1994), 8.

78. Rankine, *Nothing in Nature Is Private*, 14.

79. Rankine, Flescher, and Casper, "Interview with Claudia Rankine."

80. Claudia Rankine, *The End of the Alphabet* (New York: Grove Press, 1998); Claudia Rankine, *Plot* (New York: Grove Press, 2001); Claudia Rankine and Juliana Spahr, eds., *American Women Poets in the 21st Century: Where Lyric Meets Language* (Middletown, CT: Wesleyan University Press, 2002); and Claudia Rankine, *Citizen* (St. Paul, MN: Graywolf Press, 2014).

81. Rankine, Flescher, and Casper, "Interview with Claudia Rankine."

82. Claudia Rankine, *Don't Let Me Be Lonely: An American Lyric* (St. Paul, MN: Graywolf Press, 2004), 56.

83. Because *Don't Let Me Be Lonely* takes on the subject of hate crime, most reviews will mention the book's connection to the scourge of American racism. But the few scholarly articles that focus on this work by Rankine gravitate much more strongly toward her use of staticky television screens and stills from news programs, for example, as a commentary upon modern image-production and consumption. Emma Kimberley, for example, argues that "*Don't Let Me Be Lonely* is an explicit poem of protest against contemporary targeted uses of word and image," and Kevin Bell, writing in *The Global South*, focuses on Rankine's use of "noise," claiming (in an argument that looks somewhat like many critical arguments about John Ashbery) that Rankine's work is deliberately designed to deconstruct itself, in the process "forc[ing] consideration of the reflective insistence silently structuring the material dimension of the figural." Bell turns toward what this consideration might mean for marginalized populations near the end of the article, arguing that the mediated "dispossession" of reality with which Rankine grapples could serve as an example of how the dispossessed, more broadly, might similarly struggle to articulate (and thus free) themselves.

The only scholar that deals explicitly with Rankine's treatment of racial violence and subjectivity is the poet Dawn Lundy Martin, in a dissertation manuscript entitled "Saying 'I am': Experimentalism and Subjectivity in Contemporary Poetry by Claudia Rankine, M. NourbeSe Philip, and Myung Mi Kim." Martin focuses on Rankine's use of "racial melancholia" and the fractured subjectivities that are the product of America's history of racial violence. Rankine's "I" is multiple and shifting in *Don't Let Me Be Lonely*, Martin maintains, because "the very conditions within which melancholia is made present breaks down the I/we dialectic replacing the autonomous speaking subject with other more fluid experiences of the self." Emma Kimberley, "Politics and Poetics of Fear after 9/11: Claudia Rankine's *Don't Let Me Be Lonely*," *Journal of American Studies* 45, no. 4 (2011): 782, https://doi.org/10.1017/S0021875811000958; Kevin Bell, "Unheard Writing in the Climate of Spectacular Noise: Claudia Rankine on TV," *The Global South* 3, no. 1 (2009): 94; and Dawn Lundy Martin, "Saying 'I Am': Experimentalism and Subjectivity in Contemporary Poetry by Claudia Rankine, M. NourbeSe Philip, and Myung Mi Kim" (PhD diss., University of Massachusetts Amherst, 2009), 38.

84. Aimé Césaire. *Aimé Césaire: The Collected Poetry*, trans. Clayton Eshleman and Annette Smith (Berkeley: University of California Press, 1983), 45.

85. David Levi-Strauss, "A Sea of Griefs Is Not a Proscenium: On the Rwanda Projects of Alfredo Jaar," *Nka: Journal of Contemporary African Art* 9, no. 1 (1998): 38–43.

86. Levi-Strauss, 43.

87. Elena Shtromberg, "'I Will Not Act before Understanding. Context Is Everything.': The Work of Alfredo Jaar," *Los Angeles Review of Books*, December 8, 2013, http://lareviewofbooks.org/essay/i-will-not-act-before-understanding-context-is-everything-the-work-of-alfredo-jaar/.

88. Rebecca Macmillan, "The Archival Poetics of Claudia Rankine's *Don't Let Me Be Lonely: An American Lyric*," *Contemporary Literature* 58, no. 2 (2017): 176. See also the similar argument made in Tana Jean Welch, "*Don't Let Me Be Lonely*: The Trans-Corporeal Ethics of Claudia Rankine's Investigative Poetics," *MELUS: Multi-Ethnic Literature of the U.S.* 40, no. 1 (2015): 124–48.

89. Reed, *Freedom Time*, 102, 107.

90. Reed, 132.

91. Rankine, Flescher, and Casper, "Interview with Claudia Rankine."

92. Rankine, *Don't Let Me Be Lonely*, 21.

93. Cornel West, "Black Strivings in a Twilight Civilization," in *The Cornel West Reader* (New York: Basic Books, 1999), 102.

94. Instead, the book is blurbed by none other than Jorie Graham, who calls it a "terrifying account of our lives."

95. West, "Black Strivings in a Twilight Civilization," 98.

96. West, 108.

97. West, 97.

98. Marjorie B. Garber, Beatrice Hanssen, and Rebecca L. Walkowitz, eds., *The Turn to Ethics* (New York: Routledge, 2000), ix.

99. Rankine, *Don't Let Me Be Lonely*, 47.

100. Rankine, 117.

101. Jacques Derrida, *On Cosmopolitanism and Forgiveness* (New York: Routledge, 2001), 41–42.

102. Rankine, *Don't Let Me Be Lonely*, 48.

103. Derrida, *On Cosmopolitanism and Forgiveness*, 49.

104. Rankine, *Don't Let Me Be Lonely*, 91.

105. See Bell, "Unheard Writing in the Climate of Spectacular Noise," 97–98.

106. Sarah Boseley, "Mbeki Aids Denial 'Caused 300,000 Deaths,'" *The Guardian*, No-

vember 26, 2008, sec. World news, http://www.theguardian.com/world/2008/nov/26/aids-south-africa.

107. Rankine, *Don't Let Me Be Lonely*, 117.
108. Rankine, 117.
109. Rankine, 118.
110. Cornel West, *The Cornel West Reader* (New York: Basic Books, 1999), 554.
111. Rankine, *Don't Let Me Be Lonely*, 84.
112. Georg Wilhelm Friedrich Hegel, *Outlines of the Philosophy of Right*, ed. Stephen Houlgate, trans. T. M. Knok (Oxford: Oxford University Press, 2008), 102–8, 154–62.
113. Hegel, 159.
114. Hegel, 160.
115. Rankine, *Don't Let Me Be Lonely*, 56.
116. Rankine, 57.
117. Rankine, 57.
118. Rankine, 120.
119. Hartman, qtd. in Walcott, *The Long Emancipation*, 3.

Chapter 5. Archival Authorizations

1. Susan Howe, *The Whispered Rush, Telepathy of Archives* (Blaney Lecture), 2012, http://www.youtube.com/watch?v=wuxF23jFkOk&feature=youtube_gdata_player. A modified version of this lecture was eventually expanded into a short book, *Spontaneous Particulars: The Telepathy of Archives*, in 2014.
2. For example: the guiding work behind one of Howe's earliest poem-books, *Hinge Picture*, was as she notes Edward Gibbon's *Decline and Fall of the Roman Empire*—an academic work to be sure, but one that is of course not housed exclusively in university special collections. Susan Howe, *Frame Structures: Early Poems, 1974-1979* (New York: New Directions Publishing, 1996), 1. For more on Howe's specific referentiality, see Will Montgomery, *The Poetry of Susan Howe: History, Theology, Authority* (New York: Palgrave Macmillan, 2010).
3. The books that do populate this generic niche tend to be rich combinations of rigorous scholarly thinking and an unwillingness to separate that kind of thinking from the affective labor that drives it forward. See William Carlos Williams, *In the American Grain* (Norfolk, CT: New Directions, 1925); Lyn Hejinian, *The Language of Inquiry* (Berkeley, CA: University of California Press, 2000); Susan Stewart, *Poetry and the Fate of the Senses* (Chicago: University Of Chicago Press, 2002); Christina Sharpe, *In the Wake: On Blackness and Being* (Durham, NC: Duke University Press, 2016); Dionne Brand, *The Blue Clerk: Ars Poetica in 59 Versos* (Durham, NC: Duke University Press, 2018); Charles Bernstein, *Content's Dream: Essays, 1975-1984* (Evanston, IL: Northwestern University Press, 2001); and Charles Bernstein, *Attack of the Difficult Poems: Essays and Inventions* (Chicago: University of Chicago Press, 2011).
4. Susan Howe, "Susan Howe Papers" (1992 1984), Box 12, Folders 1-8, Beinecke Rare Book and Manuscript Library, Yale University, Folder 2. That figure, compared to the sums commonly offered to temporary lecturers in today's universities, should be deeply sobering.
5. Susan Howe, *My Emily Dickinson* (New York: New Directions, 2007), 11.

6. See in particular Virginia Jackson's *Dickinson's Misery*. Howe herself, writing the opening paratext for the 2007 reissue of *My Emily Dickinson*, notes that she "wouldn't rely on Thomas H. Johnson's editorial decisions for Dickinson's line breaks or variant readings." Howe, *My Emily Dickinson*; Virginia Jackson, *Dickinson's Misery: A Theory of Lyric Reading* (Princeton, NJ: Princeton University Press, 2005).

7. For a good summary of these claims, see Perloff's essay on "the lyric subject" in *Differentials*. Charles Altieri also puts this relationship between the avant-garde and the "tradition" against which it rebels into perspective when he notes that "once poetic values become dominant they tend to organize discourse in such a way that even those with very different commitments find themselves compelled to shape their work so that it addresses these central issues." Marjorie Perloff, *Differentials: Poetry, Poetics, Pedagogy* (Tuscaloosa, AL: University of Alabama Press, 2004), 130; and Charles Altieri, *Self and Sensibility in Contemporary American Poetry* (Cambridge: Cambridge University Press, 1984), 5.

8. Susan Howe, *The Midnight* (New York: New Directions Books, 2003), n.p.

9. Stephen Collis, *Through Words of Others: Susan Howe and Anarcho-Scholasticism* (Victoria, BC: ELS Editions, 2006), 10.

10. Interestingly, Collis writes very convincingly about dialectical poetics from a more abstract standpoint: writing for *Lemon Hound* in 2013, he is much more willing to call a spade a spade, on both sides of the (however problematic) "traditional/avant-garde" divide. Smartly contextualizing the rhetoric of conceptualist poetry in terms of its relationship to capitalistic rhetorics of "innovation," Collis argues for a poetry that can be recognizable to capital while strenuously critiquing it—the latter imperative being what separates this potential poetry from the more purely stylistic "hybrid" poetry of which he is also skeptical. Stephen Collis, "Towards a Dialectical Poetry," *Lemon Hound*, September 27, 2013, http://lemonhound.com/2013/09/27/stephen-collis-towards-a-dialectical-poetry/.

11. Susan M. Schultz, "The Stutter in the Text: Editing and Historical Authority in the Work of Susan Howe," *How2* 1, no. 6 (2001), https://www.asu.edu/pipercwcenter/how2journal/archive/online_archive/v1_6_2001/current/readings/encounters/schultz.html.

12. See also Peter Nicholls' piece on "Susan Howe and American History." Nicholls, like almost all critics of Howe, emphasizes Howe's outsider status, asserting that Howe must be "at odds with any academic discipline that founds its 'history' on the finality of definitive editions"—a condemnation of academic disciplinarity that seems too strenuous. Peter Nicholls, "Unsettling the Wilderness: Susan Howe and American History," *Contemporary Literature* 37, no. 4 (December 1, 1996): 597, https://doi.org/10.2307/1208773.

13. See Marjorie Perloff, "'Collision or Collusion with History': The Narrative Lyric of Susan Howe," *Contemporary Literature* 30, no. 4 (December 1989): 518–33, https://doi.org/10.2307/1208613.

14. Kathy-Ann Tan, *The Nonconformist's Poem: Radical "Poetics of Autobiography" in the Works of Lyn Hejinian, Susan Howe and Leslie Scalapino* (Trier: WVT, Wissenschaftlicher Verlag Trier, 2008), 12.

15. Perloff, "Collision or Collusion with History," 519.

16. Oren Izenberg, "Poems In and Out of School: Allen Grossman and Susan Howe," in *The Cambridge Companion to American Poetry Since 1945*, ed. Jennifer Ashton (Cambridge: Cambridge University Press, 2013), 197.

17. Izenberg, 190.

18. Srikanth Reddy, *Changing Subjects: Digressions in Modern American Poetry* (Oxford : Oxford University Press, 2012), 48.

19. Reddy, 50.

20. Reddy, 51.

21. Howe, *The Midnight*, 18.

22. Susan Barbour, "'Spiritual Hyphen': Bibliography and Elegy in Susan Howe's *The Midnight*," *Textual Practice* 25, no. 1 (2011): 148, https://doi.org/10.1080/0950236X.2010.495847. In *Mal d'Archive* (*Archive Fever*), Derrida examines the deconstructive and anarchic impulse as "death drive" in standing opposition to the conservationist "archival desire," the latter of which "is to have a compulsive, repetitive, and nostalgic desire for the archive, an irrepressible desire to return to the origin, a homesickness, a nostalgia for the return to the most archaic place of absolute commencement." The anarchism in archive *fever*, then, is the destruction contained in the very repetition of archival motions: the creation of the archive is always already its dissolution in "reimpression." Jacques Derrida, *Archive Fever: A Freudian Impression* (Chicago: University of Chicago Press, 1996), 91.

23. Lynn Keller and Susan Howe, "An Interview with Susan Howe," *Contemporary Literature* 36, no. 1 (1995): 1–34, https://doi.org/10.2307/1208952.

24. Gillian White, *Lyric Shame: The "Lyric" Subject of Contemporary American Poetry* (Cambridge, MA: Harvard University Press, 2014).

25. White, 36.

26. Robert Lowell, *Life Studies and For the Union Dead* (New York: Farrar, Straus and Giroux, 2007), 17–18; Howe, *Frame Structures*, 3; and Perloff, *Differentials*, 146.

27. Howe, *Frame Structures*, 22.

28. Howe, 64–65.

29. Howe, 72.

30. Howe, 16.

31. Howe, 16.

32. Howe, "Susan Howe Papers" Folder 1.

33. Howe, Folder 1.

34. Howe, Folder 3.

35. Howe, *The Midnight*.

36. See Brian Reed, "'Eden or Ebb of the Sea': Susan Howe's Word Squares and Postlinear Poetics," *Postmodern Culture* 14, no. 2 (2004), https://doi.org/10.1353/pmc.2004.0010; and Kapalan P. Harris, "Susan Howe's Art and Poetry, 1968-1974," *Contemporary Literature* 47, no. 3 (October 2006): 440–71.

37. Howe, *The Midnight*, 7.

38. Howe, 9.

39. Howe, 22–23.

40. Howe, 23.

41. Howe, 93.

42. For a thorough overview of this history, see Ricardo L. Punzalan and Michelle Caswell, "Critical Directions for Archival Approaches to Social Justice," *The Library Quarterly* 86, no. 1 (January 2016): 25–42, https://doi.org/10.1086/684145.

43. Howe, *The Midnight*, 15.

44. Malachy Postlethwayt, *The Universal Dictionary of Trade and Commerce, with Large Additions and Improvements, Adapting the Same to the Present State of British Affairs in America Since the Last Treaty of Peace Made in the Year 1763; with Great Variety of New Remarks and Illustrations Incorporated Throughout the Whole: Together with Every Thing Essential That Is Contained in Savary's Dictionary: Also, All the Material Laws of Trade and Navigation Relating to These Kingdoms and the Customs and Usages to Which All Traders Are Subject* (London: W. Strahan, 1774).

45. Robert Lowell, "Robert Lowell Accepts the 1960 National Book Award for Poetry for Life Studies," National Book Foundation, 1960, https://www.nationalbook.org/robert-lowells-accepts-the-1960-national-book-awards-in-poetry-for-life-studies/.

46. Howe, *The Midnight*, 120. See also the opening gambit of *Pierce-Arrow*, which finds Howe shivering in the basement of Yale's Sterling Memorial Library, going through Peirce's papers on microfilm before examining the manuscripts themselves at Harvard. Confronted with a copy card reader that will require her Yale Library card, Howe describes the small electronic-text "HELLO" of the reader thusly: "in all their minute and terrible detail these five little icons could be teeth." Susan Howe, *Pierce-Arrow* (New York: New Directions, 1999), 5.

47. Howe, *The Midnight*, 121–22.

48. Howe, 121–26.

49. Howe, 122.

50. For a fine overview of this history, see Shirley Lim, "The Strangeness of Creative Writing: An Institutional Query," *Pedagogy* 3, no. 2 (2003): 151–69.

51. Howe, *The Midnight*, 127.

52. Howe, 129.

53. Howe, 130.

54. Howe, 72.

55. Howe, 59.

56. Susan Howe, *The Birth-Mark: Unsettling the Wilderness in American Literary History* (Hanover, NH: Wesleyan University Press, 1993), 158. In this interview, Howe goes on to confirm that she believes that history is an "actuality," one that can of course be falsified but whose archive is nonetheless full of "uncompromising details."

57. Howe, *The Midnight*, 60.

58. A representative example, from that same interview with Edward Forster: speaking of the culture at Harvard when her father professed there, she repeatedly refers to it as "false to women in an intellectual sense," referring to the fact both that it was impossible to be taken seriously as a woman scholar and that women were critically neglected by such critical luminaries as F. O. Matthiessen. In a later interview, she returns to the moment of the earlier one, contemporaneous with the publication of *The Birth-Mark*, saying "during the 1980s, I was angry about male editorial meddling even in the work of twentieth-century poets such as H. D. and Lorine Niedecker. The editorial history of Emily Dickinson's manuscripts was an issue that especially troubled me, and still does." Howe, *The Birth-Mark*, 161; Maureen N. McLane, "Susan Howe, The Art of Poetry No. 97," *Paris Review*, Winter 2012, http://www.theparisreview.org/interviews/6189/the-art-of-poetry-no-97-susan-howe.

59. Howe, *The Midnight*, 85.

60. Howe, 79.

61. Howe, 66.

62. This last comes from one of Hardy's diary entries, where he is told by W. D. Howells that at Longfellow's funeral, an aging Emerson said "I've known him these forty years; and no American, whatever may be his opinions, will deny that in—in—in—I can't remember the gentleman's name—beat the heart of a true poet." It is an evocative passage—not only of the tragedy of memory loss but also of a more abstract fear (that Howe certainly had) of artistic oblivion, of being swallowed up by time such that no one remembers your name. Howe, 144.

63. Howe, 137.

64. In a conversation with the performance artist Joan Jonas and the scholar Jeanne Heuving, Howe puts it this way: "That's like me, endlessly revising a poem. If you could see what it takes—thousands of pieces of paper to get four lines, a total obsession! But that's the obsessive way I work, and I have to keep doing it." Joan Jonas, Susan Howe, and Jeanne Heuving, "An Exchange between Joan Jonas, Susan Howe and Jeanne Heuving," *How2* 2, no. 3 (2005), http://www.asu.edu/pipercwcenter/how2journal/archive/online_archive/v2_3_2005/current/workbook/joans/media/Interview.pdf.

65. In a different context, Michel-Rolph Trouillot frames the "narrativization of history" as something that, in a process of hegemony-maintaining alchemy, transforms overdetermined layers of individual and collective experience into singularly authoritative "fact": "a narrative of power disguised as innocence." To rewrite "fact," one must shift one's focus to historical production as such—that is, the story of the storytelling. Michel-Rolph Trouillot, *Silencing the Past: Power and the Production of History* (Boston: Beacon Press, 1995), 114.

66. Michel Foucault, *The Archaeology of Knowledge*, 1st ed. (New York: Pantheon Books, 1972), 126.

67. Foucault, 123.

68. Lynn Keller, "An Interview with Myung Mi Kim," *Contemporary Literature* 49, no. 3 (October 1, 2008): 343.

69. Myung Mi Kim, *Commons* (Berkeley: University of California Press, 2002), 4.

70. Timothy Yu has also noted similarities between Kim and Howe in a wide-ranging overview of recent Asian American poetry, which builds on his previous work in Asian American poetry and the avant-garde. Timothy Yu, "Asian American Poetry in the First Decade of the 2000s," *Contemporary Literature* 52, no. 4 (2011): 826, https://doi.org/10.1353/cli.2011.0040.

71. Kim, *Commons*, 13.

72. Kim, 42.

73. Kim, 44, 107.

74. Kim, 7.

75. Kim, 4.

76. Myung Mi Kim, *Under Flag* (Berkeley, CA: Kelsey St. Press, 1998), 30.

77. Kim, *Commons*, 107.

78. This is a term that Kim uses herself when talking about her more documentary impulses: as she tells Lynn Keller, she is less interested in the "document as artifact" (a state-

ment that distinguishes her sharply from Howe) and much more interested in the way in which "documents evoke the possibility of encounter." Keller, "An Interview with Myung Mi Kim," 345.

79. Kim, *Commons*, 37.

80. Kim, 107.

81. On the cultivation of avant-garde literature in Providence, see McGurl's discussion of "technomodernism" and its presence at Brown in the 1990s. Mark McGurl, *The Program Era: Postwar Fiction and the Rise of Creative Writing* (Cambridge, MA: Harvard University Press, 2009), 45–46.

82. Jena Osman, *The Character* (Boston: Beacon Press, 1999), 3.

83. Jena Osman, *Public Figures* (Middletown, CT: Wesleyan University Press, 2012).

84. Siobhan Phillips, "All Together Now," *Boston Review*, January 1, 2012, http://www.bostonreview.net/poetry/siobhan-phillips-carr-kocot-mlinko-osman.

85. Jena Osman, *The Network* (Albany, NY: Fence Books, 2010), 3.

86. Osman, 30.

87. Osman, 30.

88. Osman, 30.

89. Osman, 31.

90. Osman, 32.

91. Osman, 33.

92. Catherine Taylor, *Apart* (Brooklyn, NY: Ugly Duckling Presse, 2012), 9, 32, 91.

93. Taylor, 84.

94. Taylor, 71.

95. Taylor, 91.

96. Taylor, 55.

97. Taylor, 127.

98. Taylor, 128.

99. Cf., in the enduring critical conversation with Foucault's conception of the archive, Agamben's "Archive and Testimony," from *Remnants of Auschwitz*: "to bear witness is to place oneself in one's own language in the position of those who have lost it, to establish oneself in a living language in the position of those who have lost it . . . [i]t is not surprising that the witness' gesture is also that of the poet, the *auctor* par excellence. Hölderlin's statement that 'what remains is what the poets found' (*Was bleibt, stiften die Dichter*) is not to be understood in the trivial sense that poets' works are things that last and remain throughout time. Rather, it means that the poetic word is the one that is always situated in the position of a remnant and that can, therefore, bear witness." The "impossibility of speech" inheres in the dialectic of the remnant, that which is both lost and found, which both authorizes and dismantles the possibility of the witness-bearing subject. Giorgio Agamben, *Remnants of Auschwitz: The Witness and the Archive* (New York: Zone Books, 1999).

100. Taylor, *Apart*, 150.

101. Such extreme interpretations of the verb "to translate" have long been practiced by poets particularly concerned with formal innovation, comprising a wide stylistic spectrum of "hermeneutic" methods. See Robert Lowell, *Imitations* (New York, NY: Farrar, Straus and Cudahy, 1961); Gertrude Stein, *Before the Flowers of Friendship Faded Friendship Faded*

(Paris: Plain Edition, 1931); Jack Spicer, *After Lorca* (San Francisco, CA: White Rabbit Press, 1957); Ezra Pound, *Cathay: Translations, for the Most Part from the Chinese of Rihaku, from the Notes of the Late Ernest Fenollosa, and the Decipherings of the Professors Mori and Ariga* (London: Elkin Mathews, 1915); Celia Thaew Zukofsky and Louis Zukofsky, *Catullus (Gai Valeri Catulli Veronensis Liber)* (London: Cape Goliard Press, 1969); A. Dragomoshchenko, *Description* (Los Angeles, CA: Sun & Moon Press, 1990); A. Dragomoshchenko, *Xenia*, trans. Lyn Hejinian and Elena Balashova (Los Angeles, CA: Sun & Moon Press, 1994); and Robert Kelley, "EARISH," rk-ology.com, 2006, http://www.rk-ology.com/Earish_-_Paul_Celan.php.

102. Christian Hawkey, *Ventrakl* (Brooklyn, NY: Ugly Duckling Presse, 2010), 8.

103. Hawkey, 106.

104. Marjorie Perloff, "Channeling Georg Trakl: Christian Hawkey's 'Ventrakl,'" *The Los Angeles Review of Books*, May 17, 2011, https://lareviewofbooks.org/review/channeling-georg-trakl-christian-hawkeys-ventrakl/.

105. Hawkey, *Ventrakl*, 8–9.

106. Hawkey, 121.

107. In Charles Bernstein, ed., *The Politics of Poetic Form: Poetry and Public Policy* (New York: Roof Books, 1990), 24. Drawing together vanguardist difficulty and contextual explanation, Andrews cogently demonstrates how linguistic experiments that aim toward "social unbalancing" can reflect (and thus draw attention to) larger social and ideological structures.

108. Hawkey, *Ventrakl*, 60.

109. Hawkey, 62.

110. Hawkey, 120.

111. Walter Benjamin, "On Language as Such and on the Language of Man," in *Selected Writings, Volume 1: 1913-1926.*, ed. Marcus Paul Bullock and Michael W. Jennings, trans. Edmund Jephcott (Cambridge, MA: Harvard University Press, 2004), 71. In this earlier essay, Benjamin lays the groundwork for what would become both "translatability" and "pure language" (*die reine Sprache*) in "The Task of the Translator."

112. Hawkey, *Ventrakl*, 78.

Coda. Toward an Aesthetics of Disciplinarity

1. This reference barely needs a citation at this point, but I refer here to Berlant's notion that optimism can contain within it a preemptive sense of the desired object's loss, and further, that that object is *itself* an obstacle to one's flourishing even as it makes available the conditions for one's possibility. Lauren Berlant, "Cruel Optimism," *Differences* 17, no. 3 (2006): 20–36, https://doi.org/10.1215/10407391-2006-009.

2. Kornbluh's most recent book on the constructive power of literary realism is an exhilarating intervention into current debates over literary form; I am using the very broadest terms of her argument here. See Anna Kornbluh, *The Order of Forms: Realism, Formalism, and Social Space* (Chicago: University of Chicago Press, 2019), 162.

3. Jonathan Kramnick, *Paper Minds: Literature and the Ecology of Consciousness* (Chicago: University of Chicago Press, 2018); Jonathan Kramnick and Anahid Nersessian, "Form and Explanation," *Critical Inquiry* 43, no. 3 (2017): 650–69, https://doi.org/10.1086/691017.

4. A representative sample of works that aim not to do away with disciplinary expertise but rather to extend its reach and purview is essentially impossible, but in the interests of recent proof, consider Christina Sharpe, *In the Wake: On Blackness and Being* (Durham, NC: Duke University Press, 2016); Manu Samriti Chander, *Brown Romantics: Poetry and Nationalism in the Global Nineteenth Century* (Lanham, MD: Bucknell University Press, 2017); Sarah Dowling, *Translingual Poetics: Writing Personhood Under Settler Colonialism* (Iowa City: University of Iowa Press, 2018); and Sonya Posmentier, *Cultivation and Catastrophe: The Lyric Ecology of Modern Black Literature* (Baltimore: Johns Hopkins University Press, 2017).

5. Indeed, part of what motivates Kornbluh's study of *realist fiction* is the desire to get out from under the hegemony of poetry when it comes to formalist treatments of literature. I thus don't suggest here that its dominance should be reasserted but rather, and much more mildly, that there are reasons for this dominance that don't preclude other ways to point to literary form. Kornbluh, *The Order of Forms*, 12–13, 45.

6. I refer here to Sedgwick's critique of critique, in which she seeks to move beyond critical paradigms that begin with the assumption that texts have designs upon the reader, and that the job of the critical reader is to ferret out and expose them. Eve Kosofsky Sedgwick, "Paranoid Reading and Reparative Reading, or, You're So Paranoid, You Probably Think This Essay Is About You," in *Touching Feeling: Affect, Pedagogy, Performativity* (Durham, NC: Duke University Press, 2003), 123–53.

7. Louis Menand, *The Marketplace of Ideas: Reform and Resistance in the American University* (New York: W. W. Norton & Company, 2010), 108.

8. Menand's account is historical rather than formal (despite his acknowledgement that a discipline is, in fact, a form). Specifically, he traces the "disciplined" disciplinarity of the immediate postwar period (he calls it the Golden Age) and argues that the scientistic, rational frameworks that had characterized even humanities departments dissolved under the pressure of their own claims to autonomy. He places the blame, as it were, for this disciplinary dissolution—after which, he claims, things became more "anti" or "post" disciplinary—on the old scapegoats, structuralism and deconstruction. One of the pitfalls of this approach is that one ends up tied to a model that views form as symptomatic of content; Menand's argument is, in essence, that a "discipline" is simply a methodological paradigm adequate to its content at a given time, and that any shift in the paradigm must somehow run counter to the notion of a discipline as such. Counter, that is, until the shift gets reabsorbed into the discipline and thus alters its boundaries. I have no qualm with the latter characterization of historical change; there's no way to argue that (for example) gender studies didn't significantly alter the horizon of possibilities for what counted as an object of inquiry in literary studies. It's also true, in a narrow sense, that such an inclusion alters the range of acceptable methodological approaches to those objects. But what Menand's account fails to consider is the degree to which gender studies and literary studies always already *shared* a type of methodological habitus. Menand, 81–91.

9. Anthony Reed, *Freedom Time: The Poetics and Politics of Black Experimental Writing* (Baltimore: Johns Hopkins University Press, 2014), 210.

10. Natalia Cecire, *Experimental: American Literature and the Aesthetics of Knowledge* (Baltimore: Johns Hopkins University Press, 2019), xvii.

11. Nathaniel Mackey, *Splay Anthem* (New York: New Directions Book, 2006), ix.

12. Mackey, 21.

13. Mackey, 22.

14. Mackey, 51.

15. Jasper Bernes, *The Work of Art in the Age of Deindustrialization* (Stanford, CA: Stanford University Press, 2017), p. 156.

16. Mackey, *Splay Anthem*, 55.

17. Mackey, 125.

18. Bernes, *The Work of Art in the Age of Deindustrialization*, 156.

19. Sarah Brouillette, "Academic Labor, the Aesthetics of Management, and the Promise of Autonomous Work," *Nonsite*, May 1, 2013, http://nonsite.org/article/academic-labor-the-aesthetics-of-management-and-the-promise-of-autonomous-work.

20. Leigh Claire La Berge, *Wages Against Artwork: Decommodified Labor and the Claims of Socially Engaged Art* (Durham, NC: Duke University Press, 2019), 11. "The aesthetic" is also another term (alongside "autonomy") that Brouillette hopes to "reclaim from corporate application."

21. Jennifer S. Cheng, *House A* (Oakland, CA: Omnidawn, 2016), 114.

22. Anne Boyer, *A Handbook of Disappointed Fate* (Brooklyn, NY: Ugly Duckling Presse, 2018), 11.

23. See Victor Shklovsky, "Art as Technique," in *The Critical Tradition: Classic Texts and Contemporary Trends*, ed. David H Richter (Boston: Bedford/St. Martin's, 2007), 775–84.

24. Alvin Ward Gouldner, *The Future of Intellectuals and the Rise of the New Class: A Frame of Reference, Theses, Conjectures, Arguments, and an Historical Perspective on the Role of Intellectuals and Intelligentsia in the International Class Contest of the Modern Era* (New York: Seabury Press, 1979). To reiterate from the outset of this study, it should be noted that the formation of the "New Class," as Gouldner has it, is distinctly nonidentical to academic humanists but rather contains also the technocratic "intelligentsia" (medical doctors, technology workers, etc.). This wide umbrella heightens Gouldner's sense of the internal contradictions of his analytic object yet further.

Index

academic, the: and "academic poetry," 90, 176, 193; and "academic readers," 53, 74, 81; and African American creative writers, 120, 121, 123, 125, 128, 132, 133; and African American literary criticism, 126, 136–38, 144; and anxiety, 7; and archives, 166, 178, 190; and John Ashbery, 47, 50–52, 72; and aura, 140; and the avant-garde, 5, 167, 171, 199, 204, 206, 208, 209, 212–14; and Charles Bernstein, 37; and citational networks, 162; and community, 71, 76, 111; and conceptual poetry, 8; and consciousness, 77, 78; and contradictory meanings of, 3; and creative writing programs, 1, 38, 39; and critical thinking, 18; and critique of individualist ideologies of authorship, 11, 106; defined, 3; and difficulty, 60, 93; and disciplinarity, 146, 181, 186; and freedom, 101; as genre, 12, 85; and Alvin Ward Gouldner, 23; and Harvard University, 30–32; and humanities, 10, 116, 153, 179; and job market, 33, 43, 45; and labor, 2, 4, 87, 98, 178, 189, 207, 211; and legitimacy, 46, 203; and literary criticism, 102, 117; and literary historicism, 17; and Robert Lowell, 40, 42; and mainstream poetry, 14; and optimism, 43, 163; and outsiders, 169; and politics of, 44; as profession, 165, 176; and professionalization, 55, 73, 97; and reading, 56, 58; and reflexivity, 6, 35, 160; and research, 196, 198; and the self, 82, 112, 167, 188; and self-reading, 82; and solidarity, 67; and Wallace Stevens, 21, 27, 28, 30, 31, 33; and theory, 59; and vanguardism, 15

access, 67, 80, 98–101, 108, 110, 135, 167
accessibility, 67, 73, 125
Adams, John Quincy, 92, 174
adjunctification, 43, 102, 236n47
Adorno, Theodor W., 50, 67–70, 78, 118, 230n63, 231n68, 239n83
affect, 10, 144, 211; and affect theory, 43; and African American literature, 123, 126, 142, 153, 160, 161; in John Ashbery's work, 57,

64–68, 75–77, 232n81; and authorial affects, 179; and autobiography, 181, 195; and counterculture, 211; in Christian Hawkey's work, 201; in Susan Howe's work, 165, 172, 182, 187, 188; and labor, 4; and negative affects, 6, 173; and research, 198, 200
Aggrey, James Kwegyir, 129
Alexander, Elizabeth, 89
Althusser, Louis, 88
Altieri, Charles, 64
Andrews, Bruce, 202
apartheid, 157, 158, 198
Aristophanes, 77
Arnold, Matthew, 1, 80, 215n2
Ashbery, John, 10, 11, 13, 15, 47, 58, 59, 61, 134; and academia, 51; and act of reading, 52; and Mei-mei Berssenbrugge, 53, 54, 82–85; and Harold Bloom, 58; and "Fantasia on 'The Nut-Brown Maid,'" 53, 62–64, 67, 69–72, 74, 75, 141; and *Flow Chart*, 56; and Jorie Graham, 89, 90, 97, 98, 112, 135, 239n71; and *Houseboat Days*, 49, 61; and Susan Howe, 17, 172, 211; and "Litany," 53, 69–81; and reception, 57; and reflexivity, 9, 10, 13; and reputation for difficulty, 50, 60; and *Self-Portrait in a Convex Mirror*, 49, 53, 62–64, 226n1, 239n71; and *Some Trees*, 53, 56
Association of Writers & Writing Programs, 38, 40
atopia, 104
aura, 85, 100, 102, 106, 140, 142
austerity, 45
autonomy, 6, 78–81, 111, 115–18, 124; and Theodor Adorno's aesthetic theory, 70; and African American literature, 124; and John Ashbery, 78; and Pierre Bourdieu, 232n96; and critical thinking, 92; and contingency, 98; and "fiction of autonomy" in creative writing programs, 42; and individuality, 115; and Louis Menand, 254n8; and poets in academia, 40, 111, 118, 222n54; and solidarity, 81; and universality, 79, 116; and value, 66

autopoesis, 28
Auyong, Elaine, 57
avant-garde, the, 73, 116, 132, 133, 212–14; and African American poetry, 121, 122, 132, 133, 151, 163; and American academy, 3; and anxiety, 7; and John Ashbery, 53, 67, 84; and authorial subject, 167, 173; and Peter Bürger, 6, 9; and conceptualism, 8; and creative writing programs, 36; and difficulty, 3; and genre, 12, 13; and Jorie Graham, 16, 98, 111; and Susan Howe, 11, 164, 166, 171, 189; and humanities, 44, 46; and John Keene, 135, 144, 146; and labor, 2, 4, 212–14; and literary studies, 45, 93–94, 207–9; and literary theory, 58; and Jena Osman, 193, 194; and politics, 5; and Wallace Stevens, 21, 25, 35, 43; and Catherine Taylor, 199; and tradition, 40; and the university, 177, 189, 204

backlash, 26, 31, 45
Badiou, Alain, 135
Baker, Houston, Jr., 125, 126
Barbour, Susan, 172
Bard College, 51, 135
Barnard College, 148
Barth, John, 88
Barthes, Roland, 193
Batuman, Elif, 88
Baudelaire, Charles, 129
Beckett, Samuel, 78
Benjamin, Walter, 146, 203, 238n68; and aura, 140; and Susan Howe, 164; and naming, 63; and "On Language as Such and On the Language of Man," 109
Bergman, David, 51, 52
Berlant, Lauren, 205, 253n1
Bernes, Jasper, 56, 210, 211
Bernstein, Charles, 42; and critical thinking, 24; and "A Defence of Poetry," 37; and "Official Verse Culture," 14; and SUNY Buffalo Poetics Program, 36, 38, 165, 176, 177
Berssenbrugge, Mei-mei, 16, 53, 54, 81–86, 155, 233n11
Bérubé, Michael, 131, 132
Bethel University, 135
Bin Laden, Osama, 161
Black Arts Movement, 125, 128, 130, 132, 142
Black Mountain College, 7

Blackmur, R. P., 40, 66
Black studies, 44, 122, 125, 142
Bloom, Howard, 24, 58
Boggs, Abigail, 44
BOMB (magazine), 135
Boston University, 41
Bourdieu, Pierre, 33, 56, 78, 219n16, 228n22, 232n96
Boyer, Anne, 213
Breslin, Paul, 59
Brodsky, Joseph, 151
Brooklyn College, 51
Brouillette, Sarah, 9, 212
Brown University, 82, 193
Bürger, Peter, 6, 9
Butler, Judith, 137

Calinescu, Matei, 112
canon, the, 47, 166, 229n42; and African American literature, 122, 124–26, 136, 138, 144, 155; and canon wars, 45; and literary criticism, 58, 133; and modernism, 14, 25, 26, 28, 46
Cantos (Ezra Pound), 28, 128
Cavell, Stanley, 36
Cecire, Natalia, 209, 216n20
Celan, Paul, 151
Césaire, Aimé, 149, 151–53
Cheng, Jennifer S., 212
Clare, John, 52
Coetzee, J. M., 151
Cole, Henri, 147
Collis, Stephen, 169, 170, 172
Columbia University, 82, 147
conceptualism, 7, 8
confessional poetics, 192, 195, 198, 202; and the avant-garde, 171–73; and Susan Howe, 168, 177, 182, 184, 188; and sincerity, 105, 167
Cornell University, 88
Costello, Bonnie, 52, 91
Cottom, Daniel, 52
craft, 114, 122, 140, 168, 225n85; and avant-garde poetics, 36; and creative writing workshops, 26, 38, 87, 91, 99, 102; and pedagogical labor, 94, 95, 97, 116, 117; suspicion of, 41
creativity, 212; and Charles Bernstein, 38; and pedagogy, 41, 114; and Wallace Stevens, 33, 34, 47
Creeley, Robert, 165, 177

Critchley, Simon, 27
"critical thinking," 111, 205, 206, 237n62; and epistemology, 29, 108; and genre, 12; and pedagogy, 106; reclamation of, 11, 13, 18, 24, 62, 92
cultural capital, 14, 44, 68, 112, 183

Dasein (magazine), 128
Davis, Charles T., 122
deconstruction, 15, 59, 69, 101, 138, 139
Deleuze, Gilles, 58, 83
de Man, Paul, 58, 59, 222n54
Derrida, Jacques, 17, 58, 59, 83, 101, 146, 249n22; and Claudia Rankine, 151, 156, 157–60, 162; and "Signature Event Context," 132, 136, 243n59; and Gayatri Spivak, 138, 139, 241n23
Diallo, Amadou, 161
dialogic, the: and Theodore Adorno, 70; and African American poetics, 140, 210; and John Ashbery, 53, 56, 62, 63, 71, 72; and Paulo Freire, 106, 107; and Jorie Graham, 108; and the social, 75
Dickinson, Emily, 17, 165–67, 169, 176, 182–87, 196
disciplinarity: as aesthetic, 205; and African American studies, 128, 146; and epistemological plurality, 208; and Susan Howe, 181, 184; and interdisciplinarity, 206; and poetry, 207, 209, 212, 213
discursivity, 13, 43
disenchantment, 86
Donnelly, Timothy, 147
Douglass, Fredrick, 123, 124
Driskell, David, 144–46
Dryden, John, 129
Du Bois, W. E. B., 126, 155
Duchamp, Marcel, 8

Eeckhout, Bart, 21, 26
ekphrasis, 96, 135, 143, 144
Eliot, Charles W., 31, 222n47
Eliot, T. S., 7, 26, 31, 52, 94, 105, 123
elitism, 13, 54, 74, 155
Emanuel, Lyn, 88–90, 96
"Embarkation for Cythera" (Lorenzo Thomas), 129, 130
empiricism, 65, 184, 185, 194, 200
Enlightenment, 21, 155
Epstein, Andrew, 51, 223n68
Everett, Percival, 120, 121

Fence (magazine), 135
Fernandez, Ramon, 35
financial crisis of 2008, 45
Filreis, Al, 31, 32
Fischer, Dexter, 122
Fish, Stanley, 12
Fisk University's First Black Writers' Conference, 130
Floyd, George, 45
forgiveness, 157–59
form, literary, 41, 65, 86, 196, 212, 214; and African American literary expression, 120–25, 143, 144, 146, 149, 151; and critical reading, 82; and critical thinking, 3, 9, 11, 70; dialogic, 62, 140; and formal devices, 97; and formal innovation, 16, 72, 98, 112–13, 151, 193, 252n101; and formalism, 40, 94, 131, 133, 206, 254; and gender, 103; in Susan Howe, 29, 91, 168, 169; and labor, 4, 53, 139; and modernism, 64; and poetry's place in literary studies, 207–9; and Wallace Stevens, 34, 35, 43; and the university, 2, 7, 10
Foucault, Michel, 188, 206
fragmentation, 11, 21, 142, 190, 193, 199, 212; in Susan Howe, 29, 170, 174, 175, 179, 181
Frankfurter, Felix, 176
Freire, Paulo, 106, 107, 221n46
Fugitive poets, 39
fussiness, 60

Gates, Henry Louis, Jr., 122–26, 146
gift, the, 100, 101, 104
Gilliam, Sam, 144–46
The Given and the Made (Helen Vendler), 95
Glissant, Édouard, 197
Goethe, Johann Wolfgang von, 129
Goldsmith, Kenneth, 7, 8
Gouldner, Alvin Ward, 77, 79; and contradictory character of intellectual class formation, 23, 73, 214; and culture of critical discourse, 22, 24, 55, 207; and "New Class" thesis, 54, 219n16, 255n24
Graff, Gerald, 39, 68
Graham, Jorie, 93, 94, 98–101, 119; and critical thinking, 108, 116, 135; and *The End of Beauty*, 16, 89–92, 102–4, 106, 107, 111, 113; and pedagogy, 5, 10, 13, 16, 87; and philosophy, 95, 109, 112, 113, 115; and "Pollock and Canvas," 96, 97; and relationship with readers, 105, 114; and secret

Graham, Jorie (*cont.*)
  knowledge, 110, 111, 118; and the university, 148, 165, 189, 193
Gramsci, Antonio, 138, 197
Grossman, Allen, 171
Guillory, John, 14, 36, 44, 116

Hall, Donald, 42
Hall, Stuart, 18
Halpern, Dan, 147
Hammer, Langdon, 41
Harlem Gallery (Melvin B. Tolson), 127–32
Hartman, Saidiya, 137
Harvard University, 36, 38, 50, 51, 58, 82; and African American intellectuals, 155; and Jorie Graham, 92; and Susan Howe, 165, 166, 176, 181, 183, 250n58; and Wallace Stevens, 14, 19, 20, 28, 30–32, 43
Hass, Robert, 85
Hawkey, Christian, 17, 189, 199–204, 213
Heaney, Seamus, 92
Hegel, G. W. F., 59, 67, 68, 151, 160–62
Heidegger, Martin, 65, 93
Hejinian, Lyn, 194
Herd, David, 63
Higginson, Thomas Wentworth, 183
Holmes, Oliver Wendell, 176
Holocaust, the, 104
Houghton, Arthur A., 166, 181–83, 185, 187
Howard University, 128
Howe, Mark DeWolfe, 165, 176
Howe, Susan, 24, 201, 208, 211; and the archive, 164, 183–85, 193, 200; as avant-garde poet, 8, 13; and *The Birth-Mark*, 196; and "Chanting at the Crystal Sea," 175; and Foucault, 188; and *Frame Structures*, 173, 174; and "impersonal" poetry, 189, 190, 194; and the lyric, 11, 17, 29, 197; and *The Midnight*, 168, 169, 172, 177–82, 186, 187; and *My Emily Dickinson*, 166, 167, 169, 176; and relationship with the university, 165, 167, 170, 171, 204
Huehls, Mitchum, 57
Hughes, Langston, 133
Humboldt, Alexander van, 45
Hyde, Lewis, 101

immanence, 27, 33
institutionality, 3, 35, 45, 111, 146
interdisciplinarity, 206

Iowa Writers' Workshop. *See* University of Iowa Writers' Workshop
Ithaca College, 196
Izenberg, Oren, 171

Jaar, Alfredo, 152, 153
James, Henry, 123
Jameson, Fredric, 197
jargon, 60, 82
Javadizadeh, Kamran, 153, 225n84
jazz, 122
Judy, Ronald A. T., 122–25, 127

Kant, Immanuel, 143, 146, 244n67
Keats, John, 80, 81, 164
Keene, John, 140, 147, 149, 151, 244n67; and "Analysis II," 142, 143; and autobiography, 16, 121, 131; and deconstruction, 139, 140, 143; and Norman Pritchard, 133, 134, 138; and reflexivity, 10, 13; and *Seismosis*, 132, 133, 135–37, 141; and the university, 123, 144, 146
Keller, Lynn, 173
Kempf, Christopher, 3, 225n85, 226n90
Kennedy, John F., 104
Kenner, Hugh, 21
Kermode, Frank, 112, 239n72
Kim, Myung Mi, 17, 200; and academic self, 167; and *Commons*, 189–93; and Claudia Rankine, 151, 161; and Catherine Taylor, 196, 197
Kindley, Evan, 39, 66, 219n18
Koch, Kenneth, 88, 89
Koller, Katherine, 51
Konstantinou, Lee, 101, 236n42
Kornbluh, Anna, 205, 206, 253n2, 254n5
Kramnick, Jonathan, 57, 206, 208
Kristeva, Julia, 160

La Berge, Leigh Claire, 4, 5, 211, 212
Lacan, Jacques, 59
Language poetry, 8, 14, 37, 217n25, 218n20, 223n61, 223n68
Larson, Magali Sarfatti, 55
Lasky, Dorothea, 147
Lauterbach, Ann, 72
Lentricchia, Frank, 20
Levinas, Emmanuel, 151, 162
Levi-Strauss, David, 152, 153
libraries, 17, 164, 166–69, 171, 180–83, 185–87, 190

Libretto for the Republic of Liberia (Melvin B. Tolson), 127–29, 131
literary theory, 14, 58, 111, 115, 124, 133; and capital-T Theory, 59, 61, 66, 79, 95, 132, 139, 140, 154
Llorens, David, 130
Lolordo, Nick, 51, 53
Longfellow, Henry Wadsworth, 174, 251n62
Louima, Abner, 161
Lowell, Robert, 40, 41, 42, 153, 174, 178, 181
Lyotard, Jean-François, 143, 146
lyric, the, 140, 194, 196, 197, 201, 202, 248n7; and John Ashbery, 59; and autobiography, 17; and critical thinking, 11; and Jorie Graham, 93; and Susan Howe, 29, 174, 178–81, 187; and John Keene, 140; and lyric essay, 193, 197; and "lyric I," 10, 167, 170; and "lyric shame," 173; and Claudia Rankine, 148–50, 153, 154, 163; and Wallace Stevens, 28, 34; and "workshop poem," 14

MacArthur grant, 92
Mackey, Nathaniel, 60, 124, 125, 127, 209, 210, 241n14, 244n67
Macmillan, Rebecca, 154
Mandela, Nelson, 157, 158
Mann, Paul, 6
Manning, John, 184, 187
Manning, Mary, 177, 186, 187
Marcuse, Herbert, 20
Martin, Theodore, 7
Marx, Karl, 5, 11, 138
Maryland Institute College of Art, 135
Mayers, Tim, 95
Mbeki, Thabo, 159
McClatchy, J. D., 147
McCrae, Shane, 147
McDonald, Gail, 4
McGann, Jerome, 24
McGurl, Mark, 3; and academic labor, 87, 88; and non-white creative writing, 123, 124; and reflexivity, 6, 10; responses to, 215n4; and suspicion of creative writing programs, 1, 39
McHale, Brian, 37
McVeigh, Timothy, 156, 157, 158
Menand, Louis, 208, 222n47, 254n8
metaphor, 17, 33, 54, 100, 144, 173, 195, 224; and African American poetics, 241n16; and John Ashbery, 65, 70, 76, 77; and avant-garde poetics, 8, 208; and Mei-mei Berssenbrugge, 82, 84, 85; and creative writing workshops, 42; and formalism, 224; and Jorie Graham, 102, 107, 117; and Wallace Stevens, 32
MFA programs, 3, 135, 136, 144, 196, 201; and Mei-mei Berssenbrugge, 53, 82; and Jorie Graham, 90, 92, 94; and Myung Mi Kim, 167, 189; and "MFA vs NYC," 1; and Claudia Rankine, 147, 148, 153, 163; and SUNY Buffalo Poetics Program, 165
Mitchell, Nick, 44
modernism, 50, 66, 132; and "Afromodernism," 131; and John Ashbery, 50; critique of, 20; and historicization of, 15, 28; and Romanticism, 23; and Wallace Stevens, 25, 26, 47; and the university, 14, 25, 30, 31
Molesworth, Charles, 93
Moore, Marianne, 31, 171, 172
Moten, Fred, 137
motherhood, 102, 103, 148, 236n46
Myers, D. G., 39, 42, 91, 95, 224n73

n+1 (magazine), 1
Nabokov, Vladimir, 87, 88, 100
Naropa University, 135
Native Son (Richard Wright), 120
neoliberalism, 4, 57
Nerssessian, Anahid, 206
"New Class," 22, 23, 54, 55, 219n16. *See also* Gouldner, Alvin Ward
Newcomb, John Timberman, 26
New Criticism, 15, 26, 53, 79, 231n67
New Directions (publisher), 176
New Formalism, 94
New Historicism, 170
New Negro Poets (anthology), 133
Ngai, Sianne, 82
Nielsen, Aldon, 128, 130, 134
Nietzsche, Friedrich, 129
Nka: Journal of Contemporary African Art, 106, 152, 192
North, Joseph, 46
Notebook of a Return to the Native Land (Aimé Césaire), 151
notes (citational practice), 9, 154, 187–90, 195; and footnotes, 7, 128, 129, 193, 198
Nowak, Mary, 189

Ohio State University, 135
Olmsted, Frederick Law, 177, 182, 184–87
Olson, Charles, 165
Orr, David, 92

Osman, Jena, 17, 167, 189, 193–97, 200
Otten, Thomas J., 113, 114
Outside in the Teaching Machine (Gayatri Chakravorty Spivak), 90, 138

Pale Fire (Vladimir Nabokov), 88
parenting, 102, 104
pastiche, 28, 129, 133
Pater, Walter, 20
Paterson (William Carlos Williams), 28
Perloff, Marjorie, 61, 94; critique of creative writing programs, 38–40, 42; on Christian Hawkey, 201; on Susan Howe, 170, 171, 174; on Ezra Pound, 21, 29; on Wallace Stevens, 25
Papageorgiou, Vasilis, 58
pedagogy, 115, 139; and craft, 95, 97; direct discussion of, in poetry, 89; and Paulo Freire, 106–8; and the gift, 100; and mysticism, 99, 114; and Gayatri Spivak, 90; and the uncertain, 81; and "uncreative writing," 8. *See also* teaching
Peirce, Charles Sanders, 167, 179, 183, 185, 187
perception, 83, 84, 97, 192; and the Dogon peoples of Mali, 143, 244n67; and "lyric shame," 173; and modernism, 20, 25
phenomenology, 6
Philip, M. NourbeSe, 189, 245n83
philology, 27, 28, 194
Place, Vanessa, 7
Plath, Sylvia, 40, 181, 224n77
Plato, 70, 143, 146
Poetry (magazine), 59, 89
Porter, Lavelle, 120
Pound, Ezra, 7, 21, 28, 29, 31; and the *Cantos*, 128; and Wallace Stevens, 25, 26; and translation, 200, 203
pragmatism (American philosophical tradition), 29, 30
pregnancy, 102, 236n46
Princeton University, 93, 155
Pritchard, Norman, 133, 134, 138
process, 70, 91, 102, 105, 107, 140, 160, 168, 192; and craft, 95; and critical reading, 82, 105; and critical thinking, 8–12, 17, 93, 114, 119, 153; and ekphrasis, 96; and experimental poetics, 51, 54, 60, 62, 69, 70; and history, 197; and naming, 108, 210; and pedagogy, 30, 40, 102, 115, 201, 203; and perception, 83, 143; and poetic labor, 189, 198; and

"Process" (John Keene), 132, 133, 135, 136; and reflexivity, 72, 116; and research, 180, 181; and resistance, 160, 212; and secrecy, 118, 119; and self-portraiture, 112; and subjectivity, 193
professional-managerial class, 23, 219n19
progress, 4, 7, 231n79
pronouns, 71, 79, 81
Protestant work ethic, 21
Pulitzer Prize, 92

Rancière, Jacques, 198
Rankine, Claudia, 16, 123, 165, 245n83; and *Citizen*, 149, 153; and critical distancing, 143, 149; and critical thinking, 13; and *Don't Let Me Be Lonely*, 149, 150, 151, 153–62; and expectation of autobiography in African American writing, 121; and reflexivity, 9; and the university, 10, 131, 147, 148
rationality, 27, 118
Rawson, Claude, 59
reading, 12, 49, 55, 56, 86, 174; and "academic readers," 53; and African American literary theory, 122, 124; and John Ashbery, 52, 54, 57, 62, 69, 70, 72–78; and Mei-mei Berssenbrugge, 82–86; and close readings, 6; and critical reading, 63, 67, 75, 76, 213; and critical thinking, 108; definition of, 99; and Christian Hawkey, 202; and Susan Howe, 174, 182, 185; and Myung Mi Kim, 190, 192, 193; as labor, 5, 16, 56, 94, 207–9; and libraries, 164, 167, 182, 183; and literary theory, 59, 170; and Nathaniel Mackey, 210; and modernism, 28; professional, 15, 55, 71, 94, 99, 100; and Claudia Rankine, 154, 156, 158, 160; and reading public, 38, 50; and reflexivity, 10, 55, 58, 60, 68; and Catherine Taylor, 198
real, the: and John Ashbery, 75; and Jorie Graham, 114, 116–18; and Wallace Stevens, 27, 29, 47, 219n13
realism, 130, 137, 144, 146, 253n2
Reddy, Srikanth, 21, 23, 171, 172
Reed, Anthony, 4, 154, 240n4
reflexivity, 111; and John Ashbery, 53, 64, 65, 72; and critique of self-expression, 9; and genre, 10; and institutionalization of literary theory, 58; and justice, 199; and pedagogy, 106, 116; phenomenology of, 6, 109; and postmodernism, 101; and Wallace Stevens, 14, 25–27, 47

Reitter, Paul, 43, 45
research, 174, 178, 181, 184, 186, 211; and academic labor, 87, 99, 100; as commodity, 5; and Christian Hawkey, 200–203; historical, 166, 173, 180; and Myung Mi Kim, 192, 193; and libraries, 164, 167, 169; and marginalia, 187; and non-autobiographical poetry, 189; and Jena Osman, 194, 195, 196; and productivity, 212; and state support of, 205; and Catherine Taylor, 198
Ritter, Kelly, 39, 42
Roffman, Karin, 51
Rojas, Fabio, 125, 126
romanticism, 22, 23, 46, 47, 60
Rowlandson, Mary, 166
Rukeyser, Muriel, 189
Rwanda, 152
Ryan, Robert Cashin, 18

Santayana, George, 20, 29, 31–33, 36
Scalapino, Leslie, 194
Schultz, Susan M., 170
secrets, 16, 92, 98, 107, 110–12, 118, 238n70, 239n72
Sedgwick, Eve, 208, 254n6
self-portraiture, 103, 107–12, 117, 118
sentimentality, 60
Sexton, Anne, 40
Shapiro, David, 59, 60, 62, 70
Shockley, Evie, 125, 127
Silliman, Ron, 1, 17, 195
South Africa, 149, 157–60, 196, 198
Spahr, Juliana, 36, 149
Spellman, A. B., 130
Spillers, Hortense, 125, 126, 127
Spinoza, Benedict de, 29
Spivak, Gayatri Chakravorty, 12, 13, 83, 90, 138, 139
Stackhouse, Christopher, 132, 135, 140, 141, 144–46, 243n51
Stein, Gertrude, 25, 29, 31, 151, 166
STEM, 33, 138
Stepto, Robert, 122, 124, 126
Stevens, Wallace, 28, 36, 43, 48, 62, 218n10, 219n13; and John Ashbery, 50, 51, 62; and "Comedian as the Letter C," 34; and "The Emperor of Ice-Cream," 32; and Susan Howe, 29; and "The Idea of Order at Key West," 35; and "Man Carrying Things," 21, 28, 30; and "The Man with the Blue Guitar," 27; and modernism, 25; and "Of Modern Poetry," 30; and Claudia Rankine, 151, 160; and reflexivity, 15; and romanticism, 46; and "Sailing After Lunch," 22; and George Santayana, 31–33; and "This Beautiful World," 47; and the university, 10, 14, 19, 20, 23, 27, 38; and "The Weeping Burgher," 25, 26
SUNY Buffalo: and Charles Bernstein, 36, 38, 216n12; and Susan Howe, 164, 165, 176, 182, 183; and Myung Mi Kim, 189, 190, 192; and Jena Osman, 193, 196

Tan, Kathy-Ann, 170
taste, 6, 93, 234n17
Tate, Allen, 40, 41, 224n71
Taylor, Catherine, 17, 167, 189, 196–200
Taylorization, 214
teaching, 89–91, 106, 116, 148, 165; and African American poetics, 127, 148; and John Ashbery, 51; as "calling," 4; and contradiction, 91, 92, 102; as day job, 88; difficulties of, 115, 117; and figure of the creative writing professor, 89, 116; and Paulo Freire, 106; as gift, 100, 101; and Jorie Graham, 87, 92, 94, 96, 97, 105, 113; and Robert Lowell, 41; and motherhood, 103, 104; and Marjorie Perloff's critique of, 38; and poetic labor, 4, 15, 16, 99, 207, 209; and Gayatri Spivak's *Outside in the Teaching Machine*, 90, 138; and "teaching lore," 39. *See also* pedagogy
techne, 29, 95
Thomas, Lorenzo, 121, 128–31, 133, 134
Tolson, Melvin B., 121, 127–34, 162, 242n24, 242n38
Trakl, Georg, 200–203
Twombly, Cy, 135

Ugly Duckling (publisher), 196
Umbra group, 128, 242n26
"uncreative writing," 8, 29, 147
universality, 74, 77, 79, 80, 115
university, the, 30, 51, 59, 66, 81, 205; and academic labor, 88, 101; and academic reading, 50; and the African American avant-garde, 122, 123, 132, 133, 148, 151, 162; as *atopia*, 104; and contemporary poetry, 2, 3, 6, 9, 204; contradictory character of, 37, 44, 121; and Enlightenment subjectivity, 21; and experimental poetry, 26; as "500 pound gorilla," 1; and Harvard curriculum in early

university, the (*cont.*)
    twentieth century, 31; and modernism, 14, 30; and neoliberalism, 35, 66, 206; and professionalization of creative writing, 17, 39, 40; and relations of production within, 5, 33; and resistance within, 45, 47; and Wallace Stevens, 20; and theory, 59
University of Houston, 148
University of Iowa Writers' Workshop, 59, 189; and Jorie Graham, 90, 92, 94, 100, 104; and history of creative writing programs, 40, 165; and Claudia Rankine, 148, 154; and self-expression, 41
University of Pennsylvania, 36
University of Rochester, 51

valuation, 2, 53, 169
Vanderbilt University, 39
Vanderslice, Stephanie, 39, 42
Vendler, Helen, 25, 93, 94, 95, 109, 114
Vincente, Esteban, 52
Voigt, Ellen Bryant, 89
von Schlegell, David, 165, 174

Walcott, Rinaldo, 121
Watteau, Jean-Antoine, 129
Wellmon, Chad, 43
West, Cornel, 151, 155, 156, 158–60
White, Charles W., 144, 145, 146
White, Gillian, 10, 173
whiteness, 194, 196–99, 225n84; and the academy, 120, 123, 127, 128; and African American poetics, 131, 134, 153; and violence, 151, 156, 157, 159; and white supremacy, 136, 207
Whitman, Walt, 59, 61
Williams, William Carlos, 28, 164, 153
Wittgenstein, Ludwig, 107, 202
Wright, C. D., 189
Wunderlich, Mark, 87

Yale University, 124, 148, 155, 165, 167, 176, 177
Yale Younger Poets award, 53
Yeats, W. B., 185, 186

Zona, Kirstin Hotelling, 93
Zuba, Jesse, 51, 53

This page is a continuation of the copyright page. The following excerpts appear in the book:

John Ashbery, excerpts from *Houseboat Days*. Copyright © 1975, 1976, 1977, 1999 by John Ashbery. Reprinted by permission of Georges Borchardt, Inc., on behalf of the author.

Charles Bernstein, excerpts from "A Defense of Poetry," from *All the Whiskey in Heaven: Selected Poems*. Copyright © 2011 by Charles Bernstein. Reprinted with permission of Farrar, Straus and Giroux. All rights reserved.

Mei-mei Berssenbrugge, excerpts from "Forms of Politeness" and "Texas," from *I Love Artists: New and Selected Poems*. Copyright © 2006 by Mei-mei Berssenbrugge. Reprinted with permission of University of California Press.

Lynn Emmanuel, excerpts from "I told my student Kimber Lester if you cannot actually write," from *Noose and Hook* © 2010. Reprinted with permission of the University of Pittsburgh Press.

Jorie Graham, excerpts from "On Difficulty," "Imperialism," "Pollock and Canvas," "Self-Portrait as Both Parties," "Self-Portrait as the Gesture Between Them [Adam and Eve]," "Self-Portrait as Adam and Eve," "To the Reader," and "The Veil" from *The End of Beauty*. Copyright © 1987 by Jorie Graham. Used by permission of HarperCollins Publishers.

Susan Howe, "Chanting at the Crystal Sea," from *Frame Structures: Early Poems 1974–1979*. Copyright © 1996 by Susan Howe. Excerpts from *The Midnight* by Susan Howe. Copyright © 2003 by Susan Howe. Reprinted by permission of New Directions Publishing Corp.

John Keene, excerpts from "Aura," "Self," "Metaphysics," "Analysis I," and "Analysis II" from *Seismosis* (1913 Press, 2006). © John Keene, 2021. All rights reserved.

Robert Lowell, excerpts from "During Fever" and "Commander Lowell" from *Collected Poems*. Copyright © 2003 by Harriet Lowell and Sheridan Lowell. Reprinted by permission of Farrar, Straus and Giroux. All rights reserved.

Nathaniel Mackey, "Song of the Andoumboulou: 60" and "Song of the Andoumboulou: 40" from *Splay Anthem*. Copyright © 2002, 2006 by Nathaniel Mackey. Reprinted by permission of New Directions Publishing Corp.

Jena Osman, excerpts from "The Franklin Party," published in *The Narrative* (Fence Books, 2010). Reprinted with permission.

Excerpts from poems by Norman H. Pritchard from *The Matrix* (2021), Catherine Taylor from *Apart* (2017), and Christian Hawkey from *Ventrakl* (2010). Reprinted with the permission of Ugly Duckling Press.

Claudia Rankine, excerpt from "Birthright," from *Nothing in Nature Is Private*. Copyright © 1994 by Claudia Rankine. Reprinted with the permission of The Permissions Company, LLC, on behalf of the Cleveland State University Poetry Center. And Claudia Rankine, excerpts from *Don't Let Me Be Lonely: An American Lyric*. Copyright © 2004 by Claudia Rankine. Reprinted with the permission of The Permissions Company, LLC, on behalf of Graywolf Press.

Wallace Stevens, excerpts from "The Man with the Blue Guitar," copyright © 1937 by Wallace Stevens; "Man Carrying Thing," copyright © 1954 by Wallace Stevens and copyright renewed 1982 by Holly Stevens; and "Sailing After Lunch" from *The Collected Poems of Wallace Stevens* by Wallace Stevens, copyright © 1954 by Wallace Stevens and copyright renewed 1982 by Holly Stevens. Used by permission of Alfred A. Knopf, an imprint of the Knopf Doubleday Publishing Group, a division of Penguin Random House LLC. All rights reserved.

Lorenzo Thomas, excerpts from "Embarkation for Cythera," from *The Collected Poems of Lorenzo Thomas* © 2019 The Estate of Lorenzo Thomas. Published by Wesleyan University Press. Used by permission.

LITERARY THEORY & CRITICISM BOOKS FROM HOPKINS PRESS

Experimental
American Literature and the Aesthetics of Knowledge
Natalia Cecire

A compelling revision of the history of experimental writing from Pound and Stein to Language poetry, disclosing its uses and its limits.

Hopkins Studies in Modernism Series

Freedom Time
The Poetics and Politics of Black Experimental Writing
Anthony Reed

Experimental poetry and prose by Black writers rejects traditional interpretations of social protest and identity formation to reveal radical new ways of perceiving the world.

The Callaloo African Diaspora Series

Craft Class
The Writing Workshop in American Culture
Christopher Kempf

The hidden history of the creative writing workshop and the socioeconomic consequences of the craft labor metaphor.

press.jhu.edu

 @JHUPress

 @HopkinsPress

 @JohnsHopkinsUniversityPress

www.ingramcontent.com/pod-product-compliance
Lightning Source LLC
Chambersburg PA
CBHW020642230426
43665CB00008B/282